D0886984

Language Diversity and
Language Contact

Language Diversity and Language Contact

Essays by Stanley Lieberson

**Selected and Introduced
by Anwar S. Dil**

Stanford University Press, Stanford, California   1981

Language Science and National Development

A Series Sponsored by the
Linguistic Research Group of Pakistan

General Editor: Anwar S. Dil

Stanford University Press
Stanford, California
© 1981 by Stanley Lieberson
Introduction and compilation © 1981 by the
Board of Trustees of the
Leland Stanford Junior University
Printed in the United States of America
ISBN 0-8047-1098-8
LC 80-53223

Contents

Acknowledgments

The Linguistic Research Group of Pakistan and the General Editor of the Language Science and National Development Series are deeply grateful to Professor Stanley Lieberson for giving us the privilege of presenting his selected writings as the sixteenth volume in our series established in 1970 to commemorate the International Education Year.

We are indebted to the editors and publishers of the following publications. The ready permission on the part of the holders of the copyrights, acknowledged in each case, is a proof of the existing international cooperation and goodwill that gives hope for better collaboration among scholars of all nations for international exchange of knowledge.

National Development, Mother-Tongue Diversity, and the Comparative Study of Nations; with Lynn Hansen. American Sociological Review 39. 523-41 (1974), with permission of the American Sociological Association.

The Course of Mother-Tongue Diversity in Nations; with Guy Dalto and Mary Ellen Johnston [Marsden]. American Journal of Sociology 81. 34-61 (1975), with permission of The University of Chicago Press. © 1975 by The University of Chicago.

A Societal Theory of Race and Ethnic Relations. American Sociological Review 26. 902-10 (1961), with permission of the American Sociological Association.

National and Regional Language Diversity. Actes du Xe
Congrès International des Linguistes (Bucharest: Editions de l'Académie de la République Socialiste de Roumanie, 1969), pp. 769-73,
with permission of the publisher.

Language Diversity in a Nation and Its Regions; with James
F. O'Connor. Multilingual Political Systems: Problems and Solutions,
ed. by Jean-Guy Savard and Richard Vigneault (Quebec: Laval University Press, 1975), pp. 161-83, with permission of the publisher.

Bilingualism in Montreal: A Demographic Analysis. American Journal of Sociology 71. 10-25 (1965), with permission of The
University of Chicago Press. © 1965 by The University of Chicago.

Language Shift in the United States: Some Demographic
Clues; with Timothy J. Curry. International Migration Review 5(2).
125-37 (New York: Center for Migration Studies of New York, Inc.,
1971), with permission of the publisher.

Linguistic and Ethnic Segregation in Montreal. International
Days of Sociolinguistics, Second International Congress of Social
Sciences of the Luigi Sturzo Institute (Rome: Istituto Luigi Sturzo,
1970), pp. 753-82, with permission of the Institute.

Domains of Language Usage and Mother-Tongue Shift in
Nairobi; with Edward McCabe. International Journal of the Sociology
of Language 18. 69-81 (The Hague: Mouton, 1978), with permission
of the editor and publisher.

Procedures for Improving Sociolinguistic Surveys of Language
Maintenance and Language Shift. International Journal of the Sociology
of Language 25. 11-27 (The Hague: Mouton, 1980), with permission of
the editor and publisher.

Language Questions in Censuses. Sociological Inquiry 36.
262-79 (1966), with permission of Alpha Kappa Delta.

An Extension of Greenberg's Linguistic Diversity Measures.
Language 40. 526-31 (1964), with permission of the Linguistic Society
of America.

The Anatomy of Language Diversity: Some Elementary Results. Interethnic Communication, ed. by E. Lamar Ross, Southern Anthropological Society Proceedings, No. 12 (Athens: University of Georgia Press, 1978), pp. 32–48, with permission of the publisher. © 1978 by The University of Georgia Press.

How Can We Describe and Measure the Incidence and Distribution of Bilingualism? Description and Measurement of Bilingualism: An International Seminar, ed. by L. G. Kelly (Toronto: University of Toronto Press, 1969), pp. 286–95, with permission of the publisher.

Forces Affecting Language Spread: Some Basic Propositions. Language Spread: Studies in Diffusion and Social Change, ed. by Robert L. Cooper (Bloomington: Indiana University Press, forthcoming 1981), with permission of the Center for Applied Linguistics.

EDITOR'S NOTE

These essays have been reprinted from the originals with only minor changes made in the interest of uniformity of style and appearance. In cases where substantive revisions have been made, proper notation has been added. Misprints and mistakes appearing in the originals have been corrected in consultation with the author. In some cases references, notes, and bibliographical entries have been updated. Footnotes marked by asterisks have been added by the Editor.

Introduction

Stanley Lieberson was born on April 20, 1933, in Montreal. He grew up in Brooklyn, New York, in a multilingual family and early in life became aware of the reality of language as an ethnic and social marker. After his early education in the New York public schools and two years at Brooklyn College, he transferred to the University of Chicago, where he earned his Master's degree in Sociology in 1958 and his Ph. D. in 1960. In 1959 he joined the University of Iowa as Instructor in Sociology and became actively involved in research at the Iowa Urban Community Research Center. Two years later he moved to the University of Wisconsin, where in 1966 he became Professor of Sociology. In 1967 he transferred to the University of Washington, where he also served as Director of the Center for Studies in Demography and Ecology (1968-71); and from 1971 to 1974 he was Professor of Sociology at the University of Chicago, serving also as Associate Director of the Population Research Center. Since 1974 he has been Professor of Sociology at the University of Arizona at Tucson.

Lieberson spent the summer of 1970 as Visiting Professor at Stanford University, and the year 1979-80 as Claude Bissell Distinguished Visiting Professor at the University of Toronto. He has served actively in editorial and advisory positions for a number of professional journals, notably Social Problems (1965-67), Sociological Inquiry (1965-67), American Journal of Sociology (1969-74), Sociological Methods and Research (1971-), Language in Society (1972-74), International Journal of the Sociology of Language (1974-), Canadian Journal of Sociology (1975-), Language Problems and Language Planning (1977-), and Social Forces (1980-). He received a Guggenheim fellowship in 1972-73. He has served on the Committee on Sociolinguistics of the Social Science Research Council (1964-70), the Board of Directors of the Population Association of America (1969–72), the Government Statistics Committee of the American Sociological Association (1968–73), and the Advisory Committee on Sociology of the National Science Foundation (1978–81). He was elected to serve as President of the Sociological Research Association for 1980–81.

Lieberson's first publication, a paper on ethnic groups and the practice of medicine published in 1958, was followed in 1959 by a paper on ethnic segregation and assimilation written in collaboration with his dissertation director and mentor, Otis Dudley Duncan. The following year saw the publication of Metropolis and Region, a monumental study by Duncan and four of his associates, including Lieberson, whose main contributions were to the sections dealing with economic functions and the interregional flow of funds. Some years later Lieberson followed up his work on the project by collaborating with Beverly Duncan on Metropolis and Region in Transition (1970). This volume aimed at measuring changes in the ecological system and the role of cities in the national economy, and the relation of metropolitan growth to regional differentiation of the economy. Lieberson was particularly interested in the financial system of the United States and the changing role of various cities in that system.

An earlier book of Lieberson's, Ethnic Patterns in American Cities (1963), the revised version of his dissertation, is a study of ethnic segregation in ten American cities based on data from the censuses of 1910 to 1950. Praised by reviewers for its useful discussion of the contact mechanism in diffusion and for its careful statistical analysis of demographic material, it remains to this day a standard work on sociocultural assimilation and integration.

In 1964 a seminar on sociolinguistics held at Indiana University brought Lieberson into contact with linguists and other scholars concerned with developing the interdisciplinary area of sociolinguistics. The problems raised by these scholars interested him, and stimulated his work in this area. In 1966 he edited a special issue of Sociological Inquiry entitled Explorations in Sociolinguistics, which was reprinted the following year as a special number of the International Journal of American Linguistics and also published as a book by Indiana University Press. A collection of thirteen major papers by leading sociolinguists that constituted a pioneering effort to build a bridge between linguists and social scientists in general, Explorations proved to be a landmark in the development of sociolinguistics. Lieberson's paper, on "Language Questions in Censuses" (chapter 14 in this volume), proposed new ways of evaluating the accuracy of census returns on bilingualism and using them to make sociolinguistic inferences.

Another opportunity that helped deepen Lieberson's understanding of the role of language in sociocultural identity was his experience as an invited observer of the five-nation language survey of East Africa in 1968. This survey gave him a firsthand insight into the use of sociolinguistic resources in planning for better national development, and led to suggestions for improving the methods and procedures of sociolinguistic surveys (chapter 13).

Lieberson's paper "Bilingualism in Montreal: A Demographic Analysis" (chapter 8), a pilot study for a project on societal bilingualism and ethnic identity maintenance and shift in Canada, attracted the attention of the newly appointed Canadian Royal Commission on Bilingualism and Biculturalism, which gave him a research assignment and supplied him with invaluable statistical cross-tabulations from the 1961 census. His book Language and Ethnic Relations in Canada (1970) offers a wide-ranging ecological perspective on Canadian society, with its visible interplay of language, ethnic relations, and demographic processes. Inevitably, because of the sensitive political nature of the language problem in Canada, the book has had its detractors. But Language recommended it as required reading for social scientists and educators concerned with bilingualism, and it has since proved helpful to the study of language and ethnic problems in many another nation.

The essays selected for this volume represent Lieberson's most significant work on bilingualism and its social causes, on language and ethnic relations in their sociocultural context, and on methods and models of sociolinguistic research. Although he has succeeded better than perhaps any other scholar of our time in dealing quantitatively with the societal context of bilingualism, and in particular with mother-tongue maintenance and shift, a proper recognition of his accomplishment must also take into account his theoretical insights, especially those involving the role of ethnicity in language diversity. Lieberson holds that language contact between ethnic groups is a major source of linguistic diversity, and that the socio-linguistic consequences typically reflect the nature of the ethnic relations involved (chapter 4). Among his other notable contributions to sociolinguistic theory are his expansion of Joseph Greenberg's concept of language diversity measurement, and his formulation of formal models of the role of language in the integration and differentiation of the various regions of a nation-state. Few indeed are the language scientists who can match the sociolinguistic achievements of this gifted sociologist.

Anwar S. Dil

United States International University
San Diego, California
October 18, 1980

Language Diversity and
Language Contact

Part I. Ethnic Diversity and National Language

1 | Language and Ethnic Relations: A Neglected Problem

Multilingual societies are found in all parts of the world, in older nations as well as the newly created states, in both the present and in man's past. Currently there is more than one viable language spoken in such countries as Belgium, Switzerland, and the Soviet Union in Europe, Canada, Bolivia, and Guatemala in the new world, India, the Philippines, and Cyprus in Asia, and South Africa, Nigeria, and the Congo in Africa. Diverse populations gave up their mother tongues in the course of a few generations in the United States, but ethnic groups in many nations have kept their distinctive languages for centuries. Even in the United States, the Pennsylvania Dutch, the Mexicans, and the French maintain linguistic enclaves which survive to the present day.

The political and social situation created by linguistic diversity ranges from the harmony of Switzerland, a nation created before the days of modern nationalism (Mayer 1956; McRae 1964), to India, where the entire political fabric is torn with linguistic conflict. Although both represent extremes, there is usually at least some conflict and dissent within multilingual nations. Linguistic inequality occurs in areas such as Belgium where only two tongues are significant as well as in nations which are so diverse that some tongue must be favored as a lingua franca (Kloss 1966a). Although equality between linguistic groups is sometimes achieved in official political terms, it is rare either socially or economically. Moreover language differences are usually accompanied by racial or ethnic differences, thereby often becoming hopelessly entangled in broader issues.

When peoples with different languages are brought together under a common political entity, whether it be through voluntary migration or by means of conquest and invasion, generally one group is in a more favorable position than others, and likewise one language enjoys a stronger position in schools and the government, in the economy, and socially. Where populations have migrated into a situation of linguistic and ethnic subordination, there normally is much less difficulty since the option of migration back to their home country provides a safety valve. Conflict is often both longer and of greater severity in multilingual societies containing peoples who were overrun by an expanding group, in colonies, and in new nations whose boundaries were carved by European empire builders (Lieberson 1961). In the latter instance, although the flag of imperialism is down, groups find they are incorporated into a nation where some other group is dominant.

Three broad solutions are possible in a multilingual society for those whose native tongue is subordinate. One is to evolve toward the dominant group, to give up the native language and reduce—if not completely eliminate—the ethnic identity it often symbolizes. Immigrants to Canada after the British conquest are following this path in varying degrees. Another solution is to reduce the handicaps facing speakers of a given language by reforming the societal institutions. This may take place through changes in the educational system, political provisions, substates, economic reform, and the like. After the adoption of Hindi as the language of India's national unity, the central government has repeatedly been forced to acknowledge the demands of other groups for linguistic self-determination, beginning with the creation of a Telegu-speaking state in Madras in 1953 (Bram 1955: 54). The third solution is most explosive of all, namely, abandoning the existing nation through outmigration, revolution, separatism, or expulsion of the dominant language group. The disintegration of the Austro-Hungarian empire was facilitated by the diverse peoples within its boundaries who had maintained their languages despite political conquest (Delgado de Carvalho 1962: 77). The French in Canada, a conquered people who are subordinate in virtually all respects except their official political status of linquistic equality, are veering in recent years toward institutional reforms if not complete separation.

Recognizing the wide range of sociological problems involved in the contact between racial and ethnic groups with different mother tongues, this volume* develops a set of ecological propositions about the nature of linguistic pluralism, the forces which maintain such societies, and those which work toward unilingualism. The framework is then applied to the Canadian setting, focusing on two related but conceptually distinct events: first, the forces which determine how groups will adapt to the presence of others who speak different tongues; second, the long-run factors which determine whether pluralism will be maintained or evolve into a unilingual society.

Language, Race, and Ethnic Relations

Much bad anthropology has been made by thus carelessly taking language and race as though they went always and exactly together. Yet they do go together to a great extent. Although what a man's language really proves is not his parentage but his bringing-up, yet most children are in fact brought up by their own parents, and inherit their language as well as their features.

—Sir Edward B. Tylor, 1881

An association does exist in the world between ethnic groups and languages, although some scholars have gone too far by suggesting that speakers of language are members of a common race (see the discussion by Thompson 1961: 228). Very likely the forces of isolation in the period prior to widespread literacy and mass communication helped to create the conditions necessary for both new peoples and new tongues. As Znaniecki (1952: 7-8) observes, the maintenance of a cultural complex such as a language requires prolonged direct contacts among those who use it. In many instances, the word for an ethnic group is either identical to or has the same root as the word for their language, for example French, German, Polish. Thus the Germanic tongue once used by Jews in many parts of Europe is sometimes popularly referred to as "Jewish" rather than "Yiddish."

This tendency in an earlier period to associate language and pronunciation with specific ethnic and racial groups led to some

---

*Stanley Lieberson, Language and Ethnic Relations in Canada (New York: Wiley, 1970).

extreme positions such as the assumption that Jews were incapable
of acquiring the spoken language of any European country because of
physical differences in the anatomy of their speech and hearing organs
(Fishberg 1911: 388-90). The German word "mauscheln" referred to
both the peculiar pronunciation of Jews as well as vulgar speech.
Fishberg himself advances the more plausible position that these
differences in pronunciation were due to the isolation of Jews after
the development of ghettoes and the perpetuation of these differences
by the absence of non-Jewish teachers.

Since so many instances come to mind where ethnic groups
in contact are linguistically distinct and, likewise, where a common
tongue is shared by different ethnic groups, debate over this issue is
foolhardy. The solution is very simple, but most important: while
ethnic differences are sometimes not accompanied by linguistic differences, it is rare to find two or more mutually unintelligible languages used in a society without the speakers belonging to different
ethnic groups. "In a great majority of contacts between groups speaking different mother tongues, the groups constitute, at the same time,
distinct ethnic or cultural communities" (Weinreich 1953: 91). Indeed
the overlap between ethnic and linguistic boundaries, viewed more
realistically as a dynamic relationship, is often only partial but never
random. In societies where a population has begun its shift to another
group's mother tongue, an ethnic group may not be fully distinguish-
able on the basis of mother tongue. English was the mother tongue
of nearly half the second-generation Norwegians in the United States
in 1940, for example, but the use of Norwegian as a first language
was still far more common in this ethnic group than in any other
second-generation subpopulation.

Although linguists pay considerable attention to language contact as a major factor in altering languages through interference and
borrowing (Mackey 1965: 239), the sociological setting in which language contact and bilingual behavior occurs has not received sufficient
study. There are some important exceptions, such as the contributions of Weinreich, Haugen, and Deutsch (curiously, all were published
in 1953), and, more recently, the work of Fishman and associates
(1966), but the processes affecting racial and ethnic maintenance of
language are far from fully understood. Language is of importance
for a wide array of problems, ranging from its significance in assim-

ilation to the potential for nationalism and separatism inherent in any country where groups maintain distinctive languages. Perhaps because of the remarkable speed and relative ease with which ethnic groups in the United States shifted to English, the linguistic dimension to race and ethnic relations has not received the attention from American sociologists which it merits.

The surrender of distinctive mother tongues is a necessary step in the assimilation of ethnic groups in contact. Although it is true that groups may retain their identity without a unique tongue, it is difficult to visualize complete assimilation in other areas if their native languages are maintained. In this sense language provides an important shield against assimilation. Provision for adequate education in the group's language as well as the opportunity to use their native tongue in the government are two of the special rights which groups tend to seek in order to prevent their assimilation (United Nations Commission on Human Rights, 1950, pp. 2-3). Some immigrant groups in the United States, to no avail, sought to maintain their tongues by establishing voluntary schools for their children. Understandably, from the perspective of the politically dominant ethnic group, linguistic change has been viewed as one of the prime targets for breaking down old loyalties and inducing ethnic assimilation.

Linguistic assimilation is normally an irreversible process since it is unlikely that a dead language will later be revised to the point of actually replacing its successor unless there is large-scale migration of new speakers or selective emigration. The restoration of Gaelic has been a basic part of the national policy in the Irish Free State since the nation was formed, yet the percentage speaking the tongue has "remained more or less constant since 1936 despite intensive efforts during the past quarter century" (O'Brien 1964: 4). Israel provides an exception in that Hebrew was revived from an almost exclusively religious function into a national language (Bachi 1956: 184).

Linguistic similarities can support both in-group unity and out-group distance since language serves both as a symbol of other differences and as a restriction on the communication possible between ethnic groups. Populations which differ in their native tongues often see themselves distinctive in other respects. The symbolic element to language has carried over even into major subclasses of

language families. Taking cues from German writers who argued
that the various dialects of Prussia, Bavaria, Hanover, and Austria
all formed one nation and one language, the Pan-Slavic movement
"proclaimed the affinity of various peoples, in spite of differences of
political citizenship and historical background, of civilization and
religion, solely on the strength of an affinity of language" (Kohn 1960:
ix).

The means by which communication channels are restricted
by linguistic differences is readily seen. If the ethnic groups possess
distinctive languages, then clearly monolinguals will have their communication restricted within ethnic groups. Even bilinguals will usually find communication more comfortable in the tongue learned earliest, particularly to express and understand subtleties of thought.
Since communication cannot flow as freely across ethnic boundaries
as within, ethnic origin will be partially coterminous with communication channels (Deutsch 1953). However, ethnic and communication
boundaries cannot be completely coterminous if the polyethnic society
is to exist, since, by definition, there is some interdependence between the groups.

The importance of language for race and ethnic relations is
also implicit in the view of language as a collection of symbols which
influence social behavior. This position, which has been developed in
social psychology (symbolic interaction) and anthropology, places
great emphasis on the influence language has on perception and the
thought process. If language influences cognition, then ethnic groups
with distinctive tongues may respond differently in the same social
situations. Ervin (1964) and others have provided some empirical evidence in support of this approach.

All of this suggests that some joint interaction will exist between the maintenance of an ethnic group and its distinctive language,
with each reinforcing the other. Linguistic differences, by reducing
interethnic contacts, will lower the chances of other forms of assimilation. On the other hand, an ethnic group which maintains its identity
will be more likely to retain its language. We should not lose sight of
the fact that ethnic and racial groups can perpetuate themselves without distinctive languages—witness current race relations in the United
States. But it appears safe to conclude that linguistic differences form
a major obstacle to assimilation and merger.

Nationalism

> As an independent nation, our honor requires us to have a
> system of our own, in language as well as in government.
> Great Britain whose children we are, and whose language we
> speak, should no longer be our standard; for the taste of her
> writers is already corrupted and her language on the decline.
>
> —Noah Webster, 1789; cited by Bram 1955: 56

The connection between nationalism, ethnic origin, and language is complex and merits full exploration in its own right (see
Deutsch 1953). At the risk of oversimplification, modern nationalism
is usually based on a group's actual or mythological common ethnic
past and a perceived unity of purpose and need. In countries that are
homogeneous in ethnic terms, interest in developing and maintaining
loyalties to a political entity led to programs for a national language
to be used by the entire population. A commonly shared tongue,
ideally one which is different from that held by neighboring nations,
is seen as a vehicle for the maintenance of the nation and as a bulwark
against outside influences. In Eire it was thought that a "country without its own language was only half a nation and that Ireland could not
long survive as a separate independent state if English remained the
only language of the people" (O'Brien 1964: 4). Both Hertzler (1965:
238) and Delgado de Carvalho (1962: 84-85) observed that language
was not usually an object of political or cultural struggle before the
age of nationalism.

Given this general connection between nationalism and linguistic uniformity, the problems become far more complex when
ethnic diversity is found in new nation-states. Under these circumstances, linguistic diversity is more of a threat to the broader political order and the urgency of a standard language is greater, but, on
the other hand, efforts to create a unilingual society may run into the
barrier of ethnic as well as linguistic loyalties. The nationalistic
campaign to spread Hindi as India's national language ran into severe
obstacles and internal conflict not only because of the attachment that
other languages hold but because language was confounded with ethnic
loyalties.

The dominant ethnic population may well fear other groups who maintain distinctive and "disruptive" cultural elements such as their own mother tongues. Emphasis on language has been observed in a number of nationalistic settings; Park (1922: 33) found that linguistic revivals inevitably precluded every European nationalistic movement beginning with Wales in the eighteenth century. Assimilation policies have varied greatly in multiethnic nations, ranging from coercion to tolerance, but no clear-cut path toward developing loyalties to the existent political order has been found (Royal Institute of International Affairs, 1939, chap. 16). Subordinate indigenous ethnic groups that maintain their unity, and a distinctive language would be one of the most powerful instruments for doing so, are in fact potential dangers to the maintenance of the ongoing political order since they may demand their own separate nation-state in which to fully realize mastery of their own destiny. Witness the development of a series of independent nations in eastern and central Europe after World War I. That these new nations in turn often contained "minorities" who themselves wished to achieve national independence is reminiscent of the current dilemmas which face many of the newly independent nations of Africa and Asia.

Distinctive languages among ethnic groups will in themselves intensify the difficulties of maintaining loyalties to the larger political body since one form of friction is commonly the position of each group's language in the schools, courts, documents, legislature, and other arms of the government. French Canadians have complained of the inferior status of their language in Canada outside of Quebec (Royal Commission on Bilingualism and Biculturalism, 1965, chap. 4) As Chapter 3 of this volume* makes clear, there is no question that French occupies a minor position in the political system of most of the provinces. The point is that distinctive groups which maintain strong ties, such as that afforded by their own language, are always a potential threat to the national order. Not only will groups with their languages intact maintain a degree of cohesiveness, which makes it more likely and more possible for them to reject the national concept imposed on them by some other group, but the existence of distinctive tongues itself provides a breeding ground for potential conflict

---

*Stanley Lieberson, Language and Ethnic Relations in Canada (New York: Wiley, 1970).

Perspective

Competition is inherent between languages in contact because the optimal conditions for their native speakers are normally incompatible. In the simplest setting in which there are two mother tongues in a population each speaker would like to use his tongue as widely and as frequently as possible. For those whose native tongue is A, this would occur if the entire population had A as its mother tongue or if native speakers of B all become bilingual. The same set of optimal conditions, however, hold for those with B as their mother tongue, except that the languages are reversed. Hence each increment in the number of native B speakers is unfavorable to the optimal conditions for A's and vice versa. Moreover, bilingualism among the entire population is a solution not normally encountered. As bilingualism among A's rises, the need is reduced for B's to learn A, since it is increasingly possible for monolingual B's to use their mother tongue in communicating with native A speakers. Bilingualism among some A's, by decreasing the chances of B's learning A, will increase the need for bilingualism among their A compatriots who have remained monolingual.

Details about the influence of bilingualism and population size on linguistic maintenance need not concern us here since they are developed in later chapters. The important point is to recognize an inherent competition between languages in contact, based on the fact that the optimal linguistic conditions for the speakers of each tongue are incompatible. Since the gains that one language makes are to the detriment of the other, there is competition. Kelley (1966: 5) reports that the establishment of Hindi as the official language of India is opposed by those intellectuals with other native tongues who fear that this will place them at a disadvantage in competing for government positions.

Nationalism in a society dominated by A's requires not only that B's learn A, but that A replace B as their native tongue. The role of language in the maintenance of ethnic boundaries is too important, from the perspective of groups seeking to maintain their boundaries, for such a loss to be readily accepted, but a group will maintain its mother tongue only with a loss in potential communication accompanied by disadvantages in the economic, social, political, and

educational spheres. The economist Albert Breton (1964) has advance
the intriguing thesis that nationality or ethnic origin may be viewed as
investment which, in the absence of confiscation, is at a cost to the
group.

Language also enters into other forms of competition as a
potential asset in the market place, the political order, or the social
realm. In the same way that trading stamps are used by merchants
to obtain a competitive edge, so too will language play a role in these
normal forms of competition in multilingual communities. If many of
the workers who deal with both mother-tongue populations are bilingual, this will be seen as a "natural" outcome in a community such as
Montreal in which there are sizable numbers of monoglots in both
tongues. What is crucial is the existence of linguistic competition.
What forces A speakers to acquire B is not only a population who prefer B, but the existence of B-speaking competition. In normal economic competition this will be sufficient cause; once there is competition between sellers and a sizable B-speaking market it will become
advantageous to learn B even if all competitors are initially A monoglots.

In turn, this means that the degree of bilingualism will reflect some sort of interaction among those who create the market and
those who seek to meet it. If, for example, only A's require a given
service, but it is provided by both A's and B's, then the B speakers
will become bilingual unless they monopolize a specialty within the
service. The linguistic demands of the population will become less
influential in determining the linguistic abilities of those in a monopo-
listic institution. Hence, governments may be unresponsive to the
demands of a linguistic group if the group is so small that the gain
for politicians by learning their language or supporting policies advan
ing the group's interest will be outweighed by the loss in votes from
the dominant linguistic group. This latter consideration is by no
means trivial in the case of a monopoly such as a government since
its policies may be viewed as an instrument affecting language competition; for example, decisions with respect to education can improv
or weaken a mother tongue's position. By strengthening a tongue
through the provision of good educational facilities and programs a
government also weakens another tongue, since, as we have observed
the languages are in competition, whether overtly or not. Govern-

ments, we may hypothesize, will do this only when the composition of their constituency is such as to force this or where the group whose needs are not met is able to threaten the maintenance of the society and its functions. From this perspective, national governments of multiethnic societies must weigh their policies in terms of the possibility, actual or potential, of either a revolution or a separatist movement.

Equilibriums

Languages may be thought of as expanding or contracting over space and among peoples within a given area. If all the factors influencing the size of each mother-tongue group and the degree of bilingualism among native speakers of each language were to remain constant, then some form of equilibrium would result such that the position of each language would become stabilized over time. This is unlikely in any society and virtually impossible in most societies because of the constant flux and shift in such relevant conditions as the birth rate, immigration and emigration, the economy, the areal distribution and concentration of the populations, technology, changes in the needs of the labor force, and levels of educational achievement. However, each societal change may be viewed as directing a new influence on the state of the languages in contact that would lead to a new linguistic equilibrium if no further changes occurred. Each change alters, to some degree, what had been the path of linguistic balance in the society. It may accelerate the decline of one of the tongues or it may reverse the trend; it almost surely will help one language more than the other. Moreover each shift that is unfavorable to a language will require counterbalancing changes if the tongue is to maintain its initial position.

The equilibrium of a population aggregate must be distinguished from that of the individuals who constitute the aggregate. The entire population is the essential concern here, namely, the number of native speakers of each tongue and the extent of bilingualism among each mother-tongue component. In point of fact, these may remain rather steady over a long span of time although individuals fluctuate in the course of their lives. An individual may add one or more additional languages to his mother-tongue skills as he reaches certain ages and,

as is the case in Canada, also later forget or lose some of his acquire
tongues. Yet the analysis of individual fluctuations in linguistic ability
will provide important clues to the importance of various social forces
in influencing the linguistic status of the aggregate. Shifts in the linguistic abilities of cohorts, individuals of a given age traced through
a span of time, can provide useful insights into the relative importanc
of educational institutions, labor force requirements, preschool exper
iences, and the like (Lieberson 1965).

Bilingualism

Mutual intelligibility must develop between racial or ethnic
groups with different native tongues because of the economic, political
and social interdependencies found in any society. Bilingualism, eith
in the form of learning another group's tongue or some pidgin, is
therefore a necessary product of language contact. The actual freque
of bilingualism and the degree it is concentrated among one of the
mother-tongue groups may vary greatly, however. In a dual economy
in which groups living side by side are involved in essentially differen
economic systems (see Boeke 1955), the possibility exists of very littl
bilingualism since there may be very minimal intergroup contact.
When a nation's linguistic groups are highly specialized in the niches
they fill, then a much greater frequency of bilingualism in one or both
populations may be expected if there is considerable interdependency
between the groups. Basically, the behavior of bilinguals determines
whether a multilingual society will become unilingual or remain pluralistic for generations or even centuries. In working out the forces
that maintain linguistic diversity and those that support a one-languag
society, bilingualism will occupy a good part of our attention, as both
a dependent and an independent variable.

Bilingualism in the United States was an intermediate step
between the arrival of non-English-speaking immigrants and the estab
lishment of a nation in which nearly all speak the same tongue. The
immigrants or their children acquired English as a second language;
then somewhere in the interchange between generations only English
was passed on to their children. Elsewhere bilingualism has not led
to unilingualism; that is, sufficient numbers of children have been
brought up speaking the mother tongue of their bilingual parents to

allow the languages to persist over long periods of time. In the
Union of South Africa more than 70 percent of Europeans 7 years of
age and older can speak both English and Afrikaans (based on 1951
Census), yet both languages have maintained themselves over a number of generations; for example, between 1936 and 1951 neither language changed by more than 1 percent as the tongue used in the homes
of Europeans.

The point is that bilingualism can be an end product of linguistic contact or an intermediate stage in the transition from linguistic pluralism to unilingualism. The existence of a large number of
bilinguals among an ethnic group is a necessary prerequisite to the
shift to another tongue, yet second-language learning by itself does
not always mean that the group's mother tongue is about to fade away.
It is important to recognize that a high "exposure to risk, " i.e. a high
degree of bilingualism, cannot be equated with the actual rate of intergenerational language switching. Indeed, it is possible for the mother
tongue with less bilingualism to actually have a greater loss in the
next generation than the more vulnerable tongue (Lieberson 1965).

The forces influencing language maintenance in a pluralistic
situation are known or at least an array of factors has been drawn up
by several investigators. Kloss (1966b: 206) lists six factors in describing the United States situation: religiosocietal insulation; time
of immigration; existence of language islands; parochial schools; pre-
immigration experience with language maintenance; and former use
of the language as an official tongue before the Anglo-American period. He then goes on to list nine additional factors which "are apt to
work both ways, in some instances for and in others against language
maintenance" (p. 210). After describing some quantitative relations
between language maintenance and societal changes, Deutsch (1953,
chap. 7) discusses a series of additional factors. Bachi (1956: 202)
is able to explain a fair proportion of the variance in the use of
Hebrew in Israel among both immigrants and the native population by
means of such factors as sex, age, occupation, country of birth,
length of stay, and place of residence. Drawing on Otto Jespersen,
Hertzler (1965: 185-95) describes eleven factors that will yield "uni-
formation of language": war and military service; intermarriage; a
common religion; the language used in government; the rise of administrative, trade, and cultural centers; universal education; technologi-

cal and economic factors; physical and social mobility; and social psychological factors such as language loyalty and prestige of certain languages.

Rather than attempt to provide a new list of factors relevant to the linguistic outcome of race and ethnic relations, this study considers the quantitative importance of a minimal number of forces. La guage behavior is viewed as a form of adaptation to a set of institution and demographic conditions in the society, namely, population composition, both linguistic and ethnic, the degree of segregation, the occupational forces generated by the industrial structure of the society, and age. Although education is of great importance in societies in which schooling is widespread, its role in the maintenance of a group' language will be viewed as at least partially influenced by the forces described earlier, such as population composition.

No attempt has been made to differentiate between groups in terms of possible differences in their propensity to retain their languages. For one, "language loyalty" is impossible to determine until the social context of language contact is described and taken into account. As Haugen (1953: 280) observes, "The strongest possible motive for language learning is the need of associating with the speaker of the language. Any facts we can find about linguistic retentiveness are thus in large measure bound to reflect the degree of social isolation of the group." Whether some groups are particularly likely to retain their tongues above and beyond these social forces, Haugen not that "it seems doubtful whether we can assemble data which will be delicate enough to disentangle this factor from the others" (p. 281). It is risky to use the degree of language shifting as a measure of the group's willingness to adopt a new language, for this becomes nothing more or less than circular reasoning. The point is not to question the possibility that groups will differ in their inherent retentiveness, nor is it simply that this cannot be determined without taking the social context into account, but rather that there are certain social limitations on linguistic maintenance which operate above and beyond the group itself.

There are then two critical problems: the forces leading to bilingualism and the language transferred to children of multilingual parents. In the first problem bilingualism is viewed as a dependent variable. Granted that some second-language learning must take place in a language-contact setting, its actual frequency is influenced by the partial alternatives of economic and social segregation. The interrelations between bilingualism and segregation are critical because segregation can reduce the degree to which bilingualism is necessary by reducing the amount of interaction between language groups. Attention will be paid to the level of communication necessary for the city or region to function, given the nature of the economy and the distribution of the mother-tongue groups both spatially and by economic niches.

The second problem faced is in determining the influence bilingualism has, as an independent variable, on mother tongues of the next generation. In the final analysis the behavior of bilinguals will decide whether a society consisting of several language groups will become unilingual or instead remain multilingual for generations or even centuries. Bilingualism provides the necessary mechanism for intergenerational shifts in mother tongue since parents cannot pass on a tongue to their children unless they speak it themselves. Linguists seem to be fond of citing cases where each parent addressed the child in a different tongue or where a governess used a language not spoken by either parent, but normally the child's mother tongue will be a language which is spoken by both parents.

The family of procreation is usually the family of socialization. This means that if both mates share the same mother tongue, then the only reasonable chance that a new mother tongue will be passed on to their offspring is when both mates have acquired some second language. If the parents have different mother tongues but are bilingual in the other's language, it is unclear what language will become the first tongue of their children. If the parents have different mother tongues but only one parent is bilingual, the chances are good that the mother tongue of their children will be the one language shared by the parents. It is unlikely that the parents will have different mother tongues and neither learn the other's language, although this is a matter that students of marital bliss might wish to investigate. Basically, if it is assumed that the tongue passed on to offspring will be a language that both parents understand, it is necessary for mates who share the same mother tongue to be bilingual before they are likely to transmit a different mother tongue to their children.

In brief, if one of the native languages used in a multilingual setting is to disappear and therefore the society veer toward unilingualism, the native speakers must first acquire a second language for communication. Thus the forces influencing the frequency of bilingual ism are a natural first interest. However, since bilingualism per se does not necessarily lead to loss of the speaker's native tongue, a critical second step involves the transfer to the next generation of a mother tongue that is the second language of their parents. In this sense, and not to be confused with its technical meaning in linguistics, bilingualism may be viewed as being either "replacive" or "nonreplaci for the children of bilinguals. This distinction also implies that the forces influencing second-language learning may differ from those which determine mother-tongue shift in the next generation.

REFERENCES

Bachi, Roberto. 1956. A statistical analysis of the revival of Hebrew in Israel. Scripta Hierosolymitana, vol. 3. Jerusalem: Hebrew University.

Boeke, Julius H. 1955. Colonialism and dualism. In Andrew W. Lind, ed., Race relations in world perspective. Honolulu: University of Hawaii Press.

Bram, Joseph. 1955. Language and society. New York: Random House.

Breton, Albert. 1964. The economics of nationalism. Journal of Political Economy 72: 376-86.

Delgado de Carvalho, Carlos M. 1962. The geography of languages. In Philip L. Wagner and Marvin W. Mikesell, eds., Readings in cultural geography. Chicago: University of Chicago Press pp, 75-93.

Deutsch, Karl W. 1953. Nationalism and social communication. Cambridge: Technology Press, MIT.

Ervin, Susan M. 1964. Language and TAT content in bilinguals. Journal of Abnormal and Social Psychology 68: 500-507.

Fishberg, Maurice. 1911. The Jews: a study of race and environment. New York: Scribner's.

Fishman, Joshua A., Vladimir C. Nahirny, John E. Hofman, and Robert G. Hayden. 1966. Language loyalty in the United States. The Hague: Mouton.

Haugen, Einar. 1953. The Norwegian language in America. Phila-
delphia: University of Pennsylvania Press, vol. 1.
Hertzler, Joyce O. 1965. A sociology of language. New York:
Random House.
Kelley, Gerald. 1966. The status of Hindi as a lingua franca. In
William Bright, ed., Sociolinguistics. The Hague: Mouton.
Kloss, Heinz. 1966a. Types of multilingual communities: a discus-
sion of ten variables. Sociological Inquiry 36: 135-45.
_____. 1966b. German-American language maintenance efforts.
In Joshua A. Fishman, Vladimir C. Nahirny, John E. Hof-
man, and Robert G. Hayden, Language loyalty in the United
States, pp. 206-52. The Hague: Mouton.
Kohn, Hans. 1960. Pan-Slavism: its history and ideology. 2d ed.
rev. New York: Random House.
Lieberson, Stanley. 1961. A societal theory of race and ethnic
relations. American Sociological Review 26: 902-10.
_____. 1965. Bilingualism in Montreal: a demographic analysis.
American Journal of Sociology 71: 10-25.
Mackey, William F. 1965. Bilingual interference: its analysis and
measurement. Journal of Communication 15: 239-49.
Mayer, Kurt. 1956. Cultural pluralism and linguistic equilibrium
in Switzerland. In Joseph J. Spengler and Otis D. Duncan,
eds., Demographic analysis, pp. 478-83. Glencoe, Ill.:
Free Press.
McRae, Kenneth D. 1964. Switzerland: example of cultural co-
existence. Toronto: Canadian Institute of International
Affairs.
O'Brien, Denis. 1964. The restoration of the Irish language. Mon-
treal Star, August 1, p. 4.
Park, Robert E. 1922. The immigrant press and its control. New
York: Century.
Royal Commission on Bilingualism and Biculturalism. 1965. Pre-
liminary report. Ottawa: Queen's Printer.
Royal Institute of International Affairs. 1939. Nationalism. London:
Oxford University Press.
Thompson, Edgar T. 1961. Language and race relations. In Jitsuichi
Masuoka and Preston Valien, eds., Race relations: problems
and theory, pp. 228-51. Chapel Hill: University of North
Carolina Press.

Tylor, Sir Edward B. 1881. Anthropology. Reprinted by University
    of Michigan Press, Ann Arbor.
United Nations Commission on Human Rights. 1950. Definition and
    classification of minorities. Lake Success, N.Y.: United
    Nations.
Weinreich, Uriel. 1953. Languages in contact. New York: Linguis-
    tic Circle of New York.
Znaniecki, Florian. 1952. Modern nationalities. Urbana: Univer-
    sity of Illinois Press.

2 | National Development, Mother-Tongue Diversity, and the Comparative Study of Nations

In Collaboration with Lynn K. Hansen

In recent years various studies have examined the links between a nation's level of language diversity and such facets of "national development" as urbanization, industrialization, gross national product, energy consumption, literacy, and the like. Some of these studies are directly concerned with the language question (Fishman 1966; Pool 1969); in some cases their results are the incidental product of other goals (Sawyer 1967: Table 3, B; Olsen 1968: 705) or reflect an interest in the related issue of cultural pluralism (Haug 1967). Based on various cross-sectional data obtained for a relatively large number of nations, all of the above consistently indicate an inverse association between mother-tongue diversity and one or more indicators of a nation's economic and social development. Indeed, at this point the issue appears to be more a question of causal direction, namely whether these correlations mean that national development lowers language diversity or whether it means that linguistic homogeneity is a necessary prerequisite for development (Pool 1969).

This paper reexamines the basic correlations between development and language diversity. Instead of going on to issues of causal direction, we suggest that the associations reported in earlier studies are spurious in that respect. An analysis of covariance helps to explain why such cross-sectional correlations occur between variables that are not dynamically related. The results not only suggest an alternative approach to the course of language diversity in nations, but they raise basic questions about current practices in the comparative study of nations.

For purely descriptive purposes, it is appropriate to compute cross-national correlations between language diversity and

other characteristics of nations at one point in time (which is precisely the goal in several of the aforementioned papers). However,
most investigators examine such cross-sectional correlations not
merely to describe the existing pattern, but to draw inferences about
change or causality. They assume that the cross-sectional pattern
tells us something about simultaneous or lagged changes in the dependent variable that occur as the independent variables change. Indeed,
any statement about the causal links between variables implicitly
assumes that changes over time in one variable are linked to changes
in another. If this is not the case, then the causal statement would
be false or require additional modifications. Although it is a general
methodological rule that inferences about change based on data for
one point in time are risky (see, for example, Duncan et al. 1961:
160-74; Riley 1973), researchers are often caught on the horns of a
dilemma because data are available for only a single period. We are
motivated to reexamine the links between development and diversity
because in this case it is possible to use longitudinal data to examine
some of the inferences made in these earlier studies.

Cross-Sectional Analysis

        Table 1 describes the cross-national correlations around
1960 between mother-tongue diversity and seven different measures
of national development. Unlike some of the earlier studies, the
analysis in Table 1 is based on continuous variables rather than
dichotomized or polychotomous attributes. This will be particularly
useful later when an analysis of covariance model is used. Mother-
tongue diversity is measured through the use of the A index proposed
by Greenberg (1956). The A index operationalizes mother-tongue
diversity by giving the probability that randomly paired residents in
a nation will have a different mother tongue. Thus A ranges from
zero (when all members of a nation have a common mother tongue)
to 1. 0 (the impossible situation when each member of a nation has a
unique mother tongue).[1]

        The correlations shown in Table 1 indicate that the more
diverse nations are less urbanized, poorer, have lower newspaper
circulation, and greater illiteracy, consume less energy, have less
domestic mail, and are larger. In short, these cross-sectional

Table 1. Influence of Developmental Variables on Mother-Tongue
Diversity: Cross-National Analysis, Circa 1960

Independent variable	N	r_{yx}	b_{yx}	a_{yx}
		Relation between independent variable and diversity		
Urbanization	109	-.52	-.7030	.6092
Gross national product*	77	-.35	-.0001	.4730
Newspaper circulation*	102	-.43	-.0009	.4626
Energy consumption*	90	-.17	-.00003	.3503
Domestic mail*	62	-.24	-.0008	.3745
Areal size	107	.10	10^{-8}	.3541
Illiteracy	100	.49	.0039	.1770

Source: Urbanization (Davis 1969: Table A); newspaper circulation
(United Nations 1962: 648-50); energy (United Nations 1961: 278-80);
letters (United Nations 1962: 405-10); gross national product (United
States Bureau of the Census 1969: 832-33); area (United Nations 1961:
21-39); literacy (United Nations 1971: 583-90; United Nations 1964:
338-69; United Nations 1965: 704-6; Unesco 1957); mother tongue
(Rustow 1969: 94-96).

Note: Linear interpolation is used to obtain 1960 estimates
of gross national product and literacy. With respect to the latter, in
some cases it was necessary to use 1950 data. Rustow only reports
largest and second largest mother tongues. Where more than two
mother tongues were present in a nation, minimum and maximum
possible A indexes for all languages were computed and the midpoint
used for the nation. In almost all cases, the information for the two
largest mother tongues set a relatively narrow possible A index for
the nation.

*Per capita.

results are consistent with a model in which diversity and national
development are inversely linked, albeit it is not possible to deal
with causal direction. Note, however, that the correlations are not
extraordinarily high. Urbanization and illiteracy, respectively, explain 27 and 24 percent of the variance in diversity; 18 percent is
accounted for by newspaper circulation; and the other variables on

the zero-order level account for even smaller proportions of the variance in diversity.[2]

As noted at the outset, a longitudinal analysis of changes over time provides the ultimate test of whether these developmental variables and mother-tongue diversity are causally related. Although various sources provide contemporary cross-sectional data for a large number of nations, unfortunately it is much harder to obtain the necessary data over time. We have been able to piece together a longitudinal set for twenty-three European nations between roughly 1930 and 1960 as well as longitudinal data covering a relatively long period of time for eight different nations. In each case, it is possible to ask about the association between changes in mother-tongue diversity and a very limited number of developmental variables.

A Longitudinal Analysis of Europe

Kirk (1946) supplements the available European census data with estimates of mother-tongue composition and other developmental characteristics for around 1930. Coupled with 1960 data drawn from various sources (indicated in Table 1), one can determine the influence of urbanization and literacy on mother-tongue diversity during this period. The common and perhaps "intuitive" procedure for determining the effect of changes in one variable (X) between time 1 and 2 on another (Y) is to correlate their differences; thus, $r(Y_2 - Y_1)(X_2 - X_1)$. Such a procedure is increasingly recognized as fraught with difficulties (see, for example, Blau and Duncan 1967: 194–99; Hawkes 1972; Fuguitt and Lieberson 1974). Accordingly, we determine the effects of urbanization and literacy on diversity in 1960 only after taking into account each nation's level of diversity in 1930.

First and foremost, the reader should note in Table 2 that the level of mother-tongue diversity in 1960 is highly correlated with the level in 1930 (r = .88), with diversity declining during this period

$$(b_{Y_2 Y_1} = .84; \; a_{Y_2 Y_1} = -.01).$$

As Table 2 also indicates, there are only mild negative associations in the expected direction between diversity and urbanization in both 1930 and 1960. As for literacy, the results are weaker and less con-

Table 2. Changes in the Mother-Tongue Diversity
of European Nations, 1930 to 1960

	Zero order analysis		
Variables	r	b	a
Y_2Y_1	.88	.842	-.01
Y_1X_1	-.34	-.005	.39
Y_2X_2	-.18	-.003	.31
Y_1Z_1	.16	.002	.22
Y_2Z_2	-.06	-.001	.22

Net effect of urbanization and literacy

$$r^2_{y_2y_1} = .77$$

$$R^2_{y_2 \cdot y_1 x_1 x_2} = .79 \qquad R^2_{y_2 \cdot y_1 z_1 z_2} = .78$$

$$r^2_{y_2(x_1x_2) \cdot y_2} = .09 \qquad r_{y_2(z_1z_2) \cdot y_1} = .04$$

Source: Mother tongue, 1930 (Kirk 1946: 228-29); 1960 (see source in
Table 1). Data interpolated to 1930 when given for a year close to
that. Literacy, 1930 (United Nations 1960: 446-49; Kirk 1946: 263-76);
1960 (United Nations 1971: 589-90; Unesco 1957). Data interpolated to
1960 when it was necessary to use the Unesco source. Urbanization,
1930 and 1960 (United Nations 1969: 105-6). Urban percentages for
Albania and Ireland interpolated from data in United Nations 1971: 147,
150.

Y = Mother-tongue diversity.
X = Urbanization.
Z = Literacy.
Subscript 1 = 1930; 2 = 1960.

sistent; in 1930, there is a small positive association such that the more diverse nations of Europe actually had higher levels of literacy; in 1960, there is a very slight correlation in the opposite direction.

The issue at hand is whether either of the developmental variables helps us to understand the mother-tongue diversity of European nations in 1960 after the levels of diversity in 1930 are taken into account. The answer appears to be no. Roughly 77 percent of the variance between European nations in 1960 can be accounted for by taking 1930 levels of mother-tongue diversity into account. The multiple correlation with three predictors, urbanization at both time periods and diversity at the first period, is only .79. Thus, of the variance in 1960 diversity unexplained by diversity in 1930, only 9 percent can be accounted for by urbanization (based on the multiple-partial coefficient described in Blalock 1972: 458-59).

The results are even weaker for literacy; R^2 shown in Table 2 is .78, compared with an r^2 of .77 when diversity in 1930 alone is used to account for diversity in 1960. Here the multiple-partial coefficient indicates that only about 4 percent of the 1960 variance unexplained by diversity in 1930 can be accounted for by the two literacy variables. In short, the analysis of diversity changes within European nations between 1930 and 1960 indicates a general decline, but virtually no connection with either of the developmental variables for which data could be obtained.

These results clearly fail to support the developmental hypotheses derived from cross-sectional data, but there are some severe limitations. First, one may argue that the normal relationship between diversity and either urbanization or literacy is disrupted because the period includes World War II. The consequences of the war on differing ethnic mortality, redistributions, nationalistic processes, and the like were no doubt massive. Second, such a brief span of time hardly permits the testing of any lags, for example the effect of pre-1930 urbanization changes on diversity shifts between 1930 and 1960. Further, what occurs in Europe may not be representative of other parts of the world (although such an interpretation in itself would mean a major alteration of the developmental approach). Finally, there are certain demographic limits on the degree of mother-tongue change during a 30-year span which is a function of the proportion of the population at the second period who were alive in 1930.

Since mother-tongue change is normally an intergenerational phenomenon (Lieberson 1965; Lieberson 1970), the maximum possible change
is affected by the demographic replacement of the population and this
is not a trivial issue for relatively short time spans.

Longitudinal Case Studies

Most of these objections may be overcome by the careful
analysis of trends over a relatively long period of time in both diversity and national development for the limited number of countries with
such information. It is possible to trace mother-tongue diversity in
eight nations over periods ranging up to nearly one hundred years.
Minor boundary changes in all cases are not adjusted, but the figures
for India are based on 1961 boundaries retrojected back to 1911; and
the pre-World War I data for Hungary and Finland are likewise based
on their boundaries after World War I. If the developmental approach
is valid, not only should trends in diversity and the developmental
characteristic be related in the hypothesized direction, but more
critically fluctuations from these general trends should be associated
(either simultaneously or with a suitable lag).

Urbanization

Trends in urbanization are available for all eight nations.
Because of the small number of time points, no attempt is made to
employ an elegant time series analysis, rather graphs are presented
in Figure 1 for each nation. Inspection of these graphs permits the
reader to consider also various lag hypotheses in which diversity
either precedes or follows changes in urbanization.

In three nations the trends themselves are not even in the
hypothesized direction, with diversity remaining relatively stable
over a long period during which urbanization rises. In Canada, for
example, the A index fluctuates between .54 and .60 during the 1921-61
period. By contrast, the graphs show that urbanization has increased
steadily over a much longer period. The sizable numbers of non-
English- and non-French-speaking immigrants to Canada during part
of this period are not fully responsible for the sharply divergent trends
in urbanization and mother-tongue diversity. This is due to the fact

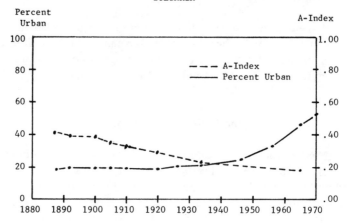

BULGARIA

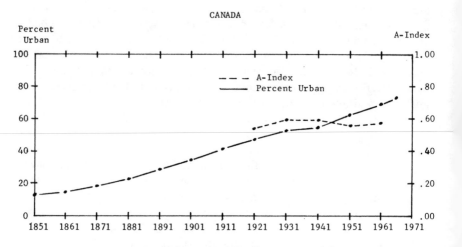

CANADA

Fig. 1. Urbanization and mother-tongue diversity

Sources for urbanization: Bulgaria (People's Republic of Bulgaria 1970: 3, 6; United Nations 1971: 147); Canada (Stone 1967: 29; United Nations 1971: 140); Finland (Central Statistical Office 1971: 8; United Nations 1971: 148–49); Hungary (Weber 1967: 101; United Nations 1952: 181; United Nations 1960: 148; United Nations 1972: 148; India (Registrar General 1964: 54, 181); Switzerland (Bureau fédéral de statistique 1970: 12; United Nations 1971: 151; United Nations 1971: 149); Turkey (United Nations 1952: 178; United Nations 1972: 146); U.S.S.R. (Weber 1967: 107; Eason 1956: 641; United Nations 1971: 154). Sources for mother-tongue diversity: Lieberson, Dalto, and Johnston 1975).

FINLAND

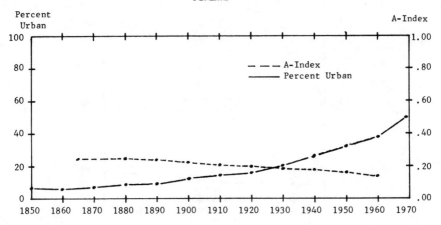

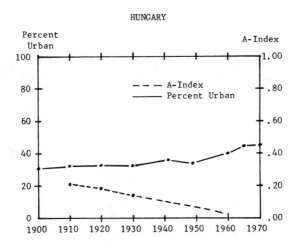

Figure 1 (continued)

27

INDIA

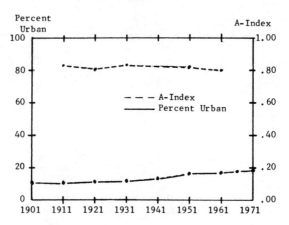

SWITZERLAND

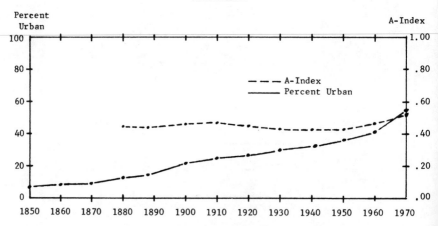

Figure 1 (continued)

28

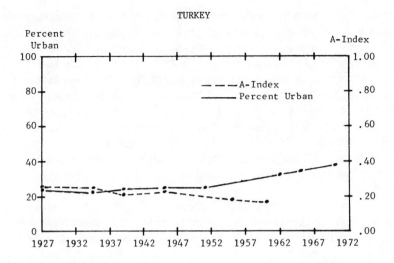

TURKEY

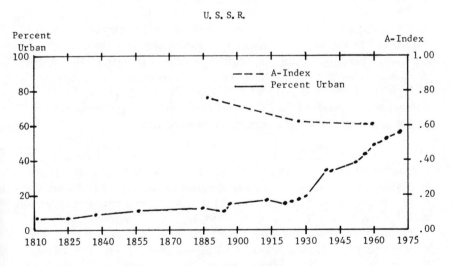

U. S. S. R.

Figure 1 (continued)

that the French mother-tongue component has been a relatively
stable proportion throughout this period (Lieberson 1970: 34). Likewise, Switzerland experienced a steady increase in urbanization from
6.4 percent in 1850 to 54.6 percent in 1970, but diversity has fluctu-
ated over a narrow range without apparent trend between 1880 and the
present. (The rise in diversity between 1960 and 1970, reflecting
immigration from elsewhere in Europe, is no problem since the
relationship is in the opposite direction from what would be expected
from the cross-sectional results.) Although the results for India are
less dramatic, there is a trendless and highly stable level of diversity
during a period in which urbanization has a gradual increase.

        In four of the nations, Bulgaria, Hungary, the Soviet Union,
and Turkey, diversity declines over time and urbanization increases.
However, with or without a suitable lag, fluctuations from these
trends are generally not associated. (The reader must bear in mind
that the key test hinges on whether deviations in the general trend
over time are related for the two variables.) In Bulgaria, the decline
in diversity is no different in the 1887-1930 period (during which urbanization increases most gradually) as in the period since then (when
urbanization rises far more rapidly). In similar fashion, the decline
in Russia's diversity between 1897 and 1926 is actually slightly more
rapid than in the 1926-57 period. Yet urbanization in the latter period
increased far more rapidly. Mother-tongue diversity in Hungary
declines steadily since 1910, but observe that urbanization barely
changes between 1900 and 1950. Turkey's fluctuations in diversity
exhibit no similarity to its fluctuations in urbanization—the latter
indicating a fairly smooth development over time.

        Of the eight nations, only Finland appears to show any simi-
larities between its diversity and urbanization patterns. Except for
the 1865-80 period, diversity has declined steadily, with the absolute
drop increasing somewhat in the most recent decades. Urbanization,
with the exception of the 1850-60 comparison, rises throughout the
period and also has generally higher increments during the most
recent decades. Developments in Finland appear to be compatible
with the notion that diversity is generally associated with urbanization—
particularly with a causal lag such that urbanization precedes a decline
in the A index.

Nevertheless, the longitudinal results for these eight nations hardly support the developmental-diversity propositions drawn from cross-sectional analyses. In seven of the eight cases, fluctuations in diversity appear unrelated to urbanization—a finding which is consistent with the 1930-60 analysis of Europe.

Literacy

For six of the eight nations it is also possible to compare changes in literacy and mother-tongue diversity over time (Figure 2). Again the results largely fail to support the links hypothesized from cross-sectional comparative studies. The stable level of mother-tongue diversity in Canada is in sharp contrast with the decline of illiteracy. In Bulgaria, Turkey, Finland, and the Soviet Union, there are downward trends in both diversity and illiteracy, but the fluctuations are unrelated. In Russia, for example, diversity dropped somewhat more rapidly between the 1897 and 1926 censuses than in the more recent period, but the opposite holds for changes in illiteracy. In Bulgaria, the decline in illiteracy is far steadier than changes in diversity over time. Illiteracy in Turkey shows a steady decline between 1935 and 1950, a period during which there was little net change in diversity. Both phenomena decline sharply during the first half of the 1950's but this is followed by a deviation in the trends afterward. Likewise, inspection of the graph for Finland indicates the fluctuations in the downward trends are not associated.

Both illiteracy and diversity decline so smoothly in Hungary that it is impossible really to talk about fluctuations. Thus, Hungary is the only nation for which the data are not inconsistent with the developmental approach. It is unfortunate that literacy data could not be obtained for Switzerland and India. The stability in the first country's level of diversity would almost surely deviate from its illiteracy trends during the period since 1880. Although it is not possible to obtain illiteracy data for India that take into account the boundary used for diversity, the general trend in India's illiteracy rates was downward during the period; from 93.5 percent illiterate in 1901 to 80.7 in 1951 (Unesco 1957: 58-59). It is quite likely that illiteracy data for a spatially comparable India would show a gradual decline which runs counter to the stable level of diversity shown in Figure 1.

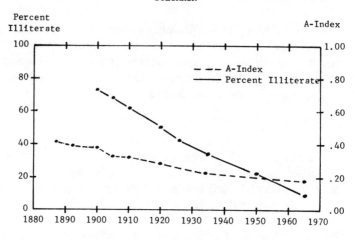

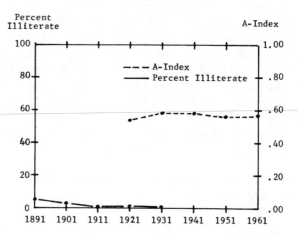

Fig. 2. Illiteracy

Sources: Bulgaria (Unesco 1957: 42, 118; Kirk 1946: 263; United States Joint Publications Research Service 1958: 13; United Nations 1972: 532); Canada (Dominion Bureau of Statistics 1936: 1064; Unesco 1957: 42); Finland (Bureau Central de Statistique de Finlande 1928: 47; Kirk 1946: 264; Unesco 1957: 29, 44); Hungary (Unesco 1957: 147; United Nations 1964; United Nations 1972: 534); Turkey (Unesco 1957: 67; United Nations 1964: 375; Cohn 1970: 152); U.S.S.R. (Joint Economic Committee, Congress of the United States, 1962: 244; Lorimer 1946: 198-99).

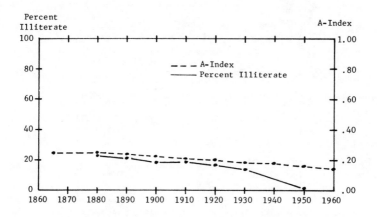

FINLAND

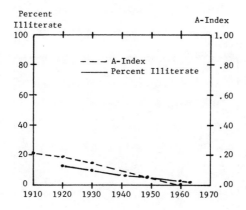

HUNGARY

Figure 2 (continued)

33

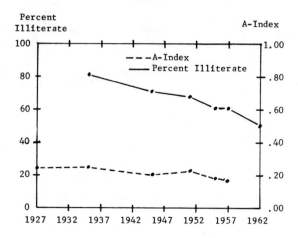

TURKEY

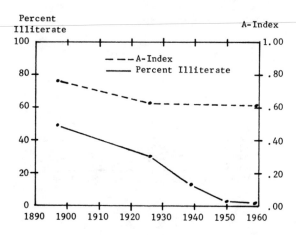

U. S. S. R.

Figure 2 (continued)

Although available for a smaller number of cases, a variety of other developmental variables were compared with diversity whenever possible. These include: density (Canada, Finland, and Switzerland); railroad mileage (Finland and Turkey); dependency on agriculture (Switzerland); and national income (Switzerland). The results are generally consistent with those reported above. Thus, a longitudinal analysis of diversity changes over time fail to support the developmental hypotheses derived from cross-sectional data.

In all fairness, one must note that these results are hardly conclusive. First, the longitudinal analyses are largely for European nations. (To be sure, the range in urbanization and literacy covered with these nations is rather wide.) But more critical is the quality of the data. In some cases they are based on published estimates and in other cases on less than fully consistent procedures. Moreover, national politics sometimes affects how a census will enumerate and report the mother-tongue distribution of a nation (Kirk 1946: 224-26). The introduction of errors normally works against the investigator when he or she is looking for correlations generated by a given theory. But in this case, random errors will tend to support the thesis that national development has essentially no impact on trends in mother-tongue diversity.

Accordingly, an additional step is necessary before we can feel free to reject developmental explanations of changes in mother-tongue diversity. Namely, some account is required of how it may be true that the developmental factors considered above do not affect mother-tongue diversity while at the same time cross-sectional correlations are obtained between such factors and diversity.

An Alternative Interpretation of the
Cross-Sectional Correlations

Under certain special conditions, cross-sectional comparisons between nations could be used to infer the consequences of longitudinal change. Visualize a scatter diagram showing diversity and urbanization for a set of nations. Suppose all nations at time 1 are clustered together in one corner because they all are highly diverse and likewise all have low levels of urbanization. Suppose an investigator finds a substantial negative cross-sectional correlation between these characteristics at time 2 such that highly urbanized nations are low on mother-tongue diversity whereas A indexes remain high in the less urbanized nations. Under such circumstances, the negative correlation at time 2 would reflect the contramovement in urbanization and diversity since time 1.

But this hypothetical situation differs from the one encountered here in two fundamental ways. First, we have no reason to think that the set of nations examined through a cross-sectional study were all alike at some earlier point. In other words, a European nation presently low in mother-tongue diversity and high in urbanization no doubt was less urbanized two hundred years ago, but it does not follow that its mother-tongue diversity was once exceptionally high. Second, nations are both born and disappear. Hence, there are nations included in the cross-sectional correlations for 1960 which were not independent entities until after World War II. Insofar as the mother-tongue diversity and developmental characteristics of new nations entering the system differ from older surviving nations, all sorts of spurious cross-sectional correlations may develop which reflect the changing forces of nation-making rather than a causal link between development and diversity.

If the basis of nation-making has changed through time, perhaps some of the original cross-sectional correlations reported in Table 1 can be accounted for by taking age into account. This is no trivial consideration given the fact that 131 nation-states were generally accepted as independent in mid-1967, compared with seventy at the start of World War II (United States Department of State 1967). Accordingly, an analysis of covariance model is used to examine the cross-sectional correlations between language diversity and the various developmental variables after taking into account year of independence (dichotomized into those achieving independence before and after 1945).[3] The within-class correlations obtained after the effects of age are taken into account drop considerably from the total correlations reported between all nations (Table 3). The total cross-sectional correlation between diversity and urbanization is -.52, for example, but the within-class correlation is -.29. Thus, the cross-national variance in diversity explained by urbanization drops from 27 to 8 percent. Illiteracy gives the next highest total correlation with diversity (r =

Table 3. Correlations Between Developmental Variables
and Mother-Tongue Diversity after Age of Nation Is
Included: Cross-National Analysis, Circa 1960

Independent variable	r				r^2	
	Total	Old	New	Within	Total	Within
Urbanization	-.52	-.23	-.41	-.29	.27	.08
Gross national product*	-.35	-.11	-.25	-.11	.12	.01
Newspaper circulation*	-.43	-.28	-.27	-.23	.18	.05
Energy consumption*	-.17	.05	-.34	-.01	.03	.00
Domestic mail*	-.24	.13	-.40	.06	.06	.00
Areal size	.10	.25	.19	.19	.01	.04
Illiteracy	.49	.31	.30	.30	.24	.09

Source: See Table 1.
*Per capita.

.49). Here the drop is to .30, with only 9 percent of the variance between nations in their diversity accounted for by this factor after age of independence is adjusted. In effect, the last column of Table 3 indicates that only a very small part of the international comparisons between nations can be accounted for by any of the seven independent variables after age is taken into account.

What happens is that diversity and the various developmental variables are all associated with age of nation. Indeed, the correlation ratio between diversity and age of nation actually accounts for slightly more of the variance (.29) than does the simple total correlation between diversity and urbanization. The analysis of covariance generally indicates that much of the association between developmental variables and mother-tongue diversity disappears after age of nation is taken into account. It is as if there are two clusters of nations, with one cluster consisting of pre-World War II nations that are generally more developed and less diverse than the second cluster of post-World War II nations. The correlations between diversity and development are created because these two separate clusters exist, but it is only a slight overstatement to say that within each cluster there is essentially no association between the developmental characteristics and mother-tongue diversity.[4]

Characteristics at Birth

One further step must be taken before the age factor can be used to resolve the apparent contradiction between the longitudinal and cross-sectional results. Namely, are older nations less diverse and more urbanized than newer nations simply because the basis of nation-making has changed? If the answer is yes, then there is good reason to conclude that the cross-sectional findings are without causal implications. On the other hand, the differences between older and newer nations may mean that the former had longer periods of independence in which both to develop and impose a nationalistic policy on the lesser language groups. Thus, a comparison between old and new nations at the present time is not sufficient. In addition, we must ask whether older and newer nations were different at "birth," that is, when they respectively gained independence.

Such an analysis can be carried out for only a limited period backward in history since it becomes progressively harder to obtain the relevant data. Banks and Textor (1963) list thirteen nations obtaining independence between 1914 and 1945 and forty-six nations obtaining independence after 1945.[5] The results clearly indicate that the older set of nations were far more urbanized and less diverse at their time of independence than were the newer nations.

The degree of urbanization at the time of independence was estimated for each of the thirteen interwar nations largely through the use of backwards extrapolation. (For the most part conservative estimates were used which work counter to the results reported.[6]) For the "new" nations, the estimated percent urbanized around 1960 was used (see source in Table 1). Since urbanization has generally been increasing and because many of these new nations were established a few years earlier, the net result is a very conservative estimate of the differences. The median percent urbanized in the older nations at the time of their independence is 21.0, compared with 14.3 in the new nations. In 62 percent of all possible old-new pairings, the old nations were more urbanized at the time of independence.[7]

One cannot determine the level of diversity at the time of independence for many of the old nations. However, current differences are so massive as to make it almost certain that the older nations were less diverse at the time of independence than were the new ones. The median A indexes presently are .15 for old nations, compared with .66 among those nations gaining independence after World War II. In 81 percent of the paired comparisons, the new nations have higher levels of diversity. Such a substantial gap presently between the nations is unlikely to have occurred simply through a decline in diversity among the older nations since their independence. As indicated below, diversity does not generally decline that rapidly.

In short, there is solid evidence that much of the association between national development and language diversity found cross-sectionally is due to the presence of two clusters of nations: those obtaining independence after World War II tend to be high in diversity and low in the standard measures of development; the opposite holds for nations that were independent before the end of World War II. Once age of nation is taken into account, the initial cross-national correlations tend to disappear. This could merely mean that the older countries have had a longer time in which to develop and impose national policies that reduce mother-tongue diversity. However, the available evidence does not support this conclusion. Rather, at their respective periods of independence, the previous cohort of nations were not as diverse or as undeveloped as the new cohort. In all fairness, the analysis does not rule out the possibility that cohorts of old and new nations also differ in their rates of change after independence as well as in their characteristics at the time of independence. In either case, the evidence seriously undermines the developmental interpretation of diversity change.

Implications for Comparative Research

Several issues are raised by these results. First, what does affect the course of mother-tongue diversity in nations? Second, why has the process of nation-making changed over time? Finally, what does the inconsistency between cross-sectional and longitudinal patterns mean for the widespread use of cross-sectional data in comparative research? The remainder of this paper will consider the latter problem, drawing on language data insofar as they help illustrate various points. An alternative approach to the course of mother-tongue diversity will be reported elsewhere (Lieberson, Dalto, and Johnston 1975).

One implication is rather obvious, but bears repetition since it is generally ignored. Namely, serious errors may occur when causal inferences are based on a static set of cross-sectional data. It is perfectly appropriate to seek cross-sectional correlations if one wishes to examine the current association or pattern between charac-teristics, but it is a totally different matter to use such data to draw inferences about causal models of change.[8] Regretfully, this propen-sity to use cross-sectional data as if they represent longitudinal pro-cesses is widespread. The well-known Burgess concentric zone hypothesis, for example, is a theory about processes over time. Yet, as Haggerty (1971) points out, the hypothesis is commonly tested with cross-sectional gradients that do not deal with changes in urban struc-ture over time. Likewise, the vast bulk of research reported in sev-eral recent compendiums of quantitative comparative research on nations is based on cross-sectional data (Russett et al. 1964; Merritt and Rokkan 1966; Dogan and Rokkan 1969; Gillespie and Nesvold 1971). Although the limitations of such results are generally recognized by the authors, they usually proceed to draw inferences about causal developments over time. The results reported above, in this sense, challenge a basic assumption of such studies.

The reader may object that cross-sectional materials are the only data available for a large number of nations. Hence, not only is it true that cross-sectional causal inferences may be correct, but no alternative exists until time series become more common. All this is true, but two simple procedures can improve such research. First one can use longitudinal case studies to examine the inferences drawn from cross-sectional results. In many problems, at least some tem-poral data sets can be gathered for a limited number of nations. To be sure, the available cases may be nonrepresentative or fail to cover the entire range of cross-national variance in the characteristics. Moreover, there are inherent sampling risks with a small number of longitudinal cases. Nevertheless, causal inferences based on cross-sectional data will be far more convincing if they are at least consis-tent with the available longitudinal results.

Another fruitful procedure stems from the use of a nation's year of independence as a control to determine if the cross-sectional correlations remain unchanged. As noted earlier, the year of a nation's independence is a surprisingly fuzzy concept and requires a clearer operational definition. Nevertheless, just as cities established after the spread of automobiles have a physical structure different from those established earlier, similarly nation-states formed in certain periods will be different "at birth" on some characteristics from those established at other times. This is clear in the case of mother-tongue diversity. More generally, cross-sectional correlations may reflect the distinctive combinations of attributes among different cohorts of nations rather than represent any patterns of change that occur after they are established. If age of nation essentially eliminates the cross-sectional correlations, substantial doubt is cast on their use for more than descriptive purposes. Unless there is longitudinal evidence that the variables are more likely to change after independence, cross-sectional inferences of causal change are probably inappropriate if the analysis of covariance indicates that age of nation eliminates the correlations.

The Stability of Nations and Their Populations

Finally, our earlier concern with the year of a nation's independence raises an issue that goes far beyond the statistical problems inherent to causal inferences drawn from cross-sectional data. When confined to a set of nations existing at a given point in time, major sources of change are excluded that occur through the birth, death, and fluctuating boundaries of nations as well as massive population movements across these boundaries. For example, there are nation-states which disappear as separate entities through conquest (Lithuania, Latvia, Estonia, and several times for Poland) or through amalgamation (Tanganyika and Zanzibar; Serbia and Montenegro). In other cases, political entities are splintered (the Austro-Hungarian and Ottoman Empires, or the separation of Eastern and Western Pakistan). Further, there have been massive population movements (the populating of the Western Hemisphere) with enormous consequences for mother-tongue diversity and other characteristics of nations. It is unlikely that these boundary and population changes occur randomly or that they are of no consequence for the new entities which result. In the case of language, we would speculate that conquest and migration generally raise diversity; separatism lowers diversity. The comparative study of nations, when restricted to a single point in time, ignores events which are in themselves one of the major sources of change for at least some characteristics of nations.

In the case of mother-tongue diversity, the A index in the Austro-Hungarian Empire was .84 in 1910, about the same level as contemporary India. The A indexes are much lower in some of the major new political configurations stemming from the disintegration of this Empire, for example Hungary (.19 in 1920) and Austria (.05 in 1934). Likewise, the A index of Pakistan was .62 in 1951, but diversity was then only .04 in the part that later became Bangladesh. Such rapid changes in diversity are far in excess of what generally occurs within nations that maintain boundaries intact. The rate of change for diversity over time is relatively slow. Projecting an analysis of past changes into the future, it would take about five hundred years for A to decline from .62 to .04 (for sources and computations involved, see Lieberson, Dalto, and Johnston 1975). Thus one major source of change occurs simply through territorial recombinations of existing language groups.

In short, the comparative analysis of nations is often based on the untested assumption that cross-sectional correlations may be used to infer longitudinal processes. In the case of language diversity we have found that this assumption generates erroneous conclusions. Hence, the results challenge the existing paradigm under which such comparative studies operate. Further, such an analysis overlooks the processes affecting the birth and death of nations, the stability of their boundaries, and international migration. These events are of considerable importance—at least for the course of mother-tongue diversity.

NOTES

The assistance and helpful suggestions of Guy Dalto and Mary Ellen Johnston [Marsden] are gratefully acknowledged. An earlier draft benefited from the comments of Allen D. Grimshaw, Charles E. Bidwell, and Peter J. Burke.

[1] Although random interaction is hardly a realistic expectation, this hypothetical condition generates an excellent way of describing mother-tongue diversity. The A index was one of the few descriptive statistics found by Goodman and Kruskal (1959: 155) to have specially desirable operational qualities.

[2] All correlations reported here and elsewhere in the paper have been inspected for non-linearity.

[3] Year of independence obtained from Banks and Textor (1963).

[4] Illiteracy yields the highest correlation with diversity among old nations, accounting for 10 percent of the variance. Among new nations, urbanization correlates most closely with diversity, accounting for 17 percent of the variance.

[5] The year of independence for nations is not too clean a concept, despite its apparent simplicity. In the case of Greece, for example, does one go back to classical times? To do so would involve overlooking its later conquest as part of the Roman Empire as well as nearly four centuries of subordination to Turkey. The successful Greek war of independence from the Ottoman Empire early in the nineteenth century is generally used to mark the independence of Greece. But in turn this means ignoring the 1941-44 period during which it was occupied by Germany, Italy, and Bulgaria. The addition of new territories to a nation, when relatively minor, is usually not conceived as creating a new date of independence. Thus, one would not base Greek independence on the additions of Epirus, Crete, and parts of Macedonia and Thrace after the Balkan wars or the addition of the Dodecanese Islands after World War II. In the case of the United States, independence is popularly held to begin late in the eighteenth century, although most of its current territory was not part of the nation at that time. On the other hand, the establishment of Yugoslavia is generally traced to 1918, but two of its important components, Serbia and Montenegro, had become independent in the latter part of the nineteenth century. In other cases, for example Syria and Lebanon, the year of independence is ambiguous since the split from total domination did not come entirely at one point in time such as would occur in a revolution. As indicated earlier, we have used the classification provided in Banks and Textor (1963). This at least gives us an independent determination without creating the danger that the position advanced here has been aided by our own arbitrary calculation of a nation's independence.

[6] There are a variety of problems inherent in estimating the percent urbanized at the year of national independence. Urban definitions are not fully comparable between nations or for the same nation over time. The figures were obtained by retrojection of later urbanization percentages for Czechoslovakia, Iceland, Irish Free State, and Poland (from United Nations 1952: Table 6). The same source was used to interpolate comparable figures for Finland and Hungary. Iraq was estimated by retrojection of figures reported in United Nations 1960: Table 9; Mongolia by retrojection of figures in United Nations 1972: Table 5; Yugoslavia by retrojection of figures in United Nations 1952: Table 6, and United Nations 1960: Table 9. No basis of direct estimation could be obtained for Lebanon, Saudi Arabia, Syria, or Yemen. Accordingly, very conservative procedures were used which are biased against the results obtained. Namely, urbanization was estimated on the basis of only the larger cities in Syria and Lebanon; and it was assumed to be nil in the remaining two countries at the time of independence.

[7] For details on this method of comparing two populations, see Lieberson 1975.

[8] See, for example, the criticisms made in Morris Janowitz 1964: 18–23.

REFERENCES

Banks, Arthur S., and Robert B. Textor. 1963. A cross-polity survey. Cambridge: M.I.T. Press.

Blalock, Hubert M., Jr. 1972. Social statistics. New York: McGraw-Hill.

Blau, Peter M., and Otis Dudley Duncan. 1967. The American occupational structure. New York: Wiley.

Bureau Central de Statistique de Finlande. 1928. Annuaire statistiqu de Finlande, 1928. Helsinki: Bureau Central de Statistique de Finlande.

Bureau fédéral de statistique. 1970. Annuaire statistique de la Suisse. Basel: Birkhäuser Verlag.

Central Statistical Office. 1971. Statistical Yearbook of Finland, 1970. Helsinki: Central Statistical Office.

Cohn, Edwin J. 1970. Turkish economic, social, and political change. New York: Praeger.

Davis, Kingsley. 1969. World urbanization, 1950-1970. Vol. 1,
    Basic data for cities, countries, and regions. Berkeley,
    Calif.: Institute of International Studies.
Dogan, Mattei, and Stein Rokkan, eds. 1969. Quantitative ecological
    analysis in the social sciences. Cambridge: M.I.T. Press.
Dominion Bureau of Statistics. 1936. Seventh census of Canada,
    1931, vol. 1. Ottawa: J. O. Patenaude.
Duncan, Otis Dudley, Ray P. Cuzzort, and Beverly Duncan. 1961.
    Statistical geography. Glencoe, Ill.: Free Press.
Eason, Warren W. 1956. Population growth and economic develop-
    ment in the U.S.S.R. In Joseph J. Spengler and Otis Dudley
    Duncan, eds., Demographic analysis. Glencoe, Ill.: Free
    Press, pp. 634-51.
Fishman, Joshua A. 1966. Some contrasts between linguistically
    homogeneous and linguistically heterogeneous polities.
    Sociological Inquiry 36 (Spring): 146-58.
Fuguitt, Glenn V., and Stanley Lieberson. 1974. Correlation of
    ratios or difference scores having common terms. In Her-
    bert L. Costner, ed., Sociological methodology, 1973-74.
    San Francisco: Jossey-Bass, pp. 128-44.
Gillespie, John V., and Betty A. Nesvold, eds. 1971. Macro-
    quantitative analysis. Beverly Hills, Calif.: Sage.
Goodman, Leo A., and William H. Kruskal. 1959. Measures of
    association for cross classifications. Journal of the Ameri-
    can Statistical Association 49 (Dec.): 732-64.
Greenberg, Joseph H. 1956. The measurement of linguistic diversity.
    Language 32 (Jan.-Mar.): 109-15.
Haggerty, Lee J. 1971. Another look at the Burgess hypothesis:
    time as an important variable. American Journal of Sociol-
    ogy 76 (May): 1084-93.
Haug, Marie R. 1967. Social and cultural pluralism as a concept in
    social system analysis. American Journal of Sociology 73
    (Nov.): 294-304.
Hawkes, Roland K. 1972. Some methodological problems in explain-
    ing social mobility. American Sociological Review 37 (June):
    294-300.
Janowitz, Morris. 1964. The military in the political development
    of new nations. Chicago: University of Chicago Press.
Joint Economic Committee, Congress of the United States. 1962.

Dimensions of Soviet economic power, Part II. Washington, D. C. : Government Printing Office.

Kirk, Dudley. 1946. Europe's population in the interwar years. Princeton, N. J. : Princeton University Press.

Lieberson, Stanley. 1965. Bilingualism in Montreal: a demographic analysis. American Journal of Sociology 71 (July): 10-25.

_____. 1970. Language and ethnic relations in Canada. New York: Wiley.

_____. 1975. Rank-sum comparisons between groups. In David Heise, ed., Sociological methodology, 1976. San Francisco: Jossey-Bass, pp. 276-91.

Lieberson, Stanley, Guy Dalto, and Mary Ellen Johnston [Marsden]. 1975. The course of mother-tongue diversity in nations. American Journal of Sociology 81 (July): 34-61.

Lorimer, Frank. 1946. The population of the Soviet Union: and prospects. Geneva: League of Nations.

Mettitt, Richard L., and Stein Rokkan, eds. 1966. Comparing nations, the use of quantitative data in cross-national research. New Haven: Yale University Press.

Olsen, Marvin E. 1968. Multivariate analysis of national political development. American Sociological Review 33 (Oct.): 699-712.

People's Republic of Bulgaria. 1970. Statistical yearbook, 1970. Sofia: National Information Office.

Pool, Jonathan. 1969. National development and language diversity. La Monda Lingvo-Problemo 1(3): 140-56.

Registrar General. 1964. Census of India, 1961, vol. 1, Part II-C(i). New Delhi Registrar General.

Riley, Matilda White. 1973. Aging and cohort succession: interpretations and misinterpretations. Public Opinion Quarterly 37 (Spring): 35-49.

Russett, Bruce M., Hayward R. Alker, Jr., Karl W. Deutsch, and Harold L. Laswell. 1964. World handbook of political and social indicators. New Haven: Yale University Press.

Rustow, Dankwart. 1968. Language, modernization, and nationhood-an attempt at typology. In Joshua A. Fishman, Charles A. Ferguson, and Jyotirindra Das Gupta, eds., Language problems of developing nations. New York: Wiley.

Sawyer, Jack. 1967. Dimensions of nations: size, wealth, and politics. American Journal of Sociology 73 (Sept.): 145-72.

Stone, Leroy O. 1967. Urban development in Canada. Ottawa:
    Dominion Bureau of Statistics.
Unesco. 1957. World illiteracy at mid-century. Paris: United
    Nations Educational, Scientific, and Cultural Organization.
United Nations. 1952. Demographic yearbook, 1952. New York:
    United Nations.
_____. 1960. Demographic yearbook, 1960. New York: United
    Nations.
_____. 1961. Statistical yearbook, 1961. New York: United
    Nations.
_____. 1963. Statistical yearbook, 1962. New York: United
    Nations.
_____. 1964. Demographic yearbook, 1963. New York: United
    Nations.
_____. 1965. Demographic yearbook, 1964. New York: United
    Nations.
_____. 1969. Growth of the world's urban and rural population,
    1920-2000. New York: United Nations.
_____. 1971. Demographic yearbook, 1970. New York: United
    Nations.
_____. 1972. Demographic yearbook, 1971. New York: United
    Nations.
United States Bureau of the Census. 1969. Statistical abstract of the
    United States, 1969. Washington, D.C.: Government Print-
    ing Office.
United States Department of State. 1967. Status of the world's
    nations. Washington, D.C.: Government Printing Office.
United States Joint Publications Research Service. 1958. Statistical
    yearbook of the People's Republic of Bulgaria, 1956. New
    York: United States Joint Publications Research Service.
Weber, Adna Ferrin. 1967. The growth of cities in the nineteenth
    century. Ithaca, N.Y.: Cornell University Press.

3 | The Course of Mother-Tongue Diversity in Nations

In Collaboration with Guy Dalto and Mary Ellen Marsden

This paper describes the course of mother-tongue diversity observed in nations over time and then interprets the patterns found.[1] Owing to such widespread processes as immigration, colonialism, and territorial conquest, some degree of linguistic diversity is probably found within the vast majority of nations at one time or another. Moreover, language diversity is of enormous consequence for the ver maintenance of a nation-state—to say nothing of assimilation or the institutional structure of a nation. Accordingly, there arises the issu of what affects the course of mother-tongue diversity. Perhaps the most influential approach stems from the work of Karl Deutsch (1953) on social mobilization. His thesis is far too complicated for an adequate summary here, but essentially his is a "developmental" approac suggesting that the course of mother-tongue diversity is affected by changes in such characteristics as urbanization, industrialization, literacy, political power, and the demographic strength of the various language groups residing within a nation's boundaries. Although Deutsch includes longitudinal case studies, much of his contribution consists in specifying a wide variety of factors that should be considered in any analysis. Cross-sectional correlations between language diversity and various developmental characteristics such as urbanization, industrialization, technology, and literacy tend to support the developmental approach (for a review of such studies, see Lieberson and Hansen 1974).

There is now some reason to question the utility of a develop mental approach in accounting for the course of mother-tongue diversity. As noted above, most of the statistical support for such an approach is derived from cross-sectional correlations. When actual changes in the level of diversity and various developmental characteristics are studied, little association is found (Lieberson and Hansen 1974). Indeed, even the cross-sectional correlations appear to reflect the changing nature of nation building and tend to collapse after a co- hort effect, age of nation, is taken into account. If there is serious doubt about the developmental interpretation, the fundamental task of explaining the course of mother-tongue diversity remains before us. Moreover, there is the further issue of understanding why normally powerful macrosocial characteristics such as urbanization, industriali- zation, and the like have so little consequence for the course of mother- tongue diversity in nations whereas they appear to affect intranational variation. With these goals in mind, we first attempt to describe and summarize the course of mother-tongue diversity in nations and then consider alternative interpretations.

Basic Trends

Any serious attempt to understand the course of mother- tongue diversity must begin with an analysis of the actual changes ob- served within nations. Accordingly, a variety of sources were used to measure mother-tongue composition within as many nations as possible for at least two points in time. Although nations sometimes differ in their definitions of mother tongue, wherever possible we have sought information reporting the language first learned in childhood. Diversity trends were obtained for 35 nations, covering periods rang- ing from about 100 years (Finland, 1865-1970; Switzerland, 1880-1970) to only five years (Latvia, 1925-30). Diversity is quantified through use of the A index proposed by Greenberg (1956). This measure oper- ationalizes diversity by giving the probability that randomly paired members of a nation will have different mother tongues. Thus A ranges from 0 (complete homogeneity) to 1.0 (the level approached were each person in a nation to have a unique mother tongue).[3] In view of the sizable task involved and because the data may prove of value to others, the basic A indexes and sources are presented in Table 1.

Combining initial and later A indexes with the length of time elapsed, the goal at this point is simply to summarize and describe the course of mother-tongue diversity within each nation. An approach described by Coleman (1968: 433) permits the use of regression tech-

TABLE 1

Mother-Tongue Diversity of Nations

Nation	Year	A Index	Change in A per Annum	Largest Tongue	Source
Albania	1938	.142	—.00191	.9248	2
	1960	.100		.9500	6
Austria	1910	.241	—.00438	.8695	8
	1934	.051		.9741	2
	1960	.020		.9869	6
Belgium	1910	.549	+.00017	.5162	1
	1920	.543		.5119	1
	1930	.540		.5100	2
	1960	.555		.5000	6
Bulgaria	1887	.419	—.00313	.7375	1
	1892	.396		.7567	1
	1900	.384		.7713	1
	1905	.349		.7956	1
	1910	.326		.8122	1
	1920	.291		.8338	1
	1934	.236		.8679	2
	1965	.186		.8972	7
Canada	1921	.540	+.00008	.6216	8
	1931	.598		.5700	8
	1941	.595		.5639	8
	1951	.565		.5911	8
	1961	.577		.5845	8
	1971	.564		.6020	8
Costa Rica	1950	.051	+.00090	.9738	3
	1960	.060		.9700	6
Cyprus	1931	.322	+.00169	.8025	8
	1960	.371		.7708	4
Czechoslovakia	1910	.561	—.00141	.5948	1
	1921	.512		.6550	1
	1930	.507		.6620	2
	1960	.480		.6700	6
Denmark	1930	.041	+.00063	.9787	2
	1960	.060		.9700	6
Dominican Republic	1950	.039	+.00006	.9800	3
	1960	.040		.9800	6
Estonia	1922	.238	—.00283	.8684	1
	1934	.204		.8889	2
Finland	1865	.246	—.00118	.8572	8
	1880	.253		.8523	8
	1890	.241		.8607	8
	1900	.231		.8674	8
	1910	.212		.8802	8
	1920	.201		.8870	8
	1930	.190		.8940	8
	1940	.180		.9004	8
	1950	.163		.9109	8
	1960	.141		.9240	8
France	1931	.265	—.00017	.8541	2
	1960	.260		.8600	6
Germany	1910	.150	—.00245	.9204	1
	1933	.018		.9906	2
	1960	.000		.9933	6
Greece	1907	.059	—.00058	.9702	1

TABLE 1 (*Continued*)
MOTHER-TONGUE DIVERSITY OF NATIONS

Nation	Year	A Index	Change in A per Annum	Largest Tongue	Source
	1928	.137		.9284	2
	1960	.040		.9767	6
Hungary	1910	.213	—.00364	.8838	8
	1920	.192		.8956	8
	1930	.149		.9209	2
	1960	.036		.9824	4
India	1911	.803	+.00040	.4048	8
	1921	.820		.3853	8
	1931	.829		.3741	8
	1951	.812		.3954	8
	1961	.837		.3586	8
Italy	1931	.061	—.00141	.9687	2
	1960	.020		.9900	6
Latvia	1925	.472	—.00600	.7125	1
	1930	.442		.7316	2
Liechtenstein	1950	.029	+.00330	.9854	3
	1960	.062		.9683	5
Netherlands	1930	.043	+.00190	.9778	2
	1960	.100		.9500	6
Norway	1930	.039	—.00165	.9801	2
	1950	.006		.9968	3
Pakistan	1951	.619	+.00250	.5452	3
	1961	.644		.5201	4
Philippines	1948	.851	—.00008	.2475	3
	1960	.850		.2411	4
Poland	1931	.502	—.00938	.6891	2
	1960	.230		.8800	6
Portugal	1930	.008	—.00027	.9956	2
	1960	.000		1.0000	6
Rumania	1930	.454	—.00677	.7300	2
	1956	.247		.8623	4
	1966	.221		.8779	7
South Africa	1946	.864	+.00021	.2063	3
	1960	.867		.2037	4
Spain	1930	.508	—.00210	.6605	2
	1960	.445		.7300	6
Sweden	1930	.018	+.00073	.9907	2
	1960	.040		.9800	6
Switzerland	1880	.442	+.00046	.7135	8
	1888	.440		.7138	8
	1900	.460		.6976	8
	1910	.471		.6918	8
	1920	.448		.7089	8
	1930	.438		.7191	8
	1941	.427		.7260	8
	1950	.435		.7211	8
	1960	.474		.6935	8
	1970	.531		.6494	8
Turkey	1927	.246	—.00219	.8641	8
	1935	.252		.8602	8
	1955	.187		.8990	4
	1960	.173		.9070	5
	1965	.181		.9021	7
USSR	1897	.761	—.00222	.4431	8
	1926	.633		.5726	8
	1959	.618		.5944	8

TABLE 1 (*Continued*)

MOTHER-TONGUE DIVERSITY OF NATIONS

Nation	Year	A Index	Change in A per Annum	Largest Tongue	Source
United Kingdom	1930	.050	−.00033	.9725	2
	1960	.040		.9800	6
Yugoslavia	1931	.444	+.00032	.7361	2
	1953	.447		.7319	3
	1960	.455		.7300	6

SOURCES.—(1) Tesnière 1928; (2) Kirk 1946; (3) United Nations 1956; (4) United Nations 1964; (5) United Nations 1965; (6) Rustow 1968; (7) United Nations 1972; (8) appropriate census or statistical yearbook for the nation.

NOTE.—Data for Austria, Czechoslovakia, and Hungary in 1910 are all based on post–World War I boundaries. All data for India are based on postindependence boundaries; results would differ somewhat if separately reported Indian mother tongues were combined in cases where they may be merely dialects of the same language. No attempt has been made to adjust for linguistic differentials in migration to or from each nation.

niques to estimate the amount of change per year under the assumption that diversity shift is simply a uniform function of time. By regressing the earliest A index (and all succeeding ones for the same nation) on the number of years elapsed since the first index, the amount and direction of yearly change is derived from the regression coefficient. If only two diversity measures are available for a nation, the result is identical with that obtained by subtracting the earlier index from the later one and dividing by the number of years intervening.

The direction and magnitude of change for each specific nation are given in Table 1. A negative value indicates a decline, and a positive value indicates an increase in diversity. The former is the case for the majority of nations, 21 out of 35, with the largest declines (−.003 per year or greater) recorded by European nations: Poland, Rumania, Latvia, Austria, Hungary, and Bulgaria. It is tempting to attribute the relatively rapid declines experienced by these countries to the boundary changes and forced expulsions associated with the two world wars as well as the differential mortality experienced by various ethnic groups during the second war. However, we shall test these effects more formally later. The increases found for 14 nations are generally smaller in absolute magnitude and do not suggest any clear-cut pattern. In some nations—for example, Switzerland and Canada—the increases clearly reflect new immigration which has increased the level of diversity; in others the small changes may be due to linguistic differentials in fertility and mortality or may simply be the product of enumeration and reporting errors that mask a highly stable linguistic balance.

Limits to the Study

Before turning to the factors affecting linguistic change, it is best to deal with certain technical considerations and limitations which have a bearing on the interpretation of the results. First, small differences between nations in the inferred yearly amount of change are of substantial consequence over a long period of time. For example, India's earliest A index (.803 in 1911) is only .042 greater than that for Czarist Russia (.761 in 1897), but the changes abstracted for these countries lead to an increase of .04 and a decline of .22, respectively, in the course of a century (obtained through multiplying the annual amount of change by 100). This is important because errors are likely in any census or population estimate—to say nothing of the special problems encountered in the enumeration or reporting of language data (see Kirk 1946: 224-26; Lieberson 1966). If diversity changes slowly (ignoring signs, the arithmetic mean change for 35 nations is .0019), then the true change occurring during short periods may be masked and distorted by measurement error (see Coleman 1968: 453, n.13).

Since far from all of the world's nations are included, another limitation occurs because there is no way of determining whether nations without longitudinal diversity data are systematically different from the 35 nations for which such figures are reported. As might be expected, a relatively large number of the latter are located in Europe. However, it will be possible at least to test whether their changes are different from those non-European countries included in our study after the appropriate geopolitical controls are exercised.

Mother-tongue change occurs largely in the shift between parent and child (Lieberson 1970). Since a nation's most recent A index includes some unknown number of residents alive at the time when the earliest A was measured, differences between nations in the magnitude of their demographic turnover alone could affect the values of the basic dependent variable. In order to determine the seriousness of this problem, turnover was crudely estimated by taking the age distribution in each nation for the most recent period and the number of years elapsed since its earliest reported A index. If 30 years have passed between the earliest and the most recent A index, the percentage of the population under 30 in the latter period gives the

TABLE 2

REGRESSION OF DIVERSITY CHANGES ON SELECTED CHARACTERISTICS

INDEPENDENT VARIABLE	NATIONS (N)	REGRESSION COEFFICIENT	
		Actual	SE
Population turnover	28	—.00149	.00233
Initial A	35	—.00139	.00170
Largest mother tongue	35	.00065	.00208
Segregation	19	.00451	.00242
Net of initial A	19	.00794	.00508
Languages in school	28	.01735	.00359
Urbanization (earliest)	31	.00075	.00349
Urbanization (longitudinal)	29	—.00468	.16263
World War II	35	—.00182	.00083
Europe–non-Europe	35	—.00173	.00094
Net of World War II	35	—.00094	.00109
Age of independence	34	—.00188	.00099
Net of World War II	34	—.00174	.00099
Boundary changes	35	.00296	.00217

relative numbers subject to mother-tongue change. The correlation between demographic turnover and the change in diversity is nil among the 28 nations for which we could obtain the necessary age distribution ($r = -.102$), with about 1 percent of the variance in diversity change accounted for.[3] (The regression coefficient and its standard error are reported in Table 2 for all correlations.) Although this is an extremely crude measure of turnover, it does suggest that differences between nations in demographic turnover are not seriously affecting the values obtained for the dependent variable.

Finally, the reader should be cautioned that this study omits diversity changes due to the political disintegration of empires. A case study of the Austro-Hungarian Empire makes it clear that the ensuing political nations may have diversity levels far lower than the A index found in the earlier political unit (Lieberson and Hansen 1974). Moreover, the changes in diversity due to these political developments are far more rapid than the shifts normally observed within a nation's relatively stable boundaries. In this regard, the study is confined to changes occurring in the absence of major political fissions.

Despite these acknowledged limitations, to our knowledge the figures in Table 1 form the most extensive set of geographic and temporal quantitative data ever reported on longitudinal changes in mother tongue diversity. Although the possibility of errors in the data rules out any expectation that all of the reported variance between nations can be fully explained, these change figures provide the basic dependent variable of the study as we determine whether various characteristics of nations help account for the course of mother-tongue diversity.

National Characteristics

Initial Level of Diversity

Even a cursory inspection of Table 1 reveals that the absolute level of diversity varies considerably, ranging from extreme heterogeneity (in nations with A indexes in the neighborhood of .8) to almost complete homogeneity (where A is virtually zero). One would expect the demographic pull exerted on the numerically smaller languages to be greatest in those nations which are initially less diverse or in which a substantial proportion of the population already holds the numerically largest mother tongue (to be called "LT"). Accordingly, it is important to determine at the very outset whether differences between nations in the level of diversity or the size of LT help explain changes in A during the ensuing years.[4]

Despite these expectations, no pattern is found when the magnitude of change is correlated with the earliest A index for the 35 nations. In fact, r is -.141, indicating that highly diverse nations tend to have somewhat larger declines than the more homogeneous countries. However, since only 2 percent of the variance in the dependent variable is explained, we need not worry too much about interpreting the sign of this correlation. Since a nation's level of diversity has a strong inverse relation to the size of its largest mother tongue, it is not surprising that the correlation between change and LT is also extremely weak (r = .038).[5]

How can one account for the fact that neither the initial level of diversity nor the size of the largest mother tongue affects the level of change in nations? An important clue lies in the differential changes occurring among the numerically smaller languages. A decline in diversity usually involves an increase in the proportion of the population with the largest mother tongue. In nations with more than two mother tongues, the rate of loss among the lesser ones varies inversely with their relative size. Increases in LT for nine nations with five or more mother tongues were accompanied by declines in virtually all of the remaining languages. But the rate of decline varied inversely with the relative size of these lesser tongues. Thus a gain in the largest mother tongue is disproportionately derived from the smaller languages in such multilingual nations. If the numerically weaker languages contribute relatively most to the initial gains in LT, more of the later increments have to be drawn from the larger of the remaining language groups. Further, it is reasonable to speculate that the spatially less concentrated native speakers of various lesser tongues are the first to shift. Hence, as LT gains it must convert the more resistant segments of the other language groups who live in fairly isolated locales supported by a relatively high degree of linguistic homogeneity.

Thus the pull of the largest mother tongue expands as its proportion of the population increases, but this pull is counterbalanced by the fact that the remaining segments of the population are presumably more resistant to shift than the children of those compatriots who had changed earlier. To be sure, it would be nothing short of magic to think that an increase in the demographic strength of LT is exactly counterbalanced by the reduction of the remaining groups into a hard core of resistance. When more precise measurements are available and a broader set of change data gathered, no doubt it will be possible to modify this conclusion. But the present evidence suggests that the two forces are essentially countervailing, thereby generating virtually no association between the course of mother-tongue diversity and the initial level of A or LT in the nation.

Segregation

As with most social divisions, mother-tongue groups tend to differ in their locations within subparts of a nation. Indeed, the subareas generally have lower levels of linguistic diversity than the nation as a whole (Lieberson and O'Connor 1975). The issue at hand is whether the spatial isolation of language groups has some bearing on the degree of mother-tongue shift. There is good reason to expect such an influence, since physical isolation is almost certain to gener-

ate greater social isolation—a point well recognized in the ecological
literature on race and ethnic relations. Social isolation would result
in more contact with linguistic compatriots, less pressure to acquire
and use some other language, and therefore a lower rate of mother-
tongue change between generations.

Data were obtained on the mother-tongue distributions within
the largest political subdivisions of 19 nations (see Table 3). Wherever
possible, the earliest available subarea data were used, but in some
instances it was necessary to use more recent materials.[6] The isolation of numerically smaller languages from a nation's largest tongue
was measured through the P* index proposed by Bell (1954), which
gives the isolation from the LT group of all other language groups
combined. A value of 1.0 is obtained if the lesser languages are so
isolated that they are all found in subareas where no LT members are
located. The lowest value of P* occurs if the largest mother-tongue
group is distributed within each subarea in the same proportion as in
the entire nation. The latter condition is never found, but the minimum possible P* does vary with the relative size of the largest mother
tongue in a nation. Thus the level of isolation among other tongues is
related to the diversity of the nation (r is .876 between the P* and A
indexes, and the regression is P* = .063 + 1.041 A). By comparing
the actual P* value in each nation with that expected on the basis of
the above regression equation, one can determine whether the lesser
languages are unusually isolated or relatively dispersed for a country
with a given level of diversity. For example, with an A index of .253
in Finland for 1880, the above regression equation would predict that
the isolation of the non-Finnish mother-tongue population would be
.326—a level only slightly smaller than the P* of .345 found for 1880.
In Bulgaria, on the other hand, language isolation for 1900 is .381,
compared with the .463 predicted by the regression of P* on Bulgaria's
level of mother-tongue diversity. The opposite holds for Switzerland;
non-German mother-tongue groups have an isolation index of .750,
compared with the .523 expected on the basis of the nation's level of
diversity.

There is a propensity for diversity to decline more rapidly
in nations with low levels of linguistic isolation. The correlation of
.427 is modest, with 18 percent of the variance in diversity change explained by this factor. This correlation holds, albeit at a somewhat

TABLE 3

Selected Characteristics of Nations

Nation	Segregation (Year)	Language Availability for Instruction	Urbanization Initial	Absolute Change	Rural and Diversity Correlation	Boundary Ratio
Albania	N.A.	0.9248	.100	.210	N.A.	1.00
Austria	.1334 (1910)	0.8694	.396	.104	.1748	1.00
Belgium	.7850 (1910)	0.9450	.510	.150	N.A.	1.09
Bulgaria	.3810 (1900)	0.7567	.188	.282	N.A.	1.16
Canada	.5866 (1921)	0.8880	.495	.265	.1321	1.04
Costa Rica	N.A.	N.A.	N.A.	N.A.	−.0061	1.00
Cyprus	.2027 (1931)	0.9831	.191	.169	−.2940	1.00
Czechoslovakia	N.A.	0.9838	.200	.280	N.A.	0.91
Denmark	N.A.	0.9787	.340	.130	N.A.	1.00
Dominican Republic	N.A.	N.A.	N.A.	N.A.	−.2680	1.00
Estonia	N.A.	N.A.	.290	N.A.	N.A.	1.00
Finland	.3446 (1880)	N.A.	.069	.311	−.5502	0.89
France	N.A.	0.8541	.390	.240	N.A.	1.00
Germany	N.A.	0.9204	.617	.103	N.A.	0.66
Greece	.1602 (1951)	0.9590	.270	.160	N.A.	2.04
Hungary	.2040 (1910)	1.0000	.323	.077	N.A.	1.00
India	.8853 (1911)	1.0000	.103	.077	.2584	1.00
Italy	N.A.	0.9686	.360	.120	N.A.	0.97
Latvia	.3681 (1930)	N.A.	.346	N.A.	N.A.	1.00
Liechtenstein	N.A.	N.A.	N.A.	N.A.	N.A.	N.A.
Netherlands	N.A.	0.9778	.490	.310	N.A.	1.00
Norway	N.A.	0.9800	.260	.060	N.A.	1.00
Pakistan	.9778 (1951)	1.0000	.114	.016	−.5115	1.00
Philippines	.9742 (1948)	N.A.	2.41	.059	N.A.	1.00
Poland	.5137 (1931)	0.6890	.210	.270	N.A.	0.80
Portugal	N.A.	0.9956	.210	.020	N.A.	1.00
Rumania	.3995 (1956)	0.7300	.130	.250	−.1580	0.81
South Africa	.8132 (1960)	1.0000	.363	.107	.3789	1.00
Spain	N.A.	0.6605	.300	.130	N.A.	1.00
Sweden	N.A.	0.9916	.250	.480	N.A.	1.00
Switzerland	.7504 (1880)	0.9855	.133	.407	.4059	1.00
Turkey	.4441 (1955)	0.8641	.242	.098	.0960	1.00
USSR	.8241 (1897)	1.0000	.152	.328	−.3902	*
United Kingdom	N.A.	0.9932	N.A.	N.A.	N.A.	1.00
Yugoslavia	.5694 (1953)	1.0000	.090	.190	N.A.	1.00

Note.—An index of 1.00 was assigned to countries claiming elementary education available in all mother tongues. The correlation between percentage rural and diversity for subareas was computed for three political units not included in the basic 35-nation sample. These are Guatemala, 1940, $r = -.1102$; Scotland, 1961, $r = .0309$; Wales, 1961, $r = .4120$. Segregation index for Greece based on 1951 census data giving language currently spoken (such data are not used for table 1).

* Between 1897 and 1926, the Russian boundary contracted (ratio is 0.94). Between 1926 and 1959, the boundary expanded (ratio is 1.06).

weaker level, when the close linkage mentioned earlier between segregation and a nation's A index is taken into account. The partial correlation between language change and segregation is .365 after the level of diversity is taken into account. Thus nations with a rapid drop in diversity also tend to have less isolated lesser tongues than might be expected on the basis of their A indexes. On the other hand, if the lesser languages are relatively highly isolated, then diversity tends to go down at a slower pace or shows some small upward movement. In Switzerland, not only do the lesser tongues have an unusually high level of isolation but also the A indexes remained stable until the recent increases caused by immigration (see Table 1).

With 13 percent of the variance between nations accounted for by segregation (based on the partial correlation), this association suggests that a relatively high degree of isolation among lesser tongues tends to reinforce those languages, thereby retarding the decline in a nation's diversity. It would be a mistake, however, to view segretation differences between nations as a more or less random event which in turn has independent consequences for language change. As will be argued later, certain types of linguistic contact situations are especially likely to generate high levels of language segretation at the outset. Moreover, in some instances, the delineation of a nation's political subdivisions may reflect pressures from the linguistic groups themselves. Thus political subdivisions are sometimes modified in order to reduce conflicts between language groups and avoid schisms.

Such modifications are illustrated by both the changes in India after independence and recent developments in the Swiss canton of Berne. Kelley (1966: 299) reports that the high overlap between language groups and state boundaries within India is in no small way due to the successful pressures from various language groups to reorganize state boundaries along linguistic lines. The predominantly Telegu-speaking state of Andhra was created in 1953, with part of its boundary running through the city of Madras (Bram 1955: 54). Likewise, in order to meet the demands of its French mother-tongue residents, in 1974 a new canton was carved out of predomiantly German Berne. When one considers that the Congress of Vienna had put the French Jura region into Berne nearly 160 years earlier, it is clear that only a high level of linguistic retention over the years in Switzerland made this recent event possible.[7] In short, although it is reasonable to assume that the level of linguistic segregation at a given time has consequences for the magnitude of diversity change that follows, there is more than a simple one-way relationship: the level of segregation will also reflect social forces exerted by the language groups as well as certain initial conditions of linguistic contact that will be discussed below.

Political Recognition

As the discussion of subnational boundaries suggests, there
is good reason to expect a complex set of interactions between the
course of linguistic diversity and the language policies of nations.
On the one hand, there are a number of instances in which a nation's
language policies have a profound effect on its language groups.
Bahasa Indonesia was successfully introduced as the national language
of Indonesia after independence from the Dutch (Bickley 1973: 88).
When Italy was unified in 1860, only 2.5 percent of the population were
italofoni (speakers of standard Italian), according to De Mauro's estimates (see Hall 1964: 91). The rediscovery of a distinctive written
Norwegian occurred only after the separation of Norway from Denmark
following Napoleon's defeat (Haugen 1966: 28-29). On the other hand,
pressures from language groups may lead to important modifications
of the political order. In the early 1960's linguistic borders were
established for various parts of Belgium in order to recognize the
Dutch-, French-, and German-speaking areas. In turn, parts of
these regions are divided into subareas which also provide special
recognition of linguistic minorities, for example French in the Flemish region (see Steinberg 1967: 828, 832). In a more harmonious vein,
recognition of Romansch as the fourth national language of Switzerland
was designed to bolster this tongue in its struggle for survival (McRae
1964: 8-9).

In this paper it is impossible to consider the entire range of
complex two-way causal relations existing between various government policies and the social, economic, and demographic positions of
the linguistic groups. Instead, a single indicator of governmental
policy is employed here, the languages used for instruction in the
lower grades of each nation. Judging by the number of multilingual
nations that have conflicts over language policies in their schools, we
are reasonably confident that this is an important indicator. For 28
nations, we determined the languages available as a medium of instruction in at least some part of the country (derived largely from UNESCO
1958). Coupled with the mother-tongue distributions in each nation,
this information permits us to determine the proportion of the country's population with mother tongues used for schooling purposes (see
Table 3).[8]

There is a sizable correlation, r = .692, between this political-educational measure and the course of mother-tongue diversity. Nearly 50 percent of the variance between nations in the course of mother-tongue diversity can be accounted for by this factor. Sizable annual declines in diversity occur when relatively small proportions of the population have their mother tongue recognized as a medium of instruction. By contrast, the declines tend to be more modest in nations where larger proportions of the population have their mother tongues recognized to some degree as mediums of instruction. This result is tricky. Not only is the cause-effect direction uncertain, but also, it should be recognized, school attendance was rather minimal in some nations. Moreover, there are often subregional differences in the availability of education, to say nothing of the wide variation both between and within nations in the frequency of school attendance. At this point all one can conclude is that governmental policies, at least as measured by the availability of educational resources in the language groups represented, are related to the course of mother-tongue diversity.

Urbanization

As noted at the outset, the origin of this paper lies in recently gathered evidence that the widely held developmental approach does not appear to have much explanatory power in dealing with longitudinal language changes (Lieberson and Hansen 1974). However, the study in question largely considered the linkage between mother-tongue diversity and various developmental variables on a case-study basis for a limited number of nations with relatively lengthy sets of A indexes. Accordingly, as a further test of this conclusion, the effect of urbanization will be considered here, simply in terms of its ability to account for the observed changes in diversity.

The urbanization level was determined for a year as close as possible to the initial A index for each country (see Table 3). For 31 nations, the correlation between urbanization and changes in the A indexes is essentially nil (r = .027). In sharp contrast with the results obtained for both segregation and language policy, the initial level of urbanization in a nation fails to predict later changes in the A indexes. Even when the absolute changes in A are correlated with the absolute

changes in urbanization over roughly the same span of time, the conclusion remains unchanged (r = -.029 for 29 nations).

The results for urbanization, since they run counter to expectations
generated in many static investigations involving cross-national comparisons as well as specific nations, will be discussed in greater detail below. But one clue is provided by the correlations between
mother-tongue diversity and rural population within the subareas of
nations (see Table 3). In Finland, Pakistan, and Russia, there is a
fairly sizable negative correlation between the level of mother-tongue
diversity in subareas and the percentage of the population who are
rural. In other words, the urbanized parts of these nations tend to be
more diverse than the rural areas. However, the opposite holds for
Wales, Switzerland, and South Africa, with the level of diversity higher
in the more rural subparts of the nation. Moreover, in many of the
nations, there is little association one way or the other between the
level of diversity in the subareas and the percentage of residents who
are rural. Too much can be made of this finding, since the number of
subareas is often rather small, the results are static, the spatial units
are large, and the positive associations may reflect reductions in
urban diversity. However, with eight nations exhibiting negative correlations and an equal number with positive associations, the results
raise a serious challenge to the common assumption that urbanization
nearly always generates substantial linguistic mixing.

Geopolitical and Temporal Changes

        Clues about various macrosociological forces may be inferred
from the relation between the course of mother-tongue diversity and
either temporal or geopolitical factors. Because of the limited number
of nations with longitudinal diversity data, the analysis will be simple
and, in some cases, far from definitive.

Temporal Analysis

        The first issue is whether there are world-wide pressures
affecting mother-tongue maintenance that have themselves changed
through the years. For each of the older nations with A indexes available over fairly long spans of time, the changes in A from the earliest

period to about 1930 can be compared with changes from that point until the most recent period.[9] If the general pressures for homogeneity have changed, then the level of shift should be generally greater in one period than the other. The results for 13 nations fail to indicate such a change. Among nations with relatively long histories, the movement toward linguistic homogeneity has not accelerated in recent decades. For seven nations the movement is more downward (or less positive) in the earlier period, but the opposite holds for six nations. Given the general thrust toward economic and technological development among these nations in recent decades, this result is consistent with the general failure, cited earlier, of developmental factors to account for cross-national changes in diversity.

Four Geopolitical Factors

The variables considered here are the experience of World War II, differences between European and non-European nations in the course of diversity, age of national independence, and boundary changes and forced population movements. Before turning to the specific variables, it is important to recognize certain limitations. It is obvious that such attributes as German occupancy, European location, and age independence tend to be correlated. Among the 16 nations listed by Banks (1971: 297-99) as having attained independence between 1914 and 1945, 11 are European. Moreover, many of these were occupied by Germany in World War II. Owing to the basically small number of cases under study, 35 nations, the analysis beyond the initial zero-order associations will be necessarily restricted and hence is far from definitive.

As noted earlier, there is good reason to expect the World War II experience to have affected the course of mother-tongue diversity. During that period the policies followed by Nazi Germany and its allies clearly resulted in differential mortality experiences within nations for various ethnic (and hence linguistic) groups. Accordingly, there is the expectation that diversity in such nations will tend to drop more rapidly than elsewhere. Using a dummy-variable approach (where 1 = occupied in World War II by Germany or a European ally; 0 = other nations), a correlation of -.363 is obtained.[10] Thus the nations so affected tend to have greater declines in mother-tongue diversity.

Again using a dummy-variable approach (where 1 = European and 0 = non-European nations, with Russia arbitrarily included among the former), a correlation of -.320 is obtained with diversity change. This indicates that European nations tend to have larger declines in diversity than other nations included in our data set. At least some correlation in this direction is to be expected, given the World War II effect noted above. Hence, it will be important to consider whether differences between European and other nations hold after the World War II effect and other factors are taken into account.

It was noted that recent diversity changes in older nations have not been more rapid than those of earlier periods. However, one cannot infer that time per se is irrelevant. Rather, there is still the question of whether cohorts of nations obtaining independence in different eras, and hence under different nation-making conditions, also differ in the course of diversity which they experience. Perhaps the most fascinating issue in this regard concerns the many Asian and African nations obtaining independence after World War II. At this point, unfortunately, very little can be said about such countries, since suitable longitudinal mother-tongue data for the postindependence period are available for only three of these nations (India, 1951-61; Pakistan, 1951-61; Philippines, 1948-60).[11]

However, with the minimal data available, we can determine whether there is evidence of a "cohort effect" among nations in their diversity changes. Using the classification scheme of Banks and Textor (1963: 75-76), we can place all but one of the nations in one of four different periods in which independence was achieved: before 1800, 1800-1913, 1914-45, and after 1945. Looking at the mean level of diversity change within each set of nations, in all but the penultimate category the levels are well within one standard error of the mean for all nations. The rate of decline among nations achieving independence between 1914 and 1945 is far more rapid than in any other category (a mean of -.020770 compared with a mean of -.001164 for all 35 nations). Using a dummy-variable approach (where 1 = independence between 1914 and 1945, 0 = independence in all other periods), a correlation of -.325 is found. This is a mild association indicating that diversity tends to drop more rapidly among those countries established during the interwar period.

Associated with the periods following both world wars was a massive set of boundary changes and forced population transfers across both older and recently created boundaries. Unfortunately, it is difficult either to quantify or to ascertain the extent of such changes and their linguistic consequences. Accordingly, it was necessary to rely on a very crude measure which hardly taps the full consequences of these changes for the reported course of mother-tongue diversity in nations. Covering the periods for which diversity indexes are available in each nation, we determined the changes in physical area encompassed by each nation (based on data reported in Banks 1971). Poland, for example, encompassed 120 thousand square miles in 1960, compared with 150 thousand in 1930 (the dates referring to the latest and earliest years for which A indexes are available). Dividing the latest by the earliest areal data, we obtain a ratio of contraction or expansion depending on whether it is, respectively, below or above unity. Thus the ratio for Poland, 0.8 (see Table 3), indicates a substantial contraction in boundaries during the period covered.

There is good reason to expect this variable to be less than satisfactory. First, there are forced population movements of linguistic consequence without boundary changes. Second, even where there is territorial expansion or contraction, the population involved may be relatively unimportant in a linguistic sense, as, for example, when Newfoundland was added to Canada. Finally, there may be simultaneous additions and subtractions to a nation which have important linguistic consequences but are recorded only as a net change. Accordingly, it is important to note that our variable does at least operate to some degree in the direction expected. The correlation between the territorial-change measure and the course of linguistic diversity is .230, indicating that contracting nations tend to experience sharper drops in linguistic diversity.[12]

Further Analysis

There appears to be no special difficulty in interpreting the effect of World War II on language shift among nations. This variable accounts for about 13 percent of the variance in mother-tongue change, and the regression coefficient is more than twice its standard error (see Table 2). Although the boundary index accounts for only 5 percent of the variance in diversity change and its regression coefficient is little more than its standard error, we are not inclined to discount the consequences of border change and forced population movements. For reasons indicated above, the boundary measure is probably a poor indicator of such changes. Accordingly, a case study of the effect of such changes on the A index is of considerable interest.

Between the czarist census of 1897 and the USSR census of 1926, Russia lost Finland, Estonia, Latvia, Lithuania, and part of what became Poland, as well as territories acquired by Rumania and Turkey (Saucerman 1937: 97). Given the linguistic composition of the areas sliced out of czarist Russia, obviously such changes would affect the fairly sharp drop in A between 1897 (.761) and 1926 (.633). Using the fairly detailed boundary changes reported in the Comité exécutif de la Conférence des membres de la constituante de Russie (1921) and Saucerman (1937), we can adjust the mother-tongue data available for subareas in 1897 to account for later political developments. The 1897 A index for Russia, if adjusted for later boundary changes, would be .684. Thus 60 percent of the entire reported decline between 1897 and 1926 is due to changes in Russia's boundaries rather than a true shift in mother-tongue composition among the population continuing to reside within the country.[13] Such a detailed analysis is not possible for each nation, but the Russian case leaves us reasonably confident that one source of diversity change is simply changes in national boundaries and forced population transfers. Insofar as boundary contractions tend to involve the loss of lesser linguistic groups, our expectation is that mother-tongue diversity will appear to decline at a relatively rapid rate under these circumstances.

Given the World War II effect on diversity change, do the remaining two geopolitical factors hold up? For European/non-European differences in change, obviously the war is a relevant control. The correlation between Europe and change drops from -.320 to -.163 after World War II is taken into account. Not only is just 2.5 percent of the variance accounted for by this factor, but also the partial regression coefficient is smaller than its standard error (see Table 2). At least in the sample of nations reported here, there is every indication that European nations do not generally differ from other countries in their diversity changes after the effect of World War II is taken into account.

For similar reasons, it is necessary to consider whether the zero-order dummy correlation between age of independence and diversity still holds after the war is taken into account. Not only are the nations attaining independence between 1914 and 1945 in our data set all European, but also German occupation played an important role in the sharp declines in diversity observed for such countries as Poland. However, in this case the partial correlation between date of independence and change is -.309 after the World War II effect is taken into account. Moreover, the partial regression coefficient is nearly twice its standard error (see Table 2).

Why should there be a cohort effect among nations such that those attaining independence between 1914 and 1945 have more rapid declines in diversity? There are several possible answers, but all one can do at this point is speculate. The possibility exists that the cohort effect is purely an artifact of the available data. This would be so if nations in each "birth cohort" universe had identical change distributions during a given period, but differed systematically in the samples included in our longitudinal data sets. Another possibility is that the thrust toward linguistic homogeneity is more successful in the early periods following independence than in later decades. If such were the case, the finding here would be an artifact of the absence of early postindependence data for other cohorts of nations. On the other hand, there is a good chance that some true cohort effect does exist, as it would if the basis of nation making changed over time in a manner having consequences for the later course of mother-tongue diversity. Many of the nations established during this period were outgrowths of intense nationalistic and ethnic movements within subareas of larger political entities. As a consequence, important forced population movements may have occurred after independence in many of these new central and eastern European nations.

Additional Issues

No attempt has been made to apply a broader multivariate approach, since such a complex, recursive system would require a far larger number of nations with available data. Accordingly, the results thus far are reasonably straightforward. Along with education and segregation, there is indication that war, boundary changes, and forced migrations also affect the course of mother-tongue diversity. In addition, one cohort of nations appears to have a more rapid decline in diversity than those attaining independence during other periods. On the other hand, there is no indication that urbanization can help explain differences between nations in their longitudinal changes in diversity. Likewise, change among European nations is about the same as elsewhere after the special effects of World War II are taken into account.

But these results do raise two important issues. First, why is the downward movement in diversity generally so slow? On the basis of the mean annual change in diversity among 35 nations, it would take about 500 years for A to decline from .62 to .04. Second, it is surprising that such a basic developmental variable as urbanization has little influence on the course of mother-tongue diversity within nations. Why would this be so when such an attribute is among the most powerful variables used in contemporary macro-national research? We shall conclude by suggesting answers to these two questions.

The Speed of Change

Whether a change is judged as "slow" or "rapid" depends on the standard of comparison used by an observer. The decline in mother-tongue diversity is obviously slow in most nations shown in Table 1 compared to that in the United States and a limited number of other countries. For the descendants of literally tens of millions of immigrants, English became the mother tongue in a matter of a few generations (Lieberson and Curry 1971). It is reasonable to ask how it came about that the shift was so rapid in the United States compared with that in the vast majority of nations.

In studying the course of race and ethnic relations within a nation, it is important to examine the origins of the contact situation. One fundamental step is to distinguish groups that are politically and economically superordinate from those that are subordinate in these institutional domains.[14] Likewise, at the time of contact one can also distinguish between migrant and indigenous populations, "indigenous" referring to groups with established social institutions—not necessarily the earliest groups known to have inhabited a given area. From these distinctions, one can develop a theory which suggests that the course of race and ethnic relations will be different in settings where the subordinate group is indigenous as opposed to those where the migrant populations are subordinate (Lieberson 1961).[15]

    In the most simplified context, consider the four types of groups: (1) indigenous superordinate, (2) migrant superordinate, (3) indigenous subordinate, and (4) migrant subordinate. It is unlikely that much, if any, mother-tongue shift will occur among the first two groups. Almost certainly a group enjoying both political and economic dominance will be in a position to ensure that its linguistic position is maintained. Bilingualism may occur, but this is not the same as mother-tongue shift. At the very most, one can normally expect only an extremely slow rate of mother-tongue change among such groups. What about subordinate groups? If they are indigenous at the time of contact, as were the American Indians or the French Canadians (after the latter were conquered by the British), it is unlikely that they will change rapidly. Initially, subordinate indigenous groups usually attempt to pursue preconquest activities through their established set of institutions and, moreover, tend to be spatially isolated. Migrant subordinate groups, by contrast, are the only groups expected to show relatively rapid rates of mother-tongue shift. By "rapid" we mean a change in mother tongue among a substantial part of the population in the course of only a few generations. First, migration into a setting of subordination means a movement away from the established institutions and social order of the group. Second, the populations are often under considerable pressure from the dominant group either to assimilate or to adapt to the new order.

    If three empirical conditions held, this theory would provide an interpretation of why the decline in mother-tongue diversity is generally slow when compared with that among immigrants in the United States. It would be necessary to show that only a small part of the mother-tongue diversity observed in most nations is derived from migrant subordinate groups, that mother-tongue shift among subordinate migrants is unusually rapid compared with the changes observed in Table 1, and that such shifts are not generated merely by such special factors as unique economic and mobility opportunities, extensive public education, and the like. A survey of such patterns throughout the world is beyond the purview of this project, but it is our impres-

sion that the diversity observed in many parts of the world is largely
derived from the presence of different indigenous groups in established
and long-standing enclaves. These language groups had been brought
into a single political entity through one group's dominance over neighboring peoples, political acts of unification, or creation of multilingual
colonies such as occurred in much of Africa and Asia. In contrast, it
is our impression that subordinate migrant groups were a specially
important source of linguistic diversity in several nations in the Western Hemisphere as well as some others such as Australia in the post-
World War II period. Thus very likely the source of a substantial
part of the linguistic diversity in most nations is not primarily derived
from the migration of groups into a subordinate situation. However,
substantiation of this view entails a complex research problem that
we cannot deal with in this paper. Regarding the second and third empirical issues raised above, both the United States and Canada provide
excellent opportunities for determining not only whether migrant subordinate groups have unusually rapid rates of mother-tongue shift, but
also whether indigenous subordinate groups in the same national context are much slower.

United States. Since there is no adequate census question on
the mother-tongue composition of the entire United States population
over time (no A indexes are reported in Table 1), our efforts must be
confined to the mother-tongue composition of specific segments of the
population. In view of the extremely high cross-national correlation
between A and LT (the proportion of the population with the nation's
largest mother tongue), use of the latter attribute will cause little
difficulty. Among second-generation whites in the United States in
1940, 52.6 percent reported English as their mother tongue. This
contrasts with an estimated 25.0 percent among their immigrant parents.[16] This shift can be crudely compared with a mean yearly increment in LT proportion of .00077 abstracted for 35 nations. At this
rate of change, it would have taken approximately 350 years for the
shift toward English to occur. Although the comparison of intergener
ational change with yearly LT change is hardly ideal, the differences
are so great as clearly to suggest that the immigrant experience of
the United States was extraordinarily rapid.[17]

One might argue that a rapid shift in the United States reflects such unique forces as early universal education and the high

rates of social and spatial mobility. It is therefore instructive to look at several indigenous subordinate groups in the United States. Most of what is presently the state of Louisiana was purchased from France in 1803. Yet in 1940 there were still nearly 300,000 French-mother-tongue residents located there. Just over 20 percent of the third- and later-generation whites in the state reported French as their mother tongue. Although more recent data suggest acceleration in linguistic assimilation, the maintenance of French occurred for a very long period during which "there have been very few immigrants of French tongue into the area" and "the language has been oral and completely subordinated to English in school" (Bertrand and Beale 1965: 42).

The Spanish-speaking population of the United States consists of several analytically distinct elements. Of particular interest here are the old Spanish who were established in the Southwest long before it was conquered by the Anglos. Since it is impossible to use census data to draw such a distinction, use of ecological patterns is of value. Conquered in 1846 during war with the United States, New Mexico probably provides the closest approximation to the behavior of this subordinate indigenous component. Although we have no data on the ethnic origins of the Native White of Native Parentage population (third or later generation), it is noteworthy that nearly 45 percent reported Spanish as their mother tongue in 1940. If every third- or later-generation white in the state were of Spanish origin, it would mean close to half had not shifted mother tongues by 1940. Since presumably a fair proportion of these were not of Spanish origin, clearly a much larger proportion of the conquered Spanish had not shifted.

As far as we can determine, mother-tongue data are not available in early periods for the very first indigenous subordinate group in the United States, the American Indian. However, one indication of their slow rate of shift is the proportion unable to speak English. As recently as 1900, slightly more than 40 percent of American Indians could not speak English (U.S. Bureau of the Census 1922: 1250). When one considers the length of time under subordination and the fact that no doubt a sizable part of those able to speak English still retained their Indian mother tongue, it is clear that mother-tongue shift was far slower than for the subordinate immigrant groups. Thus the United States provides a striking case in which the subordin-

ate migrant groups shift very rapidly at a rate far in excess of that
obtained in our general results. Nevertheless, within the same nation, indigenous subordinate groups such as the old Spanish, American
Indians, and Louisiana French have changed at a far slower rate.

Canada. The data are of a different nature for Canada, but
the conclusion remains unchanged. Mother-tongue data are available
for 17 specific ethnic categories in 1961, but without regard to number
of generations lived in Canada (see Dominion Bureau of Statistics
1963). The British (a dominant migrant group) have the highest mother
tongue retention, well over 98 percent. Among subordinate indigenous
groups, the French and the Eskimos and Indians (the latter two groups
together in the Canadian Census report), the percentages with their
ancestral mother tongue are 89.6 and 71.4, respectively. Mother-
tongue retention among the French ethnic group is second only to that
among the British. Likewise, the Indian-Eskimo figure exceeds that
for all but two of the migrant subordinate ethnic groups. It is possible
to show that even the two exceptions are probably due to the sizable
recent immigrant component among the Italian and Chinese groups.[18]
In Canada, as well as the United States, mother-tongue retention is
much stronger among the indigenous subordinate groups than among
migrant subordinate populations.

To be sure, case studies of two countries hardly can be
viewed as a systematic test of the proposition that mother-tongue
change tends to occur far more rapidly among migrant subordinates
than among indigenous subordinates—to say nothing of the assertion
that the latter are the main source of linguistic diversity in most nations of the world. Nevertheless, if anything, these results for Canada and the United States understate the profound differences between
migrant and indigenous subordinate groups in their retention of pre-
contact mother tongues. In Canada, for example, on the average,
many of the migrant subordinate groups have been in the nation for
only a few generations. Thus the proportion who have changed is not
only substantially higher than among the indigenous groups, but also
the latter have far more generations of settlement in Canada in the
period since British dominance began.

Urbanization

The results reported earlier in this paper, as well as a more extensive longitudinal study (Lieberson and Hansen 1974), appear to contradict a large number of case studies which find that mother-tongue change is more rapid in the urban parts of a nation (see the studies cited by Fishman et al. [1966: 433], as well as more recent work by Tabouret-Keller [1968], Lieberson [1970], Lewis [1972], Cooper and Horvath [1973], and Silver [1974]). Moreover, the absence of an association between urbanization and language change partially runs counter to the social mobilization approach advanced by Deutsch (1953). With improved data, contradictions may prove to be more apparent than real. Many of the case studies use cross-sectional intranational data to draw causal inferences, and such a procedure is subject to serious error (see, for example, the cautions indicated by Silver [1974: 96]). If the basic question is whether urbanization per se accelerates mother-tongue change in nations over time, then cross-sectional urban-rural comparison within nations is not necessarily a valid level of analysis for testing such a proposition. In contrast, urbanization is measured both cross-sectionally and longitudinally in this paper. Although the more extensive longitudinal study cited above also failed to find any influence, one could argue that the causal lags are perhaps longer than the time spans covered (generally no more than 100 years). Resolution of this sticky issue ultimately calls for more elaborate analysis, but we wish to suggest a perspective that may help.

It is entirely possible that inferences drawn from both sets of data are valid. It may well be true that mother-tongue change is relatively more rapid in the urbanized parts of some or even all nations. At the same time, rapid urbanization in some of these nations may strengthen the long-term resistance to change for all members of a specific group throughout a nation. If this is so, we can expect a number of case studies to report a positive linkage between urbanization and change within a nation, but a comparative analysis of a large number of nations to yield weak correlations veering toward the positive or negative side according to the relative numbers of nations included from each set.

Whether such an interpretation is valid raises empirical questions yet to be resolved. However, good grounds exist for considering this a plausible approach. First, there is evidence that mother-tongue change is not exceptionally rapid in some urban centers. In three of the four major Indian cities located outside the major Hindi-speaking areas, Kelley (1966) finds relatively little usage of Hindi (or Urdu) as a second language. Since mother-tongue change need not occur even if there is bilingualism, clearly there is no evidence of mother-tongue shift in these centers. In Canada there has been a massive movement of French Canadians from rural areas to the urban centers, with Montreal being the most important destination (Lieberson 1970). Although the French acquired English as a second language, the level of mother-tongue change between generations is very low (Lieberson 1965). Indeed, in recent years the confrontation between the French and the English has intensified, and there is evidence that this in turn has strengthened the political, economic, and educational resources of the French language. Likewise, urbanization increased substantially in Belgium between 1866 and 1947 (from 36 per cent to 63 percent of the population). Yet during much of this period there was only a small increment in the degree of multilingualism in the nation. After a modest decline in monolingualism, from 91 percent in 1880 to 81 percent in 1900, there was a period of stability through 1930 (also 81 percent) followed by a slight drop to 77 percent by 1947.[1] If two Belgians were randomly paired in 1947, they would have a common language (Flemish, French, or German) in 61.3 percent of the pairs (based on the H index proposed by Greenberg [1956]). This is barely higher than the H index for Belgium in 1890 (60.8) and not much higher than the index for the earliest period available (57.2 in 1880).

Further challenge to the proposition that urbanization accelerates language change is the observation by Fishman et al. (1966: 443) that ethnic consciousness has been primarily an urban phenomenon. "Language revival movements, language loyalty movements, and organized language maintenance efforts have commonly originated and had their greatest impact in the cities." This alternative perspective in which urbanization is seen as creating ethnic awareness rather than leading to mother-tongue shift, is developed more extensively in Fishman (1972). With regard to Belgium, it is noteworthy that Flemish and German received extensive safeguards during the period of rapid urbanization. Dutch was not recognized as an official language until 1898. In 1932, the subregional rights of each language were established, with more than one being maintained in areas with a sufficient minority. As mentioned earlier, in 1963 the linguistic boundaries of Belgium were set by law. In this regard, a careful reading of mobilization theory indicates that urbanization need not always accelerate language shift, but if sufficiently rapid may actually retard the changes (Silver 1974: 91). After reviewing studies of Nigeria, Indonesia, India, and Mexico, LeVine (1963) concludes that urbanization per se need not lead to the dissolution of traditional cultures. He goes on to assert that "urbanization combined with the political competition of new nationhood sometimes intensifies interethnic rivalries and hostilities that had been dormant in the rural setting" (1963: 285). Greenberg also found little evidence of massive language shifts in the urbanization and mixture of various language groups in much of Africa (1965: 57).

Aside from the important fact that urbanization within a nation need not uniformly affect all of the linguistic groups in the same manner (see, for example, Linz and de Miguel 1966), there are a variety of factors to consider, such as the degree of linguistic homogeneity in each specific city, the occupations engaged in and the economic handicaps faced by each language group, the isolation of mother-tongue groups within each city's subareas, and the economic functions performed in the urban places (Tabouret-Keller 1971: 202-3). It therefore seems to us that the key issue is not urbanization itself, but the conditions under which its consequences will favor or undermine linguistic diversity.

In short, the urban areas of at least some nations may experience a higher rate of language change than the rural regions, but there is reason to believe that urbanization in at least some nations has nationalistic, political, and economic consequences which intensify resistance to change and then spread back into the hinterlands (see Inglehart and Woodward [1972: 374-75] for an even more complex non-linear theory). Under these circumstances, a language group's migration into large urban centers may retard long-term change even when there is a differential rate between the urban and rural areas.

NOTES

We are indebted to James S. Coleman and Donnell M. Pappenfort for helpful suggestions.

[1] John de Vries wrote a detailed criticism of this paper ("Comment on 'The Course of Mother-Tongue Diversity in Nations,'" American Journal of Sociology 83, No. 3 (Nov. 1977): 708-14). Lieberson replied to it in his "Response to de Vries's Comment," the same issue of American Journal of Sociology, pp. 714-22. Only two of de Vries's criticisms were accepted by Lieberson, who agreed that de Vries was correct that seven of the 114 data points reported in the paper were wrong and that in some cases the causal linkage between segregation and changes in language diversity was based on unjustified temporal assumptions. Lieberson reconsidered these matters with appropriate adjustments and found that the initial conclusions in the paper remained unchanged. For more details, see these two articles.

[2] For further discussion of this measure, see Goodman and Kruskal (1959: 155) and Lieberson (1969).

[3] Here and elsewhere in the paper, scatter diagrams were inspected for non-linearity. Since the dependent variable includes both positive and negative changes, it is a bit awkward to describe the interpretation to be placed on the sign of the correlation. A negative sign means that sharper declines tend to be associated with high values of the independent variable and smaller declines or increases in the dependent variable tend to be associated with low values of the independent variable. The opposite holds for positive correlations.

[4] A method for determining this effect is provided by Coleman, but it requires the assumption that the pool of nations all have the same set of rates (1968: 437).

[5] The cross-sectional association between LT and A in nation is very close, but not linear. The correlation is $-.995$, with $A = .907095 - .899178 (LT)^2$. Since researchers and data compilations often use the proportion of the population with LT as a crude measure of the nation's linguistic diversity, it is important to note the closeness of such a linkage. However, it must be recognized that LT is an excellent non-linear indicator of A.

[6] Throughout the paper, the dependent variable is recomputed with an appropriate time span when the earliest available data for the independent variable are later than the nation's earliest A index.

[7] For an account of the political developments leading to this new canton, see Chicago Sun-Times (June 23, 1974), p. 50; New York Times (June 24, 1974), p. 23.

[8] Wherever possible, the instructional information is based on the same period as the nation's earliest available A index. Needless to say, there may be distortions between reported and actual practices with respect to languages available as mediums of instruction.

[9] The nations included and the time divisions are: Austria (1910-34, 1934-60); Belgium (1910-30, 1930-60); Bulgaria (1887-1934, 1934-65); Canada (1921-31, 1931-71); Czechoslovakia (1919-30, 1930-60); Finland (1865-1930, 1930-60); Germany (1910-33, 1933-60); Greece (1907-28, 1928-60); Hungary (1910-30, 1930-60); India (1911-31, 1931-61); Russia (1897-1926, 1926-59); Switzerland (1880-1930, 1930-70); Turkey (1927-35, 1935-65). The Coleman method was applied if more than two data points were available within each span.

[10] Although Estonia and Latvia were conquered by Germany during World War II, they were not given a one in the dummy-variable analysis because their A indexes end before World War II.

[11] Longitudinal data are available for a fourth nation achieving independence after World War II, Cyprus, but the period covered includes preindependence changes.

[12] Because Russia's boundaries contracted around World War I and expanded after World War II, we treated the changes separately for this nation and applied the appropriate A indexes in each case.

[13] Initial gross change = .761 - .633 = .128. Change in the 1897 A index after adjusting for later boundary changes = .761 - .684 = .077. Percentage of total reported decline attributed to boundary changes = (.077/.128) (100) = 60.

[14] Such a distinction does not always hold. For example, the Chinese in Thailand maintained economic dominance at the same time as the Thai ethnic group was dominant politically.

[15] For a considerably more elaborate typological development of contact situations, see Schermerhorn (1970). This typology has been applied to language contact by Verdoodt with similar conclusions (1971).

[16] The proportion of immigrant parents with English mother tongue is inferred through a standardization based on English mother-tongue data for foreign-born whites in 1940 by specific country of birth and weighted by the country-of-origin distribution for the second

generation (native whites of foreign or mixed parentage). An earlier period was not used because of changes in the mother-tongue definition employed by the Bureau of the Census (Kiser 1956: 314). Use of cross-sectional data to draw longitudinal inferences is subject to errors if the mother-tongue composition of immigrants has changed over time or because of linguistic differentials in mortality, fertility, or international migration (see Taeuber and Taeuber 1967). Unless otherwise indicated, language data for the United States are derived from U.S. Bureau of the Census (1943).

[17] On the basis of the distribution for the 35 nations, even at two standard errors above the mean, it would take slightly over 200 years for a change of this magnitude to occur.

[18] Among the Italian-mother-tongue population of Canada, slightly more than 75 percent were foreign-born. Assuming that all of the foreign-born population with Italian mother tongue are also of Italian ethnic origin, Italian would be the mother tongue of only 38 percent of the Canadian-born Italian ethnic group. This is a substantially lower level of retention than for the indigenous subordinate groups. Because of data limitations, analogous calculations are not possible for the Chinese. But if all of the Chinese-born in Canada are assumed to have Chinese as their mother tongue, this would mean that 54 percent of the Canadian-born Chinese ethnic group have their ancestral mother tongue. Again the retention is lower than that experienced by the indigenous groups.

[19] Urbanization figures obtained from UNESCO (1957: 183).

REFERENCES

Banks, Arthur S. 1971. Cross-polity time-series data. Cambridge: MIT Press.

Banks, Arthur S., and Robert B. Textor. 1963. A cross-polity survey. Cambridge: MIT Press.

Bell, Wendell. 1954. A probability model for the measurement of ecological segregation. Social Forces 32 (May): 357-64.

Bertrand, Alvin L., and Calvin L. Beale. 1965. The French and non-French in rural Louisiana. U.S. Dept. of Agriculture Bull. 606.

Bickley, Verner C. 1973. Cultural aspects of language imposition in Malaya, Singapore, and Indonesia. In Richard W.

Brislin, ed., Topics in culture learning, vol. 1. Honolulu: East-West Center.

Bram, Joseph. 1955. Language and society. New York: Random House.

Coleman, James S. 1968. The mathematical study of change. In Hubert M. Blalock, Jr., and Ann B. Blalock, eds., Methodology in social research. New York: McGraw-Hill.

Comité exécutif de la Conférence des membres de la constituante de Russie. 1921. Mémoire sur le Traité de Riga. Paris: Presse Franco-Russe.

Cooper, Robert L., and Ronald J. Horvath. 1973. Language, migration, and urbanization in Ethiopia. Anthropological Linguistics 15 (May): 221-43.

Deutsch, Karl W. 1953. Nationalism and social communication. Cambridge: MIT Press.

Dominion Bureau of Statistics. 1963. 1961 Census of Canada, population, language by ethnic groups. Ottawa: Queen's Printer.

Fishman, Joshua A. 1972. Language and nationalism. Rowley, Mass.: Newbury House.

Fishman, Joshua A., Vladimir C. Nahirny, John E. Hofman, and Robert G. Hayden. 1966. Language loyalty in the United States. The Hague: Mouton.

Goodman, Leo A., and William H. Kruskal. 1959. Measures of association for cross classifications. II. Further discussion and references. Journal of the American Statistical Association 54 (March): 123-63.

Greenberg, Joseph H. 1956. The measurement of linguistic diversity. Language 32 (Jan.-March): 109-15.

_____. 1965. Urbanism, migration, and language. In Hilda Kuper, ed., Urbanization and migration in West Africa. Berkeley: University of California Press.

Hall, Robert A. 1964. Review of Storia linguistica dell'Italia unita by Tullio De Mauro. Language 40 (Jan.-March): 91-96.

Haugen, Einar. 1966. Language conflict and language planning: the case of modern Norwegian. Cambridge: Harvard University Press.

Inglehart, R., and M. Woodward. 1972. Language conflicts and political community. In Pier Paolo Giglioli, ed., Language and social context. Harmondsworth, Middlesex: Penguin.

Kelley, Gerald. 1966. The status of Hindi as a lingua franca. In
    William Bright, ed., Sociolinguistics. The Hague: Mouton.
Kirk, Dudley. 1946. Europe's population in the interwar years.
    Princeton, N.J.: Princeton University Press.
Kiser, Clyde V. 1956. Cultural pluralism. In Joseph J. Spengler
    and Otis Dudley Duncan, eds., Demographic analysis.
    Glencoe, Ill.: Free Press.
LeVine, Robert. 1963. Political socialization and culture change.
    In Clifford Geertz, ed., Old societies and new states.
    New York: Free Press.
Lewis, E. Glyn. 1972. Multilingualism in the Soviet Union. The
    Hague: Mouton.
Lieberson, Stanley. 1961. A societal theory of race and ethnic
    relations. American Sociological Review 26 (Dec.): 902-10.
_____. 1965. Bilingualism in Montreal. American Journal of
    Sociology 71 (July): 10-25.
_____. 1966. Language questions in censuses. Sociological
    Inquiry 36 (Spring): 262-79.
_____. 1969. Measuring population diversity. American Socio-
    logical Review 34 (Dec.): 850-62.
_____. 1970. Language and ethnic relations in Canada. New
    York: Wiley.
Lieberson, Stanley, and Timothy J. Curry. 1971. Language shift in
    the United States: some demographic clues. International
    Migration Review 5 (Summer): 125-37.
Lieberson, Stanley, and Lynn K. Hansen. 1974. National develop-
    ment, mother tongue diversity, and the comparative study
    of nations. American Sociological Review 39 (Aug.): 523-
    41.
Lieberson, Stanley, and James F. O'Connor. 1975. Language diver-
    sity in a nation and its regions. In Jean-Guy Savard and
    Richard Vineault, eds., Multilingual political systems:
    problems and solutions. Quebec: Laval University Press.
Linz, Juan J., and Amando de Miguel. 1966. Within-nation differ-
    ences and comparisons: the eight Spains. In Richard L.
    Merritt and Stein Rokkan, eds., Comparing nations: the use
    of quantitative data in cross-national research. New Haven:
    Yale University Press.
McRae, Kenneth D. 1964. Switzerland: example of cultural coexist-
    ence. Toronto: Canadian Institute of International Affairs.

Rustow, Dankwart. 1968. Language, modernization and nationhood—an attempt at typology. In Joshua A. Fishman, Charles A. Ferguson, and Jyotirindra Das Gupta, eds., Language problems of developing nations. New York: Wiley.

Saucerman, Sophia. 1937. International transfers of territory in Europe. Washington, D. C.: Government Printing Office.

Schermerhorn, Richard A. 1970. Comparative ethnic relations: a framework for theory and research. New York: Random House.

Silver, Brian. 1974. The impact of urbanization and geographical dispersion on the linguistic russification of Soviet nationalities. Demography 11(Feb.): 89–103.

Steinberg, S. H. 1967. The statesman's year-book, 1967–1968. London: Macmillan.

Tabouret-Keller, Andrée. 1968. Sociological factors of language maintenance and language shift: a methodological approach based on European and African examples. In Joshua A. Fishman, Charles A. Ferguson, and Jyotirindra Das Gupta, eds., Language problems of developing nations. New York: Wiley.

_____. 1971. Language use in relation to the growth of towns in West Africa—a survey. International Migration Review 5 (Summer): 180–203.

Taeuber, Alma F., and Karl E. Taeuber. 1967. Recent immigration and studies of ethnic assimilation. Demography 4(2): 798–808.

Tesnière, L. 1928. Statistique des langues de l'Europe. In A. Meillet, ed., Les langues dans l'Europe nouvelle. Paris: Payot.

UNESCO. 1957. World illiteracy at mid-century. Paris: UNESCO.

_____. 1958. World survey of education. Vol. 2, Primary education. Paris: UNESCO.

United Nations. 1956. Demographic yearbook, 1956. New York: United Nations.

_____. 1964. Demographic yearbook, 1963. New York: United Nations.

_____. 1965. Demographic yearbook, 1964. New York: United Nations.

_____. 1972. Demographic yearbook, 1971. New York: United Nations.

U.S. Bureau of the Census. 1922. Fourteenth census of the United
        States: 1920, population, general report and analytical
        tables. Washington, D.C.: Government Printing Office.
_____. 1943. Sixteenth census of the United States: 1940, popula-
        tion, mother tongue. Washington, D.C.: Government Print-
        ing Office.
Verdoodt, Albert. 1971. The differential impact of immigrant French
        speakers on indigenous German speakers: a case study in
        the light of two theories. International Migration Review 5
        (Summer): 138-46.

4 | A Societal Theory of Race and Ethnic Relations

"In the relations of races there is a cycle of events which tends everywhere to repeat itself."[1] Park's assertion served as a prologue to the now classical cycle of competition, conflict, accommodation, and assimilation. A number of other attempts have been made to formulate phases or stages ensuing from the initial contacts between racial and ethnic groups.[2] However, the sharp contrasts between relatively harmonious race relations in Brazil and Hawaii and the current racial turmoil in South Africa and Indonesia serve to illustrate the difficulty in stating—to say nothing of interpreting—an inevitable "natural history" of race and ethnic relations.

Many earlier race and ethnic cycles were, in fact, narrowly confined to a rather specific set of groups or contact situations. Bogardus, for example, explicitly limited his synthesis to Mexican and Oriental immigrant groups on the west coast of the United States and suggested that this is but one of many different cycles of relations between immigrants and native Americans.[3] Similarly, the Australian anthropologist Price developed three phases that appear to account for the relationships between white English-speaking migrants and the aborigines of Australia, Maoris in New Zealand, and Indians of the United States and Canada.[4]

This paper seeks to present a rudimentary theory of the development of race and ethnic relations that systematically accounts for differences between societies in such divergent consequences of contact as racial nationalism and warfare, assimilation and fusion, and extinction. It postulates that the critical problem on a societal level in racial or ethnic contact is initially each population's maintenance and development of a social order compatible with its ways of

life prior to contact. The crux of any cycle must, therefore, deal
with political, social, and economic institutions. The emphasis given
in earlier cycles to one group's dominance of another in these areas
is therefore hardly surprising.[5]

Although we accept this institutional approach, the thesis
presented here is that knowledge of the nature of one group's domination over another in the political, social, and economic spheres is a
necessary but insufficient prerequisite for predicting or interpreting
the final and intermediate stages of racial and ethnic contact. Rather,
institutional factors are considered in terms of a distinction between
two major types of contact situations: contacts involving subordination of an indigenous population by a migrant group, for example
Negro-white relations in South Africa; and contacts involving subordination of a migrant population by an indigenous racial or ethnic group,
for example Japanese migrants to the United States.

After considering the societal issues inherent in racial and
ethnic contact, the distinction developed between migrant and indigenous superordination will be utilized in examining each of the following
dimensions of race relations: political and economic control, multiple
ethnic contacts, conflict and assimilation. The terms "race" and
"ethnic" are used interchangeably.

Differences Inherent in Contact

Most situations of ethnic contact involve at least one indigenous group and at least one group migrating to the area. The only exception at the initial point in contact would be the settlement of an
uninhabited area by two or more groups. By "indigenous" is meant
not necessarily the aborigines, but rather a population sufficiently
established in an area so as to possess the institutions and demographi
capacity for maintaining some minimal form of social order through
generations. Thus a given spatial area may have different indigenous
groups through time. For example, the indigenous population of
Australia is presently largely white and primarily of British origin,
although the Tasmanoids and Australoids were once in possession of
the area.[6] A similar racial shift may be observed in the populations
indigenous to the United States.

Restricting discussion to the simplest of contact situations, i. e. involving one migrant and one established population, we can generally observe sharp differences in their social organization at the time of contact. The indigenous population has an established and presumably stable organization prior to the arrival of migrants, i. e. government, economic activities adapted to the environment and the existing techniques of resource utilization, kinship, stratification, and religious systems.[7] On the basis of a long series of migration studies, we may be reasonably certain that the social order of a migrant population's homeland is not wholly transferred to their new settlement.[8] Migrants are required to make at least some institutional adaptations and innovations in view of the presence of an indigenous population, the demographic selectivity of migration, and differences in habitat.

For example, recent postwar migrations from Italy and the Netherlands indicate considerable selectivity in age and sex from the total populations of these countries. Nearly half of 30,000 males leaving the Netherlands in 1955 were between 20 and 39 years of age whereas only one-quarter of the male population was of these ages.[9] Similarly, over 40,000 males in this age range accounted for somewhat more than half of Italy's male emigrants in 1951, although they comprise roughly 30 percent of the male population of Italy.[10] In both countries, male emigrants exceed females in absolute numbers as well as in comparison with the sex ratios of their nation. That these cases are far from extreme can be illustrated with Oriental migration data. In 1920, for example, there were 38,000 foreign-born Chinese adult males in the United States, but only 2,000 females of the same group.[11]

In addition to these demographic shifts, the new physical and biological conditions of existence require the revision and creation of social institutions if the social order known in the old country is to be approximated and if the migrants are to survive. The migration of eastern and southern European peasants around the turn of the century to urban industrial centers of the United States provides a well-documented case of radical changes in occupational pursuits as well as the creation of a number of institutions in response to the new conditions of urban life, e.g. mutual aid societies, national churches, and financial institutions.

In short, when two populations begin to occupy the same habitat but do not share a single order, each group endeavors to main tain the political and economic conditions that are at least compatible with the institutions existing before contact. These conditions for the maintenance of institutions not only can differ for the two groups in contact, but are often conflicting. European contacts with the American Indian, for example, led to the decimation of the latter's sources of sustenance and disrupted religious and tribal forms of organization With respect to a population's efforts to maintain its social instituions we may therefore assume that the presence of another ethnic group is an important part of the environment. Further, if groups in contact differ in their capacity to impose changes on the other group, then we may expect to find one group "superordinate" and the other population "subordinate" in maintaining or developing a suitable environment.

It is here that efforts at a single cycle of race and ethnic relations must fail. For it is necessary to introduce a distinction in the nature or form of subordination before attempting to predict whether conflict or relatively harmonious assimilation will develop. As we shall shortly show, the race relations cycle in areas where the migrant group is superordinate and indigenous group subordinate differs sharply from the stages in societies composed of a superordinate indi nous group and subordinate migrants.[12]

Political and Economic Control

Emphasis is placed herein on economic and political dominance since it is assumed that control of these institutions will be instrumental in establishing a suitable milieu for at least the population own social institutions, e.g. educational, religious, and kinship, as well as control of such major cultural artifacts as language.

Migrant superordination. When the population migrating to a new contact situation is superior in technology (particularly weapon and more tightly organized than the indigenous group, the necessary conditions for maintaining the migrants' political and economic institutions are usually imposed on the indigenous population. Warfare, under such circumstances, often occurs early in the contacts between the two groups as the migrants begin to interfere with the natives'

established order. There is frequently conflict even if the initial
contact was friendly. Price, for example, has observed the following consequences of white invasion and subordination of the indigenous
populations of Australia, Canada, New Zealand, and the United States:

> During an opening period of pioneer invasion on moving
> frontiers the whites decimated the natives with their dis-
> eases; occupied their lands by seizure or by pseudo-purchase;
> slaughtered those who resisted; intensified tribal warfare by
> supplying white weapons; ridiculed and disrupted native re-
> ligions, society and culture, and generally reduced the unhappy
> peoples to a state of despondency under which they neither de-
> sired to live, nor to have children to undergo similar condi-
> tions.[13]

The numerical decline of indigenous populations after their
initial subordination to a migrant group, whether caused by warfare,
introduction of venereal and other diseases, or disruption of sustenance activities, has been documented for a number of contact situations
in addition to those discussed by Price.[14]

In addition to bringing about these demographic and economic
upheavals, the superordinate migrants frequently create political entities that are not at all coterminous with the boundaries existing during
the indigenous populations' supremacy prior to contact. For example,
the British and Boers in southern Africa carved out political states
that included areas previously under the control of separate and often
warring groups.[15] Indeed, European alliances with feuding tribes
were often used as a fulcrum for the territorial expansion of whites
into southern Africa.[16] The bifurcation of tribes into two nations and
the migrations of groups across newly created national boundaries
are both consequences of the somewhat arbitrary nature of the political entities created in regions of migrant superordination.[17] This
incorporation of diverse indigenous populations into a single territorial unit under the dominance of a migrant group has considerable importance for later developments in this type of racial and ethnic contact.

Indigenous superordination. When a population migrates to
a subordinate position considerably less conflict occurs in the early
stages. The movements of many European and Oriental populations

to political, economic, and social subordination in the United States
were not converted into warfare, nationalism, or long-term conflict.
Clearly, the occasional labor and racial strife marking the history of
immigration of the United States is not on the same level as the efforts
to expel or revolutionize the social order. American Negroes, one of
the most persistently subordinated migrant groups in the country,
never responded in significant numbers to the encouragement of migration to Liberia. The single important large-scale nationalistic effort,
Marcus Garvey's Universal Negro Improvement Association, never
actually led to mass emigration of Negroes.[18] By contrast, the indigenous American Indians fought long and hard to preserve control over
their habitat.

    In interpreting differences in the effects of migrant and indige-
nous subordination, the migrants must be considered in the context of
the options available to the group. Irish migrants to the United States
in the 1840's, for example, although clearly subordinate to native whites
of other origins, fared better economically than if they had remained
in their mother country.[19] Further, the option of returning to the home
land often exists for populations migrating to subordinate situations.
Jerome reports that net migration to the United States between the mid-
years of 1907 and 1923 equaled roughly 65 percent of gross immigration
This indicates that immigrant dissatisfaction with subordination or othe
conditions of contact can often be resolved by withdrawal from the area
Recently subordinated indigenous groups, by contrast, are perhaps less
apt to leave their habitat so readily.

    Finally, when contacts between racial and ethnic groups are
under the control of the indigenous population, threats of demographic
and institutional imbalance are reduced since the superordinate populations can limit the numbers and groups entering. For example, when
Oriental migration to the United States threatened whites, sharp cuts
were executed in the quotas.[21] Similar events may be noted with respect to the decline of immigration from the so-called new sources of
eastern and southern Europe. Whether a group exercises its control
over immigration far before it is actually under threat is, of course,
not germane to the point that immigrant restriction provides a mechanism whereby potential conflict is prevented.

    In summary, groups differ in the conditions necessary for
maintaining their respective social orders. In areas where the migra:

group is dominant, frequently the indigenous population suffers sharp numerical declines and their economic and political institutions are seriously undermined. Conflict often accompanies the establishment of migrant superordination. Subordinate indigenous populations generally have no alternative location and do not control the numbers of new ethnic populations admitted into their area. By contrast, when the indigenous population dominates the political and economic conditions, the migrant group is introduced into the economy of the indigenous population. Although subordinate in their new habitat, the migrants may fare better than if they remained in their homeland. Hence their subordination occurs without great conflict. In addition, the migrants usually have the option of returning to their homeland and the indigenous population controls the number of new immigrants in the area.

Multiple Ethnic Contacts

Although the introduction of a third major ethnic or racial group frequently occurs in both types of societies distinguished here, there are significant differences between conditions in habitats under indigenous domination and areas where a migrant population is superordinate. Chinese and Indian migrants, for example, were often welcomed by whites in areas where large indigenous populations were suppressed, but these migrants were restricted in the white mother country. Consideration of the causes and consequences of multi-ethnic contacts is therefore made in terms of the two types of racial and ethnic contact.

Migrant superordination. In societies where the migrant population is superordinate, it is often necessary to introduce new immigrant groups to fill the niches created in the revised economy of the area. The subordinate indigenous population frequently fails, at first, to participate in the new economic and political order introduced by migrants. For example, because of the numerical decline of Fijians after contact with whites and their unsatisfactory work habits, approximately 60,000 persons migrated from India to the sugar plantations of Fiji under the indenture system between 1979 and 1916.[22] For similar reasons, as well as the demise of slavery, large numbers of Indians were also introduced to such areas of indigenous subordination as Mauritius, British Guiana, Trinidad, and Natal.[23] The descendents of these migrants comprise the largest single ethnic group in several of these areas.

McKenzie, after observing the negligible participation of the subordinated indigenous populations of Alaska, Hawaii, and Malaya in contrast to the large numbers of Chinese, Indian, and other Oriental immigrants, offers the following interpretation:

> The indigenous peoples of many of the frontier zones of modern industrialism are surrounded by their own web of culture and their own economic structure. Consequently they are slow to take part in the new economy especially as unskilled laborers. It is the individual who is widely removed from his native habitat that is most adaptable to the conditions imposed by capitalism in frontier regions. Imported labor cannot so easily escape to its home village when conditions are distasteful as can the local population.[34]

Similarly, the Indians of the United States played a minor role in the new economic activities introduced by white settlers and, further, were not used successfully as slaves.[35] Frazier reports that Negro slaves were utilized in the West Indies and Brazil after unsuccessful efforts to enslave the indigenous Indian populations.[36] Large numbers of Asiatic Indians were brought to South Africa as indentured laborers to work in the railways, mines, and plantations introduced by whites.[37]

This migration of workers into areas where the indigenous population was either unable or insufficient to work in the newly created economic activities was also marked by a considerable flow back to the home country. For example, nearly 3.5 million Indians left the Madras Presidency for overseas between 1903 and 1912, but close to 3 million returned during this same period.[28] However, as we observed earlier large numbers remained overseas and formed major ethnic populations in a number of countries. Current difficulties of the ten million Chinese in Southeast Asia are in large part due to their settlement in societies where the indigenous populations were subordinate.

Indigenous superordination. We have observed that in situations of indigenous superordination the call for new immigrants from other ethnic and racial populations is limited in a manner that prevents the indigenous group's loss of political and economic control. Under such conditions, no single different ethnic or racial population is sufficiently large in number or strength to challenge the supremacy of the indigenous population.

After whites attained dominance in Hawaii, that land provided a classic case of the substitution of one ethnic group after another during a period when large numbers of immigrants were needed for the newly created and expanding plantation economy. According to Lind, the shifts from Chinese to Japanese and Portuguese immigrants and the later shifts to Puerto Rican, Korean, Spanish, Russian, and Philippine sources for the plantation laborers were due to conscious efforts to prevent any single group from obtaining too much power.[29] Similarly, the exclusion of Chinese from the United States mainland stimulated the migration of the Japanese and, in turn, the later exclusion of Japanese led to increased migration from Mexico.[30]

In brief, groups migrating to situations of multiple ethnic contact are thus subordinate in both types of contact situations. However, in societies where whites are superordinate but do not settle as an indigenous population, other racial and ethnic groups are admitted in large numbers and largely in accordance with economic needs of the revised economy of the habitat. By contrast, when a dominant migrant group later becomes indigenous, in the sense that the area becomes one of permanent settlement through generations for the group, migrant populations from new racial and ethnic stocks are restricted in number and source.

Conflict and Assimilation

From a comparison of the surge of racial nationalism and open warfare in parts of Africa and Asia or the retreat of superordinate migrants from the former Dutch East Indies and French Indo-China, on the one hand, with the fusion of populations in many nations of western Europe or the "cultural pluralism" of the United States and Switzerland, on the other, one must conclude that neither conflict nor assimilation is an inevitable outcome of racial and ethnic contact. Our distinction, however, between two classes of race and ethnic relations is directly relevant to consideration of which of these alterna-

tives different populations in contact will take. In societies where the
indigenous population at the initial contact is subordinate, warfare
and nationalism often—although not always—develops later in the cycle
of relations. By contrast, relations between migrants and indigenous
populations that are subordinate and superordinate, respectively, are
generally without long-term conflict.

Migrant superordination. Through time, the subordinated
indigenous population begins to participate in the economy introduced
by the migrant group and, frequently, a concomitant disruption of
previous forms of social and economic organization takes place. This,
in turn, has significant implications for the development of both nationalism and a greater sense of racial unity. In many African states,
where Negroes were subdivided into ethnic groups prior to contact
with whites, the racial unity of the African was created by the occupation of their habitat by white invaders.[31] The categorical subordination of Africans by whites as well as the dissolution and decay of previous tribal and ethnic forms of organization are responsible for the
creation of racial consciousness among the indigenous populations.[32]
As the indigenous group becomes increasingly incorporated within the
larger system, both the saliency of their subordinate position and its
significance increase. No alternative exists for the bulk of the native
population other than the destruction or revision of the institutions of
political, economic, and social subordination.

Further, it appears that considerable conflict occurs in those
areas where the migrants are not simply superordinate, but where
they themselves have also become, in a sense, indigenous by maintaining an established population through generations. In Table 1, for
example, one can observe how sharply the white populations of Algeria
and the Union of South Africa differ from those in nine other African
countries with respect to the percent born in the country of settlement.
Thus, two among the eleven African countries for which such data
were available[33] are outstanding with respect to both racial turmoil
and the high proportion of whites born in the country. To be sure,
other factors operate to influence the nature of racial and ethnic relations. However, these data strongly support our suggestions with
respect to the significance of differences between indigenous and migrant forms of contact. Thus where the migrant population becomes
established in the new area, it is all the more difficult for the indigenous subordinate group to change the social order.

Table 1. Nativity of the White Populations of Selected
African Countries, Circa 1950

Country	Percent of whites born in country	Country	Percent of whites born in country
Algeria	79.8	South West Africa[b]	45.1
Basutoland	37.4	Swaziland	41.2
Bechuanaland	39.5	Tanganyika	47.6
Morocco[a]	37.1[c]	Uganda	43.8
Northern Rhodesia	17.7	Union of South	
Southern Rhodesia	31.5	Africa	89.7

Source: United Nations, Demographic Yearbook, 1956, Table 5.
Note: Other non-indigenous groups included when necessary
breakdown by race is not given.
[a] Former French zone.
[b] Excluding Walvis Bay.
[c] Persons born in former Spanish zone or in Tangier are
included as native.

Additionally, where the formerly subordinate indigenous population has become dominant through the expulsion of the superordinate group, the situation faced by nationalities introduced to the area
under earlier conditions of migrant superordination changes radically.
For example, as we noted earlier, Chinese were welcomed in many
parts of Southeast Asia where the newly subordinated indigenous populations were unable or unwilling to fill the economic niches created by
the white invaders. However, after whites were expelled and the indigenous populations obtained political mastery, the gates to further Chinese immigration were fairly well closed and there has been increasing
interference with the Chinese already present. In Indonesia, where
Chinese immigration had been encouraged under Dutch domain, the
newly created indigenous government allows only token immigration
and has formulated a series of laws and measures designed to interfere with and reduce Chinese commercial activities.[34] Thompson and
Adloff observe that,

Since the war, the Chinese have been subjected to increasingly restrictive measures throughout Southeast Asia, but the severity and effectiveness of these has varied with the degree to which the native nationalists are in control of their countries and feel their national existence threatened by the Chinese.[35]

Indigenous superordination. By contrast, difficulties between subordinate migrants and an already dominant indigenous population occur within the context of a consensual form of government, economy, and social institutions. However confused and uncertain may be the concept of assimilation and its application in operational terms,[36] it is important to note that assimilation is essentially a very different phenomenon in the two types of societies distinguished here.

Where populations migrate to situations of subordination, the issue has generally been with respect to the migrants' capacity and willingness to become an integral part of the on-going social order. For example, this has largely been the case in the United States where the issue of "new" vs. "old" immigrant groups hinged on the alleged inferiorities of the former.[37] The occasional flurries of violence under this form of contact have been generally initiated by the dominant indigenous group and with respect to such threats against the social order as the cheap labor competition of Orientals in the west coast,[38] the nativist fears of Irish Catholic political domination of Boston in the nineteenth century,[39] or the desecration of sacred principles by Mexican "zoot-suiters" in Los Angeles.[40]

The conditions faced by subordinate migrants in Australia and Canada after the creation of indigenous white societies in these areas are similar to that of the United States; that is, limited and sporadic conflict, and great emphasis on the assimilation of migrants. Striking and significant contrasts to the general pattern of subordinant immigrant assimilation in these societies, however, are provided by the differences between the assimilation of Italian and German immigrants in Australia as well as the position of French Canadians in eastern Canada.

French Canadians have maintained their language and other major cultural and social attributes whereas nineteenth- and twentieth-

century immigrants are in process of merging into the predominantly
English-speaking Canadian society. Although broader problems of
territorial segregation are involved,[41] the critical difference between
French Canadians and later groups is that the former had an established society in the new habitat prior to the British conquest of Canada and were thus largely able to maintain their social and cultural
unity without significant additional migration from France.[42]

Similarly, in finding twentieth-century Italian immigrants in
Australia more prone to cultural assimilation than were German migrants to that nation in the 1800's, Borrie emphasized the fact that
Italian migration occurred after Australia had become an independent
nation-state. By contrast, Germans settled in what was a pioneer
colony without an established general social order and institutions.
Thus, for example, Italian children were required to attend Australian
schools and learn English, whereas the German immigrants were
forced to establish their own educational program.[43]

Thus the consequences of racial and ethnic contact may also
be examined in terms of the two types of superordinate-subordinate
contact situations considered. For the most part, subordinate migrants appear to be more rapidly assimilated than are subordinate
indigenous populations. Further, the subordinate migrant group is
generally under greater pressure to assimilate, at least in the gross
sense of "assimilation" such as language, than are the subordinate
indigenous populations. In addition, warfare or racial nationalism—
when it does occur—tends to be in societies where the indigenous population is subordinate. If the indigenous movement succeeds, the
economic and political position of racial and ethnic populations introduced to the area under migrant dominance may become tenuous.

A Final Note

It is suggested that interest be revived in the conditions
accounting for societal variations in the process of relations between
racial and ethnic groups. A societal theory of race relations, based
on the migrant-indigenous and superordinate-subordinate distinctions
developed above, has been found to offer an orderly interpretation of
differences in the nature of race and ethnic relations in the contact

situations considered. Since, however, systematic empirical investigation provides a far more rigorous test of the theory's merits and limitations, comparative cross-societal studies are needed.

NOTES

[1] Robert E. Park, Race and Culture (Glencoe, Ill.: The Free Press, 1950), p. 150.

[2] For example, Emory S. Bogardus, "A Race-Relations Cycle," American Journal of Sociology 35 (Jan. 1930): 612-17; W. O. Brown, "Culture Contact and Race Conflict," in E. B. Reuter, ed., Race and Culture Contacts (New York: McGraw-Hill, 1934), pp. 34-47; E. Franklin Frazier, Race and Culture Contacts in the Modern World (New York: Knopf, 1957), pp. 32ff; Clarence E. Glick, "Social Roles and Types in Race Relations," in Andrew W. Lind, ed., Race Relations in World Perspective (Honolulu: University of Hawaii Press, 1955), pp. 243-62; Edward Nelson Palmer, "Culture Contacts and Population Growth," in Joseph J. Spengler and Otis Dudley Duncan, eds., Population Theory and Policy (Glencoe, Ill.: The Free Press, 1956), pp. 410-15; A. Grenfell Price, White Settlers and Native Peoples (Melbourne: Georgian House, 1950). For summaries of several of these cycles, see Brewton Berry, Race and Ethnic Relations (Boston: Houghton Mifflin, 1958), chap. 6.

[3] Bogardus, p. 612.

[4] Price, White Settlers and Native Peoples.

[5] Intra-urban stages of contact are not considered here.

[6] Price, chaps. 6 and 7.

[7] Glick, p. 244.

[8] See, for example, Brinley Thomas, "International Migration," in Philip M. Hauser and Otis Dudley Duncan, eds., The Study of Population (Chicago: University of Chicago Press, 1959), pp. 523-2

[9] United Nations, Demographic Yearbook, 1957, pp. 147, 645.

[10] United Nations, Demographic Yearbook, 1954, pp. 131, 669.

[11] R. D. McKenzie, Oriental Exclusion (Chicago: University of Chicago Press, 1928), p. 83.

[12] See, for example, Reuter's distinction between two types of direct contact in E. B. Reuter, pp. 4-7.

[13] Price, p. 1.

[14]Stephen Roberts, Population Problems of the Pacific
(London: Routledge, 1927).
[15] John A. Barnes, "Race Relations in the Development of
Southern Africa, " in Lind, Race Relations.
[16] Ibid.
[17] Witness the current controversies between tribes in the
newly created Congo Republic. Also, for a list of tribes living on
both sides of the border of the Republic of Sudan, see Karol Józef
Krótki, "Demographic Survey of Sudan, " in The Population of Sudan,
report on the sixth annual conference (Khartoum: Philosophical Society of Sudan, 1958), p. 35.
[18] John Hope Franklin, From Slavery to Freedom, 2d ed.
(New York: Knopf, 1956), pp. 234-38, 481-83.
[19] Oscar Handlin, Boston's Immigrants, rev. ed. (Cambridge:
The Belknap Press of Harvard University Press, 1959), chap. 2.
[20] Harry Jerome, Migration and Business Cycles (New York:
National Bureau of Economic Research, 1926), pp. 43-44.
[21] See George Eaton Simpson and J. Milton Yinger, Racial
and Cultural Minorities, rev. ed. (New York: Harper, 1958), pp.
126-32.
[22] K. L. Gillion, "The Sources of Indian Emigration to Fiji, "
Population Studies 10 (Nov. 1956): 139; I. M. Cumpston, "A Survey of
Indian Immigration to British Tropical Colonies to 1910, " ibid., pp.
158-59.
[23] Cumpston, pp. 158-65.
[24] R. D. McKenzie, "Cultural and Racial Differences as
Bases of Human Symbiosis, " in Kimball Young, ed., Social Attitudes
(New York: Holt, 1931), p. 157.
[25] Franklin, p. 47.
[26] Frazier, pp. 107-8.
[27] Leo Kuper, Hilstan Watts, and Ronald Davies, Durban: A
Study in Racial Ecology (London: Cape, 1958), p. 25.
[28] Gillion, p. 149.
[29] Andrew W. Lind, An Island Community (Chicago: University of Chicago Press, 1938), pp. 218-29.
[30] McKenzie, Oriental Exclusion, p. 181.
[31] For a discussion of territorial and tribal movements, see
James S. Coleman, "Current Political Movements in Africa, " Annals
of the American Academy of Political and Social Science 298 (March
1955): 95-108.

[32] For a broader discussion of emergent nationalism, see Thomas Hodgkin, Nationalism in Colonial Africa (New York: New York University Press, 1957); Everett C. Hughes, "New Peoples," in Lind, Race Relations, pp. 95-115.

[33] United Nations, Demographic Yearbook, 1956, Table 5.

[34] B. H. M. Vlekke, Indonesia in 1956 (The Hague: Netherlands Institute of International Affairs, 1957), p. 88.

[35] Virginia Thompson and Richard Adloff, Minority Problems in Southeast Asia (Stanford, Calif.: Stanford University Press, 1955), p. 3.

[36] See, for example, International Union for the Scientific Study of Population, "Cultural Assimilation of Immigrants," Population Studies, supplement, March 1950.

[37] Oscar Handlin, Race and Nationality in American Life (Garden City, N.Y.: Doubleday Anchor Books, 1957), chap. 5.

[38] Simpson and Yinger, Racial and Cultural Minorities.

[39] Oscar Handlin, Boston's Immigrants, chap. 7.

[40] Ralph Turner and Samuel J. Surace, "Zoot-Suiters and Mexicans: Symbols in Crowd Behavior," American Journal of Sociology 62 (July 1956): 14-20.

[41] It is, however, suggestive to consider whether the isolated settlement of an area by a racial, religious, or ethnic group would be permitted in other than frontier conditions. Consider, for example, the difficulties faced by Mormons until they reached Utah.

[42] See Everett C. Hughes, French Canada in Transition (Chicago: University of Chicago Press, 1943).

[43] W. D. Borrie assisted by D. R. G. Packer, Italians and Germans in Australia (Melbourne: F. W. Cheshire, 1954), passim.

5 | National and Regional Language Diversity

This paper presents several theoretical propositions about the relationship between linguistic diversity within a nation and its subparts or regions. The propositions described below are equally valid for the relationships between any areal unit and its component parts. Thus they may be applied to a city and its districts or to a province and its counties.

The starting point is the A index, a quantitative measure of mother-tongue diversity proposed by Greenberg.[1] The index gives the probability of randomly paired inhabitants of a given country having different mother tongues. Its computation is rather simple; namely, after determining the proportions in a population with each mother tongue, A is equal to 1.00 minus the sum of squares of each proportion. An illustration of the computations is presented below in Table 1 for Switzerland. The value of A may be given a simple operational interpretation; namely, if each resident were to be paired with every other resident, A is the percentage of dyads in which a common mother tongue is absent. Thus A ranges from zero (in the situation where the entire population has the same mother tongue) to 1.00 (in the impossible situation where no two inhabitants have the same mother tongue).

The advantage of this measure is that it permits quantitative description of the degree of mother-tongue diversity existing in a given area as well as allowing for comparison between areas. In addition, this measure has been extended to permit quantitative determination of the degree of mutually shared mother tongues between two separate populations or groups.[2] Clearly, the operational meaning given to the A index is not intended to describe reality since it is

Table 1.   Computation of A Index for Switzerland, 1960

Mother tongue	Number	Proportion	Proportion squared
German	3,765,203	.70	.49
French	1,025,450	.19	.03
Italian	514,306	.10	.01
Romanche	49,823	.01	.00
Total	5,354,782	1.00	.53

$$A_t = 1.00 - .53 = .47$$

Note: Other mother tongues in Switzerland are not included in these calculations, which are for illustrative purposes.

unlikely that all residents will interact with one another with equal frequency. Rather, because of spatial and social segregation, residents will tend to interact with mother-tongue compatriots more frequently than with those whose native language is different. Nevertheless, this measure provides the investigator with a quantitative index of the exact degree of diversity existing within the nation or unit under study.

The question is naturally raised of the relationship between mother-tongue diversity on the national plane and its component subareas. In particular, will the regions which make up a nation have higher or lower mother-tongue diversity than the nation? In order to answer this question, the use of symbols will be helpful. Let each mother tongue be expressed as a proportion of the nation's total population, such that $b_t + c_t + d_t \ldots + n_t = 1.00$. Further, let the alphabetic order denote the numerical position of each mother tongue in the nation such that b_t is the largest mother tongue, c_t is the second largest, etc. Let each mother tongue in a given region, i, be expressed as a proportion of the total population of the region. Thus $b_i + c_i + d_i \ldots + n_i = 1.00$ for region i. (Note that the ordering of languages need not apply to any particular region. Thus all we know

is that d_t is greater than e_t, but d_i need not be greater than e_i.)
Further, unless noted to the contrary, the propositions presented
below assume that the regional-national differences in mother-tongue
composition are proportionate to the initial positions of the mother
tongue in the nation as a whole. That is, if d_t is smaller than d_i,
the increment in d_i is drawn from the remaining mother tongues of
the region in proportion to their size in the nation as a whole. This
is clearly an arbitrary assumption that will not fit reality in many
instances, but it does provide a means to deal with the entire problem of regional and national levels of mother-tongue diversity.

There are two basic propositions which describe the general
relationship between mother-tongue diversity in a nation and its
regions:

Mother-tongue diversity in a region will be less than for the
nation as a whole if the largest mother tongue of the country comprises a larger proportion of the regional population than of the
national population. More formally, $A_i < A_t$, if $b_i > b_t$ and if the
remaining mother tongues contribute to the increase of b_i in proportion to their size in the nation.

On the other hand, mother-tongue diversity in a given region
will be greater than in the nation if the nation's largest mother tongue
is also the region's largest tongue but by a smaller proportion of the
latter population. If some other tongue is the largest native language
in the region and its proportion of the region's population is even
larger than is the nation's leading mother tongue's proportion for the
nation, then regional diversity will be lower than diversity in the
nation. More formally, $A_i > A_t$ if $b_i < b_t$ and $c_i < b_t$, $d_i < b_t$, $\ldots$,
$n_i < b_t$. But $A_i < A_t$ when $b_i < b_t$, if $c_i > b_t$, or $d_i > b_t$, $\ldots$, or
$n_i > b_t$. Keep in mind that these propositions depend on the gains
or losses among other tongues being proportionate to their sizes.

There are several corollaries that should be noted before
the implications of these propositions are considered:

If a language (say d) occupies a proportionately larger position in a region than in the nation as a whole, but this gain is at the
expense of an even larger national language (say c) in the same region,
all other factors held constant, diversity will be greater in the region

than in the nation if $c_t > d_i$. To put it formally, if $c_t > c_i$, and $c_t > d_i > d_t$, such that $d_i = d_t + K$ and $c_i + K = c_t$, then $A_i > A_t$.

Implications

The implications of these propositions and processes are of considerable importance for the sociolinguistic understanding of the relationship between national and regional mother-tongue diversity. When the largest mother tongue of a nation comprises a relatively small proportion of the total population, that is, when the nation is highly diverse, segregation of the mother tongues into different regions will tend to make the regional levels of diversity lower than in the nation. Clearly if the nation's largest mother tongue occupies an even stronger proportionate position in a given region, then the region's diversity will be lower than that for the nation (making the assumptions noted earlier). But somewhat less obvious, a language which is numerically less important on the national scale can, under this set of conditions, be sufficiently concentrated into a region so as to also reduce the region's diversity in comparison to that of the nation.

This is to be compared with conditions when one language is the mother tongue of the vast majority of the nation's population. Under such circumstances, diversity in the regions will also often be less than that reached in the nation, but for different reasons. When there is low national diversity, it is unlikely for a region to have a sufficient concentration of one of the lesser national tongues such that c_i or d_i, for example, by itself exceeds the value of b_t. The concentration of a lesser tongue into a region at the expense of the nation's largest tongue will, more likely, raise that region's diversity over the national level. However, such concentrations will lower diversity in other areas by raising the level of b_i in many of the regions over b_t.

In short, A_i will often be lower than A_t in many regions if there is either a very high or a very low level of national diversity. High A_t nations will tend to have lower levels of diversity in regions where either the lesser national languages are concentrated or where b_i exceeds b_t. Linguistic homogeneity in a nation will also be accom-

panied by even greater regional homogeneity, but rarely will this be
in a region with a concentration of national "minority" languages.
Rather, lower levels of regional diversity will occur almost exclusively in those regions where b_i exceeds b_t. Thus the concentration of
lesser tongues in a region will be much more likely to create a region
with less linguistic diversity than the nation if A_t is high rather than
low.

This does not mean that the regions of countries with a high
A_t will have lower diversity than regions in countries with a low
national diversity. But it does suggest that regions of the two types
of countries will tend to be more alike than will the countries themselves. For example, using Greenberg's computations, the median
regional A index for Mexico is .19 and the median for the seven territories in the Caucasus is .33. By contrast, the A index for Mexico
and the Caucasus as a whole are much further apart, being .31 and
.87, respectively. Likewise, 11 out of 31 Mexican provinces have
higher levels of diversity than the nation as a whole, but only one of
the seven territories of the Caucasus exceeds the overall level of
diversity.

There is a contradiction between the political goals in many
nations and those of native speakers of each mother tongue. Political,
economic, and social benefits are usually believed to be derived from
a reduced level of mother-tongue diversity. It is not my intention to
evaluate this common political argument, but rather to contrast this
goal with the perspective of the native speakers of the various mother
tongues represented in a nation. If it is assumed that each person
wishes to optimize the use of his native tongue, then clearly segregation will be desirable for these people. For segregation of all forms—
by regions, by cities, and within cities by quarters—will increase the
usage of one's native language. On the other hand, the existence of
segregation means that each mother tongue can maximize its maintenance, but often at the cost of increasing the area's level of mother-
tongue diversity. Thus, particularly in those countries with a very
large dominant mother tongue, the concentration of speakers of a
lesser mother tongue into a region will tend to raise the region's level
of diversity above that for the nation as a whole even though it strength-
ens the position of the lesser tongue. By contrast, in more diverse
nations, where the largest mother tongue is not the native language

of so large a proportion of the population, segregation of lesser
mother tongues will be more likely to make regions less linguistically
diverse than the nation as a whole.

It is crucial to recognize that any concentration of a minority
language in a region will be more likely to lower mother-tongue diversity in the region if the nation has a relatively high level of diversity
to begin with. To put it another way, any buildup of a minority language in a region will be more likely to raise the region's A index if
the nation as a whole has a relatively low level of diversity.

These findings also make it clear how extremely diverse
nations can survive, ignoring questions of bilingualism among the
native speakers of lesser tongues and the existence of lingua francas.
It is relatively easier for regional diversity to be lower than national
diversity in countries where A_t is high, than in nations where A_t is
low. Thus one cannot assume that day-to-day interpersonal relations
in a nation with high linguistic diversity is radically different from
that in a moderately diverse nation. For the levels of national linguistic diversity, as important as they are for understanding the
political, economic, and social context of language relations in the
society, need not at all be closely related to the levels of diversity
on the local scene. The levels of mother-tongue diversity in the
regions of India and Scotland, for example, are very likely closer to
one another than are the national levels of diversity in the two nations.

NOTES

Support of a grant (GS-394) from the National Science Foundation is
gratefully acknowledged.
[1] Joseph H. Greenberg,"The Measurement of Linguistic
Diversity, " Language 32 (1956),1: 109-15.
[2] Stanley Lieberson, "An Extension of Greenberg's Linguistic Diversity Measures, " Language 40 (1964),4: 526-31.

6 | Language Diversity in a Nation and Its Regions

In Collaboration with James F. O'Connor

This paper has two goals: first, to expand on a model of the linkages between national and regional diversity reported earlier;[1] second, to examine the implications of this model with data for 22 nations. It is generally the case that the level of mother-tongue diversity within political subdivisions of nations need not be identical to that of the entire nation. Moreover, the regional levels of diversity can vary greatly from that found on the national plane. Nevertheless, the nature of a nation's mother-tongue diversity sets a number of bounds on what will occur in the political subdivisions which can be understood through the simple models presented below. Our goal then is to analyze the underlining structure of national-subnational linkages in mother-tongue diversity. With a knowledge of the bounds set by this "anatomy," it will be possible to more fully understand the complex political and sociolinguistic problems which exist in linguistically diverse nations.

The relation between national and subnational diversity is of importance for a variety of reasons. Restriction of one's analysis to the level of diversity within an entire nation is fully justified for many problems, but it is clear that such a restriction can often conceal radically different patterns within the regions and lesser subdivisions. Several investigators report situations where mother-tongue heterogeneity in a nation is greater than in many of its political subdivisions.[2] Accordingly, problems which appear on the national level in a highly diverse country may not be found within many of the subareas. Criper and Ladefoged, for example, report that the political subdivisions of Uganda are far more homogeneous than is the nation itself.[3] On the other hand, a relatively homogeneous nation may contain within it some areas where both the level of linguistic diversity and the mother-

tongue composition are far different. Policy decisions over such
matters as the medium of school instruction, mass communication,
official languages recognized in courts and other government agencies,
and the like must consider more than the level of language diversity
in the entire nation.

The actual linguistic situation in the local areas and regions
may have at least as great an impact on some phenomena as does the
national situation. The rates and direction of bilingualism cannot be
entirely understood without a careful examination of the distribution
of each mother-tongue group within a nation. If the level of mother-
tongue diversity for two nations is identical, but in one case the subregions are homogeneous and in the other they are more diverse, then
clearly the level of bilingualism will differ greatly if all the other
influences on language acquisition are held constant.

Finally, linkages between subnational and national language
diversity suggest some conclusions about the maintenance of the
existing nation and the potential for its splintering into two or more
new countries. The presence of one form or another of ethnic diversity is doubtlessly the single most important prerequisite to the dissolution of a nation.[4] Language is as likely as any ethnic characteristic to generate such separatist movements. Insofar as such movements are directed toward the creation of linguistically homogeneous
nations, the existing positions of each mother-tongue group in the
subareas is an important consideration in understanding the isolation,
and hence potential strength, of each of the mother-tongue groups.

Data and Methods

The data used here are obtained for 22 nations which at one
time or another have reported the mother-tongue composition of their
political subdivisions. In view of the theoretical concerns at hand,
the date at which the census was conducted is of minor consequence.
The terms "region" and "subdivision" are used loosely and interchangeably to refer to the largest divisions of a nation for which
mother-tongue data are given. Linguists seem to take great delight
in faulting census and other survey data on language composition,
but mother-tongue data are probably reasonably good in most instanc

since they normally refer to a relatively objective matter, that is, the language first learned in childhood. However, social pressures, interviewer biases, and other political forces undoubtedly do affect the responses.[5]

Much of the analysis to follow hinges on Greenberg's A index, an extremely simple and useful way of describing the level of national or regional diversity. This measure, which can range from zero to 1.0, describes the proportion of cases in which randomly paired residents of a specified area will have different mother tongues. If all members of a nation or some other spatial unit had the same mother tongue, then the A index would be zero since there would never be a case where random pairs had different mother tongues. On the other extreme, if each and every resident had a different mother tongue, then the A index would be 1.0 since randomly paired residents would have different mother tongues in 100 percent of the cases.[6] The A index for Canada was .56 in 1951, which means that if all residents of Canada were randomly paired with one another, 56 percent of the pairs would involve people with different mother tongues. Obviously, such a measure does not pretend to represent the actual frequency of interaction since various spatial, social, economic, and linguistic factors preclude anything approaching random contact within either a nation or its major subdivisions. However, the A index does provide a direct and simple way of summarizing and comparing the level of mother-tongue diversity within areas.[7] Suppose, for example, region X has two mother-tongue groups, one of which is 60 percent of the population and the smaller is 40 percent. Is region Y, with one mother-tongue group that is 70 percent of the population and three which are each 10 percent, more or less diverse than X? The A index provides a meaningful way for summarizing the mother-tongue composition in such cases (in this case, both regions have A indexes of .48).

Some Basic Comparisons

Among the 450 political subdivisions of the 22 nations studied, in the overwhelming majority of cases, A_i (the A index for a given region) tends to be lower than A_t (the A index in the nation). In 349 comparisons, the regional level of diversity is lower than the national level; in 101 cases, the regional level of diversity is greater than the

level in the entire nation. Thus, in slightly more than 75 percent of
the comparisons, A_i is lower than A_t. These results are not an artifact of the peculiar situation in a few nations with a large number of
subareas. Among the 22 nations studied, the median percentage of
subareas with lower levels of diversity is 73. This pattern is consistent with the expectation that the subregions will tend to be less heterogeneous than the nation because of mother-tongue segregation, the
operation of differential rates of mother-tongue shift, and the possibility that political boundaries are partially adjusted to take linguistic
factors into account.

On the other hand, the percentage of a nation's political subdivisions with lower levels of diversity is only mildly affected by the
level of national diversity. Table 1 lists each nation ranked by the
level of national diversity (col. 1) and also gives the percentage of
regions where A_i is less than A_t (col. 3). Inspection of the two columns indicates a weak relationship between the two characteristics.
In other words, the regions in rather homogeneous nations are nearly
as likely to be lower than the national level as are regions in the very
diverse countries. The product-moment correlation between the level
of national diversity, A_t, and the percentage of regions that are more
homogeneous is .49.

More significantly, viewing the percentage of regions with
lower diversity than the nation as the dependent variable, the regression coefficient is only 22.2 (the intercept is 66.87). This means
that the percentage of regions in which A_i is less than the corresponding value of A_t rises only slightly with increases in a nation's diversi
When A_t is .10 (a rather homogeneous nation), for example, the regression equation would predict that A_i would be less than .10 in 69
percent of the regions. In a nation where A_t is .50, the expectation
is that 78 percent of the regions would have A indexes less than .50.
Finally, if A_t is .85, the expectation is that 86 percent of the regions
would have less diversity than the national level. Thus, the percenta
of regions with diversity lower than the nation increases only mildly
with increments in A_t. The rate of increase is slower than the increase in the range of possible A_i values that would be less than A_t.

Is A_i usually lower than A_t because of certain inevitable
mathematical relations between regional and national diversity? The

Table 1. Percent of Divisions with Lower A Indexes
than the Nation's Level

Nation (year of census)	A_t (1)	Number of divisions (2)	Percent of divisions with lower A indexes (3)
Scotland (1961)	.0326	33	81
Dominican Republic (1950)	.0394	20	60
Austria (1934)	.0512	9	67
Costa Rica (1950)	.0513	7	86
Greece (1951)	.0852	10	70
Finland (1953)	.1630	10	80
Turkey (1955)	.1875	66	71
Mexico (1960)	.1956	32	69
Rumania (1956)	.2328	17	65
Cyprus (1931)	.3232	6	50
Wales (1961)	.3852	13	67
Hungary (1941)	.3907	44	68
Yugoslavia (1953)	.4515	6	83
Switzerland (1960)	.4748	25	84
Poland (1931)	.5043	17	65
Canada (1951)	.5647	12	83
USSR (1959)	.6175	15	80
Pakistan (1951)	.6194	6	67
Guatemala (1940)	.6626	22	91
India (1961)	.8372	21	100
Philippines (1960)	.8617	55	100
South Africa (1960)	.8655	4	75

first point to recognize is that there are virtually no bounds on the
percentage of a nation's regions with higher or lower levels of diversity than A_t, the national index. The mother-tongue composition in
each and every subregion could be less heterogeneous than the nation
as a whole in any country where A_t is greater than zero (in other

words, in any country which is not entirely homogeneous). The possibilities are nearly as great for regional diversity exceeding the national level. It is possible for all but one of the regions in each nation to be more diverse than the nation when A_t is less than 1.0. Thus, it can be shown that the number of political subdivisions with lower or higher diversity than A_t is generally not limited by a nation's level of diversity. [8]

Patterns of Lower Subnational Diversity

Although regional diversity is generally lower than national diversity regardless of the latter's level, an examination of diversity models indicates that the mechanisms generating this decline in highly diverse nations are different from those occurring in countries where A_t is lower. For convenience, let the numerically largest mother tongue in the nation be designated by the letter "b" and its proportion of the total population be indicated by b_t; c_t is the proportion of the nation's population with the second largest mother tongue; d_t the third largest, and so on. Thus $b_t + c_t + d_t \ldots + n_t = 1.00$. The subscript i will be used to designate the analogous proportions of a given subdivision's population with each mother tongue. Thus, $b_i + c_i + d_i \ldots + n_i = 1.00$ for region i. Note that b_i need not be the largest mother tongue in subdivision i. All we know is that b_t, by definition, is the largest mother tongue in the nation, c_t is the second largest, and so forth. In the case of Canada-Quebec comparisons, for example, b_t (English) is much larger than c_t (French), but in Quebec b_i is much smaller than c_i.

What are the forms whereby regional diversity will be less than national diversity? One mechanism is when the largest mother tongue in the nation is an even larger proportion of the region's population, i.e. b_i is greater than b_t. Assuming all other mother tongues in the nation maintain the same ratios to each other in the region—an assumption here and elsewhere in the model—then this will cause regional diversity to be lower than the national level. This process, whereby greater regional homogeneity is generated through an increased position of language "b" in the region, is indicated by roman number I in Table 2.

A radically different process which will also lead to regional homogeneity exceeding the national level occurs when one of the nation's lesser mother tongues is sufficiently concentrated in a region. For example, if the third largest mother tongue in the nation, language "d," is sufficiently concentrated in a region such that its proportion of the region's population, d_i, is greater than b_t, then diversity in the region will be less than the national level. In other words, A_i will be lower than A_t if a lesser tongue, say "d," is sufficiently concentrated in a region so that d_i exceeds b_t.[9] This mechanism, designated as Type II, is a radically different source of regional homogeneity. Here regional heterogeneity is lower than the nation because one of the lesser national languages is sufficiently concentrated in the region.

Two other mechanisms deserve brief mention. Another way by which A_i will be lower than A_t is when both of the above mechanisms operate, namely, where b_i and c_i (or some other lesser tongue) each exceed b_t. This form will be designed as Type III. Finally, it is possible in certain situations for regional diversity to be less than the national level without either b_i or any other mother tongue in the region exceeding b_t. This form will be designated as Type IV.

Among regions with less diversity than the nation, how frequently do each of these four processes operate? Secondly, is the level of a nation's diversity related to the type of mechanism found? The overwhelming majority of cases where A_i is less than A_t occur through process I, that is, where b_i exceeds b_t (251 out of 349 cases). This form is present in at least one region in 21 of the 22 nations shown in Table 2. Thus, a build-up of the nation's largest mother tongue (such that b_i exceeds b_t) is the most common means whereby regional diversity is reduced. The Type II mechanism is the second most common process, operating in 88 cases. Here, of course, is a radically different source of regional homogeneity. The Type III and IV mechanisms are far less frequent, occurring in three and seven regions, respectively.

Table 2 indicates that the level of a nation's diversity is related to the occurrence of these processes. Observing that the nations in Table 2 are listed in order of increasing national diversity almost all cases of lower regional diversity in the top half occur

through a Type I process. The only exceptions among the eleven
least diverse nations are one subdivision of Finland and four in Wales.
When national diversity is relatively low, regional diversity is lower
almost always when the largest mother tongue is even more concentrated in the particular region. Thus as A_t tends to be low, why will
A_i usually be less than A_t only when b_i exceeds b_t? The answer is
found in the arithmetic relations involved. Namely, A_t will be low
only if b_t is high. If b_t is high, then c_t must be low and all the more
so d_t, e_t, etc. When c_t is very low and b_t high, it takes very extreme
forms of segregation and a relatively large number of political subdivisions before it is possible for c_i or one of the other lesser
tongues to exceed b_t.

The sources of regional homogeneity in the more diverse
nations are considerably different. To be sure, except for the Republic of South Africa (which has only four primary subdivisions), all of
the more diverse nations also have some regions where diversity is
reduced through the operation of a Type I mechanism. In the Philippines, for example, there are 14 subdivisions with lower diversity
through a Type I process. Nevertheless, it is clear that the Type II
mechanism is an important factor in these diverse nations. Except
for Poland, this process operates in all of the more diverse nations.
Diversity is lower than the national level in 39 regions of the Philippines through the operation of a Type II mechanism. It is easy to see
the arithmetic reasons for this. In the more diverse nations, the
gap between b_t and the lesser tongues (c_t, d_t, etc.) will be less.
Hence, it will be relatively easy for one of these lesser tongues to
be sufficiently concentrated in a region so that its proportion of the
region's population exceeds b_t. Likewise, it is easier for such a
concentration to generate a level of regional diversity that is lower
than A_t.

The other two forms, Types III and IV, occur exclusively
in the more diverse nations, albeit they are not too common even
then. One can show that both of these forms of lowered regional
diversity can only occur in nations where national diversity is rather
high. The Type III process involves a situation in which both b_i and
c_i (or some other lesser tongue) each exceed b_t. This can only occur
if b_t is less than .5. In turn, if b_t is less than .5, then the nation's
level of mother-tongue diversity must be .52 or more. Hence, mechanism III can only occur in highly diverse nations.

The Type IV process also occurs rather infrequently, as inspection of Table 2 indicates. A_i may be lower than A_t even when the proportion of the region's population holding each specific mother tongue is in all cases less than b_t. Such an effect can never occur in a nation with two mother tongues or where for all intents and purposes two languages are the mother tongues of the overwhelming majority of the population. However, this process may occur in nations with three or more mother tongues and where there is a substantial gap between b_t and c_t, but where c_t is also substantially larger than d_t. Under such circumstances, A_i will be lower than A_t if b_i is only slightly smaller than b_t and if one of the lesser languages is the mother tongue of most of the remainder of the region's population.

What are the ramifications of these different mechanisms? Although the majority of a nation's regions are likely to be less diverse than A_t, the process through which these declines occur is related to the level of A_t. Nations with low levels of diversity almost always have greater regional homogeneity through the operation of a Type I process. Thus, the most homogeneous regions in such nations have heavy concentrations of the nation's largest mother tongue. Such regions create no linguistic threat to national stability as long as the majority language is also suitably served on the national plane. On the other hand, the more diverse nations experience lower regional diversity not only of the Type I form, but also in Type II situations whereby the largest mother tongue in the region is one of the lesser national languages. Under such circumstances, the possibility of fission exists since one of the lesser mother tongues enjoys greater territorial homogeneity than does the nation as a whole.

Patterns of Higher Subnational Diversity

Each of the four forms of subnational mother-tongue composition can also produce values of A_i that are higher than A_t. If the assumptions mentioned earlier about the relative ratios among the remaining languages are met, then diversity will inevitably be lower in regions with Type I, II, or III forms. When these assumptions are not fully met, A_i may be lower or higher than A_t. In looking at the forms present in regions where diversity exceeds the national level, our first concern is with the frequency of each type. Then we shall attempt to explain why certain Types are specially likely to raise or lower A_i.

Type IV is by far the most common pattern found in regions with a diversity level exceeding the nation's index. In the 101 regions with higher diversity, Type IV is present in all but 10 cases (Table 2). Type II occurs in eight regions, Type I is found in two regions, and Type III is not found at all. Not only is Type IV the most frequent source of higher regional diversity, but Type IV regions nearly always have this consequence. Inspection of the relevant columns in Table 2 indicates there are only seven Type IV regions with an A_i lower than A_t, compared with 91 cases where A_i exceeds A_t. By contrast, regions with Type I and II forms are almost always less diverse than the nation. Comparing the relevant columns in Table 2, for example, A_i is lower in 251 out of 253 regions with a Type I pattern and in 88 out of 96 regions with a Type II pattern. The three cases with a Type III pattern all involve lower levels of regional diversity.

Why do Types I, II, and III almost always generate situations where A_i is lower than A_t? First, observe that all three of these forms have one characteristic in common, namely, the largest mother tongue in the region has a numerical position which is superior to that held by the nation's largest mother tongue. In Type I, b_i is greater than b_t; in Type II, c_i or some other lesser tongue is greater than b_t; and in Type III both b_i and c_i (or some other language) each exceed b_t. By contrast, in Type IV, no tongue is concentrated in the region to the level reached by language "b" in the nation. In general this means that A_i will tend to drop if the concentration of any mother tongue in a region exceeds the level of b_t. On the other hand, the failure of any language in a region to reach the value of b_t nearly always means a rise in the regional level of diversity. Hence, we can restate the problem. If language "x" is the largest mother tongue in a region, then A_i will tend to be less than A_t when x_i is greater than b_t. On the other hand, if x_i is less than b_t, A_i tends to exceed A_t.

Part of the explanation is to be found in the procedure used for the computation of A indexes. Namely, the effect of an arithmetic increase in x_i over b_t will be magnified by the squaring procedure.[10] As a consequence, the remaining languages may be more concentrated in the nation than in the subdivision without necessarily raising A_i over A_t. This is particularly the case when b_t is either very large or very low.

For example, if $b_t = .8$ and $x_i = .8246$, then A_i will be lower than A_t, regardless of how concentrated the remaining tongues are in the nation and how uniformly distributed they are in the specific region. Needless to say, if the remaining tongues are not concentrated in the nation, i.e. if c_t is considerably less than .2, then the region will be less diverse if x_i exceeds .8 by an even smaller margin.

The minimum increment of x_i over b_t is inversely related to the level of b_t. When b_t is .9, then x_i need only be .911; by contrast, x_i must be .7615 when b_t is .7. Observe these minimum increments in x_i over b_t are determined under very special assumptions: that diversity among the remaining languages is minimal in the nation but maximal in the region. The spatial segregation of mother-tongue groups is the usual pattern and this will generate the opposite effect. Hence, in the case where b_t is .7, usually x_i need exceed b_t by less than .0615 in order for A_i to be less than A_t.

Starting with the other extreme, nations that are very diverse, a similar pattern unfolds, namely, when b_t is very small, x_i needs to be only slightly larger than b_t in order to assure that A_i will be less than A_t.

Under conditions where x_i exceeds b_t, it follows from this analysis that the probability of A_i exceeding A_t will increase as b_t moves away from either an extremely high or extremely low value. Inspection of Table 2 indicates that this is precisely the case. Observe that Types I and II generate greater regional diversity in four nations: Hungary, Switzerland, Canada, and the Soviet Union. The value of b_t in these nations is, respectively, .77, .69, .59, and .59. Thus there is some empirical support for the interpretation offered above. The absence of any cases where b_t is somewhat less than .5 is not damaging since only three of the nations have such values and the highest of these is only .36. Nevertheless, it is clear that a more systematic model should be developed in the future to incorporate the patterns reported above.

Average Regional Diversity

It is clear that most regions in a nation are less diverse than is the nation itself. In turn, this raises several additional questions about the linkages between regional and national diversity. What are the average levels of subnational diversity experienced by the inhabitants of these nations? Is the average regional level in a country somehow a function of the nation's A_t? Finally, are nations more alike in the average level of their regions' diversity or in their A_t indexes? In other words, how does the gap between a very diverse nation such as India and a more homogeneous nation such as Greece compare with the gap between their regions?

For each of the 22 nations we have computed a weighted average index of regional diversity to be designed as A_{ip}. The procedure for computing A_{ip} is simple and the measure can be readily interpreted. The A_i index for a given region, i, is multiplied by the proportion of the nation's population living in that region. This computation is made for each region in a nation and then summed. The sum is A_{ip}, the average index of regional diversity weighted by the population living in each region. Thus A_{ip} gives the level of regional diversity encountered by the average resident of the nation.

The relation between A_t and A_{ip} is shown in Figure 1. The abscissa of the graph gives the level of national diversity, A_t; the ordinate indicates the corresponding value for the weighted average index of regional diversity, A_{ip}. The solid diagonal line indicates what A_{ip} would be if there was no mother-tongue segregation within each nation and hence, if A_{ip} was exactly equal to A_t. Since all 22 points on the graph fall below the solid line, we observe that in all nations—regardless of their level of diversity—the regions tend to be less heterogeneous.

Although the pattern is non-linear, clearly A_{ip} is directly influenced by the level of A_t. With some notable exceptions, the average level of regional diversity tends to be a function of a nation's A_t. However, observe that as one moves along the X-axis toward higher values of A_t, the levels of A_{ip} tend to drop progressively away from the solid line in Figure 1. To be sure, there is a notable exception, South Africa, where A_{ip} is .72 (only about .15 less than its level

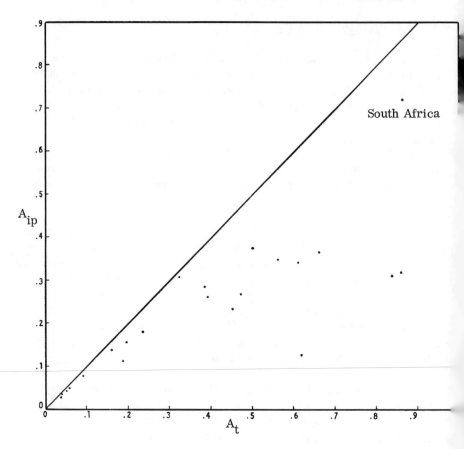

Fig. 1.   Relation between A_t and A_{ip}

of national diversity, .87). However, our model will help in account-ing for this exception. In any case, there is a general tendency for A_{ip} to rise at a decreasing rate with unit increments in the national level of diversity. Thus nations are more alike in their weighted average level of regional diversity than their differences in A_t might suggest. This graphic indication may be verified arithmetically. The average difference in A_t among the 22 nations taken pair-wise is .32. But the average difference in A_{ip} is .18.

Our diversity model helps to interpret the results shown in Figure 1 by distinguishing those parts which are mathematically inevitable from those which are the product of certain social processes. One observes that A_{ip} never exceeds A_t, but is always less. This is an artifact of the arithmetic linkages between the two indexes. If one assumes there are an unlimited number of regions in a given nation, then it can be shown that A_{ip} will range from zero to A_t. It is easy to see how these limits operate on the zero end. If there were a sufficient number of regions and if segregation was so extreme that each region was occupied by only one mother-tongue group, then A_i would be zero in every region and therefore A_{ip} would also be zero. On the other hand, it is also easy to see how A_{ip} may equal A_t. This would occur if each region had the same mother-tongue composition as found in the entire nation. Hence, each region's index of diversity would be the same as A_t; A_{ip} would, therefore, also be equal to A_t. It may appear contrary to intuition to claim that A_{ip} will never exceed A_t. Nevertheless, even if the majority of regions in a country have diversity levels in excess of A_t, this limit would still hold. The key to the explanation lies in the fact that A_{ip} is a regional average which is weighted by each region's proportion of the nation's population. Without going into the details for the inductive proof, one can conclude that the following limits operate under the assumption that there are no restrictions on the number of subareas: $0 \leq A_{ip} \leq A_t$. Accordingly, part of the pattern shown in Figure 1 is a function of certain inherent arithmetic limits such that A_{ip} must be equal or less than A_t.

Let us expand our model by considering the influence on subnational diversity due to the simple number of political subdivisions. Here our concern is with the bounds placed on A_{ip} by the number of political subdivisions in a nation. In particular, does the number of regions in some cases make it impossible for A_{ip} to reach zero? If the number of regions is less than the number of mother tongues in the nation, then A_{ip} must be greater than zero. This is easy to see. For A_{ip} to be zero, it is necessary that each mother tongue be isolated in one or more regions. Clearly, this is impossible if there are more mother tongues than regions; hence, A_i in at least one region will be greater than zero. On the other hand, if the number of regions is at least equal to the number of mother tongues, then the possibility exists for each A_i to be zero and, hence, for A_{ip} to also be zero. The number of regions is at least equal to the number of

Table 3. Nations with Minimum A_{ip} Indexes Greater than Zero

Nation	Minimum A_{ip}	Nation	Minimum A_{ip}
Costa Rica	.0008	USSR	.0615
Greece	.0014	Pakistan	.0222
Cyprus	.0010	India	.0479
Yugoslavia	.0065	Philippines	.0023
Canada	.0218	South Africa	.3701

mother tongues in 12 of the nations. The ten nations reporting more mother tongues than regions are listed in Table 3.[11] A formula has been developed for such circumstances to determine the minimum value of A_{ip}. Let R equal the number of regions; let M equal the number of mother tongues. If the mother tongues in a nation are placed in descending numerical order such that m_1 is the number of people with the largest mother tongue; m_2 is the number with the second largest mother tongue, etc., then the following equation gives the minimum A_{ip} when R is less than M:

$$\text{minimum } A_{ip} = \left[1 - \sum_{i=r}^{M} \left(\frac{m_i}{S} \right)^2 \right] \frac{\frac{S}{M}}{\sum_{i=1}^{M} m_1} \ , \ \text{where } S = \sum_{i=r}^{M} m_i$$

Put in verbal terms, the formula above indicates that the minimum A_{ip} will occur if the larger mother tongues are each in their own region exclusively and if all of the remaining mother tongues are combined in one region. Inspecting the results in Table 3, one finds that the impact on the minimum possible value of A_{ip} is rather negligible in most nations where M exceeds R. In five countries A_{ip} is still less than .01; in two countries it is about .02; in India it is about .05; in the Soviet Union it is around .06. It is not hard to understand why this is the case. Namely, under optimal conditions generated in the formula above, the smallest of the mother tongues are all combined in one region. Although that region's diversity may well be high, its proportion of the total population will be rather low and, hence, the weighted A_{ip} index will not be greatly affected. To put it another way, the formula and results in Table 3 run against the notion that a large number of mother tongues must generate a high level of diversity. This is not the case if the vast majority of them are the mother tongues of only a small proportion of the population.

Only in South Africa is the minimum value of A_{ip} substantially above zero, .37. The results for South Africa do help us in part to account for the apparent deviant case observed in the scatter diagram. If the range of possible values for South Africa's A_{ip} index is from A_t (.87) to .37 rather than from .87 to zero, then there exists a substantial bias in an upward direction. In other words, even if there was perfect segregation in South Africa along the pattern indicated by the formula above, the nation would still deviate somewhat from the general pattern shown in the scatter diagram.

In short, what does the scatter diagram in Figure 1 now tell us about mother-tongue diversity in regions? First, there is an arithmetic set of forces which tends to make A_{ip} lower than (or at most equal to) A_t. Hence, there is strong expectation that the average resident of a nation will live in a region where diversity is below the national level. Second, the isolation or segregation of mother-tongue groups within the official boundaries of political subdivisions does absorb some of a nation's diversity. This is most notable among the more diverse nations. Thus, we can observe that unit increments of A_t produce smaller and smaller unit increments in A_{ip}. The reasons for this non-linear relationship are difficult to suggest at this point. On the one hand, all of our models thus far merely indicate the maximum and minimum possible bounds; they have not generated a probability distribution based on the number and size of each region as well as the nation's mother-tongue composition. Moreover, undoubtedly the number and location of regions is at least partially a function of historic forces that also reflect the location of different mother-tongue groups. Presently, given the models used here as well as the ahistorical nature of the data employed, the non-linearity of the pattern observed in Figure 1 remains to be explained.

Mother-Tongue Unity: Regions and Nations

Of special interest is the role of language in either holding the various subparts of a nation together or, on the other hand, its role in creating cleavages within a nation. In this respect, the subnational positions of the lesser mother tongues are of considerable importance. Their spatial isolation from the numerically largest language will have considerable impact on the frequency of bilingualism and therefore the exposure to mother-tongue shift. But specially important here is the assumption that a high degree of linguistic separation will have a bearing on the maintenance and structure of the existing nation.

Suppose we consider two extreme cases: first, when mother tongues are not segregated by region; second, when there is complete segregation of these mother tongues such that each region is occupied exclusively by one mother tongue. If there is no segregation and, hence, the mother-tongue composition of each region is identical to that of the nation, then the level of diversity within each region will be identical to that found in the nation. Moreover, the mother-tongue bond between regions will be exactly the same as A_t and A_j.[12] Under such circumstances the chances of language being the basis for nationa disintegration are probably slim since the strength of any lesser tongue in each region is no greater than its strength in the entire nation.

On the other hand, consider the situation where each mother tongue is found exclusively in only one region. Under such circumstances, there will be maximum homogeneity within each region, but there will be no mother-tongue bond between regions. Under such circumstances, mother-tongue cohesion would undermine national unity. Namely, mother tongue and region would overlap completely so that members of each region shared a common language, but there would be no mother-tongue bond between regions. Such a pattern could occur in nations with various levels of A_t.

Suppose we consider a very minimal condition of subnationa strength for one of the lesser languages: namely, regions where c_i (or d_i, or some other lesser tongue) is greater than b_i. In other words, we shall assume that a very minimal prerequisite for disunit is that the nation's largest language be exceeded in number by at least one other language in the region. As our earlier analysis of Table 2 suggests, this condition is more likely to be encountered in the more diverse nations. More specifically, the five nations with the lowest A_t indexes have no regions in which b_i is less than c_i (or some other mother tongue). Four of the next five nations listed in Table 2 have at least one region where language "b" is not the largest mother tongue. Moreover, in all seven, there are regions where lesser mother tongues, for example d_i, e_i, etc., are larger than b_i. In the Soviet Union, for example, there are thirteen different mother tongues whose proportion of a region's population exceeds that of b_i. In both India and the Philippines there are 15 such languages.

The result is not particularly surprising in view of our earlier analysis of the forms by which regional diversity is reduced. However, a rather curious pattern emerges if one examines the level of mother-tongue diversity within regions where a lesser tongue has greater numerical strength than language "b." There are 16 nations with one or more regions in which c_i exceeds b_i. Comparing the average level of mother-tongue diversity within such regions in each of these nations, one finds there is no relationship between the level of a nation's diversity and the average level of diversity within these regions (tau is .02). In other words, the mother-tongue bond within these regions is generally unrelated to the nation's level of diversity. In effect, we can view the regional strength of a minority language in terms of two conditions. First, the probability of a minority language being numerically larger than "b" in a region does increase with the nation's level of diversity. However, among those situations in which it does occur, the linguistic unity within the region is not related to the level of national diversity. Hence, the mother-tongue bond within such regions among the less diverse nations is no different than among many of the more diverse nations.

There are simple structural reasons for this. Nations with low levels of diversity have the following characteristics: b_t is rather high; c_t, d_t, and other lesser tongues are therefore rather low. Hence, there will be a general tendency for c_i to exceed b_i in a region only when c_i is rather high. In turn, this means that the level of diversity within the region is relatively low. By contrast, nations with high levels of diversity are characterized by the following: b_t is relatively small; hence, c_t, d_t, etc., may be large relative to the less diverse nations.

In turn, it is easier in such nations for c_i (or d_i, etc.) to exceed b_i in a region. By "easier" is meant the degree of linguistic segregation by regions need not be as great. Thus, one can see why the homogeneous nations are less likely to have regions in which one of their lesser languages is the mother tongue of more residents than language "b." On the other hand, when such a pattern does occur, mother-tongue diversity in such regions will tend to be rather low.

Analyzing five highly diverse nations in which there are a relatively large number of tongues that are specially strong in some of the regions, we discovered a pattern that was surprising to us. This pattern may be of value in understanding the presence or absence of separatist movements. Our analysis is restricted to regions where the number of inhabitants with some lesser mother tongue not only exceeds language "b," but where the lesser mother tongue's proportion of the region's population also exceeds b_t. Therefore, the lesser mother tongue enjoys a relatively stronger position in these regions that does "b" in the nation as a whole. We determined the average A_i index in those regions where a given mother tongue's proportion of residents exceeded b_t.

Suppose we then examine the relation between the size of a lesser mother tongue in the nation and the average diversity index in those regions where its proportion of the population meets the criteria indicated above. One might expect that the larger mother tongues would tend to be in more homogeneous regions of concentration than the smaller ones. However, the pattern does not hold up very well. In Pakistan, the tau correlation is 1.0, but in the Soviet Union it is only .26, and it is actually negative in the Philippines, India, and Guatemala (-.05, -.32, and -.33, respectively). Thus, in three of the five nations, if anything the larger of the mother tongues have high concentrations in regions with a weaker linguistic bond than the smaller mother tongues. In the Soviet Union there is only a weak positive relationship. Thus, Pakistan is the only nation where the numerical size of the lesser languages is perfectly correlated with levels of linguistic homogeneity within the subareas where such languages are concentrated. We need hardly add that Pakistan has since experienced cleavage.

If one assumes that a divisive movement within an existing nation-state is most likely to be led by the larger of the lesser tongues and, in turn, that a high level of regional unity is also a factor in leading to a divisive movement, then this pattern may be of great consequence for national stability. In several of these nations, the numerically most important of the lesser mother tongues are not the languages with the greatest regional unity. Obviously, this result needs further exploration. Moreover, there are many other factors involved in the thrust toward separatism, e.g. the role of international politics in the case of Pakistan. Nevertheless, the existence of such patterns suggests possible structural features in the unity of some multilingual nations.

A Final Note

The empirical data and crude models presented in this paper describe some of the basic features in the linkages between a multilingual nation and its political divisions. We hope that they provide one of the building blocks for a thorough understanding of the complex processes by which multilingual nations are either maintained or dissolved. The simultaneous examination of both the models and the empirical data is particularly valuable. The crude models help us determine certain intrinsic limits to the possible patterns of national and subnational diversity. Since these models help one to understand the mathematical bounds which exist, this allows the investigator to distinguish those patterns which are a function of social processes from those which reflect these inherent limits. In turn, since these inherent limits do have social consequences, they may be of value in providing us with an understanding of the causes of some of these national-subnational linkages.

There are two important paths to follow. First, the models could be greatly improved through the generation of probability functions rather than merely the establishment of bounds. In turn, this would provide information on the degree to which the actual part-whole patterns in nations are the reflection of social forces. The second path is to combine these results with the many other political, social, and linguistic factors which affect the structure and stability of multilingual nations. Hopefully, this exercise will prove of use in reaching these goals.

NOTES

[1] Stanley Lieberson, "National and Regional Language Diversity," in Actes du Xe Congrès international des linguistes (Bucharest: Editions de l'Académie de la République Socialiste de Roumanie, 1969), vol. I, pp. 769-73.

[2] In addition to the paper above, see also Joseph H. Greenberg, "The Measurement of Linguistic Diversity," Language 32 (1956): 109-15; and Clive Criper and Peter Ladefoged, "Linguistic Complexity in Uganda," in W. H. Whiteley, ed., Language Use and Social Change (Oxford: Oxford University Press, 1971), pp. 145-59.

[3] Criper and Ladefoged, ibid.

[4] Stanley Lieberson, "Stratification and Ethnic Groups," Sociological Inquiry 40 (1970): 172-81.

[5] Stanley Lieberson, "Language Questions in Censuses," Sociological Inquiry 36 (1966): 262-79. Stanley Lieberson, "How Can We Describe and Measure the Incidence and Distribution of Bilingualism?" in L. G. Kelly, ed., Description and Measurement of Bilingualism (Toronto: University of Toronto Press, 1969), pp. 286-95.

[6] Because of sampling with replacement, strictly speaking the index would be slightly less than 1.0.

[7] The computational procedures are illustrated in Stanley Lieberson, "Measuring Population Diversity," American Sociological Review 34 (1969): 850-62.

[8] The consequences of a model involving the generation of random numbers might be considered here. See, for example, Karl E. Taeuber and Alma F. Taeuber, Negroes in Cities (Chicago: Aldine Publishing Company, 1965), pp. 231-35.

[9] This is precisely the case in Quebec.

[10] These computational procedures are described in Lieberson, "Measuring Population Diversity."

[11] The treatment of the residual "all other" mother-tongue category follows the procedures described in Lieberson, "Measuring Population Diversity," p. 861.

[12] A measure of mother-tongue diversity between areas is described in Stanley Lieberson, "An Extension of Greenberg's Linguistic Diversity Measures," Language 40 (1964): 526-31.

Part II. Bilingualism: Its Causes and Consequences

7 | The Causes of Bilingualism Differ from the Causes of Mother-Tongue Shift

There are several reasons to expect that the causes of bilingualism will not be automatically translated by parents into causes of mother-tongue shift. One very simple feature is the timing of bilingualism. Bilingualism ending before parenthood or occurring after parenthood will fail to undermine the mother-tongue maintenance in the next generation.

There are more complicated processes that may also generate bilingualism, but not an intergenerational shift; for example, a gap between adult male and female bilingualism is found in a number of cities and is attributed to the occupational pressures operating on men. If we make the assumption that bilingualism is necessary for both French-mother-tongue parents before an intergenerational shift will occur, the added bilingualism among adult men will not directly generate any increment in the rate of shifting among their children. To be sure, native fluency in English may offer employment advantages that lead some bilingual parents to pass on English as their child's mother tongue. Still, it is easy to see how occupational pressures will not create the same rate of intergenerational shift as some other factors leading to bilingualism.

On a more abstract plane there are four distinctive ways for factors to influence bilingualism and intergenerational mother-tongue shift. The simplest case is when a variable affects both phenomena in a consistent direction. Population composition might be visualized in this fashion. All other factors held constant, a community with a small percentage of X will tend to create bilingualism among the X group and to also raise their intergenerational rate of mother-tongue shift.

A second type of relationship occurs when a variable influences both bilingualism and retention, but in an opposite direction from expectation; for example, if a variable causes higher bilingualism but also a higher retention ratio. This is not an altogether unlikely possibility if viewed within the context of multiple causation. If a factor has a greater influence on bilingualism than retention, it may very well increase the numbers exposed to the risk of passing on a different mother tongue but lower the proportion of bilinguals whose children shift. Suppose there are 1,000 bilingual members of mother tongue X in a community and that 80 percent (800) transfer X to their offspring. Suppose, further, that some additional variable is introduced into the situation which leads a thousand more members of X to become bilingual but that 900 of these pass on their mother tongue. In effect, the total retention ratio is raised from 80 to 85 percent, $(800 + 900)/(1,000 + 1,000)$, even though the rate of bilingualism has doubled.

A third type of situation occurs when a variable influences bilingualism, but has no effect on the retention ratio. In predominantly English-speaking cities a small segment of the English-mother-tongue girls learn French as a second language, but by the time the child-bearing ages are reached many are no longer able to speak French. Accordingly, this cause of bilingualism in the particular setting has little or no effect on mother-tongue shift among the children.

A fourth type of situation is a variable that influences retention but not bilingualism. This was illustrated in the case of manufacturing and the medium of school instruction, both of which influence retention but have no effect on bilingualism in the lesser cities.

To draw an analogy visualize bilingualism as the equivalent of becoming alcoholic and visualize mother-tongue shift as the equivalent of losing one's job because of alcoholism. Suppose, like bilingualism, there are many causes of alcoholism. One cause would be "unhappiness" and another cause might be the alcoholism that results from a sales occupation in which a considerable amount of business drinking is necessary. We can visualize these two different forces operating to cause alcoholism just as we have seen more than one cause of bilingualism. Further, compared with business alcoholics, probably a larger proportion of employees who have become alcoholic because of unhappiness will be fired from their jobs. Those required to drink a moderate amount because of business reasons can probably get away with being alcoholics more than those whose source of alcoholism is unrelated to their work. Likewise, one can visualize how the different causes of bilingualism will differ in their consequences for language maintenance in the next generation.

Because very likely there is statistical interaction rather than mere additivity among these causal factors, the operation of the four types of bilingualism are complicated; for example, the influence of some variables on bilingualism and retention may be different in the lesser cities than in communities in which French is a more important mother tongue. Earlier a number of instances of "overdetermination" of bilingualism were encountered in lesser cities; that is, when a given cause of bilingualism is superfluous since virtually everyone would have been bilingual anyway. To put the point in a somewhat different manner, a factor influencing retention may have different consequences for bilingualism, depending on the operation of other forces in the community.

With better data and a more rigorous statistical approach it should be possible in the future to examine further the proposition that the factors influencing bilingualism and retention not only may differ but can have a contradictory influence on each of the two major dependent variables.
. . . .

Another theme is based on the empirical evidence offered to show that the causes of bilingualism and the causes of language shift among the children of bilinguals can be separate and distinct. The evidence offered for this proposition is admittedly based on data that are far from definitive, but the key proposition can still be restated; namely, in virtually any contact setting involving people with different native languages it is necessary for at least one segment to learn to communicate with the other. Given this assumption about the nature of society, it follows that one form or another of bilingualism will result from linguistic contact. It may take the form of learning the other group's language or it may evolve into the development of some pidgin, but, at any rate bilingualism will occur. The causes of this bilingualism are to be seen in the context of the societal conditions under which the groups interact. Such matters as the occupational pressures, compositional factors, institutional factors, and the like were shown to operate in the Canadian scene. There is no reason at this time, however, to think that they are unique to Canada.

The causes of bilingualism are distinct from the causes of language shift in the next generation. Assuming that parents are free to raise their children in any tongue they know and choose, the determinants of the language of socialization are not fully or necessarily the same as the determinants of the parents' bilingualism. The inconveniences or disadvantages suffered by the parents' failure to have complete fluency in some acquired language may lead them to try to avoid this disadvantage for their children. In many contact settings a high level of fluency may be acquired fairly early in the child's life. Also, native-like fluency in a tongue is not always all that crucial in some domains. Mother-tongue retention by the children of a bilingual couple may also be rewarded by the communication potential within the ethnic group to which they belong. Accordingly, the pressures for and against acquisition of a second language are at least partly different from the pressures operating on the parents in the tongue they use to raise their children.

NOTE

This chapter comprises selected sections from the author's Language and Ethnic Relations in Canada (New York: Wiley, 1970), pp. 238-40, 249-50.

8 | Bilingualism in Montreal: A Demographic Analysis

Montreal might be viewed as a battleground between the French language and culture of Quebec and the English-speaking Canadians and Americans who surround French Canada. This metropolitan area, containing more than 10 percent of Canada's population, is incontestably the great center of English-French contact in North America. More than 800,000 speak only the French official language, nearly a half-million speak only English, and more than three-quarters of a million are bilingual (speaking both English and French). The latter group comprises slightly more than a third of the nation's bilingual population.[1]

Perhaps "battleground" is too dramatic a term for describing French-English relations in Montreal, although the occasional acts of violence, the more frequent verbal expressions of nationalism, and the self-consciousness about language make our metaphor apt. If inherent in linguistic contact is the danger or possibility that one language will decline and the other expand, then, in this fundamental sense, Montreal, or any other multilingual setting, is a battleground.

Although we are not prepared to assert that the loss of French in Montreal would mean a decline in the importance of this language elsewhere in the province, it is reasonable to assume that Montreal facilitates the maintenance of the French tongue and the bicultural society in Canada. Since 40 percent of Quebec's population is located in this metropolitan area, Montreal is of intrinsic interest because of its sheer size. Moreover, if there is any validity to the concept of metropolitan dominance, we would expect the linguistic outcome in Montreal to influence those parts of Quebec in its hinterland. As Hughes put it, "Montreal is the port of entry from which

English influence and the industrial revolution radiate into the remote
corners of the French-Canadian world. "[2] The presence of Montreal
as a French-speaking center provides Canada with a complete French-
language society, which runs the gamut from backward rural areas to
a modern metropolis maintaining relations with the rest of the world.
The existence of this metropolis allows for a more self-contained
French community than would otherwise occur. Of considerable importance, too, is the extensive out-migration from rural French
Canada currently under way.[3] Montreal provides an outlet without
necessarily a loss of these people from the French language of the
ethnic community.

        In this paper we first examine the trends in language usage
over the past forty years and then interpret them from a primarily
demographic perspective. Our interest stems from the fact that the
encounter of different speech groups is often a concomitant of racial
and ethnic contact. The linguistic outcome in a society composed of
peoples with different tongues is by no means a foregone conclusion
in Canada or in such varied parts of the world as Belgium, Soviet
Moslem Asia, India, South Africa, Ceylon, and Paraguay.[4] Although
recognizing that many theoretical approaches are appropriate, we are
concerned here with those demographic factors that maintain a multilingual system and those that lead to monolingualism.

Bilingualism in Demographic Perspective

        If, by definition, no society can exist unless its members
are able to communicate with one another, then the development of a
bilingual population can be expected in any settlement in which different language groups reside. In this sense, bilingualism may be
viewed as an adaptation by individuals to the presence of persons with
another tongue. Although bilingualism is expected, there is no assurance that it will be of the reciprocal variety in which each group
learns a second language to an equal degree. Clearly, far more non-
English-speakers within the United States learn English than native
Americans learn the immigrant tongues.[5] Moreover, the existence
of bilingualism raises a fundamental question for Montreal or for any
similar setting, namely, "Does second-language-learning occur without a permanent change in the linguistic composition of the population,

or does it lead to a loss in the next generation in the position of one of the mother-tongue groups?"

Bilingualism may be viewed as having three possible outcomes. First, it can provide the mechanism leading to the development of a monolingual population. This is what occurred in the United States among non-English-speaking groups who migrated after the establishment of Anglo-Saxon dominance. After these groups learned the nation's language and became bilingual, somewhere along the line of linguistic transfer between generations only English was passed on and not the mother tongue of the old world. Although completion of this process may have taken several generations, clearly bilingualism was an intermediate stage between the arrival of non-English-speakers and the final loss of the foreign tongue.

Second, bilingualism may be an end product in itself. In this case, there is sufficient bilingualism to enable a population with different mother tongues to maintain the social system, but the bilingualism of parents does not lead to the loss of the mother tongue among the next generation. Rather, the next generation receives the parents' first language and merely repeats the process. Under such circumstances, two populations may be in contact indefinitely without the decline of either language.

The third possibility, which need not concern us here but will be mentioned merely for the sake of completeness, is that the speakers of one language may begin to use a simplified form of the other group's tongue (pidginization), which in turn is passed on to children as their first or mother tongue (creolization).[6] Since this is unlikely in a society such as Canada's where both languages are standardized, we shall restrict our attention to the first two possibilities. This is not to deny, of course, the incorporation into each language of loan words from the other.[7]

Data and Methods

Unless otherwise indicated, the decennial censuses of Canada are the sources for the data used in this study. Two basic language questions have been asked for a number of decades. The first con-

cerns the population's mother tongue. The census data on mother
tongue can be used as a reasonably good measure of the first language
learned. There is one difficulty, however, caused by the stipulation
that, to qualify as one's mother tongue, the first language learned
must still be understood (beginning with the 1941 census) or spoken
(1931 and earlier). Since we are dealing with a setting in which the
number of both English and French speakers is large, it would seem
reasonable to assume that nearly all persons in Montreal whose first
language was either French or English will retain sufficient knowledge
of the language so that they will meet this mother-tongue criterion of
the census takers if their first language was either of these. Very
likely part of the population who learned some other language first will
no longer be able to speak or understand it and, therefore, will have
some other language which they currently know reported as their
mother tongue. This might especially be the case for foreign-born
adults who had come to Canada as small children. When using data
from Canadian censuses, then, equating "mother tongue" and the
first language learned is open to error. However, we shall see that
this error is counter to the results reported and does not bias the
data in favor of the interpretations offered below.

The second-language question relates to the respondents'
ability to speak the official languages of Canada —English and French
—at the time of the census. The results lead to four categories: persons able to speak only English; only French; both English and French;
neither official language. The reader should note that the data on
current linguistic ability refer only to the two official languages.
Hence a person recorded as speaking "English only" may be quite
fluent in, say, German and Italian.

The difficulty in the official-language data lies in the great
simplicity of the census question, namely, "Can you speak English?
French?" We are unable to determine the subjective criteria a respondent uses when he reports his ability to speak these languages.
Moreover, there is some uncertainty about the biases of respondents.
On the one hand, there is social-psychological evidence to indicate
that English has greater prestige than French in Montreal.[8] By contrast, the recent intensification of French-Canadian nationalism and
separatism in Canada would lead us to expect an underreporting of
English-speaking ability among the French population. The frequent

exposure to the languages through acquaintances, radio and television, signs, newspapers, and conversations of strangers in public places would lead us to expect that the questions are less ambiguous for Montreal than for other parts of Canada, because Montreal residents constantly encounter a "reality check." Finally, adopting the standard demographic checks for census data, we have tested the mother-tongue and the official-language data for Canada for internal and external consistency without revealing any serious errors.[9]

As is customary with analyses over time, various adjustments, splices, and estimates to maximize comparability through the decades have been used. This is particularly important with respect to the spatial area covered. As much of the metropolitan area of Montreal as was defined in 1961 has been included for earlier periods as well. However, unlike the Standard Metropolitan Statistical Areas in the U.S. Census, Canadian metropolitan areas are not defined in terms of total counties. Hence, comparisons of the total metropolitan area would be based on dissimilar spatial units which cannot be reconciled for the different decades.

The linguist Greenberg has proposed a series of measures of linguistic diversity that can be used to determine the possibilities of communication among the population of some delimited area.[10] One of these measures, the index of communication (H), has been adapted to the Montreal study. The H gives the probability of two randomly drawn residents of Montreal being able to speak to each other in one or both official languages. Thus, an H of 1.00 would mean that all persons in the area share a mutually intelligible language. At the other extreme, we would obtain H = 0 when there was no chance of two randomly drawn persons in an area sharing the same official language. More formally, let $\underline{a}$ equal the proportion of the population speaking only English; $\underline{b}$ equal the proportion of the population speaking only French; $\underline{c}$ equal the proportion of the population that is bilingual; $\underline{d}$ equal the proportion unable to speak either official language. Then $H_W = a^2 + b^2 + c^2 + 2ac + 2bc$.

An extension of Greenberg's index has been proposed that allows us to measure the probability of communication between members of different ethnic segments of the metropolitan area.[11] Using the same scale we can determine the probability of mutually intelligible

communication between randomly selected members of two groups
as contrasted with Greenberg's measures of communication within a
group. These measures, used in tandem, allow us to determine the
extent of linguistic cohesion within populations such as the total city
or ethnic group as well as the linguistic potential between such populations. We shall use H_w to indicate Greenberg's measure of communication between randomly selected members of two populations.
For groups i and j,

$$H_b = a_i(a_j + c_j) + b_i(b_j + c_j) + c_i(a_j + b_j + c_j).$$

Trends

Communication. The H_w gives the probability of two randomly drawn residents of Montreal being able to speak to each other in
one or both official languages of Canada. For 1961, we would expect
two persons randomly selected from the metropolitan area to speak
in a mutually intelligible official language slightly less than eight out
of ten times. This is a fairly high degree of mutual intelligibility;
multilingual Brussels (Brabant), for example, has a slightly lower H
for 1947.[12] However, we should not lose sight of the fact that somewhat more than 20 percent of the time there is no shared communication possible in these languages. More striking, and contrary to the
expectations generated from the American urban experience, we find
something of a decline in H_w in the decades between 1921 and 1961
(Table 1, col. 1).

One important modification of this result must be considered,
namely, changes in H_w may reflect fluctuations in immigration rather
than a basic alteration of the linguistic processes of Montreal. Specifically, the component of the population unable to speak either official
language rises in recent decades, and much of the drop in communication may reflect this rise. In 1961 immigrants arriving during the
preceding five and one-half years comprised 5 percent of the area's
population but accounted for one-half of the population of the entire
metropolitan area unable to speak English or French.

The indexes have been recomputed in two different ways:
first, excluding all persons unable to speak either official language;

Table 1. Indexes of Communication (H) Between and Within
Selected Populations of the Montreal Area, 1921-61

Year	Within total population (1)	Within population speaking an official language (2)	Between ethnic groups			
			British		French	
			French (3)	Other (4)	Other (5)	
1921[a]	.8719	.8833	.7552	.8879	.7444	
1931[a]	.8752	.8918	.7665	.9042	.7571	
1941[a]	.8598	.8656	n.a.	n.a.	n.a.	
1961[a]	.8349	.8727	n.a.	n.a.	n.a.	
1941[b]	.8294	.8361	.6362	.9278	.6830	
1951[b]	.8222	.8385	.6269	.8849	.6664	
1961[b]	.7942	.8425	.6245	.7795	.6174	

Note: n.a. : not available.
[a] Montreal and Verdun, ten years of age and older.
[b] Montreal, Verdun, and Outremont, all ages.

second, excluding the foreign-born population entirely. In either
case, no appreciable change in the degree of linguistic communication
is observed over time. In some comparisons there is a slight rise and
in others a slight decline through time (Table 1, col. 2). Since no dis-
cernible trend is found after these adjustments, we can conclude that
the decline is due to immigration. At best, however, we do not find
a substantial rise in H_w over time, although communication potential
has more or less remained constant in the forty years between 1921
and 1961.

Using the extension of Greenberg's measures described earlier, we can measure the probability of communication between members of the different ethnic segments of Montreal. We observe a rise
between 1921 and 1931 in the chance of British-French interaction in a
mutually intelligible language (Table 1, col. 3). This is not the case
in more recent decades—witness the slight decline from .6362 in 1941

to .6245 in 1961. Moreover, for the entire metropolitan area in 1961, in only six out of ten cases could we expect two people to share a common official language. On the basis of the data available, there is no reason to think that the communication potential between British and French groups in Montreal has been rising.

The British have much closer linguistic links with other ethnic groups in Montreal than do the French (cf. Table 1, cols. 4 and 5). The closer linguistic communication of other groups in general with the British is a result of the greater affinity of these groups for learning English than for learning French. We shall consider this matter in greater detail later. Because of extensive immigration, we are not inclined to take too seriously the drop in H_b for "other" ethnics between 1941 and 1961.

These results indicate that linguistic cohesion between the major ethnic populations is only moderate, although cohesion within the British and French groups is extremely high. For the metropolitan area in 1961, communication potential within the British and the French ethnic groups is .97 and .98, respectively. In short, language is a major factor in maintaining ethnic cleavage in the city. We should note, however, that the probability of communication between the French and the British ethnic groups in the Montreal metropolitan area is still nearly three times greater than H_b between Algeria's Europeans and Moslems in the period preceding the Algerian revolution.[13] Other ethnic groups in Montreal have mainly veered toward the English language and the British ethnic population. Their linguistic unity is not sufficiently high to maintain a residual third ethnic force in Montreal. Linguistic unity for the entire Montreal area appears to be static after we take into account the influence of immigration, which tends to depress the H indexes because of the numbers unable to speak either official language.

Official language distribution. H indexes, being summary measures, may fail to disclose important trends in language usage because different combinations of official-language distributions may yield the same index values. Examination of the basic data indicates that there has been a drop in both the monolingual English and bilingual percentages, accompanied by a rise in the segment speaking French only. For example, Montreal-Verdun-Outremont dropped

from 24 to 19 percent monolingual English and from 42 to 39 percent
bilingual in the twenty years between 1941 and 1961. At the same time,
the percentage speaking French only rose from 34 to 39 (Table 2,
panel A). These trends hold regardless of the areal basis upon which
the comparisons are made.

There are striking differences between ethnic groups in
their official-language distributions. The French are far more bilingual than are the British (cf. Table 2, panels B and C). Through
time it appears that the British population has at least maintained its
degree of bilingualism, whereas bilingualism has declined among the
French. We should note that the French nevertheless remain more
bilingual than the British in 1961.

Other ethnic groups in Montreal occupy an intermediate position between the two leading ethnic populations, but they definitely
favor English. They are more likely to speak French than are the
British, although an overwhelming segment speak English only rather
than French only (Table 2, panel D). Similar to the strengthening of
the French language among the French ethnic population observed
earlier is a sharp decline since 1941 among other ethnics in the percentage speaking English only and a doubling in the small percentage
speaking French only.

It is difficult to account for these trends in a quantifiable
fashion since the necessary cross-tabulations are not available. We
should recall, however, that there has been a growing movement from
rural Quebec to urban Quebec—particularly to Montreal. The fact that
rural French Canadians living in more homogeneous settlements are
less likely to learn English than are their Montreal compatriots would
help explain the drop in bilingualism and the rise in monolingual
French-speakers among the French Canadians in Montreal. In 1961,
for example, only 9.7 percent of the French ethnic population in rural
Quebec was bilingual. We must note that internal migration probably
does not fully account for the decline in French bilingualism, since we
have also observed a recent increase among immigrants in their propensity to learn French. It would appear that the French Canadians,
although still subordinate to the British in the economic world, have
risen somewhat, and this may make knowledge of French more useful
than it has been for Montrealers. We are told, for example, of a

Table 2.   Percentage Distribution of Official Language
by Ethnic Origin, Montreal Area, 1921-61

Population and official language	Montreal and Verdun, 10 years of age and older				Montreal, Verdun, and Outremont, all ages		
	1921	1931	1941	1961	1941	1951	1961
A. All groups:							
English only	25.2	25.9	23.7	18.7	23.9	22.1	19.0
French only	21.9	20.5	28.2	32.5	34.0	35.8	39.0
English & French	51.9	52.7	47.8	46.6	41.7	41.1	39.1
Neither	0.9	0.9	0.3	2.2	0.4	1.0	2.9
B. British:							
English only	71.4	71.4	n.a.	n.a.	70.2	70.6	67.1
French only	0.7	0.5	n.a.	n.a.	1.3	2.0	2.8
English & French	27.9	28.1	n.a.	n.a.	28.5	27.4	29.9
Neither	0.0	0.0	n.a.	n.a.	0.0	0.0	0.2
C. French:							
English only	0.2	0.5	n.a.	n.a.	0.7	1.1	1.0
French only	34.3	32.7	n.a.	n.a.	51.7	52.8	55.4
English & French	65.6	66.8	n.a.	n.a.	47.6	46.1	43.4
Neither	0.0	0.0	n.a.	n.a.	0.0	0.0	0.2
D. Other ethnics:							
English only	53.3	53.8	n.a.	n.a.	55.9	50.7	44.4
French only	5.0	3.7	n.a.	n.a.	5.3	5.6	10.8
English & French	34.5	35.9	n.a.	n.a.	36.1	37.2	31.4
Neither	7.3	6.7	n.a.	n.a.	2.7	6.6	13.4

Note: n.a.: not available.

department store that at one time made no attempt to hire clerks who
knew French on the grounds that the French Canadians could not
afford to shop in its high-priced store. The bilingual Montreal class
ified telephone directories are relevant here. Under the English-
language category "Department Stores" there are twenty-eight differ
ent listings in 1938. Under the French equivalent "Magasins à Rayor
we find only four listings. In the 1964 Yellow Pages, we find forty-fi

companies listed under "Department Stores" and forty-nine under
"Magasins à Rayons."[14] To be sure, the number listed as true department stores must be taken with a grain of salt; however, it is
clear from inspection that all of the major downtown stores are now
in both the French and the English listings. The possibility of distortions in the census data due to French nationalism should be considered
as accounting for the decline in bilingualism among French Canadians.
We are inclined to minimize this explanation for several reasons.
First, this decline was observed before the recent increase in nationalism. Second, the most recent census was conducted before French-
Canadian separatism reached its apex. Finally, if a segment of the
population knows English but refuses to speak it, then for many functional purposes such people are equivalent to those who know only
French.

Considering that in 1961 French was the mother tongue of
nearly two-thirds (65 percent) of the metropolitan population and
English the mother tongue of little more than one-fifth (22 percent)
of the population, it is clear that the position of the French language
is far from being as strong as we might expect simply on the basis
of the composition of Montreal's population. The number speaking
French only amounts to 60 percent of the 1.4 million persons whose
mother tongue is French (FMT). The monolingual English population,
by contrast, amounts to 93 percent of the 495,000 persons whose
mother tongue is English (EMT).[15] For 1961, it is estimated that 28
percent of EMT British males were bilingual. On the other hand,
about 48 percent of the FMT French males were bilingual.[16] Equally
lopsided differences are found for females, although they are of a
lower magnitude. In other Canadian cities, where the relative numbers with French and English mother tongues are reversed, French
fares far worse as the lesser language than does English in Montreal.
In Moncton, N.B., for example, where French is the mother tongue
of about a third of the population and English the mother tongue of
nearly all the remaining two-thirds, only about 4 percent of EMT
British males have learned French, whereas nearly 90 percent of
FMT French males were bilingual in 1961.

Intergenerational Maintenance

If bilingualism is to lead to the demise of one of the languages, then the second language of some bilingual parents must be passed on as the mother tongue of their children. If bilingualism is to be the end product of linguistic contact, then the mother tongue of bilingual parents must be passed on as the mother tongue of their children. To simplify the problem, we will consider three elements in our model of linguistic maintenance.

First, the proportion in each mother-tongue group that is bilingual clearly influences what we might call the "exposure to risk." We observed for the two leading ethnic groups that a far larger proportion of FMT residents learn English than EMT residents learn French. For all fathers of small children in Montreal-Verdun in 1961 we estimate that about 35 percent of those with EMT have learned French, whereas about 49 percent of FMT fathers are estimated to be bilingual.[17] In the previous two decades these differences in exposure to risk were even greater. French is subject to a far greater "exposure" than is English in the sense that proportionately more of the French are potential spreaders or carriers of the English language than the English are of the French language. The relative degree of bilingualism among the different speech groups is critical, since it is reasonable to assume that only bilingual parents face an option in the tongue they pass on to their offspring.

Second, we should consider the degree to which each bilingual group passes on the acquired non-mother-tongue language to their offspring, what we might call the "rate of intergenerational language-switching." It is most important that the actual behavior of bilinguals with respect to language transfer be distinguished from the rate of bilingual exposure. The sheer fact that the FMT group is more bilingual than is the EMT group does not necessarily mean that a larger proportion of French bilinguals pass on a second language to their children. In fact, it is possible for the two sets of rates to be reversed so that there is a net decline in the language of the linguistic population with the smaller degree of actual bilingualism. This can occur if proportionately more of its bilingual members than of the bilingual component of the other language group actually pass on a second language.

Third, we should examine the <u>fertility</u> rates separately for the monolingual and bilingual subpopulations of each mother-tongue group. There can be a higher rate of language-switching among the bilingual segment of a mother-tongue group without a decline in the language if this segment's fertility rates are relatively low compared with those of the monolingual members. In this sense, we must always distinguish between aggregate and individual assimilation. It is possible for individuals to assimilate and yet for their group to maintain itself or to expand in size.[18]

There are additional variables that might be added to this simplified analytical model, such as differentials in mortality and internal and international migration. However, the three elements described above—exposure to risk,rate of intergenerational language-switching,and fertility—appear to be the major factors to consider in the Montreal situation.

If we compare the mother-tongue distribution of small children (Table 3, cols. 1-3) with that of women in the childbearing ages (Table 3, cols. 4-6), we find that the higher degree of bilingualism among the FMT population has not led to a net switch to English among the children. In all periods, a larger proportion of small children than of women in the childbearing ages have French as their mother tongue. In 1951, for example, 67.9 percent of the women had French as a mother tongue, whereas 70.1 percent of the children were reported as having French. The position of the English language is somewhat inconsistent, in some decades being slightly better than its rank among women of childbearing ages would suggest and in other instances poorer (cf. Table 3, cols. 1 and 4). The erosion of other mother tongues is quite apparent; in each decade their overall position among small children is weaker than the position among adult women. The net results of our intergenerational analysis indicate that French is not merely holding its own but is actually gaining between generations.

Before interpreting this finding, it is necessary to consider the differentials in fertility between language groups—particularly since the French have higher fertility rates than the non-French ethnic component of Montreal.[19] As a crude approximation we have determined the mother tongues we would "expect" among children under five years of age knowing their ethnic origins and the cross-tabulation

Table 3. Percentage Distribution of Mother Tongue of Children under 5 (Actual and Expected) and of Women in the Childbearing Ages, Montreal and Verdun, 1941-61

Year	Children under 5 years (actual)			Women, 15–44 years			Children under 5 years (expected)		
	English (1)	French (2)	Other (3)	English (4)	French (5)	Other (6)	English (7)	French (8)	Other (9)
1941	19.8	73.0	7.2	23.9	66.1	10.1	20.4	70.9	8.7
1951	24.8	70.1	5.0	23.0	67.9	9.0	21.2	70.0	8.8
1961	16.5	70.7	12.9	17.3	68.4	14.3	14.5	70.8	14.7
1961 (MA)a	22.6	68.3	9.0	22.0	65.9	12.1	20.2	68.5	11.3

Note: Cols. 7–9 based on ethnic origin of children under five and the relationship between ethnic origin and mother tongue for all males in the area.
a Entire Census Metropolitan Area.

between mother tongue and origin for males in the metropolitan area.
Using Westergaard's method of standardization, we derive the "expected" mother-tongue distribution of children under five given in columns 7-9 of Table 3.

Several comments are called for before discussing the results. First, we standardized on the basis of males rather than
females because ethnic origin in the case of mixed offspring is traced
through the male lineage in the Canadian census enumerations. Second, the cross-tabulation between origin and mother tongue is not
available for specific age categories. Consequently, the standardization rates incorporate to some extent the very data examined for
small children. Since children under five do not comprise a large
segment of the population, we are not too greatly hampered by this
departure from the ideal.[20] Finally, the available data do not allow
for the control of differences in fertility between monolinguals and
bilinguals within each ethnic population. This has important implications, which we will discuss shortly.

Controlling for fertility differences between ethnic groups,
we find the French language has about held its own (Table 3, cols. 2
and 8). In both 1951 and 1961, the position of French among children is
within 0.2 percent of the figure we would expect on the basis of the
ethnic origins of the youngsters. In 1941, the number of FMT children
is even greater than what we would expect on the basis of ethnic fertility differentials. The gain for French in the two most recent decades
among adult women, however, is not due to a net transfer to French
among the bilingual parents of Montreal. Rather, it appears largely
to reflect the higher fertility rates of ethnic groups with sizable numbers of native French-speakers.

By contrast, ethnic fertility differentials are clearly unfavorable to the maintenance of English. In each period the percentage of
children we would expect to have English as a mother tongue falls
below the percentage of women in childbearing ages with this mother
tongue (cf. Table 3, cols. 4 and 7). In the last two decades, however,
the English language has more than held its own when we consider the
lower fertility of ethnic groups with large numbers of EMT adults
(cf. Table 3, cols. 1 and 7). In 1951, for example, taking fertility into
account, we would expect 21.2 percent of children to have English as

a mother tongue whereas actually 24.8 percent were reported as learning this language first. The excess was more than enough to compensate for lower fertility in 1951 and results in the percentage of small children with English exceeding the percentage of women with this language (respectively, 24.8 and 23.0 percent). The results for 1961 are inconsistent, depending on whether one includes the entire metropolitan area in the analysis. What is clear, however, is that the net intergenerational switching has been favorable to English but that much or all of the gain is wiped out by the lower fertility rates.

Although the data relevant to the question of whether fertility differentials aid or handicap other mother tongues are inconsistent (Table 3, cols. 6 and 9), there is little doubt that other languages in general fail to hold their own. Whether the mother tongues of children (col. 3) are compared with those of women in the childbearing ages (col. 6) or with those expected among children on the basis of ethnic differentials in fertility (col. 9), the results clearly show a drop in other mother tongues among small children. If anything, the extent of this drop is probably understated, since many small children were either born in a country where English was not spoken or were born in Canada of relatively recent immigrants who had not yet sufficiently mastered one of the official languages to use it for speaking to their children.

It is very difficult to estimate fertility differences between the linguistic subpopulations within each ethnic group. Overall, on the basis of indirect evidence, we would be inclined to guess that the bilingual segment has lower fertility rates. This guess is based on the following facts: First, Enid Charles finds an inverse association between fertility and income within each major ethnic population.[21] Second, there is some evidence that bilinguals tend to have higher incomes than monolinguals within both the French- and the English-speaking populations.[22] This would suggest, although by no means conclusively, that the bilingual segments of Montreal's FMT and EMT populations have lower fertility than their monolingual compatriots. Under such circumstances, the exposure-to-risk rates overstate the danger to the mother-tongue populations of bilingualism.

The intergenerational language-switching rate is more elusive than the two elements of the model considered thus far. Indeed, we do not have available the basic data needed for determining the switching rates for the bilinguals of each mother-tongue group. We do wish to note, however, that if the languages are maintained between generations in a simple two-language-contact setting with some switching between generations, then if fertility is equal it can be shown that actually the bilinguals of the group with lower exposure to risk are experiencing a higher rate of intergenerational language-switching than is the group with the larger percentage of bilingual parents. It is reasonable to assume that, in a bilingual setting such as Montreal, some parents do in fact pass the second language on as their children's mother tongue. Under such circumstances, if the FMT population is more bilingual than the remainder of the population and if switching is equal in each direction, then it follows that the rate of switching is higher for the bilingual non-FMT population than for the bilingual FMT population.

One important consideration in interpreting the maintenance of both English and French through the generations is the fact that men in Montreal are more bilingual than women. This sex difference means that many of the bilingual members of each ethnic group are married to monolingual mates who share only the same mother tongue. Insofar as this occurs, the high incidence of bilingualism is reduced as a contributing force to language transfer, because only one of the mates can use the second language with their children. Sex differences in bilingualism within a largely endogamous population help to maintain the common mother tongue of the mates in the next generation, since this would be the one language that both parents could use with the children.

Of course, marriages across mother-tongue lines are considerably more complex in their possibilities. Marriages between EMT and FMT mates will often involve a cross between Catholic and non-Catholic. If the ties of the Roman Catholic church are strong enough so that frequently mates will agree to a Catholic education for prospective offspring, intermarriage will not harm French-language maintenance in Montreal, since the Catholic school system is overwhelmingly French-speaking.[23]

Table 4. Percentage Bilingual, by Age and Sex, Montreal Area, 1931–61

| | Males | | | | | Females | | | | |
| | Montreal-Verdun | | Montreal-Outremont-Verdun | | | Montreal-Verdun | | Montreal-Outremont-Verdun | | |
Age	1931 (1)	1941 (2)	1941 (3)	1951 (4)	1961 (5)	1931 (6)	1941 (7)	1941 (8)	1951 (9)	1961 (10)
0–4	4.1	5.7	5.7	3.3	2.5	4.0	5.6	5.7	3.4	2.5
5–9	18.2	11.3	11.5	9.7	9.9	18.0	11.5	11.8	9.7	9.6
10–14	43.4	22.2	22.6	20.5	22.4	41.4	21.9	22.3	20.1	21.9
15–19	62.4	51.4	51.7	50.6	49.6	54.7	43.1	43.5	44.5	46.7
20–24	67.2	67.1	67.2	64.9	59.4	53.3	51.5	51.7	48.2	44.4
25–34	61.9	68.8	68.8	68.8	59.7	49.0	47.8	48.1	47.8	41.1
35–44	62.2	63.6	63.7	68.1	65.3	44.5	40.9	41.2	45.2	45.5
45–54	59.3	60.3	60.3	62.7	63.6	41.6	35.6	36.0	37.4	42.6
55–64	57.4	53.7	53.8	57.3	57.2	37.1	31.2	31.6	30.8	34.5
65–69	56.4	49.4	49.6	49.7	52.0	34.3	28.0	28.5	26.5	28.5
70+	51.2	42.9	43.3	42.2	44.0	31.2	24.4	24.7	23.5	24.5

Cohorts

Thus far our demographic examination has focused on inter-generational dimensions of bilingualism, namely, the language transferred by bilingual parents to their offspring. At this point, we turn to viewing second-language-learning in connection with the life span of residents of Montreal. The terms "cohort," "longitudinal," and "generational" will be used interchangeably to describe the approach employed. As opposed to the more commonly encountered cross-sectional analysis, a longitudinal study allows us to determine true social change since the linguistic behavior of a population is actually traced through time.[24] By considering where in the life span second-language-learning tends to occur, we may infer the social conditions leading to bilingualism.

There are several serious difficulties involved in tracing the bilingualism of age groups through time. First, we have no way of directly controlling for the foreign-born population in Montreal and cannot readily prevent immigration between decades from affecting the analysis. Similarly, lack of available data prevents the application of controls for emigration and internal migration. The results presented are, therefore, crude cohorts which describe the process of linguistic change by age groups but which do not easily allow for the decomposition of these changes into the contributions that selective migration and mortality may have contributed to the results. With respect to mortality differentials, however, it is unlikely that these would significantly alter the results. We shall have more to say about the influence of immigration later.

Shown in Table 4 are the bilingual proportions by age and sex of the four decades 1931-61. For 1941-61, the analysis is based upon the combined cities of Montreal-Outremont-Verdun. Since data are not available for Outremont in 1931, the 1941 figures were recomputed for the Montreal-Verdun area alone.

Male cohorts. If we assume that the proportion of boys who are bilingual at the age they usually begin school falls somewhere between the proportions for the population under five and five through nine, then we would estimate that less than 10 percent speak both English and French by the time elementary school is begun. This

means that the linguistic heterogeneity of Montreal has a limited
effect in introducing bilingualism among boys at an early age. What
appears to operate is a steady push in the learning of a second official
language during the ages of mass education, some additional gain in
bilingualism in the early adult ages, and then a steady decline in bilingualism through the remaining years. Tracing male age groups between 1931 and 1941, for example, we find 4.1 percent of children under
five are bilingual (col. 1), but ten years later boys ten through fourteen years of age are 22.2 percent bilingual (col. 2). Similarly, 18.2
percent of boys five through nine are bilingual in 1931, but more than
half (51.4 percent) are bilingual ten years later. This result holds up
as well for the 1941-51 and 1951-61 comparisons (cols. 3-4, 4-5). In
addition to the rapid buildup of bilingualism through the teens, there
is some increment in the early adult ages.

This surge in bilingualism tapers off for each cohort somewhere in the twenties and early thirties and is then followed by an
actual net decline among men in the middle and later years of their
life. Men thirty-five and older in 1931 all show declines in bilingualism during the following decade (cols. 1 and 2). This interdecade
decline starts even earlier in the 1941-51 span, with men twenty-five
and over in 1941 showing declines in bilingualism ten years later.
Indeed, the age at which the decline in bilingualism begins is even
earlier by 1961. As we shall see, the decline in the age at which male
bilingualism begins to erode is explainable in terms of immigration.

These results suggest that the educational system of Montreal
which requires courses in the official language not used as the language
of instruction in the school, meets with success. This success is far
from complete, since in most decades about half of the boys fifteen
through nineteen are unable to speak both official languages. The decline that follows the school years indicates that economic and occupational forces in combination with internal and international migration
fail to fully support or maintain bilingualism among a fair number of
males. Once the supports of education and the early years in the labor
force are past, ability in both official languages begins to decline. It
is as if we were to examine knowledge of algebra by age cohorts over
time. We would expect to find a rapid rise through the school ages,
followed by a decline after the educational period, since many find
little or no need for algebra in either their occupational or their social

worlds. In similar fashion, through a fair part of the adult male span, more bilingual speakers lose their knowledge of the second language than monolinguals acquire a knowledge of the second official language.

Female cohorts. Further support for this interpretation comes from examination and comparison of bilingualism among the female age cohorts (Table 4, cols. 6-10). First, we observe that the degree of bilingualism among girls under 15 is very similar to that found for boys of the same ages. With the exception of ten- through fourteen-year-old girls in 1931, the sex differences are well under 1 percent. This suggests that the experiences of boys and girls are very similar at these ages so that the net influences of home language, neighbors, mass media, playmates, and early years of formal second-language instruction in the schools are nearly identical. Beginning with the late teens, at the age when formal education ends for many and participation in the labor force begins, we find increasing differences between the sexes in their bilingualism. By the early twenties, the sex differences in bilingualism are considerable. In 1931, for example, 43.4 and 41.4 percent of the males and females ten through fourteen are bilingual; in 1941, 67.1 and 51.5 percent, respectively, of males and females are bilingual. Percentage-point differences of about 15 are also found for 1951 and 1961 between males and females in the twenty through twenty-four age category.

The influence of male participation in the labor force and female withdrawal into the home and child-rearing can also be seen in the points at which a net decline in bilingualism occurs as well as in the lower increases in bilingualism among women. In all three interdecade comparisons we find that declines in the bilingual percentage occur at earlier ages for women than for men. This is most striking for the 1931-41 comparisons. Not until we reach men thirty-five through forty-four in 1931 do we find a cohort that declines in the succeeding ten years (62.2 in 1931 and 60.3 in 1941). By contrast, females fifteen through nineteen and older decline in bilingualism by 1941.[26] These differentials are compatible with the contention that the main supports of bilingualism are school and occupational systems, although the reader should be reminded that the evidence is hardly incontrovertible.

Immigration. Unfortunately, limitations in the available
data preclude an analysis or weighting of the specific contributions
made by such diverse institutional and demographic forces as education, occupational demands, internal migration, and immigration in
influencing the bilingualism of cohorts. It is possible, however, to
gauge through indirect means the influence of immigration in interdecade changes in bilingualism. There is little need to consider the
impact of recent immigration on bilingualism among the younger age
groups, since the rapidly rising bilingualism rates run counter to
any expectation we might have on the basis of the low bilingualism of
recent immigrants.

The decade between 1931 and 1941 affords the easiest test,
since there was very little net immigration to Montreal-Verdun. For
some age categories in 1941, less than 1 percent of the population were
foreign-born who had arrived in the preceding decade. Recent immigrants (since the 1931 census) were strongest among the thirty-five
through forty-four-year-old population, comprising 2.2 and 2.8 percent, respectively, of males and females in 1941. Even if no immigrants in the preceding decade had become bilingual—which is far
from the case—their number would have been too small to account for
the interdecade declines in bilingualism that we observe in 1941 among
men who were thirty-five and over in 1931 and among women who were
fifteen and older. We can conclude that the inferences based on cohort
changes between 1931 and 1941 are substantially unaltered by immigration during the decade.

Heavier immigration since World War II definitely influences
the cohort patterns described earlier. Among both men and women
in the age category thirty-five through forty-four in 1961, about 20
percent were immigrants who had arrived in Canada during the preceding ten years. For both 1951 and 1961 we have estimated the age-
specific bilingual percentages, excluding for each year immigrants
first arriving in the preceding decade ("recent immigrants").[26] We
shall examine these rates in order to determine whether the inferences
made earlier are valid after the effect of immigration is eliminated.

The results, shown in Table 5, indicate that no substantial
changes need be made in the cohort analysis presented earlier. In
1951 we find that the decline in bilingualism begins among men who

Table 5. Percentage Bilingual for Selected Age Groups, by Sex, Excluding Recent Immigrants, Montreal-Outremont-Verdun, 1941-61

Age	Males				Females			
	1941 (1)	1951[a] (2)	1951 (3)	1961[b] (4)	1941 (5)	1951[a] (6)	1951 (7)	1961[b] (8)
10-14	22.6		20.5		22.3		20.1	
15-19	51.7		50.6		43.5		44.5	
20-24	67.2	66.8	64.9	64.7	51.7	49.5	48.2	49.1
25-34	68.8	72.2	68.8	67.6	48.1	50.0	47.8	46.0
35-44	63.7	71.2	68.1	71.6	41.2	46.4	45.2	49.0
45-54	60.3	64.3	62.7	67.5	36.0	38.1	37.4	44.7
55-64	53.8	58.0	57.3	59.0	31.6	31.1	30.8	35.7
65-69	49.6	50.1	49.7	53.0	28.5	26.7	26.5	29.3
70+		42.5		44.5		23.7		24.9

[a] Excluding immigrants since 1941.
[b] Excluding immigrants since 1951.

were forty-five and older in 1941 (cols. 1 and 2). Among women, the decline now begins among those twenty and older in 1941 (cols. 5 and 6). In 1961, the decline for men starts with those who were thirty-five and over ten years earlier (cols. 3 and 4). The results for women are somewhat inconsistent; there is a decline for women twenty through twenty-four in 1951 but a rise between 1951 and 1961 among women twenty-five through thirty-four at the beginning of the period. However, a steady decline is observed among women thirty-five and over in 1951.

In brief, the existence of unlearning is still found among the population who were not immigrants to Canada in the intervening decades. The process of immigration tends to lower the age at which bilingualism starts to decline. In other words, the effect of large-scale immigration on cohorts is the same as if bilingualism were to start its decline at earlier ages. The decline among men is more of a middle-age phenomenon, while women tend to begin their decline in bilingualism at earlier ages. This result is, of course, compatible with the earlier interpretation of the institutional forces that maintain bilingualism in Montreal.

Comment

Racial and ethnic contact is frequently accompanied by the confrontation of peoples who speak different tongues. In the United States, with a few exceptions, we have been able to take more or less for granted the linguistic outcome of contacts with non-English-speaking peoples. Although the experience of the United States is not unique, there are far more complex linguistic situations in many parts of the world. Indeed, Canada is relatively simple compared to such nations as Nigeria, India, or South Africa.

The examination of linguistic trends in Montreal indicates a process quite contrary to the view of the city as a great mixer and melting pot of diverse cultures. Unlike most American cities, where populations with diverse linguistic origins have moved toward a monolingual status in a matter of a few generations, Montreal has maintained an equilibrium. This equilibrium is similar to that of Switzerland in the sense that it is based on dynamic demographic forces that tend to counterbalance each other.[27] It is a precarious equilibrium, since the exposure to risk is greater among the French ethnic population than among the British.

If we make the assumption that most people will not really master a second tongue unless it is learned at a relatively early age, then second-language-learning is less of a threat to the mother tongue than might otherwise be the case, since English and French languages are able to hold their own as the first language of children, and since much of the bilingualism in Canada does not occur in the very early ages or as a result of informal social contacts. Keyfitz has pointed to the handicaps that bilingual French Canadians face in the upper echelons of management or in white-collar office settings because of their lack of fluency or ease in English, which is often the language used.[28]

The constant replacement of a population through the introduction of new generations means that social change may occur without any individual changes.[29] However, we should not lose sight of
the fact that generations may be instruments of conservation. Insofar
as new members are socialized by older members, then it is equally
possible for the system to maintain itself over time indefinitely as
the newcomers who gradually replace the older members are socialized.[30] In the case of Montreal, we witness a social process of
second-language-learning in each generation that does not lead to
change through the years in the linguistic structure of Montreal.
From the perspective outlined earlier, transfer from parents to children and the stage in the life span at which bilingualism occurs are
both critical for understanding the outcome of language contact.

NOTES

This study was supported by the National Science Foundation Grant
No. G-23923. The assistance of Elaine F. Green and David Sorenson
is gratefully acknowledged.
[1] All figures based on 1961 census data.
[2] Everett C. Hughes, French Canada in Transition (Chicago:
University of Chicago Press, 1943), p. 202.
[3] Nathan Keyfitz, "L'Exode rural dans la province de Québec,
1951-1961," Recherches sociographiques, III (Sept.-Dec. 1962): 303-15.
[4] See, for example, United Nations, Demographic Yearbook,
1956 (New York: Dept. of Economic and Social Affairs, 1956), Table
9; Demographic Yearbook, 1963 (New York: Dept. of Economic and
Social Affairs, 1964), Table 10.
[5] In 1930, less than 10 percent of immigrants 10 years old and
over were unable to speak English. U.S. Bureau of the Census,
Fifteenth Census of the United States, 1930, Population (Washington,
D.C.: Government Printing Office, 1933), II; 1347.
[6] See, for example, William J. Samarin, "Lingua Francas,
with Special Reference to Africa," in Frank A. Rice, ed., Study of
the Role of Second Languages (Washington, D.C.: Center for Applied
Linguistics, 1962), pp. 54-64.
[7] For a discussion of English loan words used by French

Canadians in an outlying rural area, see Horace Miner, St. Denis: A French-Canadian Parish (Chicago: University of Chicago Press, 1939), pp. 32-35, 242-45.

[8] Wallace E. Lambert, R. C. Hodgson, R. C. Gardner, and S. Fillenbaum, "Evaluational Reactions to Spoken Languages," Journal of Abnormal and Social Psychology 60 (1960): 44-51.

[9] Stanley Lieberson, "Language Questions in Censuses" (report prepared for S. S. R. C. Sociolinguistics Seminar, Indiana University, Summer, 1964).

[10] Joseph H. Greenberg, "The Measurement of Linguistic Diversity," Language 32 (Jan.-March 1956): 109-15.

[11] Stanley Lieberson, "An Extension of Greenberg's Measure of Linguistic Diversity," Language 40 (Oct.-Dec. 1964): 526-31.

[12] Ibid., p. 528.

[13] Ibid.

[14] Bell Telephone Company of Canada, Montreal Classified Telephone Directory, July 1938, pp. 108, 223. I am indebted to G. L. Long, historian, Bell Telephone Company of Canada, for making this volume available. Yellow Pages, Montreal, September 1964, pp. 291, 552.

[15] This does not mean that 93 percent of the EMT population speak English only. Many EMT persons are bilingual but are replaced in this figure by people with other mother tongues who, of the two official languages, speak only English.

[16] Lieberson, "Language Questions in Censuses."

[17] Estimates are based on the official-language distribution of the "other" mother-tongue population in 1931 (most recent year for which such data are available) and the assumption that all EMT or FMT persons in Montreal-Verdun retain speaking ability in their mother tongue.

[18] Stanley Lieberson, Ethnic Patterns in American Cities (New York: Free Press of Glencoe, 1963), pp. 8-10.

[19] The French have higher fertility even with education and income held constant. See Enid Charles, The Changing Size of the Family in Canada (Ottawa: Dominion Bureau of Statistics, 1948), p. 105.

[20] Moreover, where there are any trends through time, the child-bearing ages would probably fall close to the mean for each ethnic group.

[21] See Charles.

[22] In a current study of want ads in Montreal newspapers, jobs that require bilinguals tend to be concentrated in categories that offer higher income.

[23] Only two of the fourteen elementary-school districts of the Montreal Catholic School District are English. See Bureau of Statistics, School Directory, 1963-1964 (Montreal: Montreal Catholic School Commission, n. d.).

[24] Among recent examples of the application of cohort analysis to empirical data are Pascal K. Whelpton, "Trends and Differentials in the Spacing of Births, " Demography 1 (1964): 83-93; Hope T. Eldridge, "A Cohort Approach to the Analysis of Migration Differentials, " Demography 1 (1964): 212-19; Beverly Duncan, George Sabagh, and Maurice D. Van Arsdol, Jr. , "Patterns of City Growth, " American Journal of Sociology 67 (Jan. 1962): 418-29; N. B. Ryder, "The Influence of Declining Mortality on Swedish Reproductivity, " in Current Research in Human Fertility (New York: Milbank Memorial Fund, 1955), pp. 65-81.

[25] Here and elsewhere, graphs have been employed to compare cohorts over time that are in different-size age categories in the two periods.

[26] The bilingual percentage for the population, excluding recent immigrants, was obtained through indirect standardization. Using the component of recent immigrants in each group as weights, the ratio of actual and standardized bilingual percentage was applied to each specific age category to estimate the bilingual percentage of the population who had lived in Canada in the preceding decade.

[27] For an excellent analysis of the demographic factors, see Kurt Mayer, "Cultural Pluralism and Linguistic Equilibrium in Switzerland, " reprinted in Joseph J. Spengler and Otis Dudley Duncan, eds., Demographic Analysis (Glencoe, Ill.: Free Press, 1956), pp. 478-83.

[28] Nathan Keyfitz, "Canadians and Canadiens, " Queen's Quarterly 70 (Summer, 1963): 163-82.

[29] Karl Mannheim, Essays on the Sociology of Knowledge (New York: Oxford University Press, 1953), pp. 276-320.

[30] See George Simmel, "Social Interaction as the Definition of the Group in Time and Space, " in Robert E. Park and Ernest W. Burgess, Introduction to the Science of Sociology (Chicago: University of Chicago Press, 1921), pp. 348-56.

9 | Language Shift in the United States: Some Demographic Clues

In Collaboration with Timothy J. Curry

Compared with the situation in many nations, a staggering number of immigrants and their descendents in the United States have given up their ancestral languages and shifted to a new mother tongue. Nearly two-thirds of the 35 million immigrants between 1840 and 1924 were native speakers of some other tongue.[1] Except for such groups as the Spanish-speaking residents of the Southwest, the Pennsylvania Dutch, the French-speaking residents of New England, and the Creoles in the Louisiana bayous, the shift to an English mother tongue was both rapid and with relatively little intergroup conflict. The conflict that did exist was confined more to battles between generations within each group rather than with the English-speaking residents.[2] Despite efforts on the part of all immigrant groups to maintain their ancestral languages, their descendents soon contributed to the growing number of English monoglots in the United States. The shift was rapid, involving but a few generations in most cases, and it was final.

Using the data available in earlier censuses of the United States, this study provides some demographic clues to the causes of this remarkable change. A complete understanding is perhaps no longer possible, but every effort should be made to determine the forces operating during the heyday of language contact in the United States. Not only does this provide us with an opportunity to understand one of the most distinctive features of American history, but it also offers valuable material for comparison with language contact in other nations.

To be sure, there are some obvious macro-societal forces operating to encourage the acquisition of English as at least a second language. Knowledge of this tongue was advantageous for economic,

spatial, and social mobility. Moreover, widespread universal education ensured that many youngsters would learn English at a very early
age. Thanks to the work of Fishman and his associates, a number of
other societal factors can be added to this list.[3] But we still need to
learn more about the nature and speed of this shift as well as the specific mechanisms whereby these macro-societal characteristics influence language behavior.

Rather than let the analysis bog down with a series of technical qualifications and cautions, certain limitations to the census data
on language should be noted at the outset. There are basically two
types of language questions that have been asked in U.S. censuses:
first, questions dealing with the language first learned in childhood,
the "mother tongue"; second, questions on the ability of the respondent to speak English, regardless of whether it is his mother tongue
or a language acquired later. Definitions and enumeration procedures
differ greatly between decades and may affect comparability of the
data over time. Moreover, not only are the data limited to certain
years, groups, and spatial units, but the census figures provide relatively few cross-tabulations. In several instances, this study uses
data originally gathered by the Dillingham Commission for the first
decade of this century. Under any circumstance, it should be clear
to the reader that shifts in the decades analyzed or variations in the
way a given variable is operationalized are simply due to the difficulties in working with these scanty, but invaluable, data.

Demographic Issues

There are two crucial demographic events necessary for
mother-tongue shift. First, non-English-speaking immigrants or
their descendents must learn English as a second language. Second,
bilingual parents must pass on English as the mother tongue of the
next generation. If only the first step occurs, but the bilingual parents
maintain their mother tongue in socializing the offspring, then a stable
multilingual situation will exist in which bilingualism does not generate mother-tongue shift.[4] With the data available in the censuses, it
is possible to offer some clues to both the factors influencing the
acquisition of English by non-English-speaking immigrants as well as
the forces affecting mother-tongue shift by bilingual parents.

Table 1. Regression Analysis of Mother-Tongue
Shift and Bilingualism

Row	Variables[a]		r_{yx}	b_{yx}	a_{yx}
	Y	X			
A	1	2	.47	.8	-3.5
B	3	4	-.26	-.5	108.2
C	1	5	-.39	.3	34.5
D	6	7	.64	85.3	12.8
E	8	9	-.49	-.1	56.2
F	10	11	.47	.5	8.9
G	12	13	.73	.9	2.7
H	14	15	.19	.2	15.4
I	14	16	.57	.5	6.2
J	17	18	.89	.6	6.3
K	19	20	-.35	-100.9	123.3
L	21	22	.88	2.9	39.7
M	23	22	.82	1.3	40.1

Note: The key presented below gives the exact nature of the variables.
The symbols Y and X indicate the dependent and independent variables,
respectively. The degree and direction of association between the
variables is described by the coefficient of correlation, r_{yx}. The coefficient of regression, b_{yx}, gives the average change in the dependent
variable that occurs with a change in the independent variable. Accord
ing to the value for b_{yx} in row A, for example, a difference between
cities of 1.0 percent in the foreign-born is associated with a difference
of 0.8 percent in those unable to speak English. The final characteristic, a_{yx}, is a constant used in the regression equation, $Y = a_{yx} + b_{yx}X$.

[a] Key to variables:

1. Percent of foreign-born whites unable to speak English, by
cities of 100,000+ population, 1910. Immigrants from English-speaking countries excluded from analysis.

2. Percent of foreign-born in each city who arrived between
1901 and 1910.

3. Percent of native males in each industry who are able to
speak English, 1908-9.

4. Percent of foreign-born males in each industry who are
able to speak English, 1908-9.

Table 1 notes (continued)

5. Percent of total population in cities of 100,000+ who are native whites of native parentage, 1910.

6. Same as variable 1, except restricted to cities where immigrants are at least 29 percent of the population.

7. Index of mother-tongue diversity, by city, 1910 (scaled so 1.1 is minimum diversity).

8. Percent unable to speak English among operatives employed in specific manufacturing industries, 1910.

9. Annual income of male operatives in manufacturing industries.

10. Percent of foreign-born males unable to speak English, by occupation, 1910. Immigrants from English-speaking countries excluded from the analysis.

11. Percent of native whites unemployed, by occupation, 1910.

12. Percent of non-apprenticed foreign-born workers unable to speak English, by occupation, 1890.

13. Percent of apprenticed foreign-born workers unable to speak English, by occupation, 1890.

14. Same as variable 10, except for 1890 and for white immigrants only.

15. Negroes as a percentage of all males in each occupation, 1890.

16. Foreign-born whites as a percentage of all males in each occupation, 1890.

17. Percent "retarded" among pupils born in the United States, with foreign-born fathers who do not speak English, 1908-9.

18. Same as variable 17, except for the children of foreign-born fathers who can speak English.

19. Ratio of "actual" to "expected" number of second-generation residents with English mother tongue, cities of 500,000+, 1940. Expected figures computed on the basis of ethnic composition.

20. Mother-tongue diversity of foreign-born, with non-English mother tongue (scaled so that minimum diversity is 1.0 and maximum is 0).

21. Mother-tongue shift from first to second generation, by ethnic group, 1940.

22. Percent of foreign-born members of the ethnic group unable to speak English, 1930.

23. Estimated percent of bilingual foreign-born who raise their children in English, by ethnic group, 1940.

Although the language outcome in the United States is known,
an examination of the magnitude of these shifts is still instructive.
In 1910, 31 percent of the foreign-born white were unable to speak
English.[5] This was a substantial increase from the 19 percent reported
in 1900, but not much higher than the 27 percent in 1890. Why the
drop-off between 1890 and 1900? Very likely it was due to the slower
increment in the foreign-born during that decade than in both the
decade immediately before and immediately after.[6] An analysis of
intercity variation suggests that immigrants had a strong propensity
to learn English after they stayed in the United States for a few years.
As a consequence, a fairly high percentage of immigrants unable to
speak English could be maintained only with sizable numbers of newcomers (Table 1, row A). With the decline in new immigrants because
of World War I and later restrictions, relatively few of the immigrants
were recent arrivals. As one might expect, the percentage of the
foreign-born in the United States unable to speak English consequently
fell sharply, reaching 15 in 1920 and then 8.5 in 1930.

Not only was there a strong thrust toward the acquisition of
English among the immigrants, but virtually no holdouts are found
among the children of immigrants. Less than one percent of the
second-generation whites in the United States were unable to speak
English in either 1890 or 1900.[7] Granted that a larger percentage of
the second generation may have been descendents of immigrants from
English-speaking nations, the very low percentage obviously means
that the acquisition of English, at the very least as a second language,
was a real issue only for the immigrant generation.

The causes of bilingualism in the second generation were not
merely a duplication of those operating on the immigrants. There is
considerable variance between cities in the frequency of English-
language-learning among the foreign-born, but the percentage of the
second-generation whites unable to speak English shows very little
association with immigrant rates in the same cities (Table 2).

Likewise, there is not much of an association between the
percentages unable to speak English among the two generations when
classified by their industries (Table 1, row B). Although the industrie
vary rather widely in the percentage of immigrant employees unable
to speak English, there is relatively little difference between second-
generation employees in these industries.

Table 2. Proportion Unable to Speak English in Cities,
Second Generation Cross-Tabulated by Foreign-Born, 1900

Cities classified by proportion of foreign-born unable to speak English	Mean proportion unable to speak English	
	Among foreign-born	Among second generation
.10+	.1957	.0065
.05 to .09	.0682	.0005
.04 or less	.0267	.0003

Note: Data based on 20 percent sample of cities with 25,000 or more
population. "Foreign-born" refers to foreign-born whites; "second
generation" refers to native whites of foreign parentage.

Causes of Bilingualism

Intercity Variations

Several features of city composition operate to influence the
variation between cities in the proportion of immigrants unable to
speak English. First, there is an inverse association with the percentage of the city population who are native whites of native parentage.
Cities where third- or later-generation whites are numerically important are also cities where few immigrants fail to acquire English
(Table 1, row C). Moreover, there is some evidence to suggest that
the absolute number of immigrants from a given group influences
their propensity to acquire English. Examination of intercity variation in the number of Italians unable to speak English suggests a non-
linear relationship such that cities with larger numbers of Italians
tend to have greater percentages unable to speak English.

The magnitude of mother-tongue diversity within the immigrant segment of a city's population is another compositional feature
that influences the acquisition of English. Diversity is measured with
Greenberg's A index, giving us a quantitative indicator of the relative
homogeneity or heterogeneity of the immigrants in the city.[8] A strong

association is found between the degree of diversity and immigrant bilingualism. Cities whose immigrant mother-tongue composition is relatively homogeneous are also cities in which the acquisition of English is relatively low (Table 1, row D). Although not shown in Table 1, this relationship holds even after the native white of native-parentage compositional factors is taken into account. Relatively homogeneous immigrant populations are less likely to acquire English since the possibility of communication through their old-world mother tongue is much greater than in a city where the immigrant groups are from diverse sources and hence do not share a common-language alternative to English.

This last finding suggests an important way in which language contact in the United States differs from many other nations. Although the nation received relatively heavy influxes of non-English-speaking immigrants, the groups came from diverse parts of the world and did not possess a single common mother tongue. Consequently, as the correlation with diversity indicates, resistance to the acquisition of English was reduced. Aside from the obvious economic and social pressures that generated an acquisition of English, one should not overlook its function as a lingua franca. In a city that is linguistically diverse because of the migration of groups with a variety of mother tongues, there is the added need to acquire some language to overcome this diversity. The strength of English as a second language among the immigrants is thus derived not only from the institutional pressures supporting English within the host society, but also the pressures to develop some medium of communication between immigrant groups with different mother tongues.

Occupations

Immigrants in various jobs differ considerably in the proportion unable to speak English. In most of the professional occupations, where education is obviously a prerequisite, virtually all of the foreign-born are able to speak English. By contrast, very sizable proportions of the immigrants in other occupations are unable to speak English. Table 3 provides some illustrative percentages for selected occupations in 1890.

Table 3. Foreign-Born White Males Unable to Speak English,
by Occupation, 1890

Occupation	Percent unable to speak English	Occupation	Percent unable to speak English
All	23	Clerks and copyists	6
		Salesmen	5
Agricultural laborers	28	Artificial flower makers	30
Miners (coal)	55	Brick and tile makers	46
Stock raisers, herders	52	Harness and saddle makers	10
Professional service	8	Iron and steel workers	33
Dentists	4	Printers, lithographers	8
Lawyers	2	Tailors	29
Bartenders	6	Tobacco and cigar factory	
Launderers	30	operatives	44
Auctioneers	4		

Note: Persons born in England, Ireland, Scotland, and Canada
(English) are excluded since it is assumed that virtually all could
speak English prior to migration.

Obviously, there are a wide variety of factors influencing
these variations. The educational prerequisites are crucial for some
occupations. In other cases, the magnitude of interaction with others
is virtually nil or else requires minimal linguistic skills. Undoubtedly,
some of the immigrants held occupations that required extensive communication, but could get along without English since their co-workers
or customers shared the same non-English tongue. But at the very
least, one can say that an ability to speak English offered the immigrant certain advantages since it meant a wider range of potential
occupational opportunities.

An important issue is whether those unable to speak English
were merely confined to certain work settings or whether they were
also handicapped in the quality of their employment. Because of the
linguistic demands in the more desirable jobs or the greater competition for them, were those unable to speak English confined to the

less desirable occupations? Using two different indicators of occupational desirability, unemployment among the native whites in each occupation, and income, the results indicate that the immigrants unable to speak English are handicapped. Those unable to speak English are more likely to be found in occupations with low incomes or relatively high unemployment rates (Table 1, rows E and F).

An unresolved issue is the extent these occupational differences are a function of factors other than selectivity along a language dimension. Do the occupational percentages reflect either different learning experiences after employment or differences between immigrant groups in the occupations that they select? There is some evidence to indicate that post-employment factors were not that influential. For some occupations, data are available on the language skills of apprentices as well as those who are presumably more experienced. Comparing apprentice with seasoned worker, there is little evidence of a sharp change in the proportion unable to speak English in these occupations (Table 1, row G). Subject to better data, this suggests that employment experience had only a moderate influence on bilingualism. Perhaps jobs requiring a knowledge of English were not opened to those unable to speak the language.

When compared with other disadvantaged strata, a puzzling difference exists in the structural basis of the discrimination against European immigrants unable to speak English. For example, the percentage unable to speak English among the foreign-born in each occupation does not correlate with the percentage of Negroes in each occupation, but does with the foreign-born (Table 1, rows H and I). The absence of an association with the first variable is to be understood partially in terms of the regional locational differences between the two subordinated groups. The nature of a sizable association for the second variable is even less adequately explained. Obviously, further research is called for on the relationship between linguistic stratification and other forms of ethnic stratification.

Overall, this occupational analysis suggests that important economic advantages existed for immigrants who could learn to speak English. The foreign-born in the better-paying occupations, as well as in those with lower levels of unemployment, tend to have very low percentages unable to speak English. Thus occupational pressures

undoubtedly increased the proportion of immigrants who learned
English. However, it is easy to overestimate the dominant role of
this factor in generating language shift. For one reason, there is no
association by occupation between linguistic ability in the first and
second generations (Table 1, row B). This means that the advantages
or disadvantages that knowledge of English offered were a superfluous
cause of English-language learning in the second generation. Occupational pressures, to be sure, influence the possibility of mother-
tongue shift between the generations. Nevertheless, there is some
basis for speculating that the occupational pressures were not necessary for the fairly complete acquisition of English among the second
generation. Very likely widespread universal education was a sufficient cause.

Other Factors

Census data cannot provide information about all of the
factors influencing the learning of English among those with some
other mother tongue. There are a few additional clues available,
however, from these data. Elsewhere, Lieberson has shown that
immigrant residential segregation influences the proportion learning
English.[9] Comparing a number of different immigrant groups within
each of ten different United States cities, those more highly segregated
also tend to have larger proportions unable to speak English. This
relationship appears to hold even after immigrant differences in their
length of residence in the United States are taken into account. Although the causal sequence is somewhat unclear, the results do indicate an inverse association between the magnitude of segregation and
the propensity to learn the host society's language. In terms of the
point made earlier about the role of English as a lingua franca among
immigrant groups with different native languages, it is significant to
note that the magnitude of segregation between immigrant groups is
related to the role of English as a linguistic bond between the groups.

Another factor that can only be touched on here is the relationship between the language skills of parents and the performance of
their children in school. Within each immigrant group, school performance is compared between the children of fathers who do not speak
English and those who do. Retardation is uniformly greater among

the first group of children (Table 1, row J). By "retardation" is meant children in a lower level class than would normally be expected for the child's age. Variations between immigrant groups in the percentage of their children who are retarded can be explained in good part by the different ethnic patterns in the use of English at home. Among those fathers able to speak English, there is considerable variation in the proportion who use it at home. In turn, the proportion of their children who are retarded is related to the propensity of their English-speaking immigrant fathers to use English at home.

What these results suggest is that the acquisition and use of English by the immigrant had an effect on the performance of their children in school. Such a relationship is hardly surprising. But it does mean an additional impetus for immigrants to learn and use English.

Mother-Tongue Shift

As noted at the outset, the causes of mother-tongue shift need not be the same as the causes of bilingualism. Or, to put it another way, the acquisition of English by the immigrants and their children does not necessarily mean that English must be passed on as the mother tongue of their offspring. In some settings, for example Montreal, bilingualism does not lead to mother-tongue shift.

There is evidence that the magnitude of mother-tongue shift from the first to the second generation is influenced by the degree of mother-tongue diversity within the foreign-born population. Table 1, row K, indicates the association between the magnitude of mother-tongue shift in the second generation (after standardization) and the A index of mother-tongue diversity among those immigrants whose mother tongue is not English. The proportion of the second generation with English mother tongue is relatively high in cities where the mother-tongue composition of the immigrants is rather diverse. By contrast, in cities with low mother-tongue diversity among the immigrants, English is the mother tongue of a relatively small segment of the second generation.

These results are extremely suggestive when contrasting the linguistic pattern in the United States with other nations. Additional evidence indicates that diversity within the immigrant population of the United States helped to generate mother-tongue shift. In nations whose language contact involves only two major groups, one might expect considerably greater resistance to shift. Certainly there are extremely diverse nations such as India that have not experienced much in the way of mother-tongue shift. But it should be kept in mind that the local contact settings in India are much more homogeneous than one might expect from just the national figures. This is due to the intense territorial segregation of language groups in India. Nevertheless, the reader must keep in mind that immigrant diversity is clearly not the only factor accounting for the distinctive quality of language contact in the United States.

The frequency of mother-tongue shift among the second generation tends also to be linked to bilingualism among the foreign-born (Table 1, row L). In other words, immigrant groups that are specially prone to learn English are also the groups with English as the mother tongue of sizable proportions of the second generation. An index of shift is used here which is obtained by comparing the percentages of the first and second generations with non-English mother tongue. The percentage for the second generation is divided by the percentage for the first generation. Thus an index value of 1.0 means no net difference between generations in the occurrence of English mother tongue. The index will tend toward zero as the relative shift to English becomes greater. It should be noted that these intergenerational comparisons do not take into account shift among the offspring of bilingual parents, but rather they reflect net cross-sectional differences between generations.

Although the data are not reported here, this type of association between the frequency of bilingualism among the foreign-born and mother-tongue shift in the second generation is also found when examining the rates for different groups within cities as well as for the nation as a whole. But all of this may appear painfully obvious at first glance, since there are both methodological and substantive reasons for expecting to find such a linkage between bilingualism and shift. If the proportion of children whose shift to English remains constant for the bilinguals of different immigrant groups, then those immigrant populations with specially high frequencies of bilingualism will also appear as the groups with high levels of intergenerational shift. One

might argue that the results are therefore an artifact of the methods
used. Moreover, on a substantive plane, one could claim that such
an association is expected if the causes of bilingualism among the
immigrants are identical to the factors influencing mother-tongue
shift between the generations.

Dealing with the methodological issue first, an examination
of the estimated proportion of bilinguals who shift mother tongues in
the second generation suggests that these results are not an artifact
of some inherent correlation due to the greater frequency of bilingualism among some groups. Rather, the groups with relatively high percentages of their immigrant members unable to speak English are
also the groups whose bilinguals are less likely to raise their children
in English (Table 1, row M). In effect, the likelihood of intergenerational shift is greater among those bilinguals in groups with the greatest frequency of second-language learning. When a sizable segment
of the immigrant generation is unable to speak English, then the bilingual parents in the group are less likely to raise their children in
English.

If a sizable segment of an immigrant group is unable to speak
English, it means a relatively greater communication loss with ethnic
compatriots if the child is raised in English. By contrast, a child
raised in the old-world language also learns English later on and is
therefore able to speak to all members of the ethnic community. On
the other hand, if the proportion of the first generation able to speak
English is rather high, then offspring raised as native speakers of
English can communicate with nearly all ethnic compatriots and there
is less reason to resist mother-tongue shift.

The relationship between shift and the percentage learning
English among the foreign-born is similar to that reported for the
various immigrant groups in Canada, but not for the French ethnic
group in that country.[10] In other words, it does not follow empirically
that the association reported above need automatically exist.

This analysis seems to suggest that mother-tongue shift is
caused not simply by the factors influencing bilingualism. Rather,
the frequency of bilingualism within the immigrant group is, itself,
an important influence on the likelihood of shift. Bilingual immigrant

in a group with a sizable percentage unable to speak English are themselves less likely to raise their children in English than are bilingual parents who belong to an immigrant group with a high level of bilingualism. Given the fact that the acquisition of English is almost universal among the children of immigrants, at least as a second language, it follows that the shift of mother tongues in the United States will take place rather rapidly from that generation on if other factors remain constant. The earlier analysis of communication advantages with ethnic compatriots also suggests that any decline in the numbers of new immigrants settling in the United States would tend to raise the rate of mother-tongue shift among the earlier settlers. In effect, newcomers unable to speak English provided an incentive for resisting mother-tongue shift among immigrant compatriots who were bilingual.

A Final Note

This study must be viewed as an effort to salvage some insights into the rather phenomenal language shift to English that took place in the United States. Unfortunately, the issues were settled long before the field of sociolinguistics began to develop. Accordingly, it is necessary to employ all available information in order to get some understanding of the American experience. There is no point in reiterating the results reported above. However, it is to be hoped they provide not only some clues to the American experience, but also some hints as to why other nations experience very different linguistic outcomes.

NOTES

This study was supported by National Science Foundation Grants No. GS-1869 and GS-394. We are pleased to acknowledge the assistance of Mrs. Lynn Hansen.
    [1] Based on data reported in U.S. Bureau of the Census, Historical Statistics of the United States (Washington, D.C.: U.S. Government Printing Office, 1960), pp. 56-59.

[2] See, for example, Einar Haugen, The Norwegian Language in America, vol. 1 (Philadelphia: University of Pennsylvania Press, 1953), chap. 10.

[3] Joshua Fishman et al., Language Loyalty in the United States (The Hague: Mouton, 1966).

[4] See, for example, Stanley Lieberson, "Bilingualism in Montreal: A Demographic Analysis," American Journal of Sociology 71 (July 1965): 10-25.

[5] Immigrants from English-speaking countries are excluded from this figure. Throughout this paper, the foreign-born will also be referred to as the "first generation." Persons born in the United States but with one or both of their parents foreign-born will also be referred to as the "second generation."

[6] See Niles Carpenter, Immigrants and Their Children, 1920 (Washington, D.C.: U.S. Government Printing Office, 1927), Table 2, p. 6.

[7] Variations by age or by sex within the second-generation population are minor.

[8] Joseph H. Greenberg, "The Measurement of Linguistic Diversity," Language 31 (Jan. -March 1956): 109-15.

[9] Stanley Lieberson, Ethnic Patterns in American Cities (New York: The Free Press of Glencoe, 1963), pp. 133-39.

[10] Stanley Lieberson, Language and Ethnic Relations in Canada (New York: Wiley, 1970). This volume along with the paper referred to in note 4 provide more elaborate statements on the demographic steps necessary for mother-tongue shift.

10 | Occupational Demands

The linguistic demands of the work-world are among the most important forces influencing the acquisition of a second language. Since virtually all able-bodied men and an increasing number of women seek jobs, the advantage one language enjoys over another in this sphere can have a profound impact on the degree of bilingualism in each mother-tongue group. Not only may language play a role in obtaining employment, but certain linguistic skills may be a vital prerequisite for advancement and higher income. Unfortunately the interaction between the linguistic demands of employers and co-workers, the kind of service or product involved, the location of the place of business, and the linguistic preferences of customers or clients involve far too many subtleties to permit a broad-gauged intercity comparison of Canadian communities. Instead, Montreal is used as a case study of the interplay between occupational demands and bilingualism.

The influence of occupational demands on bilingualism are complex. First, the importance of communication in any language will vary greatly between jobs. A laborer could get along far more easily than could a sales clerk without speaking to his co-workers or by learning a very minimal number of words. Even jobs demanding a certain level of communication can be subdivided on the basis of whether they are oriented toward co-workers or toward such outsiders as customers, clients, or the general public. A sales clerk will have a far greater need for communication with her customers than with her co-workers. A secretary, by contrast, will be fairly useless unless she can communicate with her co-workers. Occupations can also be subdivided in terms of the linguistic composition of co-workers and customers. A grocery located in the midst of a solidly French neighborhood will have very minimal demands for English-speaking clerks, whereas groceries located in an English-speaking suburb will have little need for a French-speaking employee. Occupations may themselves differ if there are any services or activities oriented particularly to one language world as opposed to the other (see Hughes 1943: 65–67, 82–83).

Occupations can be viewed as differing in the frequency of "inside" and "outside" interaction, that is, of interaction with fellow employees versus nonemployees. Occupations that involve frequent interaction with the "outside" will create a need for bilingualism when the outsiders are linguistically diverse. "Outsider" interaction will lead to bilingualism for only one of the mother-tongue segments if the outsiders tend to favor one of the languages. Likewise, among jobs that are "insider" oriented, concentration of linguistic compatriots will minimize the need for bilingualism. Ideally, occupations could be classified according to the following four criteria: (1) linguistic composition of co-workers; (2) importance of communication with co-workers; (3) linguistic composition of customers and relevant outsiders; and (4) importance of communication with customers and outsiders.

Labor Force Participation and Bilingualism

Participation in Montreal's labor force is hardly the only factor contributing to bilingualism in a city where a second language is taught in the schools, where both groups are numerically important, and both tongues are viable forces in the community. On the other hand, there is little doubt that occupational demands play an important role in generating bilingualism in Montreal. The ability to speak a second language is more common among those working than not. About 45 percent of English-mother-tongue men in the work force are bilingual, compared with 35 percent of those who are at home. Among French males, the respective percentages bilingual are 73 and 56. (In this chapter, unless otherwise noted, the data refer to the metropolitan population 15 years of age and older in 1961.) Women in the labor force are likewise more bilingual than those who are not. These data may understate the degree of bilingualism due to occupational pressures since second-language learning among school children more than 15 years of age may reflect the linguistic needs anticipated for employment.

The pressures leading to greater bilingualism among the employed are based on an interaction of other factors with occupational needs. Although work does appear to increase the need for a second language, it still affects the French more than the English. Thus, although 45 percent of the men in the labor force with an English mother tongue are bilingual, nearly 75 percent of those with a French mother tongue are bilingual. Likewise only a third of working English-mother-tongue women can speak French, whereas 60 percent of employed French women know English. Those with French mother tongue who are not in the labor force are still more bilingual than workers of the same sex with English mother tongue. The pressures favoring English are also illustrated by the languages acquired among those whose mother tongue was neither official language. The ratio between the number learning English only to the number acquiring only French is about 4 to 1.

The linkage between education and bilingualism shows that different patterns exist for Montreal's two basic groups. There is virtually no association between educational achievement and bilingualism among those of British origin, whereas bilingualism rises sharply with education in the French segment of the labor force (see Table 1). The discrepancies are striking indeed—French-Canadian men without any schooling are as likely to be bilingual as men of British origin who

Table 1. Percent of Males in the Labor Force Who Are Bilingual,
by Education

	Years of School Completed				
Ethnic Group	None	Elementary, 1+ Years	High School, 1–2 Years	High School, 3–5 Years	University, 1+ Years
British	41	44	39	38	42
French	43	58	79	89	94
Other	19	35	53	52	61

Table 2. Percent of Males Bilingual by Occupation, Employment
Status, and Ethnic Origin

Occupation	Wage or Salary Earner		Self-Employed	
	British	French	British	Frenc
Managerial	40	94	51	82
Professional and technical	33	90	60	96
Clerical	38	85	78	85
Sales	50	86	49	83
Service and recreation	35	72	56	73
Transport and communication	44	72	76	75
Farmers and stockraisers	°	°	100	46
Other primary	42	51	°	51
Craftsmen	41	64	47	71
Laborers	43	49	50	57
Total	40	72	54	81

°No males.

have attended a university. Nearly all French-Canadian men who ha
attended a university are bilingual, whereas less than half of the Bri
ish men with similar education know French. Other ethnic groups
also have a positive correlation between educational attainment and
bilingualism, although their levels of bilingualism are not so high as
among the French. Achievement of higher socioeconomic status am
the French appears to require a knowledge of English, whereas statu
and ability to speak French are unrelated for the British.

The kind of occupation held influences the degree of bilingu:
ism, but not in the same way for British and French. Unfortunately
the available data do not permit examination of specific jobs, rather
only of about 10 occupational categories, most of which can be subdivided into "wage earners" and "self-employed." The heterogeneity

of the occupational categories used cannot be stressed too greatly.
Included among the professionals, for example, are physicians, den-
tists, and lawyers—people who must orient themselves to their clientele. On the other hand, the category encompasses various engineers,
many being basically oriented toward fellow workers with little contact with the public. In addition, technicians are grouped with professionals. Differences between ethnic groups in their concentration
within the detailed occupations of a broad category can affect their
degree of bilingualism. The relevant data available from unpublished
tabulations are shown in Table 2, which gives the percentage of each
ethnic group who are bilingual tabulated by their occupation.

Regardless of occupation, the frequency of bilingualism does
not differ very much among wage earners in the British ethnic group.
The highest percentage is in sales (50) and the lowest is among professionals (33). By contrast the French range from 49 percent bilingual among laborers to 94 percent among those who are managers.
In 10 of the 11 occupational categories bilingualism is higher among
British self-employed males than among wage earners. Assuming
that employers generally have more outside contact than employees,
this offers further evidence that outside contacts provide pressure
for bilingualism. Nevertheless, the French are still more bilingual
than the British in all occupational categories, with one slight exception (self-employed in transportation and communication).

Should there be a correlation between the degree French
workers in an occupation are bilingual and the frequency of bilingualism among British men in the same occupations? There are occupations where pressure for bilingualism among one group is accompanied
by an absence of a similar pressure in the other group; for example,
it would be difficult for a French monoglot to pursue an occupation
oriented heavily toward American tourists, but the same position will
permit an English Canadian to remain ignorant of French. On the
other hand, there are jobs which put pressure on both English- and
French-mother-tongue workers to become bilingual, for example,
telephone operators or policemen. The net effect of this diversity is
a weak connection between the degree of bilingualism among the
French and British in 18 occupations $(r = -.22)$.

Because of the heterogeneity within the occupational categories, only an impressionistic interpretation can be offered here for

the variations in bilingualism between ethnic groups. Men employed
as laborers in the two groups are relatively similar in their degree
of bilingualism. This is an occupation which requires minimal interaction with either customers or co-workers. The net effect is to reduce the degree of bilingualism among the French in this occupation
to a level far below that for the labor force as a whole (49 versus 73
percent). With the British amounting to only 7 percent of laborers
in Montreal, compared with 18 percent of the total male work force,
the pressures for bilingualism among the British are perhaps slightly
greater than in occupations where English plays a more dominant
role. Thus 43 percent of the British employed as laborers are bilingual, some 3 percent more than all British men in the labor force.

The pattern for laborers is repeated by other "blue-collar"
workers such as wage-earning craftsmen and those engaged in non-
farm primary occupations. Again, there is a relatively low degree
of bilingualism among the French ethnic group and a smaller British-
French gap in bilingualism. What is noteworthy here is not the
slightly higher frequency of bilingualism among the British in these
occupations compared with those employed in other activities, but
that these occupations are marked by considerably less bilingualism
among the French compared to their overall rate.

Sales employees among both the British and French groups
are more apt to be bilingual than other wage earners. This no doubt
reflects the need to communicate with a wide variety of customers
and the advantages derived from speaking the customer's native tongue
However, the gap between the two groups in their degree of bilingualism is, if anything, slightly greater than for all wage earners. French
Canadian men employed as managers, professionals and technicians,
and clerks—all largely white-collar "office" jobs—are characterized
by an extremely high frequency of bilingualism. All but 4 percent of
self-employed professionals and 6 percent of those hired as managers
are bilingual. Employment in these occupations as a wage earner
does not yield a high degree of bilingualism among the British. Indeed
clerks and professionals are below the average for all British wage
earners. Bilingualism does rise considerably among the British who
are self-employed in these categories, probably reflecting a greater
orientation toward clients and outside markets.

The bilingual pattern among women in Montreal is fairly similar, recognizing that the actual jobs covered by these broad occupational divisions are not the same for both men and women. French women are more apt to be bilingual than British women in nearly all occupations. The pressure for bilingualism is particularly great among French women in white-collar office positions such as clerical (80 percent) and managerial wage earners (86 percent). Occupations listed under "transportation and communication" are strikingly high in the degree of bilingualism among both British and French wage earners, 57 and 90 percent, respectively. However, women in this category are largely employed as telephone operators —an occupation with a need for bilingualism among both English- and French-speaking employees.

As is the case for men, there is no particularly strong association between the frequency of bilingualism among women in the two ethnic groups. The correlation between bilingualism among British and French women by occupation is rather low, $r = .14$. When compared with their ethnic group average, in some occupations the proportion bilingual is especially low or especially high for both groups. In other occupations, relatively high rates of bilingualism are accompanied by relatively low percentages for women in the other ethnic group.

Employment Pressures

Classified advertisements in Montreal's French- and English-language newspapers provide a useful instrument for determining the existence of bilingual pressures at the time of employment. One of the great advantages of "want ads" is that they provide a clear-cut causal sequence since the prerequisites of the job are stated in advance of employment. The cross-sectional associations reported above between occupation and bilingualism may reflect the fact that acquisition of a second language is either a prerequisite, or at least an advantage, in obtaining employment in certain occupations. On the other hand, the associations may reflect the fact that persons in certain occupations are more likely to retain their bilingualism or learn a second tongue after employment. Undoubtedly all of these factors operate, but the goal here is to determine the influence of

occupational demands on bilingualism. Accordingly, the April 11
and May 2, 1964, weekend issues of the Montreal Star and La Presse
were studied.

Several assumptions are necessary. First, jobs not indicating any language requirements are assumed to be suitable for appli-
cants who can speak only the language in which the newspaper is published. This seems most reasonable, since there were no advertisements which indicated that the necessary language was the one in which
the newspaper was published. A second assumption is somewhat
stickier; namely, if the English paper carried an advertisement with
a requirement such as "must speak French" or "knowledge of French
is required, " it was assumed that the applicant had to be bilingual.
In point of fact, it is possible that the employer required someone
who spoke only French and for other reasons chose to advertise in
the English paper. It seems unlikely, however, that such advertisements would be common. Analogous assumptions were made about
want ads in the French paper. Therefore any mention of the language
other than the one in which the paper was published was taken to indicate a job in which the respondent had to know both English and French
In many instances the advertisement was less ambiguous and simply
stated that bilingualism was necessary.

There is a severe occupational bias in using newspaper classified advertisements, since there are many types of job which are
not advertised at all or infrequently at best. Use of want ads rules
out the self-employed, many professionals, jobs obtained through
employment agencies, personal contact, and the like. Jobs that have
high turnover are more likely to be represented than those with low
turnover.

Using the job description in the advertisement, each position
is placed in a standard occupational classification based on the Occupational Classification Manual, Census of Canada, 1961. Several
French manuals were also used to maximize the comparability in the
classification of want ads written in different languages. Of particular value were Classification condensée des occupations: pour les
chiffreurs de la section A, recensement du Canada, 1961 and a "Bilingual Summary Index of Occupational Divisions, Groups and Classes,
1961 Census" provided through the courtesy of the Dominion Bureau

of Statistics. Nevertheless, many occupations are not described in the advertisements with sufficient detail to make a good classification. Use was made of residual categories in each broad occupational division when a more detailed effort appeared unjustified. Want ads were not weighted by the number of positions indicated in the advertisement. Rather, each specific occupation appearing in a given ad was given a weight of one. A total of 1,509 ads were gathered from the Star and 1,433 from La Presse for the two weekends examined.

The frequency of bilingual requirements differs by language. In the English-language paper, 19 percent of the male ads and 17 percent of those for females indicate that knowledge of French is necessary. By contrast, 25 percent of male and 23 percent of female ads in La Presse require a knowledge of English. Thus the pressure for bilingualism at the time of employment is greater for French-speaking Montrealers.

Differences in the linguistic pressures operating on English- and French-speaking Montrealers are actually greater than the figures above suggest. Some of these differences are hidden by the kinds of occupations advertised in the two papers. Using for the most part a three-digit classification of occupations, the index of dissimilarity between advertisements for men in the Star and Presse is 30 and a similar index is recorded for women's want ads. If the types of occupations advertised in the two papers were identical in frequency, an index of 0 would be obtained; if complete dissimilarity existed in the kinds of jobs advertised in the two papers, then the index would be 100. Indexes of 30 mean that there is a fairly sizable difference between the newspapers in the occupations listed.

These differences in the occupations advertised in the two papers tend to conceal a stronger pressure for bilingualism in the French newspaper for specific jobs. Using Westergaard's standardization procedure, the expected percent of ads that would be bilingual in the Star is 29 if the bilingual rates for the same occupation in La Presse were to apply (Table 3). By contrast, if the bilingual rates for each occupation in the Star were to occur for jobs listed in La Presse, then only 20 percent of the want ads for men in the French paper would require bilinguals. In other words, although only 19 percent of the jobs listed for men in the English paper actually require

Table 3. Newspaper Advertisements Requiring Bilingualism, 1964

| Newspaper | Percent Bilingual | | | |
| | Male | | Female | |
	Actual	Expected[a]	Actual	Expected[a]
Montreal Star	19	29	17	38
La Presse	25	20	24[b]	12

[a]Based on occupation specific rates in other newspaper for the same sex.
[b]Differs slightly from earlier figure reported because of adjustment due to absence of rates in the *Star* for some occupations.

bilinguals, the percentage would be considerably higher, 29, if the bilingual rates for the same jobs in La Presse operated in the Star. Were jobs advertised for men in La Presse to require bilingualism no more often than the same jobs listed in the English paper, then the frequency of bilingual demands for the French would be 20 instead of 25 percent.

Differences between the two papers in the kinds of occupation advertised also understate the greater pressure for bilingualism among French-speaking women. If the bilingual rates for jobs in La Presse also occurred in the Star, then twice as many of the want ads for women in the English-language paper would require a knowledge of French as actually do (38 versus 17 percent). On the other hand, if women's want ads in La Presse had the same frequency of bilingual requirements as the same jobs advertised in the Star, then only 12 percent of the French newspaper's want ads would require bilinguals instead of 24 percent.

In summary, there is greater pressure for bilingualism in the French newspaper's job advertisements than in the English paper. Advertisements for the same occupations in the Star are less likely to ask for bilinguals than in La Presse. Although the occupations for men listed in the two papers are somewhat different, the net effect is that advertisements in La Presse require more bilingualism. La Presse lists types of jobs for women which require less bilingualism

Table 4. Weighted Mean Annual Income of Occupations Advertised,
by Newspaper, Sex, and Language Requirements, 1964

Sex	Monolingual		Bilingual		All Advertisements		
	Montreal Star	*La Presse*	*Montreal Star*	*La Presse*	*Montreal Star*	*La Presse*	Both Newspapers
Males	$3906	$3599	$4284	$4067	$3977	$3716	$3849
Females	1939	1565	2368	2281	2010	1731	1875

than those found in the Star, but this is more than compensated for by
the need for bilingualism being greater for French-speaking women.
The net effect places greater second-language learning pressure on
French-speaking women seeking employment.

One way to consider the differences in the types of jobs
offered in the two papers is to examine the income associated with
them in the 1961 Census for metropolitan Montreal. For both sexes,
the occupations advertised in the English paper tend to be better-
paying than those in La Presse, and likewise positions requiring bilinguals tend to have higher earnings than those for whom monoglots
would be suitable. Advertisements in the Montreal Star are for jobs
which pay several hundred dollars more on the average than those in
La Presse (Table 4). The differences between newspapers are somewhat greater for monolingual positions than those which require bilinguals. It is worth noting that bilingual jobs in both papers tend to be
better-paying than those which do not require a second tongue (about
10 percent better for men; 20 percent for women in the Star; and nearly
50 percent better for women in La Presse).

English speakers enjoy an advantage over the French in the
kinds of jobs offered, even when the jobs are bilingual; for example,
bilingual ads for men in the Star pay $4,284, compared with $4,067
for advertisements in La Presse for bilingual men. Despite this advantage, there are obvious rewards for bilingualism among English
speakers just as there are for bilingual French Canadians. However,
the pressure is not as great since fewer advertisements require bilin-

gualism in the Star. Moreover, better jobs tend to be advertised in
the Star than in the Presse. The reader should note carefully that the
incomes associated with the jobs in the 1961 Census are used here as
a measure of the desirability of the kinds of occupations offered in the
two papers and between those which require bilinguals as contrasted
with monoglots. Later in this chapter the actual income differences
for employed Montrealers classified by language, occupation, education, and sex are considered. The use of income data here, however,
enables us to consider the actual differences between jobs offered in
the two newspapers.

Broad Occupational Differences

The linguistic pressures vary greatly, both between occupational categories and across mother-tongue lines. Relatively few men
who are laborers, craftsmen, or in transportation, communication,
and service occupations have to be bilingual (Table 5). By contrast
the pressure for bilingualism among those in the "white-collar" world
is much greater. Around 40 percent of the ads for managers require
men who can speak both tongues (slightly more in La Presse and
slightly less in the Montreal Star). It is noteworthy that the pressure
for bilingualism is greater in the French newspaper for nearly all the
broad occupational categories, although some percentages are based
on very small numbers. With the exception of sales occupations,
where the difference is nil, and of those in occupations we could not
classify, the requirements for employment are more likely to specify
knowledge of English as a second tongue than vice versa. Particularly
striking are the occupations associated with office work; 60 percent of
the French-language ads for clerks require a knowledge of English,
whereas only half as many of the ads in the Star require a knowledge
of French. Along with professional and technical occupations, these
are the most lopsided with respect to demands for more bilingualism
from French- than English-speaking men seeking employment.

Among women the pressure for bilingualism is always greate
in the French ads than in the English newspaper. As before, there is
great variation between jobs in the degree bilingualism is required;
for example, less than 10 percent of the service jobs require knowled;
of both tongues, whereas around a third of female sales positions re-
quite bilinguals. The sharpest discrepancies between the two news-

Table 5. Number of Newspaper Advertisements and Percent Bilingual,
by Broad Occupational Categories, 1964

Occupational Division	Percent Bilingual				Number of Advertisements			
	Male		Female		Male		Female	
	Montreal Star	La Presse	Montreal Star	La Presse	Montreal Star	La Presse	Montreal Star	La Presse
Managerial	37	43	10	100	41	49	10	1
Professional and technical	11	30	13	33	150	56	56	21
Clerical	29	62	30	75	107	42	269	137
Sales	37	37	29	35	149	218	55	51
Service and recreation	10	16	4	8	118	96	238	284
Transport and communcation	13	14	22	33	46	70	9	3
Farmers and stockraisers	0	0	*	*	6	1	*	*
Other primary	*	*	*	*	*	*	*	*
Craftsmen	7	10	0	0	166	211	53	144
Laborers	0	10	0	0	11	21	6	15
Unclassified	40	11	0	25	10	9	9	4
Total	19	25	17	23	804	773	705	660

*No advertisements.

papers are for clerical workers and for professional and technical positions. Fully three-fourths of women's clerical ads in La Presse require bilingualism, whereas only 30 percent of the same jobs in the Montreal Star specify a knowledge of French.

Different kinds of occupations tend to be advertised in the two newspapers. The number of ads appearing in the Star is slightly greater than in the French paper, but differences by occupational divisions are striking; for example, the number of advertisements for professional and technical positions in La Presse is little more than a third of the number of similar ads in the Montreal Star (Table 5). There are more than twice as many listings for male clerical positions in the latter paper. On the other hand, opportunities for male sales and service workers, craftsmen, and laborers are more frequently found in La Presse. The slightly larger number of managerial advertisements in the columns of La Presse is somewhat surprising and deviates from the general pattern that emerges of favoring English in the white-collar pursuits.

Likewise women's want ads for white-collar positions tend to be placed in the Star. Clerical positions advertised in La Presse amount to little more than half the number found in the English newspaper (269 versus 137). More than two-thirds of the want ads for women in professional and technical pursuits are found in the English paper. By contrast, advertisements for female service workers and the crafts are found more often in La Presse.

Detailed Occupational Differences

Those specific occupations for which a relatively large number of ads were run provide an opportunity to get a better notion of the linguistic pressures operating as well as the tendencies to favor one newspaper over another. There were 35 requests for engineers in the Montreal Star compared with 8 in La Presse (Table 6). The percentage requesting bilinguals, although based on small numbers, is likewise unfavorable to the French. Bookkeepers and cashiers, and shipping and receiving clerks are other male pursuits that are disproportionately concentrated in the English newspaper. Moreover, the advertisements in La Presse are more likely to require bilingualism than those in the Montreal Star. Secretarial and clerical function

Table 6. Percent Bilingual and Number of Advertisements,
by Detailed Occupational Categories, 1964

Occupation and Sex	Montreal Star		La Presse	
	Percent	Number	Percent	Number
Male				
Management	37	41	43	49
Engineer	11	35	38	8
Teacher	16	25	45	11
Draftsman	11	28	0	6
Bookkeeper, cashier	33	24	71	7
Shipping and receiving clerk	10	31	40	5
Other clerical	61	23	69	13
Commercial traveler	50	52	43	49
Sales clerk	48	21	55	44
Nonspecific sales	28	43	28	81
Cook	4	27	0	30
Janitor	19	37	36	14
Driver-salesman	36	14	25	24
Taxi driver	0	22	9	23
Tailor, furrier, etc.	0	26	6	33
Metalworking	3	31	4	23
Mechanic, repairman	10	29	2	55
Laborer	0	11	10	21
Female				
Office equipment operator	9	23	27	11
Stenographer	37	62	94	31
Teacher	15	39	33	9
Clerk typist	39	66	85	34
Bookkeeper, cashier	14	44	46	13
Waitress	23	31	17	60
Other clerical	41	49	82	17
Maid	1	148	8	156
Sales clerk	36	33	57	28
Hairdresser, barber	0	21	0	2
Launderer, dry-cleaner	11	9	4	24
Spinner, weaver	0	7	0	22
Nonspecific clerical	20	15	71	28
Tailor, furrier, etc.	0	35	0	89

ªOccupations included are those containing 20 or more listings in at least one of the newspapers for a given sex. "Nonspecific" sales and clerks are residual categories for occupations which could not be classified in further detail. "Other clerical" refers to Occupational Code No. 249.

for women strongly favor English. The Star has twice the number of
ads for stenographers, clerk typists, and "other" clerical workers.
Again, ads for these occupations in La Presse are accompanied by a
much more frequent use of bilingualism as a precondition for employment. Consider that 94 percent of the listings for stenographers in
La Presse require a knowledge of English whereas only 37 percent
of ads for this position in the Montreal Star have a bilingual prerequisite. Inspection of Table 6 discloses sizable differences for other
women's office work.

Commercial travelers are fairly evenly distributed between
the papers and balanced in the proportion of ads requiring bilinguals.
This occupation tends to involve "outside" interaction with customers
from both linguistic segments. The patterns for sales clerks are not
too clear for men and women. The pressure for bilingualism, however, appears somewhat greater in La Presse.

Among occupations connected with restaurants, cooks occupy
an "inside" position, dealing almost entirely with fellow workers and
having no interaction with the public. It is easy to see why there is
little pressure for bilingualism in such listings. On the other hand,
waiters are in a very different situation, with those working in the
downtown restaurants, popular places, and the like almost certain
to encounter customers from both linguistic segments. On the other
hand, there are many restaurants in or near residential areas that
draw their clientele primarily from a locality that often contains a
predominance of one language group. Nevertheless, the results for
waitresses in Table 6 are surprising and cannot be readily explained.
Although it is possible that some occupations are so obviously bilingua
that no mention of this fact is necessary in the want ads, it is unlikely
since the author has encountered waiters and waitresses during visits
to Montreal who were obviously monolingual. It may be that there
are some who can simply record the order in either tongue, but who
are required to do little more in their second language.

The frequency of bilingual requirements for maids and hair-
dressers requires little explanation. The interaction of maids is
restricted to their employers and hence they need know only the language used in the house. Interaction for those employed in the crafts
occupations specified in Table 6 is for the most part limited to those

working in the place of employment and, moreover, these positions
would often require little conversation anyway.

Bilingualism is called for in a fair number of driver-sales-
man listings in both newspapers, with the pressure being greater on
the English. In many instances drivers-salesmen have routes including
customers speaking both languages. The infrequent mention of bilingualism in ads for taxi drivers is rather surprising, but the advantage
for bilingualism may largely be reflected in the tips obtained, rather
than affecting the driver's ability to take the rider to whatever destination is requested. The latter would require a very minimal knowledge
of numbers in the two languages and an ability to know the other tongue's
pronunciation of streets and names of popular public places. Since the
employer does not normally share in the tips, the hiring of monolingual
taxi drivers would not be a terribly significant condition from his perspective. Laborers fit nicely, with twice as many listings in La
Presse coupled with an infrequent use of bilingualism as a condition
for employment. Some of the other positions are not easily explained;
in particular, teachers and draftsmen are somewhat surprising.

Granted that the detailed occupations shown in Table 6 have
been discussed in an unsystematic ad hoc fashion, they fit into a general pattern, namely a strong bias in the white-collar positions favoring English—both in the linguistic demands and the newspaper used for
advertising positions. Blue-collar positions which do not entail frequent "outside" contacts usually are more likely to be listed in La
Presse and require bilingualism less often. Advertisements for positions dealing with the public in an unspecialized way mention bilingualism as a prerequisite in a fair proportion of the cases.

Trends Between 1939 and 1964

Want ads in 1939 were examined for the same newspapers
and then compared with 1964. In all respects the use of bilingualism
as a precondition for employment was less frequent in 1939. For both
men and women 13 percent of the positions advertised in La Presse in
1939 required bilinguals. This is little more than half the percentage
of bilingual want ads appearing in the same paper in 1964. The shift
is nowhere as great in the Star's ads for men, 19 percent in 1964 versus 15 percent in 1939, but is rather considerable for women (17 versus

9 percent). In 1939 want ads for men actually required bilingualism slightly more often in the Montreal Star than in La Presse. The greater pressure for bilingualism among French-speaking women, however, also existed in 1939. The bilingualism rates in the French newspaper are slightly lower for men in 1939 than in the English advertisements even after the standardization procedures described earlier are used. By contrast the frequency of bilingual want ads for women in La Presse is still much higher even when the occupational differences between the two papers in the ads offered are taken into account.

As in 1964, occupations requiring bilingualism tend to pay better than those for which monoglots are acceptable. Likewise, want ads for monolinguals in the Star are for higher income positions than those listed in La Presse, although the difference is slight; for example, monolingual men in the two papers differ $12. 00 in average yearly earnings (based on the cross-tabulation between occupation and income for Montreal in 1941). Table 7 indicates the average earnings associated with jobs advertised in the two newspapers.

It turns out that 1939 is hardly a desirable year for comparison with 1964 since the economic depression of the 1930's had not ended by 1939. Hence, there were relatively few want ads, even though all four weekend editions during the period between April 8 and 29 were used. Of particular significance is the fact that the kind of positions offered during a period of high unemployment may not be

Table 7. Weighted Mean Annual Income of Occupations Advertised, by Newspaper, Sex, and Language Requirements, 1939

Sex	Monolingual		Bilingual		All Advertisements		
	Montreal Star	La Presse	Montreal Star	La Presse	Montreal Star	La Presse	Both Newspapers
Males	$1198	$1186	$1406	$1314	$1229	$1202	$1214
Females	399	393	561	537	413	411	412

Table 8. Newspaper Advertisements Requiring Bilingualism,
1939 Versus Rates in 1964

| Newspaper | Percent Bilingual | | | |
| | Male | | Female | |
	Actual	Expected[a]	Actual	Expected[a]
Montreal Star	15	24	9	12
La Presse	13	30	13	15

[a]Based on application of rates in 1964 for the same newspaper to occupations listed in 1939.

too suitable for comparison. However, there is little doubt that the demands for bilingualism have basically increased in the quarter-century since 1939. If the 1964 frequency of bilingual prerequisites for employment in each occupational division are applied to the occupations advertised in 1939, 24 and 30 percent of male want ads in the Star and Presse, respectively, would have required bilinguals in 1939. These are far greater than the bilingual percentages actually encountered in 1939 (see Table 8) and clearly indicate a basic rise in the demands for knowledge of a second language among both French- and English-speaking Montrealers. Increases are observed for women as well, although not of the same magnitude. In the following section further evidence is presented that suggests bilingualism has become an increasingly important prerequisite for employment.

Language and the Customer

The bilingual Yellow Pages published by the telephone company provides a ready means for gauging the role of each language in the various commercial, industrial, and social domains of Montreal. Yellow Pages is hardly the equivalent to the information which might be obtained from an intensive and costly survey of business activities in the city. To paraphrase the telephone company slogan, we shall "let our fingers do the interviewing."

Listings in the directory suggest rather strong social segregation between the two major linguistic components of Montreal. There are 202 Roman Catholic churches and related institutions listed in Yellow Pages (the September 1964 issue is used throughout this section). Nearly 90 percent are listed under the French "Eglises" exclusively, close to 10 percent are under the English rubric only, and a handful are listed under both the English and French terms. This clearly indicates the ethnic and linguistic divisions existing within the church, for although French Canadians are the dominant group within the Catholic religion of Montreal, nearly 20 percent of the metropolitan area's Catholics in 1961 were not French.

The lack of social integration between the two language groups is also displayed by some other listings as well. Rooming houses tend to involve fairly close contact between the residents, and aversion between ethnic groups is not uncommon. Witness the reluctance in the United States to make many open occupancy laws apply to small rooming houses. There is virtually no overlap among the 593 rooming houses listed in the English or French rubrics of Yellow Pages. Only 3 percent are under both listings, 70 percent are under "Chambres à Louer," and about a quarter are under the English listing exclusively. Apartment houses reflect a less intensive form of interaction and, accordingly, 13 percent are listed under both languages, but the degree of linguistic isolation is still noteworthy. There are many more apartment house listings under English than French. Probably only more expensive apartment houses list, and this reflects the general socioeconomic positions of the two ethnic groups.

A sharp discrepancy exists between the frequency of bilingual listings among "billiard halls" and "bowling." Bowling alleys tend to be rather large commercial ventures and, although most establishments probably draw customers from one part of the city, it is still a fairly widespread area. Consequently, about three-quarters of the bowling establishments are listed under both languages. By contrast 85 percent of the billiard halls are under only one language (54 percent English, 31 percent French). It is noteworthy that billiard halls are more sociable units, since there is interaction among the players at different tables, challenges, and the establishment is more likely to serve as a meeting place and "hangout" (see Polsky 1964). Bowling

Table 9. Language Rubrics Used by Selected Activities
in Montreal's Yellow Pages, 1964

| | Percent of Listings | | | |
Category	English Only	French Only	Both Languages	(Number)[a]
Roman Catholic churches	9	88	3	(202)
Rooming houses	27	70	3	(593)
Apartments	50	37	13	(241)
Bowling	16	7	77	(103)
Billiard halls	54	31	15	(89)
Night clubs	22	36	42	(94)

[a]Organizations listed under both languages are counted only once.

involves interaction that is restricted to players in the same party or
league. Hence the activities surrounding bowling are more compatible
with a linguistically diverse set of customers than are billiard halls.
Also billiard halls probably draw their clientele from a smaller area
of the city than bowling units; hence the former's customers are more
likely to be linguistically homogeneous.

Nightclubs are rather surprising, since 40 percent are listed
under both languages. Although such clubs tend to draw from a large
part of the city and are concentrated in certain areas of Montreal, one
would expect that the use of comedians as well as singers would lead
more of them to be suitable for the speakers of only one of the two
official languages.

Retail Establishments

The frequency of double listings ranges widely between the
retail services examined in Yellow Pages (see Table 10). Retail
grocers are easiest to explain; less than 10 percent are bilisted,
about a quarter are solely under English, and two thirds exclusively
under "Epiciers-En Détail." Since grocers are ubiquitous and depend
on a relatively small trade area, the high residential segregation in

Table 10. Language Rubrics Used by Selected Retail and Wholesale
Establishments in Montreal's Yellow Pages, 1964

Category	Percent of Listings			
	English Only	French Only	Both Languages	(Number)[a]
Retail grocers	23	68	9	(1832)
Tire dealers	46	3	51	(116)
Beauty salons	18	46	35	(1084)
Retail bakers	55	19	26	(117)
Pastry shops	28	42	31	(304)
Cleaners and dyers	33	31	36	(546)
Retail shoes	26	20	54	(454)
Wholesale grocers	28	10	62	(39)
Wholesale bakers	16	16	68	(38)

[a]Organizations listed under both languages are counted only once.

Montreal affords little reason for most units to list under both languages since many deal primarily with one group. The percentages of the metropolitan population 15 years of age and older with English and French mother tongues, 23.5 and 63.1, respectively, tend to be fairly close to the percentages of grocers under each listing.

Tire dealers no doubt have larger trade areas and the fact that about half are listed under both categories is not surprising. What is noteworthy is the fact that nearly all the remaining dealers are found only under the English rubric, with less than 5 percent of all tire dealers listed under French exclusively. Granted that the socioeconomic differences between the ethnic groups are such that English-speaking Montrealers are probably more likely to own automobiles than the French, it is unlikely to be sufficient to explain such a striking discrepancy. A matter of conjecture here is that the Frenc word for tires, "pneus," may have been partially replaced by the En- glish word. Hence dealers can advertise exclusively in the English rubric without suffering too badly. Supporting this are several small inserts under the English listing which are entirely in French. It do appear that generally a number of English words for technical and mechanical subjects have become common in French usage. This is particularly striking in the case of automobile parts.

French fares better in some of the other retail trades examined, although not so well as might be expected on the basis of Montreal's linguistic composition. If the second languages spoken by the population are considered, English is almost on a par with French in Montreal. Among those 15 and over, 21 percent speak English only, 28 percent speak French only, and 49 percent are bilingual. Of course this ignores the tendency for bilinguals to favor their mother tongue, a factor which would boost the desirability for listing under French. French does very well among beauty salons and pastry shops; English is probably overrepresented among shoe stores, cleaners and dyers, and very much so under retail bakers. However, we should not lose sight of the fact that both languages are fairly well served on the retail level in Montreal. Combining the bilingual stores with those listing under English or French alone, 50 percent or more of the retail establishments are found under both languages. The only exception is groceries.

It is of interest to follow several of these retail services back a step to their suppliers. In the case of wholesale grocers 62 percent are listed under both languages. Likewise 68 percent of wholesale bakers are bilisted. In both cases the percentages are considerably higher than among the retailers. The wholesaler is less restricted in the area of the city he deals with and therefore must attempt to gain customers among retailers of both linguistic groups.

Industry

Generally, as we turn from services to industrial activities which do not deal directly with the family consumer or small retailer, the orientation toward French declines. Consider various facets of the shoe industry in Montreal (Table 11). About two-thirds of shoe manufacturers list under both languages, with the remaining third nearly all under English listings exclusively. Granted the high percentage of shoe manufacturers with double listings, one should not ignore the almost complete absence of those only under French. Taking a step (no pun intended) backward in the supply chain, there are no suppliers of shoe manufacturers' machinery, findings, laces, lasts,

Table 11. Language Rubrics Used by the Shoe Industry
in Montreal's Yellow Pages, 1964

Shoe:	Number of Listings			
	English Only	French Only	Both Languages	Total[a]
Manufacturers	34	3	73	110
Manufacturers' machinery	5	0	2	7
Findings	26	0	10	36
Lace manufacturers	3	0	2	5
Lasts	1	0	3	4
Patterns	3	0	3	6
Manufacturers' supplies	19	1	4	24

[a]Organizations listed under both languages are counted only once.

or patterns who list under the French rubric exclusively and only one
under the French equivalent of "shoe manufacturers' supplies." Combining all of these categories, 70 percent of companies in Montreal
serving the shoe manufacturers are listed only under English and near
all of the remainder are bilisted. The 30 percent with double listings
should be compared with 66 percent among manufacturers of shoes and
54 percent among retailers. The high level of double listings among
manufacturers is due to the fact that they are also oriented toward sho
retailers. Table 11 does indicate, however, the very weak position of
French in the services oriented toward manufacturers.

The textile and garment industry is important in Montreal.
Among the 250 textile wholesalers and manufacturers listed, fully two
thirds are found only in the English category, another 30 percent are
bilisted, and only 4 percent appear exclusively under the French rubr
Unfortunately Yellow Pages lists wholesalers and manufacturers together. In ancillary services, however, such as textile dyers and fin
ishers, mill equipment and supplies, printers, transfers, and broker
there are no exclusively French listings and only 21 percent of the 62
listings are in both tongues. Again, the predominance of English increases in the activities furthest removed from retail markets.

Table 12. Language Rubrics Used by Selected Heavy Industries
in Montreal's Yellow Pages, 1964

| | Number of Listings | | | |
Category	English Only	French Only	Both Languages	Total[a]
Steel	48	7	57	112
Machine tools	50	3	5	58
Plastic products	89	4	28	121
Steel foundries	13	0	4	17
Iron foundries	14	2	12	28
Brass, bronze, aluminum, and copper foundries	11	0	14	25
Foundry equipment and supplies	16	0	0	16
Chemicals	92	6	68	166
Screws	16	0	7	23

[a]Organizations listed under both languages are counted only once.

Various industrial activities which would be representative
of the positions of the two languages are listed in Table 12. One is
struck by the poor showing of French almost without exception. It
appears that in some industries French is fairly well represented
only by virtue of a large number of double listings; for example, 64
of the 112 steel companies are listed under "Acier" (7 plus 57), but
still this compares with 105 (48 plus 57) that are listed under the English category. French is not only a poor second to English in terms
of the number of exclusive listings in some industries, but fares very
poorly even when double listings are taken into account; for example,
only 8 out of 58 machine tool companies are listed in the French rubric and only 32 out of 121 companies in plastic products are found
under the French category. Incidentally, according to the pattern
observed earlier in shoes and textiles, it is of interest to note that
foundry equipment and supplies have no French listings at all. Again
we see that suppliers of goods and services that are further removed
from consumer markets are less likely to use French listings. In
Montreal generally the percentage of double listings increases from

retail to wholesale but then drops radically in the manufacturing end.
In summary, nearly all companies in the industries examined are
listed under English. In a fair number of industries a substantial
number are also listed in French, but in many industries the companies are listed only in English. Further, the listing of industrial companies exclusively in French is infrequent.

Offices

Yellow Pages provides further evidence that white-collar
activities are dominated by the English language. Nearly 80 percent
of office buildings listed in the directory are found exclusively in
English, about 15 percent are double listings, and only 5 percent are
solely under the French rubric. The vast majority of office buildings
are located in the western part of downtown, an area that tends to be
a stronghold of English in the central business district. The powerful
position of English is also reflected in listings for "Office Furniture
and Equipment, " in which about half the companies are bilisted and
nearly all the remainder are only under the English rubric. There
are 64 retailers of "Office Supplies" listed in English, of which 10 are
also found under "Bureaux-Fournitures. " Only one is listed exclusively in French.

There are 217 listings under the English category "Hotels—
Out of Town. " Under the French rubric there are only eight, five of
which are also listed in the English heading. Hence of the 110 separat
out-of-town hotels listed in Yellow Pages, more than 95 percent are
under the English category exclusively, about 1 percent are under
only the French category, and 2 percent have double listings. There
are 70 listings for hotels in the United States, all but one of which are
under the English rubric exclusively. There are 33 hotels listed for
Canadian cities outside Quebec and 31 of these are only under English
The out-of-town hotel listings reflect the lack of direct integration of
Montreal's French Canadians into the social and economic life outsid
of the province as well as the extent to which participation hinges upo
knowledge of the English language.

Trends

Using a classified telephone directory for 1939, changes for
some services can be examined over a 25-year span. The percentag

Table 13. Comparison Between Yellow Page Listings in Montreal,
1939 and 1964

| | Percent of Listings | | | | | | (Number)[d] |
| | English Only | | French Only | | Both Languages | | |
Category	1939	1964	1939	1964	1939	1964	1939
Rooming houses	100	27	o	70	o	3	(220)
Apartments	85	50	14	37	1	13	(159)
Bowling	92	16	o	7	8	77	(26)
Billiard halls	100	54	o	31	o	15	(27)
Grocers[a]	39	23	60	67	1	10	(1626)
Tire dealers	81	46	4	3	15	51	(79)
Beauty salons	39	18	48	46	13	35	(716)
Bakers[a]	49	46	33	18	18	36	(101)
Pastry shops	14	28	79	42	7	31	(14)
Cleaners and dyers	64	33	15	31	21	36	(164)
Textiles[b]	100	66	o	4	o	30	(38)
Office buildings	100	79	o	5	o	16	(39)
Office equipment[c]	88	45	o	5	12	50	(33)
Hotels—out of town	100	96	o	1	o	2	(57)

oNo listings.
[a]No distinction made between wholesale and retail in 1939; hence both categories
were combined for 1964.
[b]Comparable to "Textiles—wholesale and mfrs." in 1964.
[c]"Office Equipment" in 1939; "Office Furniture and Equipment" in 1964.
[d]Organizations listing under both languages are counted only once.

of companies listing in English only has declined for all categories
examined and the percentage listing in French only has increased in
the majority of cases (see Table 13). Without exception the proportion
of companies with double listings has also increased. In some instances these changes are minor and are due to the fact that no companies were listed in French in 1939. This was the case for "textiles
—wholesale and manufacturers," "hotels—out of town," "office buildings," and "billiard halls." Judging by the changes in office buildings
and office equipment listings, French is receiving far more recogni-

Table 14. Percent of Montreal <u>Yellow Page</u> Listings in Each
Language, 1939 and 1964[a]

| | Percent of Enterprises Listed | | | |
| | English | | French | |
Category	1939	1964	1939	1964
Rooming houses	55	30	46	73
Apartments	86	63	14	50
Bowling	100	93	8	84
Billiard halls	100	69	°	46
Grocers	40	33	61	77
Tire dealers	96	97	19	54
Beauty salons	52	54	61	82
Bakers	67	82	51	54
Pastry shops	21	58	86	72
Cleaners and dyers	85	69	36	67
Textiles	100	96	°	34
Office buildings	100	95	°	21
Office equipment	100	95	12	55
Hotels—out of town	100	99	°	4

[a]See footnotes to Table 13.

tion in white-collar activities than it did in pre-World War II Montreal.
The position occupied by each tongue is not at an equilibrium, but appears to be changing. English is still dominant, however, particularly
when the mother tongue and ethnic composition of Montreal is taken
into account.

In some instances the shifts are enormous. All but two of
the 26 bowling establishments listed in 1939 are exclusively in the
English rubric. Perhaps as a reflection of the greater prosperity
of the French Canadians in Montreal or of greater mobility due to
automobiles, a far greater proportion of the enterprises are listed
under both the English and French rubrics in 1964. This occurs even
among such locally based services as cleaners, grocers, and bakers.

Shown in Table 14 are the percentages of establishments listed under each language in the two periods. They were obtained by adding the percentage bilisted to the percentage listing exclusively under each tongue. Hence they total to more than 100 percent if any establishments are bilisted. The percentage of enterprises listed in English has declined in many instances, risen in a few such as bakers and pastry shops. By contrast, with the exception of pastry shops, in all cases the percentage of enterprises listing in French has increased. Some activities tend to make an appeal to both language groups. Fifty percent or more of the companies in the following categories are in both English and French rubrics: cleaners and dyers, office equipment, beauty salons, tire dealers, apartments, bowling alleys, bakers, and pastry shops. In 1939 only beauty salons and bakers would have met these criteria.

The reader should interpret these results carefully. These figures indicate the degree services of a given type are offered to both language groups, they do not necessarily indicate the extent to which individual enterprises pursue both groups of customers. The latter was indicated in Table 13 by the percentage of enterprises which are listed under both tongues. Among rooming houses, for example, about half the listings were in French and the other half in English in 1939. As inspection of Table 13 should make clear, this does not reflect any particular effort among many rooming houses to obtain customers from both groups. Less than 1 percent were bilisted.

This growth of double listings between 1939 and 1964 means there is increased pressure for bilingualism among those engaged in the occupations involved. This is consistent with the earlier finding that bilingualism is more frequently used as a job qualification in want ads.

Physicians

Physicians and lawyers, two of the classical professions, have both undergone the same shift toward dual listings in Yellow Pages. Less than 5 percent of all the physicians and about 20 percent of the lawyers were listed under both languages in 1939. By 1964, 30 percent of the physicians and 60 percent of the lawyers chose double

Table 15. Physicians' Listings in Montreal Yellow Pages, 1964

Listing	Specialists	Nonspecialists	Downtown East	West	All	Not Downtown
English only	28.8	35.4	4.0	63.0	49.1	26.1
French only	18.6	44.6	60.0	3.7	17.0	45.2
Both	52.6	19.9	36.0	33.3	34.0	28.7

listings. In both periods the remaining members of the two professions were split fairly evenly between English and French. Physicians
in 1964 and lawyers in both periods choosing to list under only one language were slightly more likely to elect French than English, but the
differences are slight. Considering the linguistic composition of Montreal, members of both professions are more likely to solicit English-
speaking clients or at least be oriented in their direction. It is not
clear why lawyers are more likely to have dual listings than physician.
However, one can speculate on what is probably a greater degree of
ethnic, linguistic, and religious segregation in the medical profession
than in the legal world. There is the split along hospital affiliations
as well as the religious practices that influences certain areas of
medicine such as obstetrics (see Solomon 1961; Hall 1948, 1940).

Although there is the same tendency for the ethnic origin of
a lawyer to influence the kind of practice developed, nevertheless
segregation is less complete since all lawyers must deal with the
same legal institutions. Advocates must be prepared to understand
testimony given in either English or French. Hence, more lawyers
will very likely be bilingual and thus able to pursue clients from both
linguistic groups. (I am indebted to Professor Jack Ladinsky for som
of the points made in these two paragraphs.)

In an effort to understand some of the less obvious influences
on listing practices, physicians were examined in some detail for bot
1939 and 1964. Their office locations were placed into three categori
those in the western part of the central business district; those in the
eastern section of the central business district; and those located out

side of the downtown area. The appendix at the end of this chapter indicates the census tracts included in each of the areas delineated.

Physicians segregate within the central business district along linguistic lines that correspond to the residential patterns of Montreal. Areas located east of downtown tend to be heavily French, whereas relatively more of the English speakers are located in the western part of the city. In turn, less than 5 percent of physicians in the eastern part of downtown are listed under English exclusively and a similar percentage in downtown west are listed only under French. By contrast about 60 percent of physicians in the eastern segment are listed under "médecins and chirurgiens" exclusively and a similar percentage located in western downtown are listed only under the English category. To a certain degree patients drawn to downtown physicians are attracted to two different markets depending on the language they speak.

The relationship is complex between medical practice and directory listing. Obviously, a physician with a sizable clientele among patients of a given language group may be expected to list his name in the appropriate language; one attracting patients from both groups would be expected to list under both "physicians and surgeons" and "médecins and chirurgiens." Physicians whose clientele are drawn from a narrow segment of the city would be more likely to have a linguistically homogeneous group of patients compared with those whose patients come from a broader areal base. In this connection, slightly more than half of all physicians who are specialists have dual listings compared with 20 percent of nonspecialists. Likewise, although the differences are not great, 34 percent of doctors with offices downtown are bilisted, compared with 29 percent of those located elsewhere in the city. There is a sharp difference between the English- and French-oriented segments of downtown. In each case about a third of the physicians have dual listings; however, two-thirds of the western physicians are under the English rubric exclusively. Nearly as large a percentage are under the French listing only in the eastern sector of the central business district.

There appear to be two downtowns for medical practice in Montreal. In one part the orientation is much more toward English and in the other toward French. Physicians listed only under English

are more likely to be downtown than doctors who list solely under the
French rubric. About 45 percent of all the doctors located outside the
central business districts list exclusively in French, compared with
a quarter who list only in English. The net effect, if the bilisted are
included, is that three-fourths of non-downtown physicians list under
French, compared with half in English. In the western section of
downtown less than 5 percent list only in French; in the eastern section
of downtown less than 5 percent list only in English. Both dual listings
of physicians and medical specialization were far less common in
1939. The handful of specialists sampled, however, were all bilisted
and downtown doctors were also more likely to choose double listings.

Specialists are more likely to take double listings than nonspecialists located in the same area (Table 16). Half the non-downtown specialists are listed under both linguistic rubrics, whereas 20
percent of those with general practices in the same area have dual
listings. Similar or greater differences occur in the two downtown
districts. ("Specialists" are defined as those doctors who indicate
some specialty after their name in the telephone directory.) Medical
specialization depends more on physicians' referrals than does a
general practice and hence it is easier for a specialist to obtain
patients from both linguistic groups. Moreover, there is a wider
population base necessary to support specialists and this probably
makes it more necessary for specialists to obtain patients from both
linguistic segments (Lieberson 1958).

The strong attraction of western downtown for physicians
listed under English and eastern downtown for French-listed physicians remains unaltered after differences between specialists and nonspecialists are taken into account. About three-quarters of nonspeci-
ists in western downtown are listed only under English and the same
proportion of eastern downtown physicians list only the French rubric
This holds true for 1939, when 85 percent of nonspecialists in western
downtown were listed only in English and 89 percent of those in the
eastern part were exclusively in French. (The small number of specialists and dual listings in that year precludes a more extensive tabulation for 1939.)

Office location per se does not have much effect on the likelihood of a dual listing, with the exception of the small number of

Table 16. Percent of Physicians with Dual Listings, by Office
Location and Practice, 1964

Location and Practice	Percent with Dual Listings
Downtown, East:	
Specialists	75.0
Nonspecialists	17.6
Downtown, West:	
Specialists	50.0
Nonspecialists	18.6
Not Downtown:	
Specialists	51.2
Nonspecialists	20.5

specialists located in the eastern downtown district. In fact, among
nonspecialists, those located away from downtown are more likely to
have two listings than those in either central business district (20.5
percent versus 18.6 and 17.6 percent).

Among specialists and nonspecialists alike, "English only"
doctors are most likely to be downtown, "French only" physicians
least likely, and those with dual listings occupy an intermediate position. If by limitations of language ability or intentional choice, a
physician restricts himself to an English-speaking practice, he must
draw patients from a very wide spatial area. Hence these specialists
need a central location such as that provided downtown. By contrast
a specialist who deals solely in French is less restricted to downtown
since he has a greater number of patients in the city to draw from.
This broader areal market makes it more possible for a specialist
listing only under French to locate outside of the central business district. A bilisted specialist, although needing a large population to
draw from in the same way as other specialists, can practice anywhere.
It is easy to see why nonspecialists listing only in French can more
readily locate away from downtown than "English onlys," who need to
draw on a larger spatial area because fewer of Montreal's population
are native speakers of English than French.

We should not overlook the fact that a rather large number of physicians in 1964 were listed under only one rubric. This indicates the existence of occupational segregation or dualism such that important segments of the medical profession are oriented toward providing the services needed by only one part of Montreal's population.

Changes Between 1939 and 1964

A special examination was made of changes between 1939 and 1964 of physicians who were listed in the Yellow Pages in both periods. Two noteworthy shifts occurred; they were more likely to have dual listings and to indicate a specialty in 1964. About 30 percent of physicians who were listed exclusively under either French or English in 1939 were listed under both language rubrics in 1964. The great majority of the small number of bilisted physicians in 1939 who were still practicing also retained their double listings. The trend toward specialization is also apparent, with about 28 percent of nonspecialists in 1939 listing specialties 25 years later. Bear in mind that "specialization" refers to self-declared restriction of practice, not necessarily successful completion of a residency or examinations.

Longitudinal evidence to support the earlier contention that a broader-based clientele as well as the referral system tend to encourage bilingual practices is found in the analysis of the degree of bilisting among physicians who shifted from general practice to a specialty during this period. Of those doctors listed under English only in 1939 and who later restricted their practice to a specialty, 70 percent had dual listings in 1964 (Table 17). Of those physicians who declare no specialty in either period, only 15 percent have shifted from an exclusive English listing to a dual listing. Almost the same results are obtained for physicians who were nonspecialists in 1939 and listed themselves only under the French language rubric. Only 12 percent of those remaining as nonspecialists had dual listings in 1964, whereas 68 percent of those restricting their practices were bilisted in 1964.

In summary, this consideration of physicians provides further support for the proposition that services oriented toward a consumer market in Montreal are likely to have increased pressure for bilingualism when they increase the size of the area from which they

Table 17. Listing and Practice of Physicians in 1964 Who Were
Both Nonspecialists and Singly Listed in 1939

Nonspecialists in 1939	Percent with Dual Listing, by Practice in 1964	
with Single Listing	Nonspecialist	Specialist
English only	15	70
French only	12	68

draw their clientele or customers. In the case of medicine increased
specialization leads to increased attention on the part of physicians to
the potential clientele available from both linguistic groups. The
greater frequency of dual listings among medical specialists than
general practitioners is evidence for this. In 1964 the medical profession was divided into about equal thirds among doctors listing only
in English, only in French, and those listing in both languages. Between the dual-listing practices of some physicians and the practice
of monolisted physicians locating in a segregated downtown area medical practice in Montreal provides further evidence that consumer-
oriented services do not put the population-at-large under pressure
to become bilingual, although they do affect those employed in the
economic activity being followed. The shift toward specialization between 1939 and 1964 also indicates how changes in the structure of an
occupation can alter the linguistic demands on the incumbents.

Income

One of the most important linguistic pressures generated by
the work world hinges on the income differences between the linguistic segments. The average income for both men and women in Montreal's work force is much greater for English monoglots than for
those speaking only French. The mean income for English monoglot
men in the metropolitan area in 1961 was 71 percent higher than for
those speaking French only ($5,536 versus $3,246). Women speaking
only English earn 37 percent more than those who know only the French

Table 18. Total Income by Official Language and Sex,
Montreal Metropolitan Area, 1961[a]

	Average (Mean) Income	
Official Language	Men	Women
English only	$5536	$2561
French only	3246	1867
Bilingual	4954	2515
Neither tongue	2195	1290
All workers	4720	2328

[a]Based on persons reporting income.

official language (Table 18). For each sex English monolinguals earn
the highest incomes, although the bilingual women are exceeded by
only a slight margin. Bilinguals also earn more than the average for
their sex, but by a smaller margin. People speaking only French ear
less than the average, although considerably more than those who spe
neither official language. The results for bilinguals are rather surprising, since one would expect them to enjoy advantages over monolingual speakers of either English or French.

There are some important determinants of income that co-
vary with language. The French ethnic group have less education and
are in poorer-paying jobs than the British. Although education and
occupation are clearly important determinants of income, the latter
is of a somewhat different order in the sense that French concentration in the less desirable jobs may itself reflect linguistic disadvantages. Inspection of the graph between education and income for the
different official language groups shows that English monoglots tend
to earn more than others with the same level of education (Figure 1).
Bilingual men are a fairly close second, actually exceeding speakers
of English with only an elementary school education by 17 dollars.
The French monoglots' earnings, however, are considerably lower
than the English speakers on all educational levels. The absolute ga
actually rises with education from a low of $660 among those with an
elementary school education to a high of $3,130 between English and
French monoglots with some university education. The differences

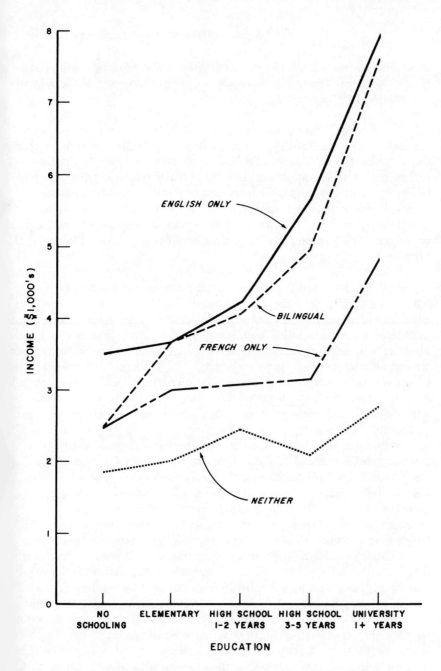

Fig. 1. Income by education and official language, males in
Montreal metropolitan area, 1961

in income between the linguistic segments of the working male population of Montreal are not to be explained simply in terms of their levels
of educational attainment.

Income differences among women tell the same story. Except
for those with no schooling, women who speak English earn more than
those speaking only French. Bilingual women are close to English
monoglots in most educational levels, actually exceeding the latter in
the very lowest and highest categories of attainment. Women unable
to speak either official language earn the least in all but one educational category. The exception, those with a university education, is
based on only 31 women who report an inability to speak either official
language.

The association between mother tongue and ethnic origin
makes it difficult, with the data available, to determine whether there
is an ethnic effect independent of the mother–tongue effect on income,
but the data are compatible with the view that native speakers of English have an edge over native speakers of French, when both are bilingual as well as when they are monoglots. Bilinguals of French
ethnic origin (overwhelmingly a population with French mother tongue)
earn less than those of British origin (overwhelmingly a population
with English mother tongue) even after education is taken into account
(Table 19). The average income for those with 3 to 5 years of high
school is more than $1,200 greater for British bilinguals than the
French ($5,818 versus $4,576). French bilinguals earn more than
their monolingual ethnic compatriots on all educational levels, but
only British bilinguals with a university education earn more than
monolingual members of their ethnic group. Hence there is a far
stronger economic incentive for bilingualism among the French.
Other ethnic groups in Montreal share with the French an incentive
for acquiring both official languages insofar as bilinguals earn more
than monolingual speakers of either French or English (with the exception of those with no schooling where the income level of English
monoglots may be suspect). Again, however, those among the other
ethnic groups who speak English only earn more than French monoglo
Granted that greater income is possible for bilinguals, English is a
more desirable first language for those whose native tongue is neithe
official language. Furthermore, the increment in income associated

Table 19. Employment Income for Men by Ethnic Group and
Official Language, Montreal Metropolitan Area, 1961[a]

Ethnic Group and Official Languages	Education				
	None	Elementary 1+ Years	High School 1–2 Years	High School 3–5 Years	University 1+ Years
British:					
English only	$3323[b]	$4077	$4498	$6074	$8830
Bilingual	2773[c]	4077	4413	5818	9116
French:					
French only	2510	3036	3048	3131	4879
Bilingual	2529	3608	3958	4576	7068
Other:					
English only	3515	3396	3779	4917	6351
French only	2474	2677	3084	3125	4506
Bilingual	2346	3783	4514	5917	7691
Neither	1857	2016	2391	2115	1687[d]

[a]Based on persons reporting income.
[b]Based on 65 cases.
[c]Based on 45 cases.
[d]Based on 64 cases.

with bilingualism is much greater among those already speaking
French than for those who are English monoglots.

Standardization for Occupation and Education

The optimal procedure for determining the effect of language
and ethnic origin on income requires that both occupation and education be taken into account simultaneously. Using the occupation-by-
education distribution of all men in the labor force, the income patterns for various ethnolinguistic segments were used to determine
the effect of language and ethnic group on income independent of occupation and education. The standardized results are shown in Table
20; for example, application of the occupation-education specific rates
for British men speaking English only would yield an average income

Table 20. Effect of Ethnic Origin and Official Language on Male
Income after Standardizing for Occupation and Education, 1961

| Ethnic Origin | Official Language | | | |
	English Only	French Only	Bilingual	Neither
British	$5124		$5041	
French		$3448	4385	
Other	4185	3260	4535	$2682

in the total male labor force of $5,124. Direct standardization in this
case may be interpreted in the following manner: If all men in the
Montreal labor force earned the same amount of money as British
monolingual speakers who held their occupation and had the same
level of education, then the average income for the male labor force
in 1961 would have been $5,124. Using the average incomes for French
bilingual men in each education- and occupation-specific category as
the norm for all employed men in metropolitan Montreal, then the
average income for men in the city would have been $4,385 in 1961.

Bilingualism is an important advantage among French-Canadian men; the standardized income is close to $1,000 greater than for
their monoglot compatriots. An even larger gap exists for other ethnic groups between French monolinguals and bilinguals, $3,260 versus
$4,535. The British monolingual earns nearly $1,700 more than the
French Canadian who knows only French. Keep in mind that these
figures are after occupational and educational differences between
ethnolinguistic groups are taken into account. As might be expected,
those unable to speak either official language are most disadvantaged
of all. Although the data are not presented here, comparisons for
specific other ethnic groups in Montreal disclose that in all instances
the bilingual members earn more than English monolinguals. Thus
it is only among the British ethnic group that the advantages of bilingualism disappear. Indeed the standardized British monolinguals are
slightly greater than their bilingual compatriots ($5,124 versus $5,04_

The average incomes for different occupational groups after
education is taken into account are shown in Table 21. French-

Canadian bilinguals earn more in all occupational categories than do
their monolingual compatriots. On the other hand, in seven of the
ten occupational categories, British bilinguals still earn less than
English monoglots. For Montreal's other ethnic groups, however,
bilinguals earn more than English monoglots, with the exception of
laborers. In turn, speakers of English only earn more than those
speaking French only. Finally, in all but two categories, those speaking neither official language occupy the lowest position in income after
educational attainment is taken into account.

Although the data are not shown, women in the labor force
have a similar pattern. Among the British ethnic group, those who
speak English only earn slightly more than bilinguals. On the other
hand, bilinguals in the French ethnic group earn more than their compatriots who are French monolinguals. Among those with other ethnic
origins, income rises from those speaking neither tongue to French
only, English only, with bilinguals highest of all.

One can only speculate why British men and women who are
bilingual earn slightly less than their monolingual compatriots. Surely,
we would not want to argue that acquisition of French will reduce the
income of British ethnics in Montreal. It may well be that the best
paying positions, those highest in an organization's hierarchy, are
those for which knowledge of French is the least necessary. Evidence
has been presented which indicates that as one turns to customers and
consumers French increases in importance. Hence the pressures for
bilingualism among the British are greater for those lower in organizations than those above them. As a consequence British bilinguals
earn less than monolinguals not because acquisition of French creates
a handicap, which it obviously does not, but possibly because those
lower in position within a given occupational and educational level are
more likely to need a knowledge of French. In this connection top
managers, technicians, and the like who are brought into Montreal
from the United States, Great Britain, and other parts of Canada are
less likely to know French but have very high income.

The earlier analysis of want ads suggested that job opportunities requiring bilingualism in the Star are somewhat more desirable
than those for which English alone is sufficient—at least as measured
by the income associated with the two types. It may well be that this

Table 21. Effect of Ethnic Origin and Official Language on Male Income for Occupations after Standardizing for Education, 1961

| | Ethnic Group and Official Language | | | | | | | |
| | British | | French | | Other | | | |
Occupation	English Only	Biling.	French Only	Biling.	English Only	French Only	Biling.	Neither
Managerial	$9570	$9171	$5361	$7100	$8293	$5293	$8511	$7606
Professional and technical	7529	7953	4818	6658	5894	4081	6679	1870
Clerical	3724	3637	2755	3501	3180	2288	3311	2314
Sales	5461	5359	3065	4605	4480	3528	5381	1563
Service and recreation	3396	3333	2550	3399	2565	2467	3097	1875
Transport and communication	4374	3948	2892	3599	3159	2871	3488	2235
Farmers and stockraisers								
Other primary[a]	2771	2818	2204	2601	2688	1861	3031	1439
Craftsmen	4293	4273	3260	3807	3476	3023	3684	2310
Laborers	2794	2627	2399	2590	2582	2413	2581	1942

[a] Excluding farmers and stockraisers.

apparent contradiction can be explained as a reflection of the advantage in bilingualism for native English speakers in obtaining certain kinds of employment, but that this advantage diminishes as they move up the hierarchy afterward. Unfortunately, one can do little more than speculate at this point since there are a number of technical considerations which themselves could explain the apparent inconsistency. The newspaper analysis is basically an ecological correlation with census income data, there is great selectivity in the jobs offered in the advertisements, and our analysis here is based on only the British ethnic population of Montreal. In connection with the last point, keep in mind that for other ethnic groups beside the French, bilingualism is associated with a distinct income advantage over monolingualism.

Some inferences about the nature of the occupational pressure for bilingualism can be drawn from the variations in income advantage which French-Canadian bilinguals enjoy over monolingual French Canadians with the same job. Among men with an elementary school education, for example, bilingual laborers earn $152 more than monolinguals, whereas the income of bilingual technical workers exceeds French monoglots by more than a thousand dollars. If French Canadians become bilingual in part because of the ensuing income advantage, there should be a strong correlation between the percentage of French Canadians in an occupation who are bilingual and the income advantage that bilinguals enjoy. Such is precisely the case, as the Spearman rank order correlations in Table 22 indicate. In the illustration cited above, for example, only 42 percent of the laborers with a grade school education are bilingual whereas 75 percent of the technicians with the same schooling are able to speak both official languages. Considering that these comparisons are between men with the same level of educational attainment, there is strong evidence that bilingualism among French Canadians tends to be a response to the presence of income advantages. When the gain in income is minor, there is a relatively low percentage of French Canadians in the occupation who can also speak English.

By contrast there is essentially no association in Table 22 between the percentage of British men who are bilingual and the magnitude of the income difference between bilinguals and English monolinguals. Thus there is further evidence for a rather persistent

Table 22. Correlation Between Income Advantage of Bilinguals
and Frequency of Bilingualism, Male, 1961[a]

Education	French Ethnic Group: Bilinguals versus French Only	British Ethnic Group: Bilinguals versus English Only
None	−.10	−.80
Elementary, 1+ years	.87	.08
High School, 1–2 years	.90	.02
High School, 3–5 years	.88	−.15
University, 1+ years	.50	.22

[a]Spearman correlations based on nine occupational categories except among British with no schooling ($N = 4$) and French with no schooling ($N = 5$).

theme: a relative absence of strong economic pressure among the
British to learn French, but the presence of a distinct gain for French
Canadians who acquire English as a second language.

Appendix

Boundaries of the Central Business
District of Montreal

Boundaries for the two downtown areas were based on a map
in the 1964 Yellow Pages which delineates districts in Montreal used
in the classified headings. By use of several street directories for
Montreal made available by the Dominion Bureau of Statistics, Liste
Des Rues, Montreal, Partie I and II, each medical office location was
placed into Enumeration Districts (and E. A.'s if the Enumeration
District was partially in one or both downtown areas) and then classified accordingly. For purposes of analysis the census tract boundaries were followed even if this meant including small areas outside the
two downtown subareas delineated in Yellow Pages. Shown below are

the census tracts, based on the 1961 tract scheme, included in each
of the central business districts delineated in <u>Yellow Pages</u>:

Downtown, West	Downtown, East
51 (includes only Enumeration Areas 1–3 of District 468)	29–50
	51 (includes only Enumeration Areas 66–68 and 112–14 of District 472)
54–62	52–53
69–72	137–39
118–21	154

REFERENCES

Hall, Osward. 1940. Types of medical careers. American Journal
     of Sociology 45: 243–53.
_____. 1948. The stages of a medical career. American Journal
     of Sociology 53: 327–36.
Hughes, Everett C. 1943. French Canada in transition. Chicago:
     University of Chicago Press.
Lieberson, Stanley. 1958. Ethnic groups and the practice of medicine.
     American Sociological Review 23: 542–49.
Polsky, Ned. 1964. The hustler. Social Problems 12: 3–15.
Solomon, David N. 1961. Ethnic and class differences among hospi-
     tals as contingencies in medical careers. American Journal
     of Sociology 66: 463–71.

11 | Linguistic and Ethnic Segregation in Montreal

Residential segregation is of great interest in any city populated by more than one ethnic or linguistic group. Spatial isolation is not only an indicator of assimilation and social distance, but is itself a vital mechanism for linguistic maintenance and ethnic continuity. Studies of the assimilation process in various American cities show fairly high and consistent correlation between the segregation of ethnic groups and intermarriage, ability to speak English, citizenship, occupational mobility, and other facets of assimilation.[1] Segregation permits ethnic and linguistic groups to minimize contact with others in activities related to residence such as neighboring, children's playmates, local services, and community institutions. Residential patterns also influence the degree speakers can maximize the use of their native tongue and avoid the need to acquire a second language. Even if bilingualism is necessary for occupational or other purposes, the range of situations in which the second tongue must be spoken can be minimized through linguistic isolation. In short, if pluralism is to remain despite the demands created by the joint participation in a single economic order, then residential segregation is an absolute necessity.

The patterns of segregation in Montreal are of greater importance than in most Canadian cities since there are few centers which approach Montreal's potential for the maintenance of both major ethnic and linguistic groups. Most Canadian cities are so overwhelmingly English or French that the numerical minority can hardly maintain themselves. At present, there is little chance that Quebec's French population or Toronto's British group will give up their native tongue. In Montreal, although French Canadians are the numerically dominant ethnic group, amounting to nearly two-thirds of the metropolitan pop-

ulation in 1961, the British number 380,000—about 18 percent of the
population. The 60,000 French Canadians residing in Toronto, by
contrast, comprise only about 3 percent of the metropolitan population.
In addition, nearly 20 percent of Montreal's residents are members of
other ethnic groups. More than 20 percent of the Italians in Canada
and over 40 percent of the Dominion's Jewish population reside in Montreal. Most of these groups strengthen the position of the English language in Montreal.

Pluralism in Montreal raises several issues which are not
normally found in U.S. cities and rarely even in Canada. In American
cities, there is usually one clear-cut "norm" or standard with which
to compare each immigrant group's residential distribution, namely,
the native whites. If information were known about later generations,
then probably the norm would be Americans of British origin. There
is even less of a problem in determining the linguistic standard since
it is clearly English. In spite of the fact that Canada recognizes the
privileged status of the English and French languages, in most cities
of Canada it is clear that one or the other tongue dominates. Adoption
of French by the Ukrainians of Winnipeg or of English by the handful
of Poles in Trois Rivières could hardly be considered a major step
toward assimilation among their neighbors. In Montreal, acquisition
of either official language or location near either the British or French
ethnic groups can be regarded as assimilation.

There are several major aims in this study of segregation in
a community which is both multilingual and multiethnic in character.
First, the current residential patterns of ethnic and linguistic groups
are measured and then compared with earlier decades so that the
present situation may be placed into an historical perspective. Second,
since there are close relationships between ethnic origin and linguistic
abilities, an effort is made to determine the role of language in influencing ethnic segregation and, conversely, the impact of ethnic segregation on linguistic residential pattern. Of particular interest is the
segregation between the monolingual French and English populations
since the pressure for learning a second language will in part reflect
their proximity to one another. Compared with most Canadian cities,
the degree of bilingualism is very high in metropolitan Montreal; more
than a third of the English-mother-tongue population 15 years of age
and older are able to speak French and nearly 60 percent of those with

French mother tongue are bilingual. The residential patterns of these bilinguals can greatly affect the positions of their ethnic groups and their native tongue. Using special census cross-tabulations, the influence of linguistic differences within each ethnic group on the residential patterns are examined. For example, do bilingual French Canadians tend to have a residential pattern which differs greatly from monolingual French Canadians? If so, does it tend to be much closer to the spatial distribution of Montreal's British population?

Data and Methods

Canadian censuses provide ethnic and official language distributions for the census tracts of metropolitan Montreal in both 1951 and 1961. Census tracts are small subdivisions of the city and suburbs, rarely containing more than 10,000 residents, which are designed to be relatively uniform in area and population.[2] The ethnic composition of Montreal's wards is also available for 1871, 1901, and 1941—with data on linguistic composition reported for the latter year.

Segregation is measured by means of the index of dissimilarity, a commonly used ecological measure of differences between the proportional distributions of groups in the spatial units of an urban area, which ranges in value from 0 (no segregation) to 100 (complete segregation). There is no segregation between two groups in a city if their distributions by census tracts are identical. An index of 100, maximum segregation, occurs only if no tract contains members of both groups, that is, if the tract holding 100 percent of the city's X population have no residents from group Y.[3] A useful way of thinking about the index of dissimilarity is that it states the percentage of one group that would have to relocate into different subareas if the two groups were to have identical percentage distributions in the city's tracts or wards.[4]

Since the index of dissimilarity is affected by the number of spatial units, comparisons between 1871, 1901, and 1941 of absolute values are difficult, owing to the changing spatial arrangements in these three years. Comparisons between 1951 and 1961 are possible if the analysis is restricted to those parts of metropolitan Montreal which were tracted in both periods and if the units are recombined so that they are spatially comparable in the two periods. Segregation measures for Montreal in 1961 have been computed in three different forms: one for the entire metropolis in 1961 (Type I); one which maximizes comparisons in segregation with as much of Montreal in 1951 as possible (Type II); and, finally, a more restricted segment of the metropolis which permits comparative standardization between decades (Type III).

Two of Greenberg's measures of linguistic diversity, H_w and A_w, have been adopted to measure respectively mutual intelligibility in an official language and mother-tongue diversity.[5] Official language data, available in 1941, 1951, and 1961, classifies each resident of the subareas into those able to speak English only, French only, both English and French, or neither official language. H_w gives the probability that two randomly drawn residents from a given neighborhood will share knowledge of one or both official languages. The measure ranges from 0, when no two people share a common tongue, to 1.0, which would occur if everyone could communicate with everyone else in a mutually understood official language. An extension of Greenberg's measure, H_b, determines the degree of mutual intelligibility between ethnic groups.[6] Using the same scale, 1.0 means that all members of one group can communicate with all members of the other group; a value of 0 means that no mutually understood language was common to the two groups. A_w and A_b are comparable measures of the mother-tongue diversity within and between groups.[7]

Finally, Westergaard's expected cases method is employed. This is a form of standardization which allows the investigator to determine the expected association between two variables after taking into account their association with a third variable. It is particularly useful in measuring the effect that linguistic differences between ethnic groups have on the actual degree of ethnic residential segregation. Analysis of the results in terms of correlation coefficients is not fully appropriate and special procedures are employed which will be described later.

Residential Segregation: Present and Past

The crucial linguistic and ethnic groups of metropolitan Montreal are highly segregated from each other. The index of dissimilarity between the British and French ethnic groups is 55.4 in 1961. This means that 55 percent of one or the other ethnic group would have to relocate themselves into different census tracts if the spatial frequency distribution of the two groups was to be identical. Likewise, segregation between the monolingual speakers of English and French is also very high—the index is 64 in 1961.

With the exception of Italians and Ukrainians, other ethnic groups are less segregated from the British than the French (Table 1, cols. 1 and 2). Northwestern European groups—Germans, Scandinavians, and Dutch—are far less segregated from the British than from the French; other European groups, although highly segregated from the British, are even more isolated from the French. Data are not available on the Jewish ethnic population for 1961; however, examination of their segregation indexes for 1951 indicates that Jews also tend to be highly segregated from the British and even more from the French.

Examination of the trends in ethnic segregation between 1951 and 1961, complicated by the changes in the tracted areas, requires recomputation of the 1961 results in order to maximize comparability between the decades (shown in cols. 3 and 4 of Table 1). Declining isolation from the French and British has been the general trend in the past decade for most ethnic groups (compare cols. 3 and 5, 4 and 6). Only the Italians and Russians have increased their segregation from both groups in the past decade. Increased segregation for nonspecified Europeans is at least in large part due to the exclusion of Jews from this category in 1951. Except for the Germans and Asians, the ethnic groups increased or decreased in segregation from both the French and British groups.

Of particular importance are the trends in segregation between the British and French ethnic groups. In 1871, these two groups were more isolated from each other in the nine districts of the city than were either from the remaining population. It is noteworthy that the French Canadian residents of Montreal were then slightly less segregated from others than were the British (28.3 and 30.5, respectively). The current segregation pattern in which the British ethnic group is more segregated from the French then from the remaining groups in Montreal had developed by 1901. The somewhat greater proximity of

Table 1. British and French Residential Segregation
from Other Ethnic Groups

| Ethnic Group | Type I | | Type II | | | |
| | 1961 | | 1961 | | 1951 | |
	British (1)	French (2)	British (3)	French (4)	British (5)	French (6)
German . . .	30,2	52,2	30,6	54,5	28,4	58,4
Italian . . .	66,3	51,0	66,3	50,1	60,8	43,9
Jewish	NA	NA	NA	NA	74,0	86,2
Netherlands . .	28,2	59,0	28,7	60,6	31,3	71,8
Polish	47,1	54,3	46,5	54,0	50,2	57,6
Russian . . .	55,7	70,2	54,6	70,5	51,9	68,4
Scandinavian .	18,6	56,4	19,1	57,9	23,1	65,0
Ukrainian . .	54,3	53,5	54,3	52,7	61,5	59,0
Other Europe .	55,9	66,9	55,8	67,6	36,8	51,7
Asiatic	52,8	55,4	51,9	54,4	53,9	50,3
Other and Not Stated . . .	38,4	63,1	37,1	63,5	41,8	65,9

NA: Not available.
Note: Jews not specified in 1961, mainly included in « Other Europe »
category.

"other" ethnics to the British rather than the French population was
also established by then, although it should be kept in mind that segregation from the British remains rather high. Presently, "other"
ethnic groups have an average segregation index of 44.7 from the
British and 58.2 from the French.

The higher the segregation between the British and French
ethnic groups, the greater must be the total segregation from these

two groups of other ethnic population in Montreal. This is due to a mathematical property of segregation indexes described elsewhere which shows that the degree of residential segregation between two groups is not independent of their spatial relationship with respect to any third group.[8] Consequently, the residential segregation indexes between some "other" ethnic group and the British and French ethnic populations must total to at least the segregation index between the latter two groups. Since the British and French are segregated to a fairly high degree, this means that it is impossible for any of Montreal's other ethnic components to be very close in residential distribution to both of these groups. In other words, if the Italians were to achieve an index of segregation of 10 from the French, then their minimum segregation from the British would be 45.4. High segregation between the British and French in Montreal means that no ethnic group can achieve very low segregation from both of these populations, although some can be highly isolated from both of these groups.

Of great significance is the fact that British-French segregation actually increased very slightly between 1951 and 1961 (based on Type II comparisons). Not only does this mean that the two most important groups of Montreal show no greater tendency toward residential proximity now than ten years ago, but the persistence of such isolation will prevent other ethnic groups from reaching close proximity to both of the city's major populations.

The closer residential patterns of northwestern Europeans than other Europeans to the British spatial distribution is also found in American cities as well as in Montreal.[9] In fact, in many Canadian cities where the French ethnic group is not important numerically and where the French language is not widely used, French-British segregation is low and more like the segregation pattern found for these two northwest European groups in American cities. For example, the indexes of segregation between these groups in metropolitan Toronto and Calgary are, respectively, only 21 and 12.

In 1961 and in the preceding two decades, the most highly isolated official language segments of Montreal have been the monolingual speakers of English and French (Table 2). While it is hardly surprising that bilinguals are less isolated from speakers of English only or French only, it is noteworthy that even those unable to speak either

Table 2. Residential Segregation
Between Official Language Components of Montreal

Year	English only and			French only and		Bilingual
	French only (1)	Bilingual (2)	Neither (3)	Bilingual (4)	Neither (5)	Neither (6)
1961, Type I .	64,3	43,4	61,9	24,6	59,4	54,0
1961, Type II .	66,0	44,3	61,3	24,9	57,8	53,4
1951, Type II .	66,6	45,1	54,4	24,0	64,7	54,4
1941	60,6	44,2	42,5	18,2	55,9	48,4

official language are less segregated from these two monolingual
groups (compare col. 1 with cols. 3 and 5). Since segregation between
the monolingual English- and French-speaking populations is even
greater than that between the British and French ethnic groups, the
total degree of isolation from these two basic speech groups by bilinguals or some other linguistic component must be high because of the
arithmetic relationship described earlier. Because 71 percent of the
bilinguals are French Canadians, the finding that bilinguals are far
more segregated from the monolingual English than from those who
speak French only is more or less to be expected. There are no great
changes between 1951 and 1961 in the magnitude of segregation between
the linguistic segments (compare rows 2 and 3), although a drop in the
segregation of those unable to speak either official language from the
monolingual French is found along with a rise in their segregation
from speakers of English only.

Linguistic segregation raises the degree of intelligible communication possible in the subareas of Montreal above that for the city
as a whole. H_W gives the proportion of randomly paired interactions
between residents in which communication through a mutually shared
official language is possible. Because of data limitations, it is not
possible to take into account communication in tongues other than English or French. Since H_W was .83 in the city of Montreal in 1941, we

would expect the same average degree of mutual intelligibility in the 35 wards if there was no segregation. In point of fact, the average H_W of .90 in the subareas was higher than that for the city as a whole. Likewise, in 1961, H_W is .79 for the entire metropolis, but averages .88 in the census tracts. In both instances, the segregation patterns tend to raise mutual intelligibility within the neighborhoods to a level greater than that for the city as a whole. If the population was randomly distributed in 1961, the frequency of mutual intelligibility would be about 10 percent less than it actually is. One solution to diversity, aside from bilingualism, is the differential location of the speech groups so that residential contacts tend to be concentrated among those with whom communication is already possible and the need for further bilingualism is reduced.

The Relation Between Linguistic and Ethnic Segregation

        In view of the differences between ethnic groups in their linguistic makeup, there is good reason to expect some association between ethnic and linguistic patterns of segregation. Knowing that the ethnic groups are segregated, then at least some degree of linguistic segregation will occur if only because the French and British ethnic groups tend to be the main carriers of the French and English mother tongues, respectively. Among the population 15 years of age and over, 96.5 percent of the French mother-tongue population were members of this single ethnic group; among the English mother-tongue population 75.9 percent were British. The tendency to favor English over French among other ethnics is illustrated by the fact that English is their mother tongue slightly more than three times as often as French. Likewise, there are some striking differences in the degree of bilingualism among the ethnic groups (Table 3). Not only is the English mother-tongue population less likely to become bilingual than those with French mother tongue, 36.1 vs. 57.8 percent, but there is considerable difference within the mother-tongue categories along ethnic lines. For example, 31 percent of native English speakers in the British group are able to speak French whereas nearly 70 percent of Italians with an English mother tongue are also able to speak French. It is noteworthy that within each ethnic group, the French mother-tongue component is usually far more likely to become bilingual than are their English mother-tongue compatriots (Table 3). The powerfu

Table 3. Bilingualism Among the Population with English or
French Mother Tongue and Official Language Distribution
Among Those with Another Mother Tongue, Population 15
Years of Age and Older, Metropolitan Montreal, 1961

Ethnic Group	Per Cent Bilingual		Official Language Distribution Among those with Another Mother Tongue			
	English Mother Tongue	French Mother Tongue	English only	French only	Bilingual	Neither
British . . .	30,6	77,7	57,2	1,7	29,4	11,7
French . . .	65,8	57,2	13,1	26,1	47,3	13,5
Other than British or French	49,1	74,8	44,3	10,8	32,0	13,0
German . . .	31,7	76,1	72,8	1,0	23,7	2,6
Italian . . .	68,7	79,7	10,6	27,3	36,2	25,9
Jewish	56,6	90,2	60,4	0,6	35,5	3,5
Ukrainian . .	54,0	88,3	53,8	5,1	37,6	3,6
All Other . .	42,4	69,1	57,2	4,5	28,6	9,7
All Groups . .	36,1	57,8	44,1	10,8	32,1	13,0

attraction of English is also demonstrated in Table 3 by looking at the
linguistic behavior of those whose native tongue was some other language. Among the Germans, for example, 72.8 percent speak only
the English official language, whereas 1 percent speak only the French
official language.

At the very least, we can say that there is some form of joint
causality operating such that ethnic origin influences linguistic segregation and, inversely, linguistic ability influences ethnic segregation.
However, from the perspective of the individual it is possible to put
some order into these relationships. Ethnic origin is a status ascribed

at birth—at least in terms of the census definition used in Canada, it
is beyond the capacity of anyone to alter his origin or that of his offspring. Of course, we know enough about racial and ethnic relations
to recognize that most people within the broad category of "white"
could change their identification without detection if they are willing
to conceal enough of their background and the cultural attributes associated with their ethnic group. Linguistic knowledge is somewhat in
a no man's land between being an ascribed or an achieved status. On
the one hand, there is no choice in the language first learned in childhood; it is the tongue used by parents in addressing the child. On the
other hand, there is some option in the languages later acquired volun-
tarily. Moreover, among bilingual parents, there is a choice in the
tongue they can use in speaking to their offspring. In view of the com-
plexities in attributing a causal link, we shall take the view that language and ethnic origin are related and, therefore, determine the
degree each factor can be used to explain the segregation patterns of
the other.

   Linguistic segregation. Shown in row 1 of Table 4 are the
indexes of segregation between each of the four official language speech
groups and the remainder of the population. The monolingual English
speakers and the population unable to speak either official language
are the most highly segregated from others; bilinguals, as might be
expected, are least segregated. Row 2 gives the indexes of dissimilar
ity for linguistic groups "expected" on the basis of the actual ethnic
residential patterns in Montreal and the cross-tabulation between ethnic origin and official language. These figures are based on the Westergaard expected cases method. Knowing the ethnic composition in
each tract and, further, the general association between official language and ethnic origins for the metropolis, the official language distribution in each tract expected on the basis of ethnic origin was deter
mined. The percentage of actual linguistic segregation which can be
explained solely on the basis of ethnic residential patterns (row 3) is
obtained by dividing row 2 by row 1. This ranges from a high of 81
percent for monolingual English speakers to a low of 47 percent for
the segregation of bilinguals. Ethnic residential patterns and the asse
ciation between origin and language fail to explain 19 percent of Englis
monolingual residential patterns, 32 percent of both monolingual Fren
and those speaking no official language, and more than half of the bili
gual pattern. Although ethnic origin is a major influence, it is clear

Table 4. Residential Segregation Between Official Language
Segments and Remainder of the Population, Actual and Expected

Year and Type *1961, Type I*	Segregation from the Remainder of the Population			
	English only	French only	Bilinguals	Neither official language
Actual Segregation Index . . .	53,5	38,0	12,9	54,6
Expected Segregation Index . . .	43,3	25,7	6,1	36,9
Per Cent Explained by Ethnic Segregation	81	68	47	68
Type III				
1961, Per Cent Explained by Ethnic Segregation	80	67	58	70
1951, Per Cent Explained by Ethnic Segregation	83	72	71	71

Note: Expected linguistic segregation index based on the ethnic residential patterns in Montreal and the cross-tabulation between official language and ethnic origin.

that linguistic segregation patterns are more than merely a function of ethnic segregation.

Comparisons are possible between 1951 and 1961 in the degree ethnic segregation explains linguistic segregation only if the analysis is restricted to a smaller segment of the metropolitan area for which the necessary cross-tabulations are available for comparable areas. Comparing rows 3 and 4 we see that the role of ethnic origin has declined very slightly for all but the bilingual population whose current residential pattern is considerably less a function of ethnic origin than it was in 1951 (58 and 71 percent, respectively).

Since the linguistic groups do not simply follow the pattern expected on the basis of ethnic segregation in Montreal, it is of interest to learn where in Montreal they tend to concentrate and what areas are avoided. One way of looking at this problem is to compare each tract's linguistic composition with that expected on the basis of the tract's ethnic composition. The scatter diagram in Figure 1 compares the percentage in each tract able to speak English only with the percentage expected on the basis of ethnic composition. Although a very high correlation exists between the actual and "expected" frequency of English monolinguals, $r = .99$, note how the regression slope exceeds 1 ($b = 1.21$). The solid line in Figure 1 indicates the function which would occur if the actual and expected percentages speaking English only were equal in each tract. Inspection of the scatter diagram shows that in areas where the ethnic composition would lead us to expect to find a small percentage of monolingual English speakers, we usually find even less. By contrast, areas where a sizable proportion of the residents are expected to be English monolinguals tend to have an even larger percentage actually speaking only the English official language. The fact that b is greater than unity means that the variance in the actual degree of monolingual English spoken in the tracts of metropolitan Montreal is explained to a smaller extent by ethnic composition than might be assumed on the basis of the coefficient of correlation. Using a procedure for decomposing the variance in such situations, about 66 percent of the variance in the percentage speaking only English is due to the joint effect of composition with other factors.[10] In short, although ethnic origin explains a large part of the distribution of English-only speakers, there is a strong tendency for English monolinguals to be located away from areas where there are relatively few expected and to concentrate in areas where a particularly large number are expected to begin with.

A similar result is obtained for the actual and expected percentages speaking French only in the tracts of metropolitan Montreal in 1961. Again, where a small percentage of French-only speakers is expected on the basis of ethnic origin, an even smaller percentage is actually found. As before, tracts whose ethnic composition leads to the expectation that a sizable segment of the population will speak French only are areas where even larger proportions are usually monolingual French speakers (Figure 2). Although the correlation is very high, $r = .95$, again the regression slope is far greater than 1, $b = 1.$

Decomposition discloses that the net effect of ethnic composition explains only 45 percent of the variance in the percentages speaking French only in census tracts, while 37 percent of the variance is due to the joint effect of composition with other factors.

There is very little association between composition and the degree of bilingualism; the correlation between actual and expected percent bilingual is only .13. After finding that the percentage speaking English tends to be greater than predicted on the basis of ethnic composition when the expectation is initially high and lower than expected when the prediction is low to begin with, then to some extent the analogous finding for the monolingual French population is not completely independent. That is, in tracts where the English-only speakers exceed the number expected on the basis of composition, then some other linguistic segment must be less than expected. Likewise, if there are fewer monolingual English speakers than expected in some tracts, then the number of at least one other linguistic component must be greater than expected in these tracts. However, the low association between actual and expected bilingualism in Montreal indicates that the findings need not necessarily have been what they were. Moreover, comparisons between the actual and expected percentage of residents speaking French only among those who are not monolingual English speakers, i.e. [(French only) ÷ (French only + bilingual + neither official language)], indicates that this phenomenon occurs even after English monolingual speakers are excluded. For Montreal's 35 wards in 1941, the percentage of French-only speakers among non-English monolinguals exceeds expectation in wards where the prediction is high, but is less than expected when a small percentage of French-only speakers is predicted on the basis of ethnic composition.

There are two interpretations, both plausible, which can be offered for the finding that the actual percentage speaking English only or French only is higher than expected in those parts of the city where the ethnic composition would lead us to expect a high proportion. This may be due to either linguistic differences within each ethnic group in the residential areas they select or it may be a result from linguistic adaptation to the area of residence. It is assumed that such high regression slopes are not due to systematic errors in the enumeration of language and ethnic origin. Also, we recognize that there are

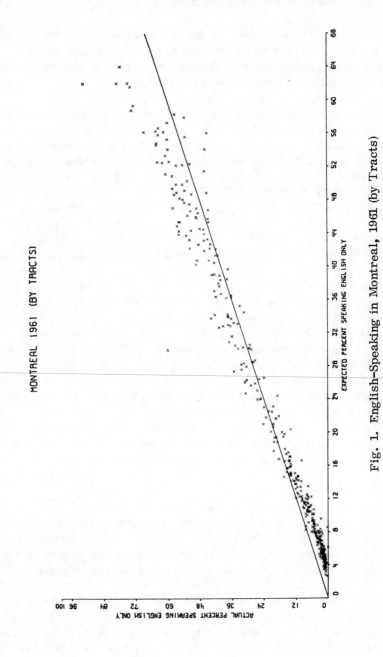

Fig. 1. English-Speaking in Montreal, 1961 (by Tracts)

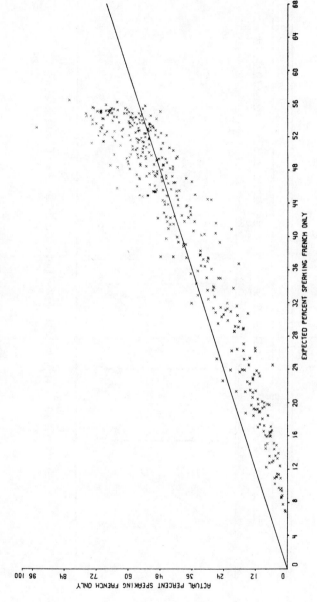

Fig. 2. French-Speaking in Montreal, 1961 (by Tracts)

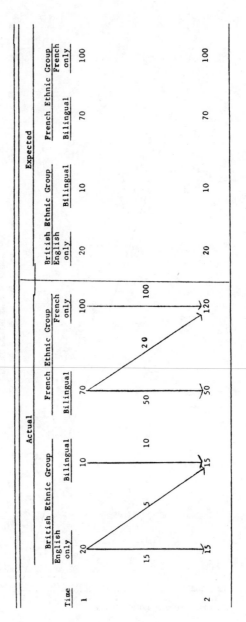

Illustration 1. Hypothetical Shifts Between Linguistic Classes

certain pressures on second-language learning which are independent
of the residential location, particularly the demands of the work world
in Montreal and the fact that both languages are taught in the Protestant
and Roman Catholic school systems.

Following is a simplified illustration of how these findings
may result from a process of adaptation to the neighborhood speech
environment, in other words, second-language learning and forgetting.
In Illustration 1, the actual and expected linguistic composition are
equal at t_1; for example, the number of monolingual English speakers,
20, is the same as the number expected on the basis of the tract's
ethnic composition. Since the hypothetical area is predominantly
French-speaking, some of the monolingual English speakers will
learn French as a second tongue if linguistic adoption occurs. The
arrows show that at a later period, t_2, five English monolinguals have
become bilingual, thus reducing the number who speak English only to
15. Likewise, because of the widespread use of French in the area
and the relatively small number of monolingual English speakers, it
is not unreasonable to expect that some of the bilingual speakers will
forget English if their first language is French. For convenience, it
is assumed that all of the British have an English mother tongue and
all French Canadians are native speakers of French. The diagram
shows a net loss among bilingual French mother tongues of 20 who are
unable to speak English by t_2. Not all French-Canadian bilinguals are
expected to forget English if only because many need this tongue for
occupational purposes. Since there has been no shift in ethnic composition, the number of French-only speakers now exceeds "expectation"
(respectively, 120 and 100) and the number of monolingual English
speakers is below "expectation" at t_2 (15 vs. 20).

Critical to this process is the fact that many Montrealers
acquire at least a smattering of the second official language through
school or elsewhere. Therefore, if they live in a residential area
which supports this second language, they will maintain or improve
their ability. By contrast, if they live in an area in which their native
tongue is more than adequate for communication, then this incipient
bilingualism will not be supported. This, of course, would be the
case for the French Canadians in the area under consideration. In
point of fact, a decline in the degree of bilingualism is found in Montreal beginning with the middle years of life.[11]

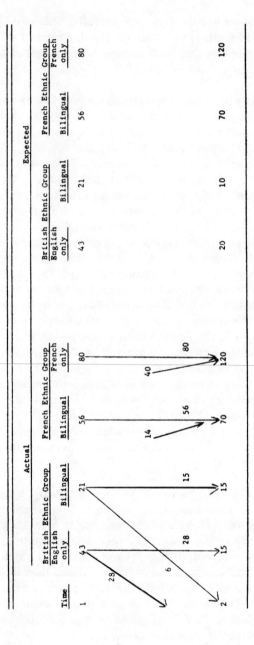

Illustration 2. Hypothetical Differentials in Migration

There is another process based on selective location within the linguistic components of each ethnic group which could yield a similar pattern. As before, in the accompanying illustration, the actual and expected linguistic distributions are equal at t_1. Because French is the dominant tongue in the tract, it is reasonable to assume that some of the monolingual English residents move to a neighborhood which is compatible with their linguistic skills. As shown in Illustration 2, 28 of the English-only speakers move out by t_2. Since bilingual members of the English mother-tongue population will not have as great an impetus to leave, only 6 English mother-tongue bilinguals are shown leaving the area by t_2. The important assumption is that the probability of net outmigration is greater for the monolingual minority than their mother-tongue compatriots who are bilingual. Likewise, it is assumed that the probability of net immigration to the tract is greater for monolingual speakers of the majority tongue than their mother-tongue compatriots who are bilingual. Thus 40 French only and 14 bilinguals have entered the tract at t_2. Since the ethnic composition has changed by the end of this second period, the expected linguistic distribution is also different, but the same excess of French-only speakers and deficit of English-only speakers over that expected is observed as long as there is selective immigration among the native French speakers and selective outmigration among the English mother-tongue population.

Either approach would be adequate if the population whose mother tongue is neither English nor French is included in our approach. In terms of the learning approach, if it is assumed that these "other" speakers learn the dominant tongue of the tracts they are located in, then this will boost the actual percentage speaking the dominant tongue over that expected for the tract. For example, if members of ethnic group X are 60 percent English speakers and 40 percent French speakers, then in a tract which is predominantly French the percentage learning this tongue among X will be greater than the city-wide rate and therefore raise the actual rate over that expected. However, the differential location hypothesis would fit here also; namely, members of ethnic group X might select residential areas in accordance with their linguistic abilities.

Very likely linguistic adaptation to the neighborhood and selective location within ethnic groups both occur. In order to deter-

mine the relative importance of these two forces, longitudinal panel-
type data are necessary so that the linguistic abilities of the population
could be traced before and after residential moves. Since such data
are not available, all that can be done here is to speculate. The most
reasonable interpretation is that monolinguals tend to move to areas
where communication is high, rather than learn a second language in
order to adapt to a different linguistic environment. Although this
means we are inclined to classify the role of second-language learning
due to residential factors as a minor influence, very likely many do
forget what knowledge they possess of a second tongue because of
little usage in their residential area coupled with an absence of occupational demands.

There are several reasons for offering this interpretation.
For one, the relatively low degree of bilingualism among small children suggests that second-language learning as a function of residential contacts is not very great. Second, bilingualism develops primarily in the school-age and early adult years, showing a net decline during most of the adult period.[12] This can be interpreted as reflecting
the primary role of schooling and occupational supports for some bilinguals rather than the influence of neighborhood contacts on the
chances of becoming bilingual. Third, the dual school system of Montreal, whereby the language of instruction is French in the vast majority of Roman Catholic schools and is English in nearly all Protestant
schools, tends to support residential selection along mother-tongue
lines for those whose native tongue is either English or French. If
location near the appropriate school is to be maximized, then there
will be a built-in form of selective residential location. Of course,
with the segregation patterns which presently exist, new schools will
be built in areas with a large concentration of potential students. In
turn, this will further encourage redistribution rather than adaptation
to the linguistic environment. Finally, we shall soon see that ethnic
residential patterns are hardly influenced by the official language
abilities of the groups once mother tongue is taken into account. This
suggests that residential patterns are based on communication in the
native tongue and that the ability to communicate in their residential
areas by means of a second language is not an adequate substitute for
most Montrealers. For these reasons, we are inclined to place primary emphasis on selective movement and redistribution as well as
second-language unlearning as the main forces leading monolingual

English and monolingual French to be concentrated in some parts of
the city to a greater degree than expected on the basis of ethnic composition. The reader should keep in mind that this is more of a spec-
ulation than a conclusion based on empirical examination of the two
alternative interpretations.

Ethnic segregation. Ethnic segregation patterns will be influenced by differences between these groups in their linguistic composition. Shown in row 1 of Table 5 are the indexes of dissimilarity
between each ethnic group and the remaining population of metropolitan Montreal in 1961. It is interesting to note that the variation between ethnic groups in their segregation is relatively low; the highest
index is for the residual "Other Europeans" category, 59.4, and the
lowest is for the German ethnic population, 37.6. The British and
French are both more segregated than all but three of the remaining
ten groups. The high value for "Other Europeans" is probably due to
the inclusion of most Jews in this category in 1961. In 1951, when data
were available separately for the Jewish ethnic group of Montreal, it
is clear that this group was strikingly more segregated than other
groups in the metropolis (their index was 78.6, while the next most
isolated group, the Dutch, had an index of 58.3).

The degree of segregation which could be expected on the
basis of the official language abilities of the ethnic groups is shown
in row 2. In the case of Italians, an index of only 13 would be obtained
if this group were to locate themselves solely on the basis of their linguistic abilities and the overall linguistic pattern of Montreal. Since
their actual index is 51.4, the percentage of Italian ethnic segregation
explained by official language composition is 13.3/51.4 = 26 percent.
Generally, a greater part of northern and western European ethnic
isolation can be explained by their official language composition than
is the case for other ethnic groups. This may be due in part to the
fact that official language data provide no information about the other
tongues which these groups may speak and which can greatly influence
the patterns of ethnic segregation. For example, more than 80 percent of the Italian ethnic group in Montreal have an Italian mother
tongue. Although the Italians rank relatively high in their degree of
bilingualism in both English and French, about 25 percent of the ethnic group speak neither official language. Since they would nearly all
know Italian, it is clear that language data based only on ability to

Table 5. Residential Segregation Between Ethnic Groups and Remainder of the Population, Actual and Expected

Year and Type	ETHNIC GROUPS												
	British	French	German	Italian	Jewish	Netherlands	Polish	Russian	Scandinavian	Ukrainian	Other Europe	Asian	Other and Not Stated
1961, Type I													
Actual Segregation Index	49,9	49,7	37,6	51,4	NA	45,9	42,2	58,5	43,1	46,3	59,4	43,8	49,2
Expected Segregation Index	35,0	35,9	27,7	13,3	NA	28,1	23,8	23,2	27,3	22,8	24,4	20,0	27,3
Per Cent Explained by Official Language Segregation	70	72	74	26	NA	61	56	40	63	49	41	46	55
Type III													
Actual Segregation Index, 1961	47,3	51,4	44,9	49,5	NA	48,6	45,5	60,1	40,0	48,1	63,2	42,5	49,3
Per Cent Explained by Official Language Segregation, 1961	72	70	65	26	NA	57	58	43	66	52	44	53	55
Actual Segregation Index, 1951	49,3	53,5	44,4	45,7	78,6	58,3	47,8	57,0	50,3	56,5	39,2	42,1	52,1
Per Cent Explained by Official Language Segregation, 1951	73	74	59	13	36	48	53	44	58	48	57	43	34

Note: Expected ethnic segregation index based on the official language residential patterns in Montreal and the cross-tabulation between official language and ethnic origin.

speak the official tongues of Canada are inadequate for interpreting Italian ethnic isolation.

Not only are the northwestern European groups less segregated than other ethnic populations in Montreal, but row 3 shows that a larger part of their segregation can be interpreted as simply a function of official language composition. Although linguistic factors account for more of northwestern European segregation, it should be kept in mind that at best 74 percent of an ethnic group's isolation (the Germans) can be accounted for in terms of linguistic differences.

Overall, there has been some decline during the past decade in the residential segregation of ethnic groups in Montreal (compare rows 4 and 6 of Table 5). Excluding the "Other Europeans" category owing to lack of comparability between the decades, seven groups registered declines and four increased during the ten years. The Dutch, Scandinavian, and Ukrainian groups showed fairly sharp drops for such a short period, while all of the increases were relatively small. Even more significant, in all but three cases the percentage of ethnic isolation accounted for by linguistic differences between the groups rose in the decade; for example, the degree of Polish segregation explained by official language composition increased from 53 to 58 percent (compare rows 5 and 7). These results suggest a long-run trend toward less ethnic isolation in Montreal and, moreover, a larger part being due to linguistic differences between the groups.

Of particular importance, however, are the segregation patterns of the British and French ethnic groups between 1951 and 1961. In both instances, there was a small decline in their segregation, although the degree their isolation is accounted for by linguistic composition also declined. It is difficult to project long-run trends on the basis of two points of time, particularly when they are ten years apart, but what evidence we have suggests that these two ethnic groups may well take an extremely long time in reducing their isolation.

In examining the influence of language on segregation between ethnic groups, it is important to remember that there are two linguistic dimensions which are relevant; ethnic groups may differ in their mother tongues as well as their current abilities in the official languages of Canada. Indeed, mother tongue reflects a linguistic aspect which is more akin to what is customarily meant by "ethnic origin" than does official language. Tabulations for the 35 wards of Montreal in 1941 provide an excellent opportunity to examine the influence of language on ethnic segregation, since data are available on both the mother tongue and official language composition of each ward. By contrast, the mother-tongue composition of tracts are not available in either 1951 or 1961.

The segregation between each of 11 specified ethnic groups was computed for 1941, generating a matrix of 55 indexes of inter-ethnic segregation. Combining the cross-tabulation between mother tongue and ethnic origin for the city of Montreal with the mother-tongue residential patterns in the wards, the relationship between actual segregation between ethnic groups and the indexes expected on the basis of mother-tongue composition of the groups can be determined. The effect of official language on ethnic residence was examined in similar fashion.

Ethnic mother-tongue composition goes a lot further in explaining the segregation patterns between ethnic groups than do inter-ethnic differences in official language composition. The product-moment correlations between actual inter-ethnic segregation and the indexes expected on the basis of mother and official language are, respectively, .93 and .17. Not only is the association much greater, but generally the indexes of segregation expected on the basis of mother tongue are far closer to the actual segregation between ethnic groups than are the indexes expected on the basis of official language composition. The average difference between the actual segregation indexes for ethnic groups and those predicted by mother tongue is 9.2; whereas the mean difference between actual segregation and the indexes predicted on the basis of official language composition is 37.0

Computation of the patterns of ethnic segregation expected on the basis of their official language composition is an unfair test in the sense that it ignores the fact that communication is possible between bilinguals and either French or English monolingual speakers. Since monolinguals and the bilingual population have different spatial distributions in the city, examination of inter-ethnic segregation in terms of the patterns expected on the basis of official language ignore the communication potential which may exist between members of two different ethnic groups. In other words, two ethnic groups can be highly dissimilar from one another in their official language composition, but have a high degree of potential communication. Accordingly, two additional measures were computed: H_b, which gives the probability of mutual intelligibility in one or both official languages when members of two ethnic groups are randomly paired together; and A_b, which gives the probability that randomly selected members of the two ethnic groups will share a common mother tongue.[13]

Again residential segregation between ethnic groups is influenced by mother-tongue similarities to a far greater degree than by potential communication in an official language. The correlation between inter-ethnic segregation (in logarithms) and A_b is -.84. By contrast, the correlation between segregation (also expressed in logarithms) and H_b is only -.39, with 16 percent of the variance explained. The partial correlations show no association between segregation and official language after mother tongue is taken into account, partial r = -.04; whereas the partial correlation between segregation and mother tongue is -.81 after taking official language communication into account.

Much of the variation in residential segregation between ethnic groups can be accounted for in terms of their mother-tongue composition whereas the independent effect of official language is nil. This suggests that the way peoples start out linguistically will greatly influence their propensities to locate near one another later, but languages acquired later in life will have little influence on ethnic segregation patterns. These findings are supported by the fact that early learning of a language is critical for most persons in determining their fluency and ability in the tongue. In terms of informal social contacts such as are likely to arise in neighborhood settings, the mother-tongue similarities between ethnic groups are of considerable importance. These results tend to support the earlier contention that linguistic groups tend to avoid each other rather than be modified by proximity to others. Later language learning plays only a minor role at best in influencing ethnic segregation patterns. Thus, in a city where a sizable part of the population learns a second language, this has little bearing on ethnic residential distributions. What is crucial is the language the child first learns, not languages learned later. There is an ecological counterpart here to the demographic fact that

most French-Canadian children start with the French mother tongue
and most children of British origin start with the English mother
tongue. Even though many later acquire a knowledge of the second
official language, these findings suggest that this has little impact on
their residential segregation and, further, very likely the groups continue to live apart.

Linguistic Diversity

        In Montreal, where every ethnic group is linguistically
diverse and, likewise, each linguistic group consists of several ethnic components, the potential importance of language for the disintegration of ethnic unity is enormous. If the segments of an ethnic
group who acquire a second tongue tend to drift away from their ethnic
compatriots who remain monolingual, then the group's basic strength
can be seriously undermined—particularly when a large number become bilingual. If ethnic assimilation occurs because of linguistic
changes, then very likely greater pressure will exist on the remaining monolingual members since their group's basic position in the
community will be weakened because of the numerical decline. Using
special tabulations run for the Royal Commission on the census tract
distributions of the various linguistic segments of each ethnic group
in metropolitan Montreal in 1961, it is possible to examine directly
the segregation patterns among the linguistic subgroups of the two
major ethnic populations. Thus we can directly test our previous
inferences about the effect of bilingualism on ethnic segregation.

        The main linguistic segments of both the British and French
ethnic groups consist of those who speak only their group's native
tongue and those who are bilingual. While it is clear that acquisition
of the second official language influences the residential pattern, the
bilinguals of each ethnic group still favor their own ethnic compatriot
over the other ethnic group. For example, the segregation index between the bilingual and English-only components of the British ethnic
group is 19.3. While this is by no means trivial, British bilinguals a:
much more highly segregated from the French ethnic population. For
example, their index of segregation from French-Canadian bilinguals
is 43.7 and from monolingual French speakers among French Canadi:
it is 55.6. To be sure, monolingual English-speaking members of th

British ethnic group are even more segregated from these components
of the French-Canadian population, respectively 59.2 and 70.3. Although it is very clear that linguistic ability modifies ethnic isolation,
for example, bilingual members of the British ethnic group are less
isolated than are their monolingual English compatriots from the
French ethnic population, the fact remains that bilingual British
Canadians are much less segregated from ethnic compatriots who
speak only English.

Likewise, although bilingualism affects the residential pattern of French Canadians, they are still closer to their monolingual
French compatriots than they are to various British segments in
Montreal. For example, French bilinguals have a segregation index
of 18.7 from monolingual French compatriots, but their segregation
from the British runs from 43.7 (British bilinguals) and higher.
Again, French Canadians who speak only French are even more highly
isolated from these components of the British group.

In short, the bilinguals of both the French and British populations are much less segregated from their ethnic compatriots with
the same mother tongue than they are from other major ethnic groups.
Thus, while bilingualism is related to the residential patterns among
both ethnic populations, the paramount factor influencing location is
still proximity to ethnic compatriots. Accordingly, knowledge of the
other ethnic group's tongue does not lead to a grand exodus of bilinguals
into the camp of their ethnic rivals. This is of great importance since
it indicates an ecological mechanism which allows both the British and
French to maintain their mother tongue among the new generation of
offspring. Although there is considerable bilingualism among both
groups and therefore an "exposure to risk" that the acquired tongue
may be passed on as the next generation's first language, the fact that
bilinguals in each ethnic group tend to locate in areas where their
monolingual compatriots are found tends to reduce this danger to the
mother tongue.

Members of the British ethnic group who are monolingual
French speakers and French Canadians who are able to speak only the
English official language are both in rather anomalous positions since
they do not share the predominant mother tongue of their ethnic compatriots, but instead are able to speak only the native language of

their ethnic rivals. Whether the product of ethnic intermarriage or assimilation into the other ethnic group, these people are essentially lost to the other ethnic group. They are much closer in residence to the other ethnic group than they are to their own ethnic compatriots. For example, French Canadians who speak English only have segregation indexes of 51.8 and 63.1, respectively, from French-Canadian bilinguals and monolingual French speakers. By contrast, their index of segregation from the British population is only 24.8. Similar results are obtained for British Canadians who speak only French; their index from other British Canadians who are bilingual is 60.3 and from British who speak only English is 71.8. By contrast, the index of segregation between French Canadians and the monolingual French component of the British ethnic group is 36.6.

Comment

If it is assumed that residential integration is an essential prerequisite to ethnic fusion and linguistic homogeneity, then the basic implication of this study is that the diversity of Montreal is destined to remain rather high in the foreseeable future. Although some decline is noted in segregation in the past decade, the maintenance of high British-French isolation on both linguistic and ethnic lines indicates not only that the main elements in Montreal will continue to go their separate ways, socially speaking, but that other linguistic and ethnic components will be forced to choose between one group or the other. Younge's observation of the two paths which other ethnic groups may take in Montreal, although made two decades ago, still applies to the current situation.[14]

Residential segregation and bilingualism are alternative means for adapting to a situation of linguistic diversity. Segregation helps to protect a group from dissolution since contact with others is reduced; bilingualism provides a potential mechanism for the loss of linguistic distinctiveness since the members may opt to pass on the learned language to their children rather than the mother tongue. For the British and French bilinguals, the finding that they still tend to reside much closer to monolingual ethnic compatriots than to the competing ethnic group suggests that there are ecological reasons for the failure of bilingualism thus far to undercut the linguistic maintenance of these two groups.

Ethnic and linguistic segregation tend to reinforce each other in the sense that the ethnic groups differ in their linguistic composition and, likewise, the linguistic groups differ from one another in their ethnic makeup. However, it should be noted that ethnic segregation is not explained solely as a function of the linguistic differences between the groups. This is to be expected since patterns of ethnic segregation are found in many cities where linguistic differences have disappeared. Nevertheless, as some of the findings reported earlier indicate, ethnic segregation is no doubt greatly increased because of the linguistic differences accompanying these groups. Likewise, although differences in ethnic composition tend to explain a fair part of the linguistic segregation found in Montreal, our analysis showed rather clearly a tendency for language groups to concentrate among themselves to a greater extent than can be explained solely by ethnic factors. The fact that people speaking different tongues tend to avoid each other helps to reduce the degree of bilingualism necessary since residential areas have higher rates of mutual intelligibility among residents than would occur if there was no segregation in Montreal.

Linguistic characteristics are but one part of the complex which comprises an ethnic group, but insofar as the ethnic groups are able to maintain their distinctive languages, then this will retard assimilation between the British and French on other dimensions as well. And insofar as the groups remain highly segregated from one another, it is unlikely that any linguistic fusion between the groups will occur.

NOTES

This study was supported by the National Science Foundation Grant No. GS-394 and by the Royal Commission on Bilingualism and Biculturalism. The assistance of Leslie G. Ibach, Deborah E. Kuhn, David Sorenson, and Patricia G. Thompson is gratefully acknowledged.

[1] Otis Dudley Duncan and Stanley Lieberson, "Ethnic Segregation and Assimilation," American Journal of Sociology 64 (Jan. 1959): 364-74; Stanley Lieberson, "The Impact of Residential Segregation on Ethnic Assimilation," Social Forces 40 (Oct. 1961): 52-57.

[2] Dominion Bureau of Statistics, Census of Canada, 1961, "Population and Housing Characteristics by Census Tracts, Montreal," Bull. CT-4 (Ottawa: Minister of Trade and Commerce, 1963), p. 3.

[3] See Otis Dudley Duncan and Beverly Duncan, "Residential Distribution and Occupational Stratification," American Journal of Sociology 60 (March 1955): 493-95.

[4] A more elegant interpretation of the index of dissimilarity is possible based on the number of each group who would have to redistribute themselves.

[5] Joseph H. Greenberg, "The Measure of Linguistic Diversity," Language 32 (Jan.-March 1956): 109-15.

[6] Stanley Lieberson, "An Extension of Greenberg's Measures of Linguistic Diversity," Language 40 (Oct.-Dec. 1964): 526-31.

[7] Ibid.

[8] Stanley Lieberson, Ethnic Patterns in American Cities (New York: Free Press of Glencoe, 1963), pp. 38-40.

[9] Ibid., chap. iii.

[10] Otis Dudley Duncan, Ray P. Cuzzort, and Beverly Duncan, Statistical Geography (Glencoe, Ill.: The Free Press, 1961), pp. 118-28; Patricia Hodge and Robert W. Hodge, "Regression Analysis of Standardized Proportions," unpublished manuscript.

[11] Stanley Lieberson, "Bilingualism in Montreal: A Demographic Analysis," American Journal of Sociology 71 (July 1965): 10-25.

[12] For data on age at which bilingualism occurs, see ibid.

[13] For convenience in presentation and comparison, the A_b index was reversed from its normal computation so as to make 1.0 equal to mother-tongue similarity and equal to no overlap between two groups in their mother-tongue composition. It should also be noted that the "other mother tongue" category was not used in cross-multiplication; that is, it was assumed that the population speaking an "other" mother tongue in one group could not speak to the population with "other" mother tongue in another group. Undoubtedly this yielded some errors; however, they are likely to be slight since most ethnic groups have very low percentages in the residual mother-tongue category. Exceptions are the Dutch and Scandinavian groups. Since the mother tongues of these groups were not specified, it was assumed that speakers in these groups who were classified in the "other" mother-tongue category spoke the groups' native language.

[14] Eva R. Younge, "Population Movements and the Assimilation of Alien Groups in Canada," Canadian Journal of Economics and Political Science 10 (Aug. 1944): 372-80.

12 | Domains of Language Usage and Mother-Tongue Shift in Nairobi

In Collaboration with Edward J. McCabe

There are two fundamental issues that must be resolved in order to understand intergenerational mother-tongue shift in multilingual societies. Since there will be no shift between parent and child without bilingualism among the former, the first issue is to understand the forces generating bilingualism. If by "mother-tongue shift" is meant that the first language learned by a child is different from the first language learned by its parent, then shift will not normally occur among the children of monolingual parents. The second major issue pertains to the forces affecting the language that bilinguals pass on to their children. It is clear that bilingualism per se need not generate shift since bilingual parents may still use their mother tongue exclusively in addressing their children. Shift between generations is sometimes very slight even in settings where a substantial portion of a mother-tongue group acquires a second language. This is precisely the case in Montreal, for example, where a sizable part of the French mother-tongue population learned English through the years, but where there is little shift because the overwhelming majority of French bilinguals still address their offspring in French (Lieberson 1965).

Dealing with the latter question, the language transferred by bilinguals, there are a variety of factors which affect the propensity of bilingual parents to pass on their own mother tongue to their offspring. Among these are: population composition, government pressure, languages available for schooling, degree of fluency in the second language, intermarriage between mother-tongue groups (see Lieberson 1970). In a number of important statements, Fishman has suggested that one of the factors affecting language shift is the domains or social settings in which a bilingual uses one or both languages (see, for example, the papers in Fishman 1972). Persons knowing one or more

additional languages besides their mother tongue need not necessarily
use all of these tongues in each social setting. Indeed such a uniform
usage is rather unlikely. The potential of analyzing linguistic behavior in terms of domains is both great and complex since there are a
wide variety of social settings as well as such issues as the language
used by subjects for thinking for various settings and functions.

     For a sample of the Gujarati mother-tongue population of
Nairobi in 1964 this paper explores the relation between linguistic
usage in various domains and the presence or absence of mother-
tongue shift. A secondary goal, based on data for a wide variety of
mother-tongue groups in the city, is determination of the degree of
bilingualism in each domain and the consistency of language choice
in these settings.

     The capital and largest city of Kenya, Nairobi was an excel-
lent setting in 1964 for an examination of mother-tongue shift and linguistic usage by domains. According to the 1962 Census, 41 percent
of the 267,000 residents were non-Africans; this includes 86,000
Asians (largely originating from India prior to its partition), 21,000
Europeans, 1,000 Arabs, and 1,600 others.[1] The Asians themselves
consist of various linguistic and religious elements; among the latter
there are 46,000 Hindus, 16,000 Moslems, 14,000 Sikhs, and 10,000
Christians. The Europeans are largely British, with small numbers
of Italians, Americans, and others present. The African population
of Kenya is quite diverse linguistically, with about one-third speaking
various non-Bantu tongues in 1962 and a number of Bantu languages
represented among the remaining two-thirds (Molnos 1969: 10). Three
of the four largest African mother tongues in Nairobi are Bantu:
Kikuyu, 66,000; Luyia, 26,000; and Kamba, 24,000. The exception
is Luo, with 25,000 members of this non-Bantu language represented
in the city.

     The project is possible only through the enormous generosity
and ingenuity of Dr. J. C. Sharman. In May and June of 1964, he conducted a language survey of students in nine of Nairobi's secondary
schools. The schools were selected not with the impossible goal of
obtaining a representative sample of all residents of the city, but in
order to assure that all of the various mother-tongue groups would
be represented. Each student given a questionnaire was asked to take

it home and obtain from each parent the following information:
mother tongue, occupation, age, and the language(s) normally used
by their father and mother when talking to the following groups of
people:

1. Other grown-ups in your family
2. Children in your family
3. African friends
4. Asian friends
5. European friends
6. At work, to the boss or seniors
7. At work, to equals
8. At work, to juniors
9. To servants, ayahs
10. African shopkeepers or assistants
11. Asian shopkeepers or assistants
12. European shopkeepers or assistants
13. At the market
14. Doctor/hospital

And

15. If they go to religious services, what language(s) are
    used there?
16. If they listen to the radio or watch television, what lan-
    guage(s) do they prefer to listen to?

In effect, the study uses pupils in secondary schools to survey the
languages used by their parents. It is an extremely economical device for estimating linguistic patterns by domains. However, the
coding of such a large number of domains separately for each parent
and the enormous variety of language choices and combinations reported meant that codification and processing of the data would entail
resources beyond those available to the Kenya Language Group.
Accordingly, thanks to the efforts of Dr. Clifford H. Prator and Dr.
Charles A. Ferguson, the senior author received the raw questionnaires several years after the survey had been conducted.

Before turning to the analysis, it is best to recognize certain
limitations in the data. In addition to the normal response problems
faced in a sociolinguistic survey, the sample derived from questionnaires administered by schoolchildren is distorted by linguistic group
and almost certainly by socioeconomic status as well. The European

Table 1. Comparison Between Census and Survey Population
of Nairobi

Ethno-linguistic group	Percent distribution	
	Survey, 1964	Census, 1962
Arabic.	.2	.4
English	19.0	7.3
Other European	2.7	.7
Gujarati.	28.2	
Hindi	4.4	
Konkani	3.5 \} 46.9	\} 32.4
Punjabi	10.8	
Kamba	0.8	8.9
Kikuyu	20.1	24.6
Luyia	2.5	9.9
Luo	3.4	9.3
Swahili	.8	.1
Other African	1.5	5.8
Other n.e.c.	2.0	.6
Total.	99.9	100.0

Note: Europeans of British, American, South African, and Irish nationality
in the Census are arbitrarily listed here as having English mother tongue.
Others n.e.c. for the Census refers to non-Africans.

and Asian groups are overrepresented in the survey at the expense
of the African population of Nairobi. More than a fifth of the sample
have European mother tongues (19.0 percent English and 2.7 percent
other European). By contrast, only about 8 percent of Nairobi's population in the 1962 Census had English or other European mother
tongues (see Table 1). Whereas nearly half of the sample population
had an Asian mother tongue (Gujarati, Hindi, Punjabi, or Konkani),
only about one-third of the census population were reported as Asian.[3]
Except for Swahili, the African groups are all underrepresented in
varying degrees. Were age adjustments made to deal only with the
adult population, the underenumeration of Africans in the survey would
be even greater since they amount to 62.5 percent of the adult population in the 1962 Census but only 29 percent of the survey population.
Even without considering economic factors, it is clear that the survey
cannot be taken as representative of the actual frequency of linguistic
choices in each domain for the entire population of Nairobi.

Language Shift

Table 2 indicates the degree of intergenerational language maintenance for each of ten specific mother-tongue groups. The strongest language is English, where 97.9 percent of the adults with this mother tongue address their children exclusively in the same language. Konkani is the weakest of the ten languages, with barely more than 10 percent of the adult mother-tongue population using only that language to speak to their offspring. Two qualifications are in order: first, we have a distorted sample and hence these shift data need not represent the behavior of the entire mother-tongue group in Nairobi; second, shift in Nairobi is more subtle than an all-or-nothing event. Many of the parents who do not use their native tongue exclusively in addressing their children instead use some other language as well as their native tongue (see the second column of Table 2). Very likely this latter condition leads to an intergenerational weakening of the mother tongue which ultimately may generate a complete shift. For example, if Konkani parents only use Konkani in speaking to their children, then no shift has occurred between the two generations. If only English is used by such parents, then a clear case of shift is observed by the generations. An ambiguous situation exists if both Konkani and English are used by the parents, but it is likely that the

Table 2. Language Usage with Children by Mother Tongue of Parent

Mother tongue	Percent of parents using their own mother tongue	
	Exclusively	With another language
English	97.9	2.1
Kikuyu	88.4	8.8
Luo	83.9	10.8
Kamba	82.6	8.7
Punjabi	75.7	17.7
Luyia	75.4	15.9
Gujarati	58.4	24.2
Swahili	56.5	8.7
Hindi	43.6	24.8
Konkani	11.2	13.3

following generation will themselves be more susceptible to shift because of dual language usage.

It is important to recognize the implications of this finding that a substantial number of parents use some other language as well as their mother tongue in speaking to their children. First, it suggests that the standard definition of mother tongue, the language first learned in childhood, may be grossly inappropriate for some sociolinguistic settings. For a substantial number of children in Nairobi there may well be no single language first learned in childhood, but rather two or even more languages. To be sure, multiple mother tongues are nothing new to linguists who cite cases of children addressed by their father in one language and by their mother in another. But the Nairobi results suggest a far more widespread pattern in which one or both parents each use two languages. Moreover, if this is borne out by observation of parental practices, the next issue may well be the domains of language usage by bilingual parents in addressing their children. Caution is in order, however, since we only know about parental practices toward their children generally and not about their practices in the first few years of childhood when the mother tongue is normally maintained. The second implication is that shift from language X to language Y may well involve an intermediary step where a generation is raised comfortable in both languages. Under such circumstances the shift may occur in several steps. First an X mother-tongue person acquires Y as a second language. Their children are raised in both X and Y. In turn, the offspring of parents with dual mother tongues may be raised exclusively or primarily in Y.

Mother-Tongue Shift and Language Usage by Domains

In determining the linkage between language usage by domain and mother-tongue shift, we shall examine the patterns just for the Gujarati group. Although there are other language groups with radically different rates of intergenerational shift, only the Gujarati mother tongue population provides a sufficiently large number of cases of shift, non-shift, and partial shift. There are 456 parents who address their children in Gujarati only, 186 who address their children in both Gujarati and English, and 129 who use only English in speaking to their children. The use of other language combinations among Gujarati parents

Table 3. Language Used with Children Tabulated by Language
Used with Other Adults in the Family

Language with adults	Number	Percent distribution: Language used with children			
		Gujarati only	English and Gujarati	English only	Total
Gujarati only	557	59.4	22.4	18.1	99.9
English and Gujarati .	87	28.7	57.5	13.8	100.0
English only	23	34.8	26.1	39.1	100.0

Note: Language usage not shown for seven adults not reporting and six adults who use both Gujarati and some other tongue in speaking to adults in the family.

is essentially nil, with 19 of the remaining 24 parents not reporting their language usage with children.

A further step was taken before turning to the analysis. Namely, it is important to eliminate parents who are simply unable to speak English and deal only with those who by choice use Gujarati in speaking to their children. In other words, we want to concentrate on language choice among those exposed to the risk of shift. Accordingly, the 456 parents using only Gujarati in talking to their children were reduced to the 365 who do indicate English usage in one or more of the domains covered in the questionnaire. Thus the analysis is confined to the linkage between language usage in each domain and mother-tongue shift among those Gujarati residents who are able to speak English in addition to their mother tongue.

Is language usage in a given domain related to the languages passed on to children in any systematic manner? This is precisely the case in the domain shown in Table 3, conversation by parents with other grown-ups in the family. Since there are only six people using a combination of Gujarati and some other language in this domain, we need only concern ourselves with the differences between three choices. Looking down the first column of Table 3, the highest mother-tongue retention rate is for those just using Gujarati in this domain (59.4 percent), with rates considerably lower for those using English only 34.8 percent or a combination of English and Gujarati

(28.7 percent). In similar fashion, the probability of using both
Gujarati and English with the children is highest for those adults
using both tongues in this domain (57.5 percent) and much lower for
other speakers. Likewise, whereas 39.1 percent of those Gujarati
who employ English only in this domain also just use that tongue with
their children, much smaller rates exist for the other speakers in
this domain.

Were the linguistic situation in each domain to just involve
choices between Gujarati, English, or a combination of the two languages, then the task would be simple. One would expect the greatest
degree of shift for those just using English only, the least for those
just using their mother tongue, and an intermediate level for those
using both languages. However, the situation is far more complex in
other domains. Consider, for example, the languages employed by
the Gujarati group in a medical situation. Again, one finds the three
simple patterns of Gujarati only, English only, and the two languages
combined. But there are also 44 persons who use a combination of
English, Gujarati, and one or more other tongues; there are 45 who
use English and one or more other tongues; 28 who use Gujarati with
at least one other tongue; and 16 who use neither Gujarati nor English
in this domain. Accordingly, the various language-usage combinations
in each domain were scaled in the following manner (in order of an
assumed scale of favoritism between Gujarati and English):

> Gujarati only
> Gujarati and other
> ⎧ Gujarati and English and other
> ⎨ Gujarati and English
> ⎩ Other
> English and other
> English only

Operating with these five different levels of linguistic preference, how closely associated is linguistic shift in each domain?
Using the statistic proposed by Goodman and Kruskal to measure
ordinal association, gamma, the linkage between linguistic usage and
mother-tongue shift is examined in each domain (reported in the first
colume of Table 4). There is considerable difference between domair
in the association between linguistic usage and shift. The association
between language usage and degree of language shift tends to be rela-

Table 4. Gammas Between Language Usage with Children
and Language Used in Different Domains

Domain	Gammas	
	First ordering	Second ordering
Adults in family	.37	.28
African friends	.09	.10
Asian friends	−.15	.41
European friends.	.42	.38
Seniors at work.	.47	.22
Equals at work	.34	.33
Juniors at work.	.39	.06
Servants.	.12	−.18
African shops	.11	.11
Asian shops	.11	.35
European shops.	.54	.54
Market	.25	.23
Hospital-doctor.	.39	.13
Religion.	−.17	.23
Radio-television	.35	.31

tively high in such domains as European shops (where gamma is .54),
in talking to seniors at work (.47), conversations with European
friends (.42), the doctor-hospital setting (.39), and juniors at work
(.39). Surprisingly the gamma between the language used by parents
in talking to other adults in the family and the language they use with
children is not as strong, .36, albeit in the expected direction. In
the case of two domains, Asian friends and religious settings, if anything, there is a negative association between our language scale and
the language passed on to children (more about this later). In any
case, the association is rather weak and this is likewise true for a
number of other domains such as language choice with African friends,
servants, African shops, and Asian shops.

If the readers find some of these patterns mystifying, they
are not alone. On the one hand, linguistic usage in a socially casual
setting such as shops might be expected to be less closely associated
with language shift among children than the more intense relations
with other adults at home. Although this would account for the low
gammas in both the African and Asian shop domains, the fact remains

that the European shop gamma is the highest of all reported in the
first column of Table 4. The ordering of linguistic favoritism employed to generate the gammas in the first column seems to have
little association with shift in the case of either African or Asian
friends and shops, but does for Europeans. Likewise language choice
with servants is of no consequence, but this is not the case for juniors
at work.

It follows from these results that perhaps the ordering of
language usage in terms of a scale of favoritism between English and
Gujarati is incorrect. Accordingly, we approached the problem empirically. Comparing each and every combination of language usage
with every other combination, we determined the relative advantage
each has in favoring Gujarati maintenance. For example, there are
12 domains in which speakers of Gujarati only and speakers of a combination of English and Other are found. In 10/12 of these, or 83 percent, the former have a higher rate of Gujarati maintenance, that is
in terms of the percentage who use just Gujarati in speaking to their
children. Applying such comparisons to each and every language
usage combination, an ordering of Gujarati favoritism may be empirically determined. The results, listed below in order of decreasing
maintenance of Gujarati, are different from our initial expectations:

Other
Gujarati and other
Gujarati only
English and other
⎧English and Gujarati and other
⎨English only
⎩English and Gujarati

The most striking finding here is that the language usage pattern in various domains that most favors intergenerational Gujarati
maintenance is the exclusive usage of some other tongue(s). In each
domain, people in this class on the average have higher rates of Gujarati maintenance than any other usage group. Working with this empirically determined ordering, the gammas were again computed for
each domain (shown in the second column of Table 4). The results
are rather interesting and complex. In some domains there is still
no substantial linkage between language usage and mother-tongue shift.
This is the case for African friends and shops. In other domains, the
gammas are roughly the same with either ordering, for example,

European friends, equals at work, the market, and radio-television. However, in some domains the results are radically different. The gamma for Asian shops changes from -.15 in the first ordering to .41 in the second ordering. A similar change is observed for Asian shops, from .11 to .35.

Theoretical Implications

Before developing a set of propositions suggested by these patterns, the reader should be reminded that their validity cannot be determined until more data are gathered on various multilingual situations. Moreover, we are only reporting associations between intergenerational shift and language usage—no direct causal linkage has been demonstrated. A definitive statement will be possible only after the detailed linguistic analysis of domains suggested by Fishman becomes widespread. However, we believe that the propositions below help account for what would otherwise appear to be anomalous results for at least the Nairobi setting.

1. Domains vary in the importance of language usage for intergenerational shift. This is true no matter how the language-usage patterns are ordered along a stability-shift continuum. Linguistic usage with African friends has relatively little bearing on mother-tongue shift no matter how the patterns are ordered. The percentage passing on just Gujarati to their children varies from 45.7 (for the 247 respondents using both English and other tongues in talking to African friends) to 59.1 for the 318 only using other tongue(s). The speakers of just English occupy an intermediate position with 54.1 percent.[3]

Thus the usage patterns in the African friend domain range only from 45.7 to 59.1 percent Gujarati retention. Compare this with the range in the domain for Asian friends. Just looking at the same three usage categories, the retention of Gujarati varies from 24.5 percent (for the 159 English-Gujarati combination users) to 94.3 percent (for the 141 people who use only other tongues in this domain).[4] The gap between English only and other speakers in this domain is nearly 40 percent, whereas it is just 5 percent in the African friends domain.

2. The linkage between intergenerational mother-tongue retention and usage of a given language (or combination) varies between domains. If the first proposition is generally true, then it follows that usage of a given language will vary between domains in its effect on shift. Among those using Gujarati only in Asian shops or in conversation with Asian friends, respectively 55 and 51 percent pass on Gujarati only to their children. By contrast, about 80 percent use this language exclusively with their children if they speak Gujarati only with either seniors or juniors at work. What we witness here is a variation between domains in the intergenerational consequences stemming from use of a given language. This in part reflects the linguistic structure of the domain. In a setting where a given language is commonly used by many people, following that norm will have a less distinctive consequence for shift than will a setting where the linguistic norms are different or where a greater diversity of linguistic usages is found. In the case of Asian shops and Asian friends, linguistic patterns commonly involve the use of Gujarati (alone or in combination); at work it is less common to use Gujarati.

3. The failure to use one's own mother tongue poses no danger for mother-tongue shift in some domains but does in others. This proposition is basically illustrated by the data just cited above. In the case of conversations with Asian friends, for example, intergenerational retention is 94.3 percent for the 141 adults who use some other tongue in this domain and do not use Gujarati. This is a higher level of retention than the 51.0 percent for those who use Gujarati only. By contrast, one need just look at Table 3 to see that in another domain the absence of Gujarati usage is strongly associated with mother-tongue shift.

4. Finally, there are a number of domains in which the rate of intergenerational mother-tongue maintenance is higher for those speakers of some other tongue than for those using only Gujarati. This runs totally against "common sense," but is borne out by the empirical results obtained in the Nairobi study where the employment of other languages in some domains is less of a threat to shift than is the usage of Gujarati. This is illustrated in the case cited above involving conversations with Asian friends as well as in a number of other domains. For example, those using Gujarati only in Asian shops have a lower level of intergenerational mother-tongue reten-

tion than those using both Gujarati and another tongue (55.2 vs. 78.7 percent). Supporting this assertion are the empirical comparisons reported in the text in terms of the relative advantages each language usage pattern has over every other specific one. The ordering of language usage patterns in terms of the degree of Gujarati retention was different from that initially expected.

In summary, the analysis of Gujarati mother-tongue maintenance in Nairobi supports the assertion of Fishman that domains are a powerful tool for analyzing language usage and language shift. Our empirical results indicate that language usage in some domains is closely linked to mother-tongue maintenance, but has relatively little bearing in other domains on the next generation. Likewise, we also find that both the absolute and relative consequence of a language usage pattern for intergenerational shift varies enormously between domains.

A second major point that will require further attention in the future is the intermediate form of mother-tongue shift. Among the Gujarati population of Nairobi there were more children whose parents spoke both their ancestral tongue and English to them than were addressed exclusively in English. In other words, much of the shift that occurs in this specific setting occurs through the introduction of both languages. Prior to this finding, we had tended to view the language first spoken to a child as largely being a case of one tongue or another. This is, of course, the common procedure—witness the usual census or demographic definition of mother tongue. Indeed, this may still be the case in most multilingual settings. However, judging by the frequency with which children report their Gujarati parents using both English and Gujarati in talking to them, this assumption may be false. Of course, we have to learn more about the actual speech patterns of parents toward their children during infancy since this may be quite different from what occurs after the offspring are older. At the very least, the use of more than one language in addressing children suggests another mechanism by which long-term shift may occur in addition to the simple change from parents' mother tongue to use of a different language with their offspring. This is a complex issue since there is also the possibility that these offspring may themselves use both languages to address their children in a process which could go on indefinitely.

NOTES

We are deeply indebted to Dr. J. C. Sharman for making his survey
data available to us. In addition, we wish to thank both Mr. Gordon
W. Clemans and Ms. Mary Ellen Johnston [Marsden] for computation
assistance. The authors are solely responsible for the analysis and
interpretation of these results.

[1] See the references for the census sources used here and
elsewhere in this discussion.

[2] Punjabi and Hindi were intentionally coded separately.

[3] Because of the small number of cases, three, linguistic
retention is not considered for those speaking Gujarati only with
African friends.

[4] For other patterns of linguistic usage the total number of
cases and the percentage addressing their children in just Gujarati
are: English only (18), 55. 6 percent; Gujarati only (247), 51. 0 percent; English-Gujarati-other (61), 63. 9 percent; English-other (12),
16. 7 percent; Gujarati-other (41), 39. 0 percent.

REFERENCES

Fishman, Joshua A. 1972. Language in sociocultural change.
         Stanford, Calif. : Stanford University Press.
Lieberson, Stanley. 1965. Bilingualism in Montreal: a demographic
         analysis. American Journal of Sociology 71: 10-25.
_____. 1970. Language and ethnic relations in Canada. New
         York: Wiley.
Ministry of Finance and Economic Planning. 1964. Kenya population
         census, 1962, advance report of volumes I and II. Nairobi.
Molnos, Angela. 1969. Language problems in Africa. Nairobi:
         East African Research Information Centre.
Statistics Division. 1966. Kenya population census, 1962. Vol. IV,
         Non-African population. Nairobi: Ministry of Economic
         Planning and Development.
_____. 1966. Kenya population census, 1962. Vol. III, African
         population. Nairobi: Ministry of Economic Planning and
         Development.

13 | Procedures for Improving Sociolinguistic Surveys of Language Maintenance and Language Shift

Surveys of language maintenance and shift take many forms, ranging in magnitude from Grierson's <u>Linguistic Survey of India</u> to small non-representative studies of informal linguistic behavior in an urban neighborhood. Sociolinguistic surveys are usually conducted with one or more of the following goals in mind: (1) a description of the existing language situation and its social correlates; (2) measurement of the direction and magnitude of sociolinguistic change within the territory under study; (3) estimation of the linguistic consequences of government policies (such as those pertaining to education or the mass media) and/or broad societal changes (such as urbanization, industrialization, and internal migration); (4) a consideration of the causal linkages occurring in the opposite direction, namely, the impact of language conditions on political, economic, and social conditions. It is important to recognize that a survey of the existing situation, no matter how well done, may answer the first of the above objectives without providing information relevant to the other questions. Indeed, it is quite easy for such surveys to generate totally misleading conclusions about the magnitude and direction of sociolinguistic change—to say nothing of the causal inferences based on such studies.

The goals of this paper are twofold: to alert researchers to some of the pitfalls faced when using these surveys to measure temporal changes and generate causal inferences; second, to describe various techniques that can be used to improve the quality of sociolinguistic surveys. There is no escaping the fact that most sociolinguistic surveys have certain census-like qualities and goals (Kelkar 1975), and hence the methods and perspectives of demography are applicable to these surveys as well.

Change and Cause

Basic epistemological factors make it extremely difficult to measure sociolinguistic change from a survey and, in turn, to infer causal patterns. Nearly all sociolinguistic studies are one-shot affairs rather than ongoing surveys which repeatedly study a population over the years. Yet any statement about "change" normally implies a sequence of events measured at two or more points in time. The absence of a temporal dimension in the typical sociolinguistic survey is not only a severe handicap when attempting to gauge sociolinguistic changes but also a serious obstacle to measuring the linguistic consequences of various governmental policies or broad societal developments. Knowledge of "cause" almost inevitably requires the study of "change" since causality here would normally mean a sequence of events over a period which spans the time before and after other changes occur. This becomes even more of an obstacle if one recognizes that the impact of a given event need not be immediate but may very well have some time lag before its consequences are fully appreciated. Accordingly, if one wishes to determine the impact of a new educational policy in the secondary schools or of the spread of elementary education into the hinterlands of a nation, there is no reason to expect that any or all of the linguistic changes will occur simultaneously with the educational changes introduced.

Before suggesting some procedures that can be introduced into most sociolinguistic surveys, consider an example of how static, cross-sectional studies may generate serious errors. Until recently it was a fairly standard "fact" that a causal linkage existed between the economic and social development of nations, on the one hand, and their degree of mother-tongue diversity. Cross-sectional comparisons consistently found that nations with high levels of mother-tongue diversity were generally lower in per capita income, energy consumption, literacy, urbanization, and the like (see, for example, the studies cited in Lieberson and Hansen 1974: 523). Indeed, the problem appeared to be one of determining the direction of causality by deciding whether a movement toward homogeneity was a necessary prerequisite for national development or whether the causal linkage was in the opposite direction such that the development processes might be expected to reduce the level of linguistic diversity in a nation (see Pool 1969). There is now fairly good evidence that essentially no

substantial causal linkage exists in either direction between changes
in a nation's development and its level of linguistic homogeneity.
When the actual changes within nations are examined with longitudinal
data, no correlation is observed between <u>changes</u> in language diversity
and <u>changes</u> in development despite the fact that a static cross-sectional correlation exists between these characteristics (Lieberson
and Hansen 1974). This was the case for European nations between
1930 and 1960 as well as for detailed case studies of some eight different nations.

Note that an inverse association clearly does exist between
mother-tongue diversity and the level of development. The correlation by no means approaches unity but is sufficiently strong to make
it appropriate to describe this as a pattern found in the world. There
would be no difficulty if one were content merely with viewing such
results as a descriptive statement, but the sociolinguist is in serious
trouble when this static cross-sectional correlation observed at a
single point in time is used to infer a causal connection implied by the
conclusion that the changes in one characteristic will be accompanied
by, or follow from, changes in the other. The apparent paradox of
finding no causal or temporal linkage between diversity and development
even when a cross-sectional association exists is resolved when one observes that the age of national independence is jointly associated with
both of these attributes. Nations formed since World War II tend to
be less developed and more diverse linguistically than those formed
before World War II. However, within each set of nations, there is
no linkage between development and diversity. Very likely the ethnolinguistic basis of nation-making has changed since 1945, and this is
the reason for the static correlations (see Lieberson and Hansen 1974:
535-38). The point of this is to illustrate how surveys based on one
point in time can be totally misleading about change and causality.

Age and Change

Given the financial and other difficulties faced in conducting
one adequate sociolinguistic survey of a nation, it is of little help to
suggest that the ideal solution for studying the dynamics of language
behavior calls for surveys conducted at two or more different times
in the same setting. However, there are several rather elementary

procedures which provide estimates of change (or its absence) even
when a single survey is used. First one must recognize that change
among individuals occurs through processes either associated with
the aging of individuals and/or through processes in which new cohort
reaching a given age differ from those who preceded them into that a
level. Examples of the first type of age-related change are those no
mally encountered in the life-style of even a completely stable societ
as individuals move from infancy through childhood, adolescence, th
young adult years, middle age, and the older ages. The second form
of age-related change has been dramatically illustrated in recent
years—at least in the Western nations—by the new values and behavioral patterns displayed among college students when compared with
the preceding cohorts of college-age people (indeed, at the moment,
it appears as if the latest college cohort is in turn radically different
from those in the turbulent sixties). If one wishes to determine the
existence, direction, and degree of sociolinguistic change, clearly it
is important to examine the association of various sociolinguistic
attributes with age.

But such a determination is only a first step since, as observed above, differences between age groups in their linguistic patterns may reflect radically different causes depending on whether
these are new developments not experienced by earlier cohorts when
they were at that age (in which case a genuine sociolinguistic change
exists) or merely a pattern of age-related changes which was experienced by the preceding cohorts as they went through the life cycle.
Suppose, from a single sociolinguistic survey, we obtain results suc
as those presented in Table 1 below. The data give the percentage of
female residents who are bilingual (able to speak both English and
French) in metropolitan Montreal by age. Given the high degree of
residential segregation between language groups in the city (Lieberso
1970a), it is understandable why relatively small proportions of youn
girls in the pre- and early-school ages are bilingual. But we note
that bilingualism increases with age until it reaches a peak among
those in the early twenties, 48.2 percent, and then declines progressively downward after that age. Can one infer that the older cohorts
of residents were simply less likely to become bilingual than those
born later? Is it the case, in turn, that the younger generations are
not becoming as bilingual as those in their twenties? Or do the high
rates for those in their twenties compared to adolescents simply me

Table 1. Percent Bilingual Among Women in the Montreal
Metropolitan Area, 1951

Age	Percent able to speak English and French	Age	Percent able to speak English and French
0–4	3.4	35–44	45.2
4–9	9.7	45–54	37.4
10–14	20.1	55–64	30.8
15–19	44.5	65–69	26.5
20–24	48.2	70+	23.5
25–34	47.8		

Source: Lieberson (1965: Table 4).

that more of the latter will become bilingual as they get somewhat
older and reach or even exceed the 48.2 percent reported for the
former? Likewise, the decline in bilingualism in the older ages may
not reflect lower bilingualism rates among those groups but merely
the unlearning of a second language analogous to the way people forget
algebra or plane geometry if they make little use of such skills in
their daily life. In this particular case, it was possible to resolve
many of these different interpretations because similar data were
available from the Canadian censuses for the decades preceding the
1951 census and for the decade following this census. For girls 10 to
14 in 1951, it was possible to determine their degree of bilingualism
when they reached the 20 to 24 age range at the time of the 1961 census; likewise, by tracing the older cohorts backward it was possible
to determine whether they had lost their ability to speak a second language or whether they were simply never as bilingual as those 20 to
24 in 1951 (see Lieberson 1965).

Retrospective Question

        Given the importance of obtaining age-specific language data,
i.e. the language characteristics for each age group cross-tabulated
by various social characteristics the researcher deems relevant, how
does one cope with the ambiguity of the results such as those shown

above? One simple step is to use retrospective questions which
thereby place a time dimension on the results. One asks not merely
about present language abilities and usage patterns but also about pas
language abilities and the past patterns of usage. Thus, one should
not determine merely if the respondent is presently able to speak lan
guage Y, but must also determine what the respondent's answer woul
have been five years ago, ten years ago, etc. In settings where the
population is unable to accurately report their age or a specified num
ber of past years accurately, the sociolinguist must still experiment
with variations of this procedure such as the use of questions which
locate the past in terms of a certain experience rather than a specifi
year; for example, what the respondent's answer would have been at
the time of puberty, marriage, first child born, first moved to this
village, etc.

Retrospective questions have many difficulties: inaccurate
recall of the linguistic phenomenon under study; uncertainty about
placing dates and years; ignorance of the names of languages. More
over, the linguist cannot test the respondent's statement about the
past whereas such an obstacle does not exist for current claims.
Nevertheless, such retrospective questions do provide a means for
determining change over time when data can be gathered at only a
single point in time. Retrospective questions have been used rather
successfully in the United States for dealing with internal migration
and occupational mobility by asking, respectively, where the respon
ent lived and the occupation held five years earlier (see, for exampl
U.S. Bureau of the Census, 1973, Appendix B: 18-19, 35). To be sur
this approach may not be applicable to all parts of the world. However, retrospective questions do permit the determination of intra-
generational linguistic change by providing a comparison between
current and past linguistic patterns among persons in a common age
cohort. Moreover, intergenerational change can also be studied this
way; for example, one can compare the language characteristics of
young adults presently with the retrospective answers given by those
who are somewhat older. In this case one can use a single survey to
provide inferences about sociolinguistic changes between cohorts.

The sociolinguist may well object to retrospective questions
on the grounds that the population in many areas cannot always give
valid answers. This is no doubt true, but one must weigh the obstac

of <u>partially</u> invalid data with the alternative of completely ignoring any inferences about either change or the consequences of societal events on language behavior. Later in the paper I will refer to some elementary methods which can be used to gauge the degree of inaccuracy in the current ages reported by respondents to the survey. Such procedures will provide an indirect test of the population's likely accuracy in recalling earlier events.

Parent-Child Changes

Another elementary step, but potentially of great value, involves cross-tabulating the language characteristics of parents with their children. One can estimate the rate and direction of mother-tongue shift between generations, a central issue in many sociolinguistic surveys, by obtaining information cross-tabulating the mother tongue of parents with that of their offspring. In many sociolinguistic settings—although by no means all—it is probably the case that the main way in which mother tongues decline and others grow (ignoring linguistic differentials in mortality, fertility, and migration) is through members of one mother tongue (say X) acquiring a speaking knowledge of another language (Y) and then passing on Y as their offspring's mother tongue. (A second source of change may well be a shift in the young pre-adult ages, but this process would be caught through the retrospective questions discussed above.) Bilingualism is a necessary precondition for such changes, but it does not follow that the acquired language, Y, will inevitably become the mother tongue of the bilinguals' children (see Lieberson 1970b). Indeed one finds nations in which a sizable percentage of the population is bilingual but where there is relatively little net shift between generations. Consider, for example, the high frequency of bilingualism among the Afrikaans and English speakers in South Africa or among the Walloons and Flemish in Belgium. Hence, not only does the surveyor want to obtain cross-tabulations between parents' and childrens' mother tongues but also additional characteristics about the parents so that it is possible to determine the social characteristics which distinguish those bilinguals who pass on the acquired language to their children from those bilinguals who do not. Obviously, the domains of language use are important here, e.g. what language is used at home, at work, among friends, etc. (see Fishman 1972; Lieberson and McCabe 1978), but also a variety of other factors are relevant such as the education of parents, composition of their community, facility in the second language, and the like.

If a variety of important sociolinguistic problems are to be studied in terms of the intergenerational changes that may occur within the family, then the implications for survey construction are enormous. Even researchers limited to a survey of only a narrow subsegment of the society, e.g. secondary school students, should make efforts to ask the respondents about the language characteristic of their parents. In village or city surveys, on the other hand, surveyors should learn not only about linguistic patterns among persons in their prime adult years but also about their offspring and, if possible, their ancestors. Finally, an interesting possibility exists when the sociolinguist not only obtains current characteristics of parents cross-tabulated by the characteristics of their children but also employs retrospective questions about the language characteristics of parents when they were the same age as the children are presently Questions of this nature provide the surveyors with another means for gauging intergenerational change. To be sure, the ability of respondents to answer such questions with reasonable accuracy will vary greatly between nations and socioeconomic subsets within nations, but such pursuits are worthwhile.

Cross-Sectional Usage of Age Data

There are many sociolinguistic questions for which neither of the above solutions is possible. Retrospective questions about phonetics, syntax, and glottochronology are virtually certain to be without value because only trained linguists could provide an explicit verbal description of the subtle linguistic qualities involved. Likewise, parental comparisons with children are either not possible or may fail to overcome the danger that the observed pattern represents changes that occur within the lifespan of the parent rather than intergenerationally. Under the circumstance, the researcher may be tempted to use age-specific language data for one point in time to draw inferences about temporal changes in language behavior. For example, although a superb scholar such as Labov has carefully distinguished age-grading from changes in "real time," some of Labov's most frequently cited statements about change in both Martha's Vineyard (1963) and New York City (1966: chap. 9) are derived from age-specific data for a single point in time. Since it is at best extremely difficult to interpret age-specific data even when they are available for several points in time (see, for example, Glenn 1976; Mason,

Mason, and Winsborough, 1976; Knoke and Hout 1976), this technique needs more careful consideration than has hitherto been the case.

At the outset one has to recognize that the age pattern observed at a single point in time may represent factors other than the existence or absence of societal changes. Not only may age differences in language behavior represent changes occurring within the life cycle and hence be found in a highly stable society, but it may also reflect temporal fluctuations in linguistically relevant forces which differ in their impact on the age groups. A classical demographic example of the latter is the effect on fertility of the onset of an economic depression. Those in the older child-bearing ages will not be deeply affected since most of their fertility would have occurred earlier, but younger women will experience a sharp drop from preceding cohorts without it being clear whether this represents a long-term shift in fertility or merely fluctuations due to the unique set of economic conditions. Accordingly, it is absolutely crucial that one recognize the misleading and totally incorrect inferences that may be generated when one uses age-specific sociolinguistic data for one time point to draw inferences about social change. The discussion below is strictly an effort to <u>minimize</u> rather than avoid the dangers of erroneous inference about sociolinguistic change.

One must first determine whether the linguistic phenomenon under study is likely to shift over one's life cycle or if it is more or less invariant with age. Recognize that the answer for most linguistic features probably falls on a continuum rather than being a simple case in which the feature never changes or always fluctuates with the aging process; to the degree that the researcher can assume life-cycle invariance, one can be satisfied that the age-specific differences do not merely reflect such life-cycle changes. Obviously the data under analysis cannot answer the question since they are for one period. However, any other temporal data set for even a related linguistic feature is helpful since it would enable one to determine the magnitude of such life-cycle changes in at least other contexts. If there is evidence that the linguistic features under study change substantially with the life cycle, I would suggest avoiding any temporal or longitudinal inferences about trends in the linguistic characteristics based on data for one point in time. Thus, as the earlier illustration made clear, one would avoid making inferences about temporal changes in bilingualism based on information gathered at one point in time. On the other hand, age-specific data on mother tongue would not be objectionable because in most contexts—except for reporting errors— it would tend to be invariant with age.

If the age differences are not due to life-cycle factors, one must then consider whether unique historical events were serious factors generating the age differences observed. A simple and helpfu tool for unraveling is to examine the detailed cross-tabulations within each age category between linguistic behavior and the factors that are supposed to be generating the changes. Do the cross-tabulations mak sense in terms of the hypothesis under consideration? For example, suppose one speculates that the decline in some language feature among the younger ages is due to increasing education in the communi ity and the shifts in language usage that accompany these changes. If this is largely the factor, then one might expect to find a cross-tabu- lation between education and language usage in each age group that is more or less similar. Indeed, if there were no interaction involved (admittedly an unlikely situation), one would expect the same cross- tabulation between education and language usage in each age group such that the age-based change was due only to the different educa- tional composition within each age category. This is, of course, a rather simplified statement, and the sociolinguist would normally expect to turn to sociologists or social statisticians for detailed help in the analysis of the survey data. But the point is extremely impor- tant: although it is impossible to be confident that the age-specific data for one point in time truly reflect the presence or absence of temporal change, one should examine the cross-tabulations between age and linguistic behavior in terms of the factors hypothesized to see if such linkages are at least consistent with the theory under con- sideration.

In summary, sociolinguistic surveys are often concerned with questions of change. In turn, the existence of "change" or its absence implies that events have been measured at more than one point in time. Yet it is unlikely that we shall have very many socio- linguistic surveys that are consistently conducted at several points in time. It is a standard procedure in many of the social sciences to examine characteristics in association with the age of the respondent No doubt such a development will occur in sociolinguistics. But even

/hen data are tabulated by age, the inferences are tricky and decep-
ive. I have suggested several basic procedures which should greatly
acilitate sociolinguistic surveys concerned with change. It is impor-
ant to recognize that such procedures are probably among the few
/ays available presently for inferring changes and the causal conse-
uences of various policies and social movements. Accordingly, even
f less than ideal, this choice may best be contrasted with an alterna-
ive in which no inferences about the degree and direction of sociolin-
uistic change are possible.

Migration

Many nations, those with highly advanced levels of technology
nd industrialization as well as the less developed countries, exper-
ence massive redistributions of their population over relatively short
pans of time. When internal migration is numerically important,
he sociolinguistic survey is apt to encounter respondents in a given
ommunity who vary greatly in their exposure to the influence of that
etting on their linguistic behavior and skills. Under the circumstances
espondents will differ greatly in their "exposure to the risk" of mother-
ongue shift, acquisition of new languages, and the like. It is there-
ore extremely important for surveyors to determine how long the
espondents have been living in their present location. For those who
ave lived their entire life in the setting, it is necessary to ascertain
he number of generations that their ancestors have lived there (at
east the first few generations are important). The ability of the
espondents to answer such questions will vary, of course, but it is
bvious that cross-tabulations with respect to language behavior should
e made in the context of the length of exposure to the social setting
n which the respondents live. For migrants from another nation, it
s clearly important to determine how long they have lived in the new
ation as well as their length of residence in the specific community.

Migration involves a second issue that appears to be generally
gnored in sociolinguistic research. Namely, migration into or out of
n area is almost always a non-random process that is selective along
arious social, demographic, and economic dimensions. There is
ittle reason to expect sociolinguistic characteristics to be exempt—
ather one might start with the working hypothesis that migrants dif-

fer from non-movers in terms of their linguistic traits as well. Thi
is of no consequence for a national survey since internal migration
would only have a bearing on where people are found, not on the num
ical distribution of linguistic characteristics in a nation. But it is a
very serious matter when one studies the sociolinguistic traits withi
a community because it is almost certain that outmigrants differ linguistically from those who remain and, likewise, that newcomers
differ from those who did not migrate to the area. (In a micro sens
the same could be said about the subareas within the community; for
example, those who move from the central city to the suburbs probably differ linguistically from those remaining in the central city.)
The importance of these factors is an open question that will require
greater empirical consideration in the future in terms of the distortions introduced. But the sociolinguistic researcher had best be
aware of this issue. For example, when one considers age differences in the linguistic characteristics within a community, it is not
at all unlikely that selective migration into and/or out of the commu
ity is deeply affecting the age pattern and, in turn, the changes inferred without considering this issue (see, for example, the studies
of change cited by Johnson 1976). If, for example, the usage of a
stigmatized phonological feature is more common among older than
younger people (see, for example, Lobov 1963: 337-38), this may
represent no temporal shift whatsoever but could be due to changing
selective outmigration by age.

Sampling Issues

        Obviously the ideal sociolinguistic survey will be one in
which there is a sizable but purely random sample of the entire population universe. It is equally obvious that such samples will be rar
given the prerequisites of generous monetary support, excellent tra
portation to all areas of the nation, established research facilities i
the nation, and the existence of a census which provides detailed information on the size and distribution of the population universe with
the subareas. Under less than ideal conditions, there will be a nece
sity to select certain areas based on such criteria as their sociologi
importance (e.g. the capital city), transportation convenience, ease
administering questionnaires (such as to secondary school students c
those enrolled in a university), or simply because the researchers

have a reasonable expectation that they will find a large concentration
of X speakers in a particular part of the country. In effect, the sociolinguistic survey becomes a series of case studies. Such procedures
are understandable and unavoidable in many settings. However, it is
extremely important to recognize the distortions generated by such
procedures when inferences are drawn about linguistic behavior in the
nation. In nations where relatively few attend secondary schools, for
example, it is almost certain that the linguistic patterns among those
who do will differ from the patterns among those of the same age who
are obliged to work. There is much to be said under such circumstances for supplementing the basic secondary school survey questionnaire with at least some studies of children of the same age who do not
attend school.

The influence of an area's linguistic composition on the patterns of sociolinguistic behavior is another example of the sampling
distortions commonly encountered in sociolinguistic surveys. Weinreich (1957) showed that the frequency and direction of bilingualism
in India tend to vary by the linguistic composition of the area. A
similar pattern emerges in other nations—indeed one even finds immigrant language behavior in the United States affected by linguistic
composition (Lieberson and Curry 1971). This is hardly a shocking
result, and, moreover, the composition factor fails to explain fully
differences between areas in the bilingualism of a given mother-tongue
group. Indeed, given the observation that bilingualism is rarely equal
or reciprocal, the effect of linguistic composition need not be identical
for each mother-tongue group. In Canada, for example, the acquisition of French will be less frequent in a city where 10 percent of the
population has English as the mother tongue than will the acquisition
of English be in a city where French is the mother tongue of only 10
percent of the population (Lieberson 1970b: 46-50). These qualifications should not, however, keep a sociolinguistic surveyor from recognizing and appreciating a very simple principle: data gathered on
500 members of a given ethnolinguistic group will almost surely not
lead to the same conclusions as data gathered from another locale on
500 members of the same group if the demographic or social context
is different. One can illustrate the implications very simply in terms
of population composition of the areas, but the group planning a sociolinguistic survey should remember that other factors such as urbanization or sources of employment may also deeply affect the linguistic
behavior observed.

I have no easy answer to the problem of non-random samples but there are several matters for the surveyors to keep in mind. First, it is important to remain fully cognizant of the fact that the sample may easily not represent other situations in which the same linguistic group is encountered. This is especially important when policy questions are involved. Second, there is an argument for including areas which are linguistically mixed as well as fairly homogeneous areas so that the influence of composition may be taken into account. Finally, the sociolinguistic surveyors should keep in mind the societal trends they believe are occurring. If, for example, there is reason to believe that members of the X mother-tongue group are now leaving their fairly homogeneous settlements and migrating to cities where the linguistic composition is quite different, then great pains should be taken to examine areas which represent both the "before" and "after" contexts.

Theoretical Voids

Many of the sociolinguistic surveys conducted thus far have been rather atheoretical, concerned primarily with uncovering the sociolinguistic "facts" as best as could be done with limited budgets, personnel problems, national governments that are likely to have certain "preferred" conclusions, and the uncertainties that invariably plague researchers engaged in a relatively new domain of scholarly activity. Given these limitations, the sociolinguistic surveyors have more than enough to do as they seek to record the patterns and describe the associations found between the linguistic and social characteristics of individuals. Nevertheless, sociolinguists must come to grips with a central theoretical issue: the societal underpinnings of linguistic behavior. On the one hand, it would be foolish to expect the sociolinguistic experience of one nation to provide an inevitable model of what another country might expect. On the other hand, it could be equally unwise to assume that each nation is so unique as to make it impossible for the experiences of one to provide clues as to the likely sociolinguistic outcome in another country. The answer calls for attempts to develop propositions about the conditions affecting language usage, shift, switching, loyalty, multilingualism, and other sociolinguistic phenomena not merely in terms of the characteristics of the individuals such as age, sex, occupation, prestige.

Rather, it is also necessary to consider the characteristics of the nation or the groups involved. Does the condition of contact, for example, affect language shift? How, if at all, does urbanization, national development, and age of nation affect these processes? Obviously, the survey of a single nation, no matter how well constructed and executed, cannot provide answers to these questions. But comparisons between various nations with such surveys or other data sources will provide some clues. For example, it has been suggested that politically and economically subordinate language groups will be far more likely to shift mother tongues in the course of a few generations if they have migrated to the situation of subordination rather than if they have been conquered or otherwise overrun by some dominant group (Lieberson, Dalto, and Johnston 1975). Likewise, in the same study, we concluded that spatial segregation had an important influence on mother-tongue maintenance but that urbanization did not. These are, of course, provisional results and, at best, suggest certain tendencies rather than an iron law without exceptions. However, it does serve to illustrate the kinds of societal propositions that are needed in order to fit together the sociolinguistic data obtained from various nations.

Direct Applications from Censuses

Evaluating the Quality of a Sociolinguistic Survey

Linguists are sometimes rather hypercritical of the language data obtained from censuses but choose to be rather uncritical when considering the quality of their own surveys. Yet there are certain demographic procedures widely used in evaluating the quality of censuses which could be put to good use for determining the validity of sociolinguistic surveys. Consider, for example, age heaping. There is a tendency in many nations for respondents to report their age in a biased manner so as to give disproportionately more numbers ending in a zero or a five rather than the remaining eight digits. The expectation would normally be that 20 percent of the population will have ages ending in either zero or five since these are two of the ten possible last digits. A very simple measure, Whipple's Index, is applied to determine the degree of age heaping in censuses, and this measure can likewise be applied to the age data obtained in a socio-

linguistic survey of the total population of a village or other settings
where in theory there should be no heaping (as opposed to a survey
of children in a specific grade or men in the army, etc.). Particularly advantageous to the sociolinguist with minimal statistical background, the Index is easy to compute and interpret (see Shryock and
Siegel 1971: 205ff for a discussion of Whipple's Index and more elegan
tests of age heaping such as Myers' blended method). A survey with
relatively little age heaping is not necessarily one with valid sociolinguistic data. However, the presence or absence of sizable heaping
does decrease or increase one's confidence in the ability of the survey to obtain reasonably accurate data. Moreover, given the argument made earlier about the utility of retrospective linguistic data,
it would be all the more critical to see if one can have reasonable
confidence in the respondents' ability to report their current ages
accurately. There are a variety of other tests described specifically
for language data in censuses which have varying applications to
sociolinguistic surveys, and these are discussed elsewhere (Lieberson 1966).

Using Censuses in Conjunction with Sociolinguistic Surveys

Finally, scholars seeking to maximize sociolinguistic knowledge about a nation which does include one or more language questio
in their census should not view the issue as one data source versus
another. Instead the question is whether the existing data can facili-
tate the sociolinguistic survey. My experience with linguists through
the years has taught me that they are almost certain to be suspicious
of the linguistic information in a census and wary of using such data.
One recognizes that most linguistic subtleties will not be caught in
anything short of a survey conducted by trained linguists. On the
other hand, there is often reason to think that census data on mother
tongue, bilingualism, and language spoken at home may provide reasonably close approximations of the "real world" even if they are distorted to some unknown degree. For communities which have undergone relatively little population change since a recent census, the
scholar has a magnificent opportunity to compare the results obtained
from his/her survey with those derived from the census figures. If
strikingly different, then a good deal of well-founded suspicion of the
census exists and should be reported accordingly. If the census and
survey results are reasonably similar, then the former should be use

more extensively in combination with the survey, for example, by employing age-specific language data in the census to deal with changes over time in the communities surveyed. Moreover, except for the most grossly distorted census, the language data should provide a sampling frame for picking locations and communities with the linguistic composition, level of literacy, industrial activities, and other characteristics desired in the populations that are to be surveyed.

In short, although most sociolinguistic survey research is less than ideal in terms of its sample, temporal features, and execution, there are a variety of practical techniques that could greatly improve such studies. Indeed, unless some of these methods are more widely employed, such studies are likely both to fall short of their potential and, moreover, to produce misleading results and erroneous inferences.

NOTE

Support of the Ford Foundation is gratefully acknowledged.

REFERENCES

Fishman, Joshua. 1972. Language in sociocultural change. Stanford, Calif.: Stanford University Press.

Glenn, Norval D. 1976. Cohort analysts' futile quest: statistical attempts to separate age, period and cohort effects. American Sociological Review 41: 900-904.

Johnson, Lawrence. 1976. A rate of change index for language. Language in Society 5: 165-72.

Kelkar, Ashok R. 1975. The scope of a linguistic survey. In Sirapi Ohannessian, Charles A. Ferguson, and Edgar C. Polomé, eds., Language surveys in developing nations. Arlington, Va.: Center for Applied Linguistics.

Knoke, David, andMichael Hout. 1976. Reply to Glenn. American Sociological Review 41: 905-8.

Labov, William. 1963. The social motivation of a sound change. Word 19: 273-309.

Labov, William. 1966. The social stratification of English in New
        York City. Washington, D. C.: Center for Applied Linguistic

Lieberson, Stanley. 1965. Bilingualism in Montreal: a demographic
        analysis. American Journal of Sociology 71: 10–25.

————————. 1966. Language questions in censuses. Sociological
        Inquiry 36: 262–79.

————————. 1970a. Residence and language maintenance in a multi-
        lingual city. South African Journal of Sociology 1: 13–22.

————————. 1970b. Language and ethnic relations in Canada. New
        York: Wiley.

Lieberson, Stanley, and Timothy J. Curry. 1971. Language shift in
        the United States: some demographic clues. International
        Migration Review 5: 125–37.

Lieberson, Stanley, Guy Dalto, and Mary Ellen Johnston. 1975. The
        course of mother-tongue diversity in nations. American
        Journal of Sociology 81: 34–61.

Lieberson, Stanley, and Lynn K. Hansen. 1974. National develop-
        ment, mother tongue diversity, and the comparative study
        of nations. American Sociological Review 39: 523–41.

Lieberson, Stanley, and Edward J. McCabe. 1978. Domains of lan-
        guage usage and mother tongue shift in Nairobi. Internationa
        Journal of the Sociology of Language 18: 69–81.

Mason, William, Karen Oppenheim Mason, and H. H. Winsborough.
        1976. Reply to Glenn. American Sociological Review 41:
        904–5.

Pool, Jonathan. 1969. National development and language diversity.
        La Monda Lingvo-Problemo 1: 140–56.

Shryock, Henry S., Jacob S. Siegel, and Associates. 1971. The
        methods and materials of demography. Washington, D. C.:
        Government Printing Office.

United States Bureau of the Census. 1973. Census of population;
        1970, Characteristics of the population. Part I, United
        States summary, section 2. Washington, D. C.: Govern-
        ment Printing Office.

Weinreich, Uriel. 1957. Functional aspects of Indian bilingualism.
        Word 13: 203–33.

14 | Language Questions in Censuses

Census data on language are of great value for many sociolinguistic problems when investigators are aware of the difficulties
and pitfalls in their usage. This paper spells out the potentials of
such data as well as the difficulties encountered. The possibility of
deriving more information from published census data than is directly
evident is considered. In addition, a schedule of questions for improving the language coverage in future censuses is presented. Also, several methods are suggested for checking the validity of available census data on language. Finally, there is a brief discussion of bibliographical sources on language data in past and present censuses.

Advantages

Since censuses provide a geographic and temporal coverage
of languages hardly ever reached by the individual researcher with
more limited funds, these data are at least the base point for many
sociolinguistic investigations—if not the source of the major independent variables. It is clear that the nation-state is one of the most important units in which to analyze the maintenance and loss of languages.
It is no accident that a number of typologies of different language contact situations have employed the nation as the social unit for classification.[1] Given the association between political and linguistic developments as well as the critical role played by education, industry,
mass communication, and arts and sciences in influencing the position
of languages and dialects, it becomes apparent that diverse sociolinguistic problems such as creolization, multilingualism, and language
standardization cannot be understood fully without some idea of the
linguistic composition in large cities, broad regions, and nations.

Moreover, there is little reason to doubt that the great territorial
division of labor and interdependency will expand within the less developed nations of the world in the future. If the linguistic outcome in
small communities and less populated areas is increasingly influenced
by and related to a much larger social context, then increasingly we
must begin our studies by turning to the language data available for
these broader areas such as those often found in censuses.

We should also keep in mind the existence for a number of
nations of census data on language which cover long spans of time.
For example, Canada's first question on language occurred in their
1901 census, and the Union of South Africa has reported data on the
language characteristics of the European population since 1918. Insofar as questions of change and stability are central concerns of sociolinguistics, the census provides a most powerful instrument for determining the past linguistic condition of the population. In this sense
we might note that the improvement of contemporary language questions in censuses will provide future generations of scholars with an
invaluable document for their studies of our own times. As the censuses are improved, an increasing number of nations will have linguistic data taken at different points in time.

Nevertheless, it is reasonable to expect that many research
efforts will remain concentrated on smaller areas and populations
such as a single village, neighborhood, or tribe. The linguistic correlations of social interaction between castes, the interpersonal domains of speech, the relation of phonological variables to social class,
and other micro-sociolinguistic problems are frequently investigated
on the basis of extremely small populations. Although the assumption
is often covert, such studies are frequently performed with broader
generalizations in mind of such a nature that the results are intended
to be representative of all villages in a nation, all parts of a city, or
all tribes in a region. The case study is often a reasonable device
for approaching such problems. However, since the very best language data in censuses are of no value for this type of study, the inves
tigator is apt to overlook the potentialities which such data nevertheless offer. Namely, use of linguistic data in the census allows the
researcher to place his findings into a broader perspective by compar
ison with other parts of the nation. In other words, in a study which
concentrates on a specific community it is still possible to determine

how typical the community is of the larger region or nation by a comparison of census data on language in these different areas. Indeed, for those nations with linguistic data in their censuses, a strong argument can be made that the census should be consulted in advance of field work so as to determine the locales which are most representative or appear to offer the sociolinguistic setting most suitable to the problem under study. It goes without saying that the census is of great value to investigators wishing to select, say, several villages or other social aggregates for comparative study.

Additional Inferences

The value of published census data is greatly enhanced when the sociolinguist is able to infer more about the social characteristics of different language users than is apparent from first appraisal of the tabulations in a census. One can draw upon the spatial distribution of the linguistic groups as well as the cross-tabulations between language data and non-linguistic characteristics to obtain relevant information about the population which is not directly evident. Since this is primarily a task for the sociologically trained sociolinguist, particularly the demographer and human ecologist, we shall be illustrative here rather than present a detailed discussion of this subject. Moreover, because this is a problem which varies with the research need and the data available in a particular census, it is not possible to provide a set of general principles.

Following a method developed by Hurd for use with Canadian language data, we shall illustrate how the skilled investigator can get more out of the published census than apparently is available.[2] In the Canadian censuses, data are given on two separate language questions: first, the mother tongue, which is the first language learned in childhood and still spoken;[3] second, the official language of the population which is determined on the basis of answers to the questions "Can you speak English? French?" Thus we have information on the first language of each member of the population and the present speaking ability in English and French. Nowhere does the census give the cross-tabulation between first language (mother tongue) and present language ability in French and English (official language). Thus, it is impossible to determine directly the degree to which a population has acquired

French or English as a second language or the extent to which speake
of a specific mother tongue have later learned the other official language.

For many age, sex, ethnic, and areal populations we have
available, then, the following information:

A = total population   D = English only official language
B = English mother tongue   E = French only official language
C = French mother tongue   F = Both English and French official
                                          languages

If we make the reasonable assumptions for Canada that virtu
ally all persons continue to report their first learned language as
their mother tongue and that persons with English or French mother
tongues retain their ability to speak the respective language, then we
can estimate the proportion of the non-English mother-tongue population who have learned English by

$$\frac{(D + F) - B}{A - B}$$

Correspondingly, the proportion acquiring French among those with
non-French mother tongue is

$$\frac{(E + F) - C}{A - C}$$

The proportion of the population with "other" mother tongues who
learn neither English nor French is

$$\frac{A - (D + E + F)}{A - (B + C)}$$

Thus, although no cross-tabulation is given between mother tongue an
current language status, Hurd used the equations above to estimate
some of the relationships and was even able to compare the proportions acquiring these tongues in different decades.[4]

Using the same set of assumptions, the present author has
developed estimating formulas for determining the minimum and max
imum degrees to which one of the official languages is learned by the

population which has the other official mother tongue. For example, the maximum percent of the English-mother-tongue segment of a population who have learned French is

$$\frac{F - (C - E)}{B}$$

The minimum percent who have learned French is

$$\frac{B - D}{B}$$

Among the population with French mother tongue, we can estimate the proportions learning English as

$$\text{Maximum} = \frac{F - (B - D)}{C} \; ; \quad \text{Minimum} = \frac{C - E}{C}$$

Using these equations, the minimum and maximum percent bilingual in the two official languages for selected metropolitan areas are shown in Table 1.[5]

Inspection of Table 1 indicates generally favorable results in the sense that we obtain fairly narrow ranges and clear-cut evidence of the greater propensity of one mother tongue over the other to learn the second official language. In some instances, such as for the

Table 1. Estimated Bilingualism in Canada, by Mother Tongue, 1961

| Metropolitan area | Percent bilingual whose mother tongue was: | | | |
| | English | | French | |
	Min.	Max.	Min.	Max.
Montreal	7	48	40	55
Ottawa	1	11	65	80
Quebec	62	80	22	23
Toronto	0	4	88	100
Vancouver	0	3	91	100

French mother-tongue population of Quebec and the English mother-tongue populations of Toronto and Vancouver, the range between minimum and maximum is very small. The only really unsatisfactory result is for Montreal, where the range for the English mother-tongue population is excessive and prevents us from determining with assurance whether the French or English mother-tongue population has a greater propensity toward bilingualism.[6]

The point of this brief excursion into the Canadian census data is that in many instances there are possibilities for doing more with the actual census data than might be apparent from the linguistic information actually reported. Insofar as this is the case, we have even greater opportunities for obtaining useful information for sociolinguistic questions. Particularly noteworthy are the possibilities of inferring individual relationships and aggregate cross-tabulations on the basis of published data by means of various correlational techniqu

Difficulties

Before leaping into the linguistic data available from census around the world, the investigator must be extremely cautious and guard against a wide range of possible errors. A number of difficulties result in one way or another from intentional distortions by the government taking the census. The fundamental potential of language as a form of national cleavage, coupled with inherent ambiguity in the terms "language" and "dialect, " have proved too tempting for some governments and have led to distortions of their language results in directions favorable to national policy. In an excellent discussion of some of the pitfalls in linguistic statistics, the demographer Dudley Kirk provides some pre-World War II examples of distortions intentionally produced to minimize or maximize a linguistic population:[8]

In the old Austrian censuses all Yiddish-speakers were classified as Germans despite the protests of Jewish minorities. In this way the apparent German minorities in Galicia and Bucovina, for example, were magnified by the presence of Jewish elements who formed the core of the urban populations in the region. The opposite objective (i.e., of minimi ing the importance of a minority) may be achieved by enume

ating dialects and fractions in detail and thereby drawing
attention away from the whole. Thus in German censuses
Kaschub and Masurian are distinguished from Polish, though
these are Polish dialects with no greater differences than
exist between German dialects to which no official recognition
is given. Similarly in Poland the inhabitants of Polesie were
arbitrarily reported as speaking a "local" language which
actually is a dialect of White Russian; in Hungary indigenous
South Slav minorities of Serbo-Croat speech were given local
names and were separately classified.

In a similar vein, English and other non-Indian languages have not
been accepted as a second language in several of the Indian censuses.[9]

There are also great difficulties created, particularly for
international comparative studies, by the different kinds of language
questions that have been used in censuses. The three basic types can
give quite different results in a country which is sociolinguistically
complex and therefore of particular interest. First, we have the
"mother tongue" type of question which usually gets at the language
first learned or used by the respondent. Second, some censuses have
asked questions on the language usually used by the individual or in
the home at the time of the enumeration. Finally, we sometimes encounter questions which are designed to determine all languages which
the individual knows.[10] It is important to recognize that the type of
question will affect the kind of results obtained. Kirk argues that,
generally, "the use of mother tongue favors minorities in the process
of assimilation, since it records the original language of the respondent and not his linguistic practices as influenced by schooling and adjustment to the dominant language. ... 'Usual' or customary language,
on the other hand, favors the dominant language."[11]

Even within these categories, there are variations between
countries in the way questions are put, which will influence the results.
For example, the 1940 census of Brazil asked the question, "Do you
speak the national language fluently?" whereas in the same year Mexicans were asked, "Do you speak the national language?" In similar
fashion, the Brazilian census had a question on language usually
spoken at home, whereas one year later the Hungarian census asked
for the language which the individual spoke best and by preference.[12]

Indeed, within the same nation, definitions have been altered which
affect comparability over time. Thus the excellent series of language
data available from the Canadian censuses are slightly marred by a
change in the definition of mother tongue such that in 1931 it was "the
language learned in childhood and still spoken by the person," wherea
in 1941 it was necessary that the respondent only <u>understand</u> the moth
tongue.[13] A more serious shift occurred in the definition of mother
tongue for the second generation in the United States. In 1910 and 192
the second generation was classified by the mother tongue of their
foreign-born parents, whereas in 1940 it was the language spoken at
home in earliest childhood by the respondent himself. Consequently,
in the earlier censuses, the second generation could not be classified
as having English mother tongue unless their foreign-born parents
used English at home before coming to the United States. By contras
the limitations were lessened in 1940 when mother tongue referred
solely to the linguistic characteristics of the second generation themselves. As Kiser has shown, this lack of comparability led to mis-
interpretation by the Census Bureau itself of the trends between 1920
and 1940.[14]

These complications due to the lack of consistency may be
improved in forthcoming censuses; since in recent years the United
Nations and the Inter-American Statistical Institute have made sugges
tions for standardizing the language questions asked, as well as inclu
ing certain valuable cross-tabulations of language data with such basi
social characteristics as age and sex.[15]

Leaving aside matters of intentional distortion by the respon
ent or government body, there is one problem which I believe deserv
more consideration than it has received thus far, namely, unintention
errors on the part of respondents due to the subjective types of questions used. Questions on mother tongue offer relatively little difficul
since it is more or less a factual question which language was first
learned. We should, however, wish to see a better opportunity presented here for valid responses for the truly bilingual or multilingual
home setting, in which it is impossible to state which language is
learned first. Undoubtedly, there are many countries where only one
language is used at home, although much of the adult population is bilingual. Thus, in the Union of South Africa, where more than 70 percent of the European population is bilingual, only 1.4 percent reporte

the use of both English and Afrikaans at home.[16] However, there are situations such as one reported by Joan Rubin about the town of Luque in Paraguay where more than half of her younger respondents reported learning both Spanish and Guarani as their first language at home.[17]

However, it is particularly with questions about the ability of the respondent to speak one or more languages that we encounter considerable difficulty in present censuses. The key shortcoming for such questions hinges upon the lack of a clear-cut operational definition of ability to speak a given tongue. As a consequence, it is difficult for the sociologist or linguist using such data to know precisely what is being measured. If a respondent indicates knowledge of a given language, does this mean a high degree of fluency or minimal ability? Similarly, it is unlikely in any intensive multilingual setting that many of the residents will be absolutely and completely ignorant of the other tongues about them. Hence, we have no way of determining what the linguistic ability of the population reporting themselves as monolingual really is. It seems most reasonable, nonetheless, to assume that the population reporting themselves able to speak a given language have a far higher degree of fluency than the segment of the population reporting themselves unable to speak the language. And, presumably, in most instances the two populations will indeed reflect true differences in their ability to communicate in the specified language.

A Proposed Schedule of Language Questions

There appear to be two possible solutions to the difficulties described above. First, a series of intensive questions designed to measure communication potential in a language could be prepared for administration to a sample of the population. For example, the respondents might be asked to give the meaning of specific words, or be given questions based on a short passage in the language in question; or they might be asked questions in the language which would be relatively independent of social status or educational level. Such an approach would call for extremely careful selection of the questions with an eye toward possible biases in favor of one language group or social category over another. It would also be difficult to measure trends over time since undoubtedly it would not be possible to use the

	Understand a Conversation	Speak Conversationally	Read Books and Papers	Write Letters
In what language(s) could the respondent				
The first language in which the respondent was able to				
Language used in the home presently (most frequent)	Conversation			
Language on the job (most frequent)	Conversation		✕	✕
Language of instruction: for respondent	Instruction		✕	✕
for children	Instruction		✕	✕
Language(s) preferred by respondent	Conversation		✕	✕
Language of religious activities	Sermon	Prayer	Liturgy	

Fig. 1. Proposed schedule of language questions for a census.
(Note: radio and television have been considered possible substitutes
for, or supplements to, the "reading of books and papers" item.)

same questions in a later census. However, such an approach would
allow for a good estimate of the linguistic ability of the population if
the questions were properly selected.[18]

A second approach would involve a revision and extension of
the census questions such that linguistic ability is sought in terms of
specific social contexts or domains. These questions, shown in Figure 1, were developed by the "multilingualism and language shift"
work group cited earlier with the goal of making questions about language usage in the census more operational. Also, we have included
a question on attitudes, i.e. language preference, although this by no
means insures that language attitudes will not distort the results
yielded by other items as well. However, insofar as these questions
refer to specific contexts and types of media, there is less chance of
distortion than when vague general questions are used on present linguistic ability or even on mother tongue. These suggestions are all

the more important as we become increasingly conscious of the arbitrary dichotomization of linguistic ability into either a monolingual or
bilingual category. Since Diebold's development of the concept of
incipient bilingualism, there has been a shift to viewing bilingualism
as belonging on a continuum from complete ignorance to mastery of
all the nuances of a second language.[19] Not only is the meaning of the
language ability question uncertain in many present censuses, but it
is difficult, for this writer at least, to determine what precisely would
be the ideal criteria. Here again, the kinds of operationalized and
specified questions listed in Figure 1 offer a far higher degree of clar-
ity, in that important domains of language usage are specified in somewhat of a behavioral framework. Since investigators will have different criteria of bilingualism in mind, the specification of linguistic
ability along behavioral and contextual lines will allow each investigator to use the criteria of bilingualism closest to his own research needs.

The figure itself requires little explanation. It is obviously
generalized in the sense that various items might be dropped, or possibly some added, for the census of a particular nation. However, it
is hoped that this chart will provide the core of questions on language
which each nation should consider in preparing their census schedules.
We have attempted to specify linguistic ability by both the media of
communication (conversation, reading, writing) and what are probably
the most important sociolinguistic contexts (childhood, home, work,
school, and religion).

Finally, we wish to emphasize that many nations could be
doing far more in the way of asking language questions on their censuses. A more detailed set of linguistic questions could be used for
those areas of a nation which are linguistically complex, while a minimal questionnaire could be employed in the linguistically more homogeneous areas. The United States, for example, should include a
more elegant set of language questions than that presently employed—
particularly for those areas with obviously more complex linguistic
situations such as the Southwest, the New York metropolitan area,
Hawaii, parts of Louisiana, and the like. Various scholarly organizations in the sociological, linguistic, and demographic professions
should make the needs for improved language data better known to
national governments and such international bodies as the United
Nations and the Pan-American Union.

If language questions in the censuses of the future are to improve, perhaps no means to their improvement will prove to be as important as the extensive use of those data which are presently available. Not only will the widespread use of these data provide an incentive for continuing and expanding such questions in the future, but through greater experience it will be possible to indicate where improvements can be made.

Validity Checks

In this section, we suggest some of the checks which may be employed by an investigator for determining the validity of the language data in a census. Aside from the obvious expedient of conducting a post-enumeration survey of greater intensity than the census itself, we can only suggest that checks of internal and external consistency may be devised for a census' language questions which may offer some clues as to the validity of the data obtained. Such checks may be particularly critical for those nations in which language is a burning political issue and in which the census could possibly be distorted or loaded in a particular direction.

Errors in the census are, of course, by no means confined to linguistic data alone. Based on a special study of this problem, it is estimated that from 4.7 million to 8.5 million persons were omitted from the 1960 census of the United States.[20] Since demographers have not generally worked with linguistic data, the tests they have developed are primarily for other characteristics of the population such as age. However, we have attempted to apply some of these procedures to the linguistic data as well as present some tests which are uniquely suitable to the subject.[21]

One type of check on the validity of linguistic data in a census is based upon their consistency with data obtained from other sources, so-called external verification. The goal is to select quantitative data from a non-census source which are believed to be valid and then compare these data with relevant census reports in order to determine if they are reasonably similar. We may illustrate this procedure by a comparison of school enrollment data with census results on mother-tongue distribution of school-age children in the Province of Quebec.

Because there are always strong possibilities that linguistic or other socially relevant groups will have differential rates of school attendance, we wish to select an age category in which nearly all children attend school. (For example, we would not care to estimate the number of college-age whites and Negroes in the United States on the basis of their respective numbers attending an institution of higher education.) Children between the ages of 10 and 14 are most suitable for our purposes since nearly all in the Province attend school; in 1961, 96.4 percent attended according to the census.

In Quebec there are two school systems, one Protestant and the other Roman Catholic. The language of instruction is English in almost all Protestant schools and it is French in the vast majority of Roman Catholic schools. Thus, if we assume that children attending Protestant schools have English mother tongue and children attending Catholic schools have French mother tongue, then we may compare the respective school systems' enrollment figures and expect these to be roughly comparable to the census data on mother tongue for children of the same age groups.

Shown in Table 2 are the percentages attending the respective school systems in the 1957-58 school year, the most recent available.[22] Using linear interpolation between the 1951 and 1961 censuses for the population 10-14, we find a reasonable correspondence with the data on the mother tongues of children in the census. Thus 85.9 percent have French as the mother tongue, 11.3 percent have English mother tongue, and 2.8 percent are children with other mother tongues who for the most part doubtlessly attend one of these school systems. When we consider that there are probably more English schools in the Catholic system than French language schools in the Protestant system, the moderate differences are readily accounted for.[23] Thus, on the basis of this consistency check with an outside source of data, we would conclude that there was no reason to doubt at least substantial validity of the census figures on mother tongue for children in the age period examined.

There are a series of checks which the demographically trained sociolinguist can apply to determine the internal consistency of language data. If the census data prove to be highly inconsistent, then serious doubt is raised about their validity. On the other hand,

Table 2. Comparison of School System Enrollment and Census Data,
Children 10-14 Years of Age, Quebec, 1957-58

School system	Percent	Percent	Mother tongue
Roman Catholic	89.6	85.9	French
Protestant	10.4	11.3	English
		2.8	Other
Total	100.0	100.0	

internal consistency does not "prove" validity as much as show that
we are unable to find any evidence of error. In this sense, the use
of internal checks is analogous to the null hypothesis in statistics.
Namely, we do not prove that the census data are correct, rather that
with respect to certain possible tests we cannot find any reason to
doubt the validity of the data. Several illustrations, again based on
the author's experience with Canadian census data, will perhaps clar-
ify procedures.

One extremely useful check is to look at consistency between
censuses on the language data. Shown in columns 1 through 3 of Table
3 are the mother-tongue percentage distributions of the population at
different ages in 1951. Thus, for example, we find among males 15-24,
55 percent have English mother tongues, about a third are French, and
somewhat more than 10 percent have some other mother tongue. If
these data are valid, then we would expect the population in the next
census ten years later to have comparable language distributions. This
assumes the following: that differences in mortality between language
groups are negligible (an assumption which may be less reasonable in
underdeveloped nations); that rates of emigration are not high or, if
high, are not selective by language group; and that the same may be
said about immigration. In the latter case, we have eliminated immigrants coming to Canada between 1951 and 1961 from the age distribution
for 1961.

Columns 4-6 show the percentage distributions for the respective age groups ten years later. For both English and French, the

Table 3. Male Cohorts by Mother-Tongue Distribution, Canada,
1951 and 1961

	1951				1961		
	Percent whose mother tongue was:				Percent whose mother tongue was:		
Age	English	French	Other	Age	English	French	Other
0–4	61.7	32.3	6.0	10–14	63.6	32.3	4.1
5–9	58.4	34.6	7.1	15–19	59.4	34.8	5.9
10–14	57.0	33.8	9.2	20–24	56.8	34.1	9.0
15–24	55.3	32.6	12.1	25–34	56.0	32.6	11.4
25–34	57.4	28.7	13.8	35–44	58.3	29.0	12.7
35–44	58.6	26.4	14.9	45–54	58.7	26.6	14.7
45–54	55.2	24.4	20.4	55–64	54.7	24.4	20.8

several cohort results are stable over a decade. In 1951, for example,
57.4 and 28.7 percent of men 25–34 years of age reported English and
French mother tongues, respectively. This compares rather closely
with the percentages of men 35–44 who ten years later in 1961 reported
these mother tongues, 58.3 and 29.0. The percentage of the population with other mother tongues does drop off in all but one age category
in the period between 1951 and 1961. This may reflect some error in
the data, say, that the foreign-born report English or French as their
mother tongue; or it may be a function of the peculiar criteria of
mother tongue (perhaps that the language still be understood); or it
may be due to some complex higher mortality among the foreign-born
who are overrepresented in the other mother-tongue category, some
returning to home countries, and others migrating to the United States
in disproportionately large numbers. Possibly all of these factors
operate. However, the overall results seem to point to reasonably
consistent language data by age over the decades. Again, we must
note that this does not prove that the census data are valid so much as
showing good consistency between censuses and suggests that if there
are errors, they are not a function of sharp shifts by age in the mother
tongue reported.

Another useful way of testing language data by internal mean involves comparisons between the sexes. If there is error in reporting official language or mother tongue, we might well expect a differential tendency between males and females. In a country receiving large numbers of immigrants, such as Canada, this is complicated by the fact that more males than females in the adult ages will be foreign-born, because many groups frequently send more male than female emigrants. Hence, for such groups we would expect more males than females to report a mother tongue corresponding to their ethnic origin. We can, however, carry out our analysis of sex differentials by restricting it to the younger ages. Let us make the following reasonable assumptions for Canada: the propensity of parents to migrate to or emigrate from Canada is not correlated with whether their small children are male or female; the survivorship ratios for males and females of each language group are roughly of a similar magnitude and correspond to the nations sending immigrants to Canada with small children. Under these assumptions, among children we would expect the sex ratio of each mother-tongue group to be close to that of the entire Canadian population. On the other hand, if there was some tendency for parents to distort the mother tongue of their children in their responses to the census enumerators, then we might expect this to be related to whether the child was male or female. Under such conditions, we would expect to find considerable variance in the sex ratio between mother tongue among children.

Inspection of the data shown in Table 4 indicates a sex ratio in most mother-tongue groups which is very close to the 104.6 for the entire Canadian population under 15 years of age. The only exception is the combined Indian and Eskimo mother-tongue population where fewer males are reported than we might expect. It is significant to note that the sex ratio for the Indian and Eskimo ethnic population is also low (102.2); however, we are unable to determine whether there is some error in reporting mother tongue so that males in this group are more likely to be omitted or whether these results are a function of a migh higher ratio of male to female deaths among this group. At any rate, with one exception, results of our examination increase our confidence in the reporting of the various mother tongues among the population.[24]

Table 4. Sex Ratio of Leading Mother Tongues Among Population
0-14 Years of Age, Canada, 1961

Mother tongue	Sex ratio*	Mother tongue	Sex ratio*
English	104.95	Russian	103.36
French	103.83	Scandinavian	106.12
German	106.11	Ukrainian	103.97
Italian	105.98	Yiddish	105.05
Dutch	106.13	Indian and Eskimo	101.29
Polish	105.13	Total population	104.64

*Number of males per 100 females.

One final application of the sex differential check will be
shown for what is the most difficult type of language data to validate,
namely, the current language ability of the population. We assume
that among infants and children we would expect to find little difference between the sexes in their ability to speak one or both official
languages of Canada. That is, in the preschool ages we would expect
the language experiences of boys and girls to be similarly influenced
by home speech, mass media, playmates, and neighbors. In the early
school years we would expect the influence of school to be relatively
similar for the sexes. Consequently, in these ages we would expect
to find very similar official language distributions for boys and girls.
By contrast, in the late teens and adult ages we might very readily
expect differentials between the sexes since presumably males are
more likely to learn or retain a second language because of their higher
rates of participation in the work force. This raises an important consideration for the sociolinguist in his testing of census data. Namely,
it is necessary to take general conditions of the society into account,
such as immigration, occupational patterns, and the like, lest the linguistic results appear to be erroneous when they are merely reflecting
these general social processes.

Shown in Table 5 are the official language distributions for
males and females in each of three age groupings where we would

Table 5. Official Language Distribution by Age and Sex,
Canada, 1961

		Proportion whose official language is:				
Age	Sex	English only	French only	English and French	Neither	Total
0-4	Male	.66844	.27979	.01665	.03512	1.00000
	Female	.66660	.28162	.01697	.03481	1.00000
5-9	Male	.68414	.26563	.04432	.00591	1.00000
	Female	.68174	.26760	.04497	.00569	1.00000
10-14	Male	.67398	.25023	.07359	.00221	1.00000
	Female	.66865	.25370	.07562	.00203	1.00000

expect little difference between the sexes, namely, 0-4, 5-9, 10-14.
Inspection of these distributions indeed discloses very similar patter
for the sexes. There is a slight tendency in all three age categories
for more males than females to be reported as speaking English only
and, by contrast, more females than males are reported as speaking
French only. The bilingual and "neither" components are very similar between the sexes. Thus our analysis suggests the possibility tha
males may be slightly overreported as English-only speakers and/or
females underreported in this category. However, we should not los
sight of the main finding that results for the two sexes are remarkabl
similar, with the greatest discrepancy being 0.5 percent (English-on
speakers, 10-14 years of age).

It may be worth repeating here that our analysis of age-speci
sex differences in the reporting of official language does not validate
the language data so much as it provides another instance where we
might readily expect selectivity between the sexes in distortion and
where we do not find any significant degree of difference between the
groups. The building up of such findings tends to raise our confidenc
in the language data that are being used. And it is through measures
such as these that the sociolinguist may test for major errors in the

language censuses with which he chooses to work. Finally, we should note that the tests which have been shown are illustrative of the internal and external checks which may be applied. The tests which an investigator should use for a specific census will very much depend on the data available in the census and on the kinds of assumptions he can reasonably make.

BIBLIOGRAPHICAL SOURCES

Since many otherwise fine university libraries appear to have scandalously incomplete collections of census volumes on a worldwide basis, it may be useful for scholars if we refer to some general sources which can provide the necessary information on which linguistic data are available in past and present censuses.

The quarterly Population Index is almost entirely bibliographical and contains a section which lists current censuses and other official statistical publications alphabetized by continent and nation.[25] In relatively short order, it is possible to learn what the recent census materials for a given nation or area have to offer in the way of linguistic data.

Two issues of the Demographic Yearbook provide excellent coverage for the period 1945–63.[26] The 1963 volume provides 37 distributions for 28 countries and territories which had language data in censuses between 1955 and 1963. The Yearbook for 1956 gives some 69 census distributions referring to 58 countries with language questions between 1945 and 1955. The Yearbook does not describe the cross-tabulations available with the language data other than by sex. However, careful indications of the type of language question used are given for each of the censuses surveyed. Further, it is possible by means of this source to determine rapidly which countries have language data in their censuses for the period under consideration.

Despite the title, "Statistics for Studying the Cultural Assimilation of Migrants, " by Max Lacroix and Edith Adams is an extraordinarily useful source on the available language data in the several decades before World War II as well as through at least part of the

"forties."[27] In the set of tables shown in an appendix, language data
are listed by type such as mother tongue, language(s) currently
spoken, etc., and also by cross-classifications which are available,
such as with age, sex, birthplace, etc. The coverage is world-wide.

There are several bibliographical sources worth mentioning
although they are more restricted in the area covered. Two fine
sources for Europe in the period between the two World Wars are
Dudley Kirk's Europe's Population in the Interwar Years[28] and a statistical appendix by L. Tesnière.[29]

Several joint publications by the United States Bureau of the
Census and Library of Congress may prove of value to sociolinguists
interested in the areas covered. A review of General Censuses and
Vital Statistics in the Americas under the direction of Irene Taeuber
covers all earlier censuses for each nation and foreign possession in
the new world through the early 1940's.[30] Two annotated bibliograph-
ies by Henry J. Dubester cover Europe between 1918 and 1948.[31] Finally, Dubester has prepared an annotated bibliography of demographic
statistics conducted in British Africa.[32]

For recent Latin American censuses, the Inter American
Statistical Institute prepares summary volumes which cover the censuses which these nations have been conducting.[33]

NOTES

Revised and expanded version of paper prepared for Sociolinguistics
Seminar, Indiana University, Summer, 1964. Suggestions by member
of the multilingualism and language shift work group are gratefully
acknowledged. Preparation of this paper was supported in part by
National Science Foundation Grant No. G-23923.

[1] For example, William A. Stewart, "Outline of Linguistic
Typology for Describing Multilingualism," in Frank A. Rice, ed.,
Study of the Role of Second Languages in Asia, Africa, and Latin
America (Washington, D. C.: Center for Applied Linguistics, 1962),
pp. 15-25; Heinz Kloss, "Types of Multilingual Communities," and
Joshua A. Fishman, "Some Contrasts Between Linguistically Homo-

geneous and Linguistically Heterogeneous Polities," Sociological
Inquiry 36, no. 2 (Spring, 1966) [= Explorations in Sociolinguistics];
Charles A. Ferguson, "National Sociolinguistic Profile Formulas,"
UCLA Conference on Sociolinguistics, 1964.

[2] Origin, Birthplace, Nationality and Language of the Canadian
People (Ottawa: Dominion Bureau of Statistics, 1929), chap. 8.

[3] This definition has been revised in recent decades.

[4] W. Burton Hurd, Racial Origins and Nativity of the Canadian
People (Ottawa: Dominion Bureau of Statistics, 1942), chap. 9.

[5] In some instances a negative number is obtained for the minimum and a figure above 100 percent for the maximum. Under such
circumstances we assume zero and 100 percent, respectively.

[6] A more detailed analysis allows us to go beyond this conclusion. However, it is not relevant to the purpose of this paper.

[7] See, for example, Leo A. Goodman, "Some Alternatives to
Ecological Correlation," American Journal of Sociology 64 (May 1959):
610-25; Otis Dudley Duncan, "Occupational Components of Educational
Differences in Income," Journal of the American Statistical Association 56 (Dec. 1961): 783-92.

[8] Dudley Kirk, Europe's Population in the Interwar Years
(Princeton, N.J.: Princeton University Press, 1946), p. 225.

[9] Uriel Weinreich, "Functional Aspects of Indian Bilingualism,"
Word 13 (Aug. 1957): 231.

[10] United Nations, Demographic Yearbook, 1956 (New York:
Statistical Office, Department of Economic and Social Affairs, 1956),
p. 34.

[11] Kirk, p. 224.

[12] United Nations, Population Census Methods, "Population
Studies, No. 4" (Lake Success, N.Y.: Department of Social Affairs,
Population Division, 1949), p. 71.

[13] Eighth Census of Canada, 1941, vol. 4 (Ottawa: Dominion
Bureau of Statistics, 1946), p. xviii.

[14] Clyde V. Kiser, "Cultural Pluralism," in Joseph J. Spengler and Otis Dudley Duncan, eds., Demographic Analysis (Glencoe:
The Free Press, 1956), p. 314.

[15] Population Census Methods, p. 69, includes a summary of
the recommendations of these international agencies.

[16] Computations derived from the 1951 Census of the Union of
South Africa.

[17] Joan Rubin, "Stability and Change in a Bilingual Paraguayan Community," paper presented to the 1963 meeting of the American Anthropological Association.

[18] I am indebted to my colleague David Heise for suggesting this approach to me.

[19] A. Richard Diebold, Jr., "Incipient Bilingualism," Language 37 (Jan. -March 1961): 97-112.

[20] U.S. Bureau of the Census, Evaluation and Research Program of the U.S. Censuses of Population and Housing, 1960: Record Check Studies of Population Coverage, Series ER60, No. 2 (Washington, D.C., 1964), p. 2.

[21] For illustrations of some of the techniques for determining accuracy in census data generally, see George W. Barclay, Techniques of Population Analysis (New York: Wiley, 1958), chap. 3; U.S. Bureau of the Census, Handbook of Statistical Methods for Demographers (preliminary edition—2d printing), by A. J. Jaffe (Washington, D.C., 1951), chap. 4.

[22] Survey of Elementary and Secondary Education. Part I of the Biennial Survey of Education in Canada, 1956-58 (Ottawa: Dominion Bureau of Statistics, 1960), pp. 70-71.

[23] For example, although almost no Protestant schools in Montreal offer classes where French is the language of instruction, two of the fourteen elementary school districts in the Catholic system are English. See Répertoire des Ecoles, 1963-64 (La Commission des Ecoles Catholiques de Montréal, no date).

[24] It should be noted that analysis of these data by more refined age categories lead to greater variance between mother-tongue groups in their sex ratios. However, it would appear that much of this is due to the relatively small numbers involved for some of the mother-tongue groups.

[25] Published by Office of Population Research, Princeton University, and the Population Association of America.

[26] Demographic Yearbook, 1956, pp. 282-94; 1963 (New York: Statistical Office, Department of Economic and Social Affairs, 1964), pp. 321-29.

[27] In Population Studies, supplement (March 1950), pp. 69-108.

[28] Kirk, Europe's Population in the Interwar Years.

[29] L. Tesnière, "Statistique des langues de l'Europe," in A.

Meillet, Les languages dans l'Europe nouvelle (Paris: Payot, 1928),
pp. 291-484.

[30] Washington, D. C., 1943.

[31] National Censuses and Vital Statistics in Europe: 1918-1939
(Washington, D. C., 1948); National Censuses and Vital Statistics in
Europe: 1940-1948. Supplement (Washington, D. C., 1948).

[32] Population Census and Other Official Demographic Statistics
of British Africa (Washington, D. C., 1950).

[33] See, for example, La Estructura Demografica de las Naciones
Americanas, vol. I, Tomo 3 (Washington, D. C.: Union Pan Americana,
1960), chap. 12.

15 | An Extension of Greenberg's Linguistic Diversity Measures

1. In 1956, Greenberg proposed eight measures of linguistic diversity designed to determine the possibilities of communication among the population of some delimited area.[1] Taking note of the considerable variance between areas of the world in their linguistic diversity, Greenberg's measures allow us to quantify this diversity on a continuum ranging from complete diversity, such that no two people speak a mutually intelligible language or dialect, to the other extreme, where all inhabitants share a common tongue. By going beyond mere verbal descriptions of an area's linguistic diversity, these quantitative measures enable us to correlate language usage with social, economic, political, and geographic factors.

Although Greenberg refers only to the linguistic diversity of spatially delineated population aggregates such as nations, states, and cities, his measures are equally applicable to any socially meaningful population delimited on a non-areal basis. Thus, we could apply his measures to the civil service of India, the Ukrainian ethnic population of the USSR, teenagers in Brussels, or Negroes in Chicago.

Greenberg's measures are all confined to diversity or communication within some defined population. In this paper, I extend Greenberg's measures to linguistic diversity or communication between two or more spatially delineated populations or between socially defined subpopulations of a larger aggregate. The measures proposed here are extensions of the probability-type indexes of Greenberg, which have merited commendation from the statisticians Goodman and Kruskal.[2] There is no difficulty in using Greenberg's measures of diversity between areas or populations; the results obtained by these procedures are fully compatible and may be compared without further adjustment.

A solution is offered for measuring interaction between groups which is applicable to all eight of the measures proposed by Greenberg. However, I will only illustrate its application with two of these measures, since the procedure is basically the same for all eight indexes.

2. Algeria before the exodus of the French provides an illustration of the application of $\underline{H}$, the Index of Communication between groups. $\underline{H}$ within groups is "the probability that if two members of the population are chosen at random, they will have at least one language in common" (1956: 112). Based on the language(s) spoken by the population ten years of age or older shown in Table 1, we find that $\underline{H}$ is .669 for the total population, .801 for the Moslem population, and 1.000 for the European population. What we find, then, is fairly high communication probability for the total population of Algeria, higher communication within the Moslem segment, and maximum communication within the European segment. We may be somewhat suspicious of the latter figure, since it indicates that not a single European is unable to speak French. We will not consider the computational procedure for these indexes, since it is based on the formula described by Greenberg (1956: 112).

The conventional $\underline{H}$ index fails to provide us with a measure of the potential communication between the two major ethnic segments of the population, Moslem and European. If we randomly select a Moslem and randomly select a European, what is the probability that they will be able to communicate in a mutually intelligible language? It is necessary to introduce a new measure to obtain this communication potential between groups. First, let us consider why $\underline{H}$ for the total population is inadequate. The $\underline{H}$ of .669 for the entire population is weighted by the relative numbers of the component segments we are interested in. In Algeria there are 5.4 million Moslems and only .8 million Europeans ten years of age or older. To the extent that there is a numerical difference, $\underline{H}$ will be weighted in the direction of the larger group. Second, $\underline{H}$ within the entire population is influenced by the communication probabilities within each segment of the population and not solely between the segments of the population: if we have a nation composed of two groups, A and B, all members of A speaking only language X and all members of B speaking only language Y, computation of Greenberg's $\underline{H}$ for the entire population would give us a

Table 1. Language Distribution, Algeria, 1948. Population 10 Years of Age and Over

	Arabic	Berber	French and Arabic	French, Arabic, and Berber	French and Berber	French	Sum
Total population	.676	.097	.064	.041	.006	.116	1.000
Moslem	.780	.112	.053	.047	.007	.001	1.000
European	—	—	.135	.003	.001	.860	.999

Table 2. Language Distribution, Belgium, 1947. Population All Ages

	F	D	G	FD	FG	DG	FDG	None	Within-group H
Brabant	.293	.309	.001	.318	.010	.002	.036	.030	.748
French areas	.837	.007	.018	.056	.023	.001	.012	.046	.866
Dutch areas	.019	.753	.002	.152	.001	.005	.030	.040	.893

Note: F = French, D = Dutch, G = German.

measure of the communication possibilities within the entire population but would tell us nothing about the linguistic possibilities between the ethnic groups.

Both of these objections can be avoided by means of the following procedure. Taking the linguistic distribution of each population as shown in Table 1, we determine the cross-products between members of the two groups who have one or more common languages. We do not take the cross-products of common language among members of the same socially or spatially defined group, as we would if we were computing the value of $\underline{H}$ within a population. Letting A, B, and F represent Arabic, Berber, and French, and letting subscript 1 represent Moslem speakers, subscript 2 European speakers, the between-group $\underline{H}$ index is $A_1(A_2 + FA_2 + FAB_2) + B_1(B_2 + FAB_2 + FB_2) + FA_1(A_2 + FA_2 + FAB_2 + FB_2 + F_2) + FAB_1(A_2 + B_2 + FA_2 + FAB_2 + FB_2 + F_2) + FB_1(B_2 + FA_2 + FAB_2 + FB_2 + F_2) + F_1(FA_2 + FAB_2 + FB_2 + F_2)$. For communication between Moslems and French, the data in Table 1 yield $.780(0 + .135 + .003) + .112(0 + .003 + .001) + .053(0 + .135 + .003 + .001 + .860) + .047(0 + 0 + .135 + .003 + .001 + .860) + .007(0 + .135 + .003 + .001 + .860) + .001(.135 + .003 + .001 + .860)$. In this case, $\underline{H}$ between the two ethnic groups is .216.

As indicated earlier, the proposed measure is based upon the same type of analysis as Greenberg's and therefore the different computational procedure does not prevent us from interpreting the results along with that obtained for $\underline{H}$ within the populations. Algeria before the revolution was a society with a fairly high degree of overall communication, .669, but with its ethnic segments sharply split. That is, communication is rather high within the groups, but low between them. If we randomly select a Moslem and randomly select a European, they possess a common language a little oftener than twice out of 10 times.

3. The between group-application of Greenberg's measures is not restricted to two groups, but can be applied to as many groups as desired. Belgium is divided into three areas: the predominantly French-speaking area (Hainaut, Liège, Luxembourg, and Namur), the predominantly Dutch-speaking area (Antwerp, West Flanders, East Flanders, and Limburg), and Brabant, which includes Brussels, in the center. Again using the $\underline{H}$ index, we can determine the probabil-

ities of communication within each area by means of Greenberg's procedure. We find H̲ fairly high within each area, although it is lowest within Brabant (Table 2). By computing intergroup H̲ along the lines suggested earlier, we find communication is fairly high between Brabant and the Dutch and French areas, respectively .695 and .639. But H̲ between the Dutch and French areas is very low, .249. It is noteworthy that H̲ within Brabant is lower than H̲ within either the French or the Dutch area. Thus we find that a population with a relatively lower communication level within may have considerably higher communication levels with other areas than do linguistically more uniform areas. Finally, the use of both within- and between-area measures indicates that communication for residents of Brabant is nearly as great with residents of the Flemish and Walloon areas of Belgium as it is with fellow residents of Brabant (.695 and .639 compared with .748).

4. The application of this between-groups approach to all the measures of diversity proposed by Greenberg can be readily summarized. In each case, we need the linguistic distribution of the subpopulations that are to be examined. Second, we obtain the cross-products between the proportions of the two social groups using the same language(s), never multiplying within a subcategory but always across subpopulations. If the method is to be weighted by some resemblance factor like that based on glottochronology, as in the B̲, D̲, and F̲ measures (Greenberg 1956: 110-12), the between-group application is similarly weighted. In each instance we obtain a measure of diversity between subgroups which is independent of linguistic homogeneity within the subgroups and which is not distorted by the relative sizes of the groups. Rather, these measures describe the diversity existing between the two subpopulations in the form of a probability statement.

5. The procedure as well as the substantive potential may be illustrated with the A̲ index of linguistic diversity. This is called the Monolingual Nonweighted Method, and described thus (Greenberg 1956: 109): "If from a given area we choose two members of the population at random, the probability that these two individuals speak the same language can be considered a measure of its linguistic diversity." The conversion into a between-groups measure of A̲ is essentially as before, namely the probability that an individual randomly drawn from

Table 3. Mother-Tongue Distribution, Norwegian Foreign White
Stock in the United States, 1940

	Norwegian	English	Swedish	All other and not reported	Total
Foreign-born	.924	.051	.012	.013	1.000
Second generation	.502	.477	.008	.013	1.000

one population and an individual drawn from a second population will
speak the same language. This will be regarded as a measure of linguistic similarity between groups. If we have the mother-tongue distributions of two or more populations and, for example, wish to measure their linguistic diversity in a manner analogous to the within-
group A measure, we obtain the cross-products of the same language
in each group. Using data for the Norwegian first and second generations in the United States, shown in Table 3, we can compare the
linguistic diversity between generations for 1940 in the following manner:[3] $(.924)(.502) + (.051)(.477) + (.012)(.008) + (.013)(.013) = .488$.
Since Greenberg's indexes, except for the $\underline{H}$ discussed earlier, are
stated in the form of probability of diversity, I will follow his procedure by subtracting the cross-products from 1; thus $\underline{A} = 1 - .488 = .512$.
The range of our index runs from 0 (where pairing members of two
groups always yields speakers of the same language) to 1.000 (where
such pairing always yields speakers of different languages). In monolingual populations $\underline{A} = 1 - \underline{H}$.

The potentialities of using a between-group measure of linguistic diversity in conjunction with Greenberg's measure for within-
group diversity are illustrated with the data shown in Table 4. The
first two columns give the $\underline{A}$ measure within the first and second generations of various foreign white groups in the United States. We
observe some fairly sharp rises in diversity within generations of
the same foreign-born group. This is particularly the case for foreign-born groups that were relatively homogeneous in their mother
tongues, such as the Norwegians, Swedes, Germans, and Greeks.

Table 4. Mother-Tongue $\underline{A}$ Indexes Within and Between First-
and Second-Generation Groups, United States, 1940

| | $\underline{A}$ index within | | $\underline{A}$ index between |
	Foreign-born	Second generation	generations
Norway	.143	.520	.512
Sweden	.122	.513	.589
Switzerland	.495	.531	.739
Germany	.124	.524	.535
Greece	.113	.529	.468
Poland	.407	.485	.476
USSR	.603	.690	.762
Lithuania	.430	.583	.555

For example, the probability is .124 that two randomly selected
German-born immigrants will have different mother tongues; the
probability is .524 that two randomly selected second-generation
Germans will have different mother tongues. In all cases there is
less linguistic unity within the second generation than the first. This
is due to the generally sharp rise in English as a mother tongue in the
second generation, while a declining but still substantial segment of
the second generation retains the old-world mother tongue (like the
Norwegians shown in Table 3). Applying our between-group measure
$\underline{A}$, we see in the last column of Table 4 the probability of mother-
tongue diversity between randomly selected members of the two generations of the same national origin. These figures are strikingly
higher than those for diversity within the first generation.

6. Shown in Table 5 above the diagonal are the $\underline{A}$ indexes
between foreign-born groups computed in the manner suggested earlier.
We find very high diversity between different immigrant groups. For
example, the probability is .998 that a Norwegian and a German immigrant will have different mother tongues. Below the diagonal are
the intergroup diversity indexes for second-generation members of
these groups. With the one exception of the Swiss-German compari-

Table 5. Mother–Tongue A Indexes Between Foreign White Groups, United States, 1940

	Norway	Sweden	Switzerland	Germany	Greece	Poland	USSR	Lithuania
Norway		.980	.996	.998	.999	.999	.998	.999
Sweden	.725		.997	.998	.999	.999	.998	.999
Switzerland	.711	.659		.353	.999	.984	.949	.984
Germany	.763	.721	.548		.999	.971	.921	.978
Greece	.808	.774	.756	.800		.999	.999	.999
Poland	.892	.872	.859	.875	.909		.887	.952
USSR	.797	.761	.710	.738	.829	.872		.918
Lithuania	.865	.840	.825	.854	.886	.904	.855	

Note: First generation above diagonal; second generation below diagonal.

son, the diversity index is always higher for the foreign-born than the second generation. For example, the probability that a second-generation German and Norwegian will have different mother tongues is reduced to .763.

On a substantive basis, these data, in conjunction with those reported in Table 4, suggest that European immigrant groups in the United States were mostly very distinct from one another in their mother tongues. Differences between first and second generations in mother-tongue composition are in the direction of breaking down the initially high linguistic barriers between nationality groups accompanied by a drop in mother-tongue unity within the nationality groups. Moreover, we have seen that the mother-tongue diversity between generations of the same foreign group is fairly substantial and far greater than the diversity within the first generation. In other words, the process of assimilation involves a rise in foreign-mother-tongue diversity within nationality groups and a drop in mother-tongue diversity between different origin groups.

7. By means of Greenberg's indexes, it is possible to determine the linguistic communication within areas or socially significant populations. By means of the indexes proposed here, it is possible to get at questions of linguistic communication between segments of a given population. These measures, used in tandem, provide an instrument for a quantitative approach to a basic sociolinguistic problem, namely the degree to which language sets populations apart so that communication within social components of a population is greater than between the components.

NOTES

I gratefully acknowledge the support of the National Science Foundation Grant G-23923.
    [1] Joseph H. Greenberg, "The Measure of Linguistic Diversity," Language 32 (1956): 109-15.
    [2] They refer to Greenberg's paper as "one of the few instances we know in which descriptive statistics are constructed so as to have

operational interpretations in the sense that we have discussed."
See Leo A. Goodman and William H. Kruskal, "Measures of Association for Cross Classification. II. Further Discussion and References," Journal of the American Statistical Association 54 (1959): 155.

[3] For convenience I assume that speakers in the small category "all other and not reported" all speak the same language in both generations.

16 | The Anatomy of Language Diversity: Some Elementary Results

One of the central aspects of racial and ethnic contact is the degree to which language sets groups apart from one another. Where mutual intelligibility between groups is low, language is a major force for the maintenance of ethnic divisions. Where ethnic or racial groups share a common tongue, on the other hand, language provides a bridge between these populations and is an important steppingstone toward the decline of other group differences. There is a danger in overemphasizing the importance of language, since clearly groups can remain separate even if they are not divided on linguistic lines. It is relevant, though, that a shared language is necessary for the assimilation or merger of groups in contact—even if it is not always a sufficient condition. Where populations do not share the same tongue, communication channels along these language lines are necessarily restricted, and even groups that are in contact do not share the same experiences or possess a very high degree of mutual intelligibility. Even if ethnic groups with different mother tongues are bilingual, the ability to share the subtle nuances and communicate freely is still restricted by the lack of a common mother tongue. This is the essential message in Deutsch's notable effort to consider the role of language in the maintenance of ethnic groups (1953).

This chapter describes a basic procedure for analyzing the degree of linguistic intelligibility possible between members of each ethnic group studied, as well as between members of different ethnic groups. The procedure is designed to analyze the three fundamental influences on communication within any linguistically pluralistic situation, namely each group's mother-tongue composition, bilingualism, and segregation or other forms of non-random interaction. The concern here is clearly not with measuring or analyzing the institutional, cultural, and normative forces that generate these phenomena or alter them—for instance, government policies, the educational system, the work world, and economic and political power. Regardless of the starting point, the effect of any of these influences must be transferred through a change in one or more of the characteristics under study here.

If, for example, the values of a group are such that its members are unusually tenacious about their language, then we would expect this to influence the isolation, or bilingualism, or mother-tongue composition of the group. Similarly, if through economic changes stronger demands are made for fluency in a given tongue, the response will ultimately be an increase in bilingualism or in isolation. In addition, a group in process of linguistic shift will first exhibit a rise in bilingualism followed in turn by a change in mother-tongue composition. My position, however, is that these three attributes are more than intervening variables; rather, they are also important causal considerations for interpreting the outcome of linguistic contact. Regardless of values, for example, the position of a language spoken by 87 percent of the population will somehow be much stronger than in another community where the same tongue is used by only 2 percent of the populace. Here we can intuitively see that holding all other factors constant in the two communities, the fundamental nature of the linguistic contact will be influenced by population composition.

This chapter consists of three parts. First, a method is presented for analyzing potential linguistic communication within an ethnic population or the total community or nation. Second, an analogous method is presented for potential linguistic communication between ethnic or racial groups. Finally, some applications of these techniques are presented in order to give the reader some illustrations of their potential value in the study of linguistic bonds within and between groups. In all of the illustrations, I will assume that there are two mother tongues represented in each group or community, designated as A and B, and that some members of each mother tongue are monolingual, designated by a subscript o for only. The subscript a designates those who speak A as a second language and b designates those who have learned B as a second tongue. Some of this may seem unnatural since there are situations where all members of a given ethnic group have a common mother tongue, or where no members are bilingual, but this example does provide all of the basi computations that would be involved in even more complicated multi-lingual social situations.

Communication Within a Community or Group: H_w

One of the simplest and most direct measures of potential speech in a shared tongue is H, the Index of Communication, propose by Greenberg. This is "the probability that if two members of the population are chosen at random, they will have at least one language in common" (Greenberg 1956: 112). H then is a basic statistical tool for describing the degree to which a population can participate in mut ually intelligible speech. Its range runs from 1.00 (where every pos-sible pair of speakers share at least one common tongue) to 0 (the unlikely extreme where every speaker possesses a different mother tongue and has not learned the language of anyone else). It is expres in operational form, a characteristic which has drawn praise from th statisticians Goodman and Kruskal (1959: 155), so that the probability of mutually intelligible speech can be stated once the linguistic abil-ities of the population are known.

H_w is computed in the following way. Following Lieberson's terminology (1965: 13), we will use the subscript w to label this mea-sure of linguistic communication within a population. Suppose there is a community (or an ethnic group) where two languages are used, s that 20 percent of the population are native speakers of A and 80 per-cent are native speakers of B. Assume that some speakers of each mother tongue have learned the second language of the community; in this case one-fourth of the A speakers can also speak B and one-eight of the B speakers can communicate in A. The subscript o is used to designate those who speak only their mother tongue, a designates thos who speak A as a second tongue, and b designates members of the por ulation who have learned B as their second language. The community is divided proportionately as follows:

$$A_o = .15$$
$$B_o = .70$$
$$A_b = .05$$
$$B_a = .10$$
$$\text{Total} = 1.00$$

H_W is simply the proportion of all pairs of persons in which one or more mutually intelligible tongue is shared. In this case,

$$H_W = (A_o)^2 + (B_o)^2 + (A_b + B_a)^2 + 2A_o(A_b + B_a) + 2B_o(A_b + B_a).$$

Thus $H_W = (.15)^2 + (.70)^2 + (.05 + .10)^2 + 2(.15)(.05 + .10) + 2(.70)$ $(.05 + .10) = .79$. If two people are randomly selected from the population, mutually intelligible communication will be possible in 79 percent of the cases. In $1.00 - H_W$, or 21 percent of the time, verbal communication between randomly interacting pairs will be impossible.

A given H_W can be achieved through different combinations of mono- and bilingualism among a population. For example, if all of the A's were monolingual, $A_o = .20$, and if the B's were distributed so that $B_o = .525$ and $B_a = .275$, then H_W would again be .79. As the example suggests, although the index describes the degree of mutually intelligible communication possible within a population, it fails to provide any information about the strength of each tongue, the relative degree of use in communication, and the separate impact on the monolingual and bilingual segment of each language group. To accomplish this, the simple situation is decomposed into the various components shown in Table 1.

First, observe that H_W is equal to the sum of components I, II, and III. In effect, communication occurs in one of three ways: through language A in situations where one or both speakers only known A (component I); through B when one or both speakers are able to use only B (II); and through either tongue where two bilingual speakers are in contact so that either language can be used (III). In the first two instances, a bilingual speaker must use the monolingual's language regardless of the former's preference if communication is to occur. Component IV gives the proportion of contact situations in which linguistic communication is impossible. This is a function of the relative sizes of the two monolingual groups, $1 - H = 2(A_o)(B_o)$. Making the fairly reasonable assumption that most bilinguals will use their mother tongue among other bilinguals with the same mother tongue, the optional component, III, can be divided into three subcategories: III_a, those cases of interaction where A will probably be favored; III_b, where B will be favored; III_c, those cases where bilinguals with different mother tongues are in contact and where no natural

Table 1. Components of the H_W Index

Component	Description	Encounter Type	Formula	Illustration
I	A must be used	(a) $A_o A_o$	$(A_o)^2$	.0225
		(b) $A_o A_b$	$2(A_o A_b)$	.0150
		(c) $A_o B_a$	$2(A_o B_a)$	.0300
	Sum: $(A_o)^2 + 2A_o (A_b + B_a)$			.0675
II	B must be used	(a) $B_o B_o$	$(B_o)^2$	.4900
		(b) $B_o B_a$	$2(B_o B_a)$	.1400
		(c) $B_o A_b$	$2(B_o A_b)$	.0700
	Sum: $(B_o)^2 + 2B_o (B_a + A_b)$			.7000
III	Option (favoring A) (a) $A_b A_b$		$(A_b)^2$	.0025
	Option (favoring B) (b) $B_a B_a$		$(B_a)^2$	.0100
	Option (no clear preference)			
		(c) $A_b B_a$	$2(A_b)(B_a)$	.0100
	Sum: $(A_b)^2 + (B_a)^2 + 2(A_b)(B_a)$			.0225
Total probability of communication				.7900
IV	No communication possible			
		$A_o B_o$	$2(A_o)(B_o)$	.2100

NOTE: Illustration based on figures given in text for hypothetical situation.

preference is evident. The sum of these three subcomponents total to III. The proportion of all contact situations in which A can be used is determined by the sum of components I and III; the proportion in which B can be used is the sum of II and III.

Communication Potential Between Ethnic Groups: H_b

For either an ethnic group or community, the components of H_W presented in Table 1 provide a means for examining the communication potential existing at a given time as well as the ramifications for communication of any specified change in mother-tongue composition or bilingualism. However, the H_W index does not determine the potential communication between the ethnic groups of a community, although it can be used to measure communication within these groups. Elsewhere, the author has shown why H_w cannot be employed in the analysis of communication between groups and, in addition, has proposed an index that is fully compatible with Greenberg's measure of within-group diversity (Lieberson 1964).

The solution essentially involves taking the linguistic distribution of each population and then determining the sum of cross-products between members of the two groups who share one or more common languages. This measure of potential communication between subpopulations, H_b, gives the probability that if one member is chosen at random from each of two populations they will have at least one language in common and therefore be able to speak to each other.

Suppose there are two languages, A and B, spoken in each ethnic group, I and J, and that bilingualism exists among members of both mother tongues. For the two groups, I and J, $H_b = I_{Ao}(J_{Ao} + J_{Ab} + J_{Ba}) + I_{Bo}(J_{Bo} + J_{Ba} + J_{Ab}) + I_{Ab}(J_{Ao} + J_{Ab} + J_{Ba} + J_{Bo}) + I_{Ba}(J_{Ao} + J_{Ab} + J_{Bo} + J_{Ba})$, where the subscripts indicate the proportion of the specified ethnic group with a given mother tongue (uppercase) and second tongue, if any (lowercase). Monolinguals are indicated by a lowercase $\underline{o}$. Thus, if $I_{Ao} = .15$, this means 15 percent of the I ethnic group have mother tongue A and are monolingual.

H_b, like H_w, has a range from 0 to 1, where 0 means no language is shared between speakers of the two groups and 1.0 would occur if all members of each ethnic group could speak to all members of the other group. Having introduced this additional measure, ethnic subscripts will distinguish between the two measures. Thus, H_i will refer to the H_w measure within ethnic group I; H_j will refer to H_w for ethnic group J; H_{ij} will refer to mutual intelligibility between the two groups; and H_{i+j} will refer to communication within the combined total population consisting of I and J members.

Based on the hypothetical language distributions shown at the bottom of Table 2, an example is provided of the computation of the index for potential communication between members of ethnic groups I and J. As was the case for H_w, the H_{ij} index is equal to the sum of three components: communication through language A in circumstances where one or both people speak only A, communication through lan-

Table 2. Components of the H_{ij} Index

Component	Description	Encounter Type	Illustration
I	A must be used	(a) I_{A_0} J_{A_0}	.0375
		(b) I_{A_0} J_{A_b}	.0825
		(c) I_{A_0} J_{B_a}	.0000
		(d) I_{A_b} J_{A_0}	.0125
		(e) I_{B_a} J_{A_0}	.0250
	Sum: $I_{A_0} (J_{A_0} + J_{A_b} + J_{B_a}) + J_{A_0} (I_{A_b} + I_{B_a})$		.1575
II	B must be used	(a) I_{A_b} J_{B_0}	.0100
		(b) I_{B_a} J_{B_0}	.0200
		(c) I_{B_0} J_{A_b}	.3850
		(d) I_{B_0} J_{B_a}	.0000
		(e) I_{B_0} J_{B_0}	.1400
	Sum: $I_{B_0} (J_{A_b} + J_{B_a} + J_{B_0}) + J_{B_0} (I_{A_b} + I_{B_a})$		.5550
III	Option (favoring A)	(a) I_{A_b} J_{A_b}	.0275
	Option (favoring B)	(b) I_{B_a} J_{B_a}	.0000
	Option (no clear preference)	(c) I_{A_b} J_{B_a}	.0000
	Option (no clear preference)	(d) I_{B_a} J_{A_b}	.0550
	Sum: $I_{B_a} (J_{B_a} + J_{A_b}) + I_{A_b} (J_{A_b} + J_{B_a})$		.0825
Total probability of communication			.7950
IV	No communication possible	(a) I_{A_0} J_{B_0}	.0300
		(b) I_{B_0} J_{A_0}	.1750
	Sum:		.2050

NOTE: Encounter type and formulas are identical and hence not shown separately. Illustration based on figures given below for hypothetical situation:

	I	J
A_0	.15	.25
B_0	.70	.20
A_b	.05	.55
B_a	.10	.00
Total	1.00	1.00

guage B in analogous circumstances for language B, and where communication is possible in either tongue because both the I and J ethnic group members are bilingual. The two subcomponents where no mutually shared language is held are also indicated.

One consequence of obtaining the H_i, H_j, and H_{ij} measures is that communication potential within each of the ethnic groups, respectively I and J, may be compared with the potential between groups. This enables one to measure the role of language as a bond setting off the ethnic groups from one another as well as its cohesive force within each group. Of particular interest is the degree of communication possible within and between the ethnic groups with and without bilingualism. The latter, based on just the mother-tongue composition of the groups, may be easily measured with procedures discussed elsewhere. Computing the $\underline{A}$ index for mother-tongue diversity—described in Greenberg (1956) for measurement within an ethnic group and in Lieberson (1964) for measurement between ethnic groups —it is only necessary that the index so obtained be subtracted from 1.0 to obtain a value that is exactly analogous to the H indexes described here. In an application based on various Canadian cities, the result is that often the mother-tongue bond is stronger between the French and British ethnic groups than it is within the French group. Bilingualism in a number of these cases has the surprising quality of raising within-group communication potential more rapidly than raising the potential for communication between ethnic groups (see Lieberson 1970: 241-45).

Some Implications

Three serious questions about these procedures should be considered. First, are there data that can be applied to these analytical techniques? Second, given the complex set of factors that affect language behavior—for instance, power, values, work pressures, mobility, and the like—are these procedures so oversimplified that they are of little value in understanding the role of language in the bonds within and between ethnic or racial groups? Third, what do they tell us about linguistic issues that are not evident from the tabulations themselves?

As for the first question, not only are there census data for several countries that provide information on mother tongue and bilingualism—Cyprus, India, and Canada, for example—but any sociolinguistic or ethnic study having field research that entailed gathering data on the language skills of the population would provide data applicable to these techniques. I have no doubt that there will be an increasing number of this type of data sets.

As for the second question, it is of course true that a complex set of factors affects the language patterns of ethnic groups in contact. The analytical procedures outlined in the two tables, however, do enable one to determine the consequences for within- and between-group communication potential under any observed or hypothetical set of conditions. One can determine, for example, the consequences of any set of changes in mother-tongue composition (due, for example, to migration) or in bilingualism (due to new industrial requirements or changes in the educational opportunity structure) or in segregation (such that members of a given group change the frequency with which they are in contact with other segments of the community in terms of where they work or live or attend school). These are powerful tools, even if the underlying causes are not directly measured, insofar as the procedures permit some consideration of the consequences that develop.

As for the implications of these components, I have listed some below that I find either not to be obvious or, if so, to be important enough that a formal proof is valuable in understanding the role of language in ethnic relations.

Mother-tongue composition. The consequence of a change in mother-tongue composition is different for communication within an ethnic group (the H_i or H_j measure) as opposed to communication between ethnic groups (H_{ij}). A unit change in mother-tongue composition due to migration, mortality, fertility, intergenerational shift, or other factors will have varying effects on communication potential within a population. For example, if there is a community where half of the populace are A's and the other half B's, then a shift of the nature that 60 percent of the population are B's will have relatively little influence on the degree of mutually intelligible communication in the community. In this case, H_w would rise from .50 to .52, a change of .02. By contrast, in a community where 80 percent are monolingual A's and 20 percent B_O's, a change to a situation where 90 percent are A_O's would raise H_W from .68 to .82, a rise of .14. In short, a change in a community where most members share a common mother tongue will have a more severe impact on overall communication than a change of equal magnitude in a community with a lower initial H_W.

By contrast, unit changes in mother-tongue composition have a constant effect on the level of interethnic communication potential. This leads to a curious paradox: a given change in a group's mother-tongue composition will not necessarily have the same consequences for within- and between-group communication potential. Indeed, as far as within-group communication is concerned, shifts in mother-tongue composition have a changing impact on communication potential.[1]

Bilingualism. Rather clearly, communication potential within a group will rise as bilingualism increases. Where all other factors are constant, H_W-type indexes will change in accordance with the degree of bilingualism among the mother-tongue populations. Less obvious are some quantitative relationships between bilingualism and mutual intelligibility. In the simple situation where only two mother tongues are present, shifts of equal magnitude between the bilingual and monolingual segments of a given mother-tongue population have an impact on H_W, which is a function of the mother-tongue composition of the community and the degree of bilingualism among the mother-tongue group held constant.

Following component IV presented earlier in Table 1, we recognize that $H_W = 1.00 - 2A_O B_O$. Since B_O and 2 are constant regardless of the initial level of A_O, a unit change in A_O will have a constant effect on H_W, which is a function of $2B_O$. Thus a unit change in bilingualism among a given mother-tongue group leads to a unit change in H_W regardless of the initial degree of bilingualism in the population undergoing a shift.

To put this into applied terms, visualize two cities in Canada; the proportion of the population who are monolingual B speakers and bilingual B's is the same in both. However, nearly all the A's in one city are bilingual while almost no A's in the second city can speak B. If an equal number of monolingual A's in the two cities now learn B, the H_W indexes for the two communities will rise equally—although they differ in their initial positions. A rise from 85 percent to 100 percent bilingualism among A's will increase H_W as much as an equal rise from 0 to 15 percent bilingualism among A's in the second city.

A second observation about the relation between bilingualism and communication within a population is that the influence on H_W of unit shifts in bilingualism among one mother-tongue population will vary in accordance with the degree of bilingualism among the mother-tongue group held constant. The greater the degree of monolingualism among one speech group, the smaller the total communication within the community or society, holding everything else constant. However, the greater will be the rise in communication with a unit increase in bilingualism among the other mother-tongue population.

This indicates that the effect of an equal degree of bilingualism will vary with the mother-tongue composition of the community and with the group that is bilingual. Let A be the smaller mother-tongue group, so that A < B; let K be the number of people who are bilingual; further, let K $\leq$ A. Then H_W will be highest where all the bilinguals K have mother-tongue A. H_W will be the lowest where all the bilinguals are members of mother-tongue B. And H_W will vary directly with A_b/K. This is shown in Table 3, where the 5 percent of the population that are bilinguals are shifted so that: first, all bilinguals are A's; second, all bilinguals are B's; and finally, half of the bilinguals are A's and half are B's. The range of H_W varies from .76 to .70 depending on which group are the bilinguals. More generally, holding population composition constant as well as the percentage of the community who are bilingual, H_W will go up as the bilingual component shifts from the larger group to the smaller.

A striking quantitative implication of this general statement deals with the degree of bilingualism in each group necessary to yield the same H_W. The H_W obtained when a given percent of the larger mother-tongue group is bilingual will equal the H_W obtained when the same percent of the smaller mother-tongue group is bilingual. This means that where there is a considerable difference in size between the two language groups, it will take a far greater number of bilinguals among the larger group to yield the same degree of mutual intelligibilit

Table 3. Variations in the Effect of Bilingualism on Communication
Potential Within a Community

Linguistic Component	A is bilingual	B is bilingual	A and B are bilingual
A_o	.15	.20	.175
B_o	.80	.75	.775
A_b	.05	0	.025
B_a	0	.05	.025
H_w	.76	.70	.729

within the community. In terms of minimizing effort, if we ignore
difficulties in learning languages, the optimum means for raising
mutual intelligibility through bilingualism is by having only the smaller
mother-tongue group become bilingual. Implications of this finding
for underdeveloped areas and other nations endeavoring to formulate
a national language policy are clear-cut. While there are many other
factors for planners and statesmen to consider, it is readily possible
to draw out a program for obtaining a given level of mutual intelligibility that involves the minimum degree of second-language learning.

It is important to recognize that the degree of bilingualism
in each mother-tongue group will fluctuate over time. Assuming
again that A is the smaller of the two mother-tongue groups, on the
basis of earlier observations we would expect net changes in bilingualism among a given number of A speakers to alter the degree of intelligibility more than a change of the same number among the B mother-
tongue group. This means that the importance of shifts in bilingualism for the total community will vary in accordance with the mother-
tongue group involved. It is possible to state the exact increase in
bilingualism necessary among one mother-tongue group to compensate
for a decline in bilingualism among the other speech group. Similarly,
if a group increases its bilingualism, it is easy to determine the drop
in bilingualism that can occur among speakers of the second mother
tongue without a decline in H_w. If we define A_o' as the number speaking A_o after a shift and B_o' as the number speaking B_o after a shift,
then these four rules apply to all two-language contact situations:

If K people shift from A_b to A_o, then the number of B_o who must become bilingual to maintain H_w at its previous level is:

$$B_o - \frac{(A_o)(B_o)}{B_o'}$$

If K people shift from A_o to A_b, the number of B_a who can become monolingual without a decline in H_w is:

$$\frac{(A_o)(B_o)}{A_o'} - B_o$$

If K people shift from B_a to B_o, then the number of A_o who must become bilingual to maintain H_w at its previous level is:

$$A_o - \frac{(A_o)(B_o)}{B_o'}$$

If K people shift from B_o to B_a, the number of A_b who can become monolingual without a decline in H_w is:

$$\frac{(A_o)(B_o)}{B_o'} - A_o$$

To illustrate the application of these formulas, consider a population of 1,000 with an initial linguistic distribution as follows: A_o is 150, A_b is 50, B_o is 700, and B_a is 100. The proportional distribution among the four language components is, respectively, .15, .05, .70, and .10, with an H_w index of .79. Suppose the monolingual B mother-tongue population declines by 140 such that B_o is now 560 and B_a is 240. Given this increase in bilingualism among the B population, how large a number of A_b speakers could shift to A_o without dropping the H_w index? Applying the last of the four equations shown above, the number equals:

$$\frac{(A_o)(B_o)}{B_o'} - A_o, \quad \text{thus} \quad \frac{(150)(700)}{560} - 150 ,$$

which equals 37.5. This is .0375 of the population. Hence, given that B_o has become .56 and B_a is .24, H_w would remain unchanged if A_o increases to .1875 (.15 + .0375) and A_b drops to .0125 (.05 − .0375).

Communication within and between ethnic groups. If there are two ethnic groups, two mother tongues in each group, no bilingual ism, and the largest mother tongue in each ethnic group is different, then communication within each ethnic population will inevitably exceed communication across ethnic lines, that is, H_{ij} will be less than either H_i or H_j. For example, if A = .9 and B = .1 for ethnic group I, and A = .1 and B = .9 for the J group, then H_{ij} will be only .18 whereas H_i and H_j will both be .82.

The exact relationship between H_{ij} and the linguistic composition of ethnic groups I and J may be determined in the two-language-monolingual context on the basis of the following formula:

$$H_{ij} = .50 + (I_A - I_B)(J_A - .50),$$

where I_A is the proportion of ethnic group I with mother tongue A; I_B is the proportion of ethnic group I with mother tongue B; J_A is the proportion of ethnic group J with mother tongue A. This formula shows the effect of changes in the linguistic composition of one group on intergroup communication when the composition of the second ethnic group remains constant. The formula also applies, incidentally, to cases where the largest mother tongue is the same in each of the two ethnic groups.

If the largest mother tongue is different in the two groups, out-group communication will be only slightly less than in-group communication when both H_i and H_j are relatively low. When in-group communication is very high for both groups, then out-group communication will be low both in an absolute sense and in comparison to the degree of mutual intelligibility within each group.

Contact settings where the numerically largest mother tongue is the same for each ethnic group are also of interest. In cases of linguistic assimilation, we would expect to find an intermediate stage where the same mother tongue is most important in each group, but where a sizable minority of the assimilating group still retains the old mother tongue. Under such conditions, the assimilating group will actually have lower mutual intelligibility among themselves than with the second ethnic population. Where two ethnic populations differ in their mother-tongue composition but both have the same numerically dominant mother tongue, then with no bilingualism we will find $H_i > H_{ij} > H_j$, if I is the ethnic group that is more homogeneous linguistically. Where two groups share the same dominant mother tongue,

but in different degrees, the situation will be one in which a decline
will be expected in linguistic unity among the more heterogeneous
group in the sense that communication within J will be lower than the
communication potential that J members have with the I group. Observe, of course, that this does not hold for ethnic group I since
their in-group communication potential exceeds the potential for that
across ethnic boundaries. Where linguistic assimilation has proceeded
far enough so that the group's most important tongue is the same as
that of the other group, we can see how tenuous unity within the assimilating group becomes.

In view of the important differences between contact settings
where the largest mother tongue is the same in both ethnic groups
and those settings where different mother tongues are dominant, we
shall refer to the former as "shared dominance" and the latter as
"distinctive dominance." In shared dominance settings, linguistic
unity within the less homogeneous ethnic group is actually lower than
it is with the other ethnic group. In distinctive dominance settings,
both ethnic groups always have higher within-group than between-
group mutual intelligibility.

Bilingualism. Acquisition of a second language by some members of an ethnic group will raise the potential for both in-group communication (assuming that not all members share the same mother
tongue) and also raise H between the ethnic groups. The first question to ask is whether in-group or out-group communication is raised
more rapidly by bilingualism. No flat answer can be given; rather,
the mother-tongue composition of the two groups determines if H_i or
H_{ij} increases more rapidly when bilingualism occurs among some
members of the I group.

The techniques presented in this paper allow one to analyze
the implications of the various possible situations. Consider a setting where only two mother tongues are found and where all second-
language learning occurs in these languages. Under these circumstances, a change in monolingualism can only occur through an opposite change in the bilingual segment able to speak both tongues. First,
we can define our H measures as follows:

$$H_i = 1 - 2(I_{Ao})(I_{Bo}),$$
$$H_j = 1 - 2(J_{Ao})(J_{Bo}),$$
$$H_{ij} = 1 - [(I_{Ao})(J_{Bo}) + (I_{Bo})(J_{Ao})].$$

Using Delta to indicate a change in value from an earlier status, we can see that a change in I_{Ao} will have the following effect:

$$Delta\ H_i = Delta\ I_{Ao}(2I_{Bo}),$$
$$Delta\ H_{ij} = Delta\ I_{Ao}(J_{Bo}).$$

Therefore, we conclude that bilingualism among members of I will raise H_{ij} more rapidly than H_i only under the following conditions:

If I_{Ab} increases, H_{ij} will rise more rapidly when $J_B > 2I_B$.
If I_{Ba} increases, H_{ij} will rise more rapidly when $J_A > 2I_A$.

Of course, were both the A- and B-speaking members of an ethnic group all to become bilingual, then H_i would equal H_{ij} since communication would be possible in all cases. For analytical purposes, however, it is advisable to restrict ourselves to the situation where members of only one linguistic segment of an ethnic group become bilingual. In terms of practical application, the formulas given above are extremely important for contact settings where there is distinctive dominance, i.e. where the dominant mother tongue is different in the two ethnic groups. If I's dominant tongue is A and J's dominant tongue is B, then the learning of a second language by the I_{Ao} population could undermine linguistic unity in I only if $J_B < 2I_B$. What this means is that bilingualism among the dominant mother tongue of one ethnic group has an impact on the relative rise of in-group versus out-group communication which depends on the compositional conditions indicated above. On the one hand, in-group unity may actually rise more rapidly than out-group unity even when the other group's dominant mother tongue is learned by the second ethnic population. Under other circumstances, bilingualism can sharply undercut the degree language provides a unifying force for the ethnic groups.

A second question follows from the answer to the first: namely, in those distinctive dominance settings where out-group communication rises more rapidly than in-group communication, with sufficient bilingualism can the H_{ij} index actually exceed H_i? The

answer is no, at least under the conditions where only one mother-
tongue segment of an ethnic group becomes bilingual. Although the
more rapid rise in intergroup communication potential through bilingualism will lead to a decline in the differential, which in some cases
may be considerable, linguistic potential will never be lower within
the groups whose members become bilingual than across ethnic lines.

Segregation. The limitations of space do not permit a thorough mathematical consideration here of the linguistic consequences
of segregation. Whether one examines residential location, work
situations, or other contact settings, it is clear that racial and ethnic
groups tend to be segregated. It is also clear that such forms of
segregation reduce the needs for communication across ethnic lines
and, in turn, thereby reduce to some unknown degree the need to
acquire a second language. As a consequence, segregation can be
viewed as an alternative to bilingualism. How much of an alternative
is a moot point, but it is at least in part affected by the groups' mothe
tongue composition. Although he works from a somewhat different
perspective, Coleman's examination of segregation is of interest here
He finds that size of group has a bearing on the magnitude of segregation necessary for members of the group to attain a certain frequency
of interaction with compatriots (Coleman 1964: 484-87). As one migh
expect, there is an inverse linkage such that less segregation is required as the group's relative size increases. If one postulates some
minimal level of communication potential needed at a given stage of
industrial and social development, the ability of groups to isolate
themselves instead of (or as a partial alternative to) becoming bilingual will vary directly with the group's size. On the other hand, the
pressure to become bilingual, holding such forces as political power
and economic dominance constant, will vary inversely with group size
Accordingly, it should be possible to work out curves whereby one
can determine the magnitude of segregation necessary as an alternative to a given level of bilingualism for a specific mother-tongue situation.

Regarding segregation, one should also note the incredible
complexity that may exist when there are linguistic differences among
members of each ethnic group. In a simple situation where there are
two mother tongues represented within an ethnic group, there will be
four separate linguistic subclasses; that is, there can be both bilingua

and monolingual speakers of each of the two mother tongues among members of a single ethnic group. Under these circumstances, the frequency of ethnic interaction does not necessarily correspond to the degree of mutual intelligibility—indeed they may very well run in opposite directions. A dilemma exists for some linguistic components of an ethnic group since the optimal form of ethnic interaction is not the optimal means for maximizing linguistic contact and, likewise, the optimal form of linguistic interaction reduces the degree of contact with ethnic compatriots from the maximum possible. Consider, for example, the ethnolinguistic situation in Montreal. Since the mother tongue of the French ethnic population is predominantly French, communication for the small number of French ethnics with an English mother tongue would hardly be raised through the maximization of contact with their ethnic compatriots. The interaction pattern among English mother-tongue members of the French ethnic population would also depend on whether they had acquired French as a second language. Far more significant numerically is the behavior of the sizable bilingual and monolingual segments of the French mother-tongue component. Since bilingual French Canadians have no need to interact with French Canadians in order to maximize their degree of mutual intelligibility, a very important consideration is whether the bilinguals differ from monolinguals in their patterns of linguistic and ethnic association. Analogous questions could be asked about Montrealers of British origin or of any other ethnic group whose members differ in mother tongue or acquired languages.

The point is that the linguistic components of each ethnic group may vary greatly in their optimal strategies for maximizing intelligibility and contacts with ethnic compatriots. Moreover, if we postulate some maximum segregation ratio possible for each ethnolinguistic segment of a community (that is, the component of an ethnic group with identical linguistic capabilities), then we will find that often the groups face a dilemma in the alternatives available to them. Even without considering the maximum self-selection possible, however, the groups face alternatives in the degree linguistic communication or ethnic contact is maximized.

Conclusion

The techniques presented allow one to analyze mathematically the role of language as a bond both between and within ethnic groups. It must be emphasized that these techniques do not allow one to deal with ultimate causes. Nevertheless, they provide analytical tools for examining the implications that any and all mother-tongue and bilingual situations have for ethnic unity. Although only touched upon here, very likely the next expansion of this procedure is an analysis of the ethnolinguistic impact of segregation in various domains such as residence, work, education, and other institutions.

NOTES

The support of the Ford Foundation, Grant 755-0669, is gratefully acknowledged.
[1] I have not attempted to provide the algebraic proofs in this paper, but the interested reader may determine the nature of the relationships by inspecting formulas shown in Tables 1 and 2 or experimenting with a hypothetical data set.

REFERENCES

Coleman, James S. 1964. Introduction to mathematical sociology. New York: Free Press.
Deutsch, Karl W. 1953. Nationalism and social communication. Cambridge: Technology Press of the Massachusetts Institute of Technology.
Goodman, Leo A., and William H. Kruskal. 1959. Measures of association for cross classifications. II. Further discussion and references. Journal of the American Statistical Association 54: 123-63.
Greenberg, Joseph H. 1956. The measurement of linguistic diversity. Language 32: 109-15.

Lieberson, Stanley. 1964. An extension of Greenberg's linguistic
    diversity measures. Language 40: 526-31.
_____. 1965. Bilingualism in Montreal: a demographic analysis.
    American Journal of Sociology 71: 10-25.
_____. 1970. Language and ethnic relations in Canada. New
    York: John Wiley.

17 | How Can We Describe and Measure the Incidence and Distribution of Bilingualism?

The kinds of questions about bilingualism that can be asked in a census or any large-scale survey are restricted by certain limitations inherent to such studies. The questionnaire must be constructed so that it can be readily understood not only by the respondents but by interviewers who will normally have no technical competence in linguistics. The goal of censuses is usually to eliminate or minimize the judgments required of the field workers. Moreover, the questions must be completed in a relatively short period of time. This means that there are many facets of bilingualism which, at least at present, cannot be measured on a general purpose census. To expect a census to tap such dimensions as interference, switching, diglossia, dialects, styles, and registers would be like listening to a soprano amplified through the sound system of ball park. There are aspects of bilingualism for which the instrument is inadequate. If a population were surveyed about their diglossia, for example, there is reason to believe that many would be unaware of, or would at least deny, their use of the low variety (Ferguson 1964: 431).

On the other hand, censuses offer certain important advantages. They can yield data on bilingualism for a far larger population than any linguist could possibly hope to interview during a lifetime of work. Moreover, the coverage is relatively more complete and less distorted than what would normally be obtained in the field. In addition, the possibility is presented of linking the data with earlier censuses of the same area as well as with other bilingual settings. In other words, censuses are not appropriate for linguistic analysis per se, but they are an excellent device for determining the frequency, distribution, trends, and social correlates of bilingualism.

One major problem about bilingualism questions in censuses pertains to the validity of the results obtained. There is the possibility of intentional distortion by the respondent because of either prestige, political, or ethnic reasons. Commenting on the adequacy of the linguistic data in the 1940 census of Brazil, Mortara (1950: 39-40) observes that the results would have been far less satisfactory after Brazil's neutrality ceased. Census results from some parts of India have been questioned on these grounds (see, for example, the discussion of Kelley 1966: 306). But even the well-intentioned respondent will often find it difficult to give a correct answer to the census taker's question about the languages he can speak. If bilingualism is not clearly defined by the profession, ranging from Bloomfield's "native-like control of two languages" on to Diebold's conception of passive-knowledge (Mackey 1962: 52), what can be expected of the linguistically naive respondent?

Thus, the problem comes down to the optimal questions about bilingualism that will minimize intentional distortion, reduce the subjectivity of the respondents' answers, and provide the researcher with meaningful information about the linguistic capacity of the population which will be most suitable for analysis with other social characteristics obtained in the census. In other words, after deciding on the most desired information about this elusive quality called "bilingualism," the goal is to develop simple questions that will reproduce as nearly as possible the results that would be obtained if expert linguists had interviewed and classified each respondent according to a specific set of criteria.

There are two other major problems in the demographic study of bilingualism besides the development of measures of linguistic ability suitable for censuses. It is necessary to also determine what other social characteristics of the respondents are relevant and worth measuring. Second, one must also know the appropriate descriptive and analytical techniques to use with the data obtained. For the moment, little need be said about these two issues since they mainly involve errors of omission rather than commission.

Attempted Solutions

Several different types of language questions have been asked on censuses which are pertinent to measuring bilingualism. These are mother tongue, language used in the home or most frequently, and ability to speak one or more languages (United Nations 1964: 39). Although only the latter question deals directly with bilingualism, the first two are important to consider since they provide crucial linguistic information about the population and may, at times, be used to infer some aspects of bilingualism. Information on only the bilingual capacities of a population, unless accompanied by data on their mother tongues, ethnic origins, or some other similar characteristic, fail to indicate which segments of the population have been acquiring additional languages. Some of the Belgian censuses provide a good illustration of these difficulties. Although reporting trilingualism as well as bilingualism and monoglots, no information is given on the native tongue of the respondents. Instead, data are reported on language preference, a very ambiguous matter. This makes it difficult to determine mother tongues of the multilingual population.

The questions used to measure bilingualism are usually rather simple and, although usually dealing with the skills of speaking and understanding, they are often ambiguous for all but the most fluent and the most ignorant. In most instances the answers are restricted to certain specific languages, although some nations instruct the enumerator to merely record the language(s) reported by the respondent. The question is often of the utmost simplicity; for example, the 1961 question on Gaelic in the census of Scotland merely asked the enumerator to check off those who speak Gaelic only or both Gaelic and English. The commentary is rather revealing: "'Speaking Gaelic' is itself an expression that was left to the interpretation of the persons supplying the information on the schedule" (General Register Office 1966: ix).

In the 1930 census of the United States an effort was made to learn if the foreign-born population could speak English. The entire set of instructions for the enumerator were as follows: "Write 'Yes' for a person 10 years of age and over who can speak English, and 'No' for a person who cannot speak English. For persons under 10 years of age leave the column blank" (Bureau of the Census 1933: 1400). In evaluating these data, the Bureau acknowledged that "determination of this ability has been left to the judgement of the enumerator, and no specific tests of the knowledge of the English language have been prescribed. The standards may therefore be subject to some varia-

tions in different parts of the country, but on the whole the replies
are believed to indicate the ability or inability to use the English language in ordinary daily activities" (Bureau of the Census 1935: 1437).

The question on bilingualism used in Canada for a number of
decades is equally simple: "Can you speak English? French?" The
Enumeration Manual, at least for the 1951 census, raises no questions
about the meaning of the question other than with respect to infants
(Dominion Bureau of Statistics 1951: 40). A slight variation of this
approach is evident in the 1960 census of Americans living overseas
where the question dealt with ability to speak any of the local languages.
The provisal was made, "If he knows only a few words of the language,
check 'No'" (Bureau of the Census 1964: xix). Likewise, in the question used for the District of Puerto Rico, "Persons were classified
as able to speak English if they reported that they could make themselves understood in English. However, persons who could speak
only a few words, such as 'Hello' and 'Goodbye,' were classified as
unable to speak English" (Bureau of the Census 1962: xx). Thus,
there is sometimes an effort made to slightly qualify the question so
as to eliminate an affirmative answer among those with very minimal
linguistic competence. Nevertheless the illustrations above are by
no means exceptional in the degree to which bilingualism is left un-
classified.

In passing it should be noted that both the Puerto Rican and
Scotland questions, although dealing primarily with the individual's
ability to speak a single specified language, can be used to draw inferences about bilingualism. In Scotland, unless a respondent indicates
that he can only speak Gaelic, it may be safely inferred that he speaks
English. Likewise, if one assumes that virtually everyone speaks
Spanish in Puerto Rico, knowledge of the English-speaking ability of
various segments of the population enables one to classify the population into those who are bilingual in both tongues. In these instances
the procedure would involve errors; for example, there will be some
Puerto Ricans who know English but not Spanish and there must surely
be recent residents of Scotland who know neither English nor Gaelic.
But clearly under some circumstances it is possible to gain a great
deal of information about bilingualism by only concentrating on one
language. To be sure, it would eliminate certain types of data which
could prove of value. This lopsided type of question would not be

appropriate in any nation where linguistic pluralism was more complex. Another economical move sometimes employed is to enumerate bilingualism in only one part of a nation; for example, the report on the Welsh-speaking population of England and Wales covers Wales only.

Attempts have been made to further restrict, and thereby specify, the meaning of the bilingualism questions. The Republic of the Philippines in their 1960 census used a conversational criterion: "Any person who can carry a simple conversation in Tagalog, English or Spanish on ordinary topics is considered 'able' (to speak) for the purpose of this census" (Bureau of Census and Statistics 1960: xxiii). A similar test of speaking ability was used in Ceylon in the 1953 enumeration except that the criteria were either an ability to conduct a short conversation or "understand and answer questions put in that language" (Department of Census and Statistics 1957: 125).

The Indian censuses have included a question on bilingualism in addition to the inquiry on mother tongue. Respondents in 1961 were asked if they knew any other language(s) with the goal of recording those which the individual "speaks and understands best and can use with felicity in communicating with others. Such language or languages will exclude dialects of the same mother tongue" (Office of the Registrar General 1965a: 437). Although up to two languages were accepted in addition to mother tongue, the published results gave only the first of the two languages. This was rather unfortunate since there was no particular ordering requested in the listings of the additional languages.

Enumerators in the Israeli census of 1948 were instructed to record all of the languages used by the respondents in daily living beginning with the one used most often (Gil and Sicron 1956: lxxi). This provides a measure of bilingualism which is distinct from the ones mentioned earlier in two important ways. First, the census dealt with the use rather than knowledge of various tongues, making it possible for a completely fluent speaker of a given tongue to not be recorded as bilingual if he did not use the language. Second, it allows for some ranking among the languages of bilinguals since the respondent has hopefully indicated the one used most.

There are several non-census studies of bilingualism which merit attention because of their enumeration procedures. The Reyburns' study of the Mosquito Coast of Nicaragua and Honduras employed an elaborate set of questions for this linguistically complex area. Two items of particular interest here are those dealing with "Communication Elements" and "Chronological Bilingualism." Communication elements are reading, writing, understanding, and speaking. The individual's ability in each language for each of these was to be determined, leading to series of different combinations which could be constructed; for example, only reading, writing and reading, understanding-reading-speaking, etc. (Reyburn 1956: 10-11).

The concept of "Chronological Bilingualism" deals with both the degree of mastery of each language and the age at which it was first acquired. Distinctions were drawn between full and partial mastery of a tongue, as well as between whether a language was first learned before or after the age of 14 (Reyburn 1956: 12). In addition, the Reyburns propose obtaining these data for four generations by asking each respondent about two preceding and one descending generation.

However, as interesting as these questions may be, nowhere is there any indication of how the interviewer is to determine the actual degree of ability in each tongue for the various communication elements. In the questionnaire used for the Nicaragua survey, for example, the interviewer simply checks off whether the respondent is fluent, satisfactory, minimal, or has forgotten (Reyburn 1956: 50). Thus Reyburn fails to give us any idea about handling the validity issue or how the naive respondent is to answer or even what the interviewer is supposed to look for in making a judgment.

The Center for Applied Linguistics in Dakar employed a worthwhile set of questions to survey the linguistic abilities of school children in Senegal. For each child, the ethnic origin of the father and mother was obtained along with the language spoken at home and any additional tongues used by the child (Wioland 1965: 20). This procedure, although less elaborate than Reyburn's, also permits determination of linguistic shifts between generations if the mother tongues of the parents can be assumed on the basis of their ethnic origin. However, again I could not find any indication of the validity of the

data obtained. Incidentally, this more limited procedure for determining intergenerational shifts is probably more practical in most
cases than questions dealing with two generations back.

Diebold, in his study of San Mateo, Mexico, developed a
100-word lexicostatistics list in Huave which he presented to the native
Huave-speaking villagers. Having previously classified the respondents into monolinguals, subordinate bilinguals, and coordinate bilinguals with respect to their Spanish-speaking ability, he then asked
them to indicate the Spanish correspondence to each Huave word on
the list. The mean number and range of correct responses for his
three categories of speaking ability of Spanish differed in the direction
which might be expected. The fact that the monolingual group, that
is, those classified as able to speak only Huave, were able to give
correct answers to about a third of the words on the list suggested to
Diebold the importance of recognizing incipient bilingualism. In addition, the possibility was raised of using this procedure in other linguis
tic surveys. But, for the moment, it should be noted that the initial
classification of speakers into the three categories of Spanish-speaking
ability was made on what were admittedly "highly impressionistic"
grounds (Diebold 1961: 104).

Critique of Attempts to Date

Questions on mother tongue deal with a linguistic characteristic which most respondents should have little difficulty in answering.
To be sure, there are certain improvements that could be made; for
example, censuses seem to never recognize the possibility that a
respondent could have more than one mother tongue. Moreover, although the United Nations has recommended that mother tongue be
defined as "the language usually spoken in the individual's home in
his early childhood, although not necessarily spoken by him at present
(Department of Economic and Social Affairs 1959: 21), it would be
worth knowing exactly why this is preferable to asking for the first
language which the respondent learned as a child. In particular, the
first question would be rather inappropriate for bilingual parents who
elect to raise their offspring in their acquired language despite the
fact that they prefer to use their native tongue among themselves.
This, it seems to me, would be an important consideration in countries with a sizable immigrant population.

Census enumerations of the single language most frequently used have varied widely, including such characteristics as language usually spoken, language best spoken, language spoken fluently, language spoken with the family, language spoken in addition to mother tongue or official language, etc. (Department of Economic and Social Affairs 1959:23). Most of these questions, which I assume are aimed at determining the primary language used by the population, are clearly ambiguous and demand difficult judgments by the respondents. It seems to me that the optimal solution would be to ask a question on language used most frequently at home. Not only is this less ambiguous than many alternatives, but it provides information on an extremely important factor in determining the bilingual character of the nation. Moreover, the linguistic situation in many other socially important settings such as work and school can be inferred if the results of the bilingualism question are cross-tabulated with suitable social characteristics of the population. Nevertheless, there is a serious consideration about the language used at home which has not received sufficient attention. Namely, a not insignificant segment of the population of many western and urbanized nations probably live alone and hence could not answer such a question without publicly admitting that they talk to themselves! In such instances, I would favor asking an alternative question such as the language favored in thinking or among friends or socially.

But the main difficulties pertain to the questions asked in connection with bilingualism. In a number of instances we have observed that the question is put so simply as to make it very unclear to the respondent or the interviewer exactly what is meant. Although linguistic ability is an admittedly difficult question to ask at best, since second-language skills range so greatly, such ambiguous questions more or less court erratic responses, considerations of prestige, and nationalistic fervor. Census reports on this problem, as some of the earlier quotations suggested, have often been rather casual about the ambiguity of their questions while at the same time confident about the validity of the results obtained.

There has been very little effort made to determine the distortions due to extraneous factors influencing the respondents. One notable exception is India, which published careful reports on the accuracy of the linguistic returns for each State, recognizing the political and ethnic agitation which occurred in some parts of the nation. Likewise, Gil and Sicron point out that the frequency in which Hebrew was indicated in the 1948 census of Israel may have been intentionally exaggerated because of the national pride during the early days of the new nation (Gil and Sicron 1956). This undoubtedly is a consideration in other countries as well.

Nevertheless, little effort has been made to examine the data on bilingualism in San Mateo disclosing that 19 percent were either subordinate or coordinate bilinguals, but all that is told about the results from the 1950 census is that less than 20 percent were bilingual in the village and surrounding area (Diebold 1961: 104). Thus, there is reason to think that the census was not too far off from the results obtained by a trained linguist, assuming that the former was not trying to include cases of incipient bilingualism.

A desirable procedure in censuses is to conduct a post-enumeration survey of a small sample of the population to probe further into their responses and then make some estimates of the accuracy of the census results with respect to the various questions asked. Although the United States Census Bureau has published a series of technical papers dealing with the 1960 census, I have not been able to find any evaluations of the mother-tongue question asked. Fishman (1966: 422) reports a "correction factor" of 1.4 for mother-tongue data in 1960, claiming these data are therefore more reliable than those for age by sex, color or race, residence in 1955, and year moved into present house. Unfortunately, he is apparently referring to the adjustments used to deal with sampling variability, a rather different matter from the issue at hand (see Bureau of the Census 1966: xii-xiii). Another failure has been in the absence of techniques for the evaluation of the internal and external consistency of the language data in censuses. In the case of age returns, the Indian census was able to use Myer's Index of Digital Preference and Whipple's Index of Concentration to evaluate the accuracy of the data. By contrast, very little has been done to develop measures of the reliability and validity of language returns, although the present author has outlined some techniques (see Lieberson 1966: 272-78).

Recent statistical developments have made it possible to infer the response variance in census questions. The Dominion Bureau of

Statistics experimented in the 1961 census with reenumeration and interpenetrating samples to derive some estimates of the consistency of the results obtained. I. P. Fellegi reports results for the mother tongue, bilingualism, and ethnic origin questions which are relatively poor compared to other items in the census. "These questions," he observes, "are quite emotionally charged in Canada, and as it turns out, the interviewers did not seem to be detached" (Fellegi 1964: 1037). It would be particularly worthwhile to know what the results might be if a less ambiguous question on bilingualism were used. Nevertheless, the results are probably not that bad by normal standards of social research. These pioneering efforts in Canada should be tried out in other countries as well. However, it should be noted that these techniques cannot be used to estimate systematic but consistent errors on the part of respondents and interviewers.

There are certain errors of omission in the gathering and reporting of bilingualism data which could be readily corrected. Some countries will not collect linguistic data for some segments of the population. Thus, for example, the Union of South Africa censuses did not ask about the African languages spoken by Europeans. Likewise, Weinreich (1957: 231) has criticized the Indian census for not accepting English as a second language—a shortcoming which was corrected in the 1961 census. I have already alluded to the frequent failure of countries to report cross-tabulations when two or more different language questions were asked on the census. But another important difficulty that could be readily corrected is the failure to cross-tabulate the language data with a wide range of social characteristics aside from just sex and age.

Based on his conception of incipient bilingualism, Diebold has criticized census data for "concealing in the category 'monolingual' some very real measure of bilingualism" (Diebold 1961: 111). In this regard, I do not think that the censuses can be properly criticized since it does not seem to me that incipient bilingualism is an appropriate dimension for censuses to tap. If the goal is to determine the social correlates of bilingualism, then to a certain degree a limited knowledge of some words in a second language is of little significance. Virtually everyone in the United States or Canada, for example, would have to be classified to some minute degree as incipient bilingual speakers of German, French, and Spanish since probably most know

a few words in these languages. Rather, it seems to me that the
basic issue is whether a language is known well enough to use conver-
sationally or in reading, etc. To be sure an incipient bilingual is
closer to this state of affairs than one who is completely monolingual,
but only as a special measure of _potential_, rather than _actual_ bilingualism, can I find much reason for demographic and other institutional
studies of bilingualism to obtain such data.

What Remains to Be Done

The most glaring weakness of census procedures is the failure to consider the validity of the data obtained on language questions.
One particular difficulty is due to the fact that linguists themselves
would probably not be in agreement on the definition of the term "bilingual." It would be foolhardy to develop here a single most adequate
definition. Rather, what has to be done is select a relevant target
and then figure out how best to measure it. I would suggest that
serious consideration be given to measuring bilingualism on censuses
in terms of an ability to carry on a social conversation in the language(s)
This would measure both the ability to understand and speak a given
tongue. In my opinion these are the kinds of linguistic skills which
would be most suitable for enumeration in censuses, given the limitations described earlier. Along with information gathered on the language used most frequently at home and the mother tongue of the
respondent, a wide range of problems could be studied which deal with
bilingualism in its demographic and institutional context. Information
on the mother tongue of the respondents' parents would be of enormous
help in inferring intergenerational shifts.

These three (or four) items, when analyzed along with the
social characteristics of the population, would provide the investigator
with many possible inferences as to language use. Many of the linguistic domains that might be studied through a lengthy questionnaire such
as that proposed by several investigators recently (Fishman 1966;
Lieberson 1966) could also be inferred by cross-tabulating linguistic
information with the relevant social characteristics. For example,
occupational pressures could be inferred by cross-tabulating linguistic
ability with the occupations reported by respondents. The impact of
education could be inferred by means of the linguistic associations

with age and years of school completed. Indeed, it is one thing to ask individuals what languages are used in the schools and it is quite different to ask whether they can engage in a social conversation in the language. Many of the influences of various domains could be determined by cross-tabulation between linguistic ability and both age and sex. For example, it was possible to compare the degree of bilingualism by these two characteristics in Montreal and infer the influence of social contacts between small children, second-language learning in schools, occupational pressures, and the experiences in middle and older ages of life (Lieberson 1965). The Scottish census of 1961 drew all kinds of inferences about the use and position of Gaelic by means of only a handful of cross-tabulations with relevant social characteristics.

My point is not that censuses and other surveys of this type are cure-alls for determining the social context of bilingualism, for obviously there are too many subtleties both to bilingualism as a linguistic phenomenon and to social contexts or domains to make this possible. Rather, it is that sociolinguists have generally failed to utilize the linguistic data available to them in censuses except for the most elementary descriptive purposes. Several important exceptions come to mind, to be sure; for example, Weinreich (1957), Fishman (1966), Kelley (1966), Arès (1964), Deutsch (1953), and Coates (1961), but overall the data remain neglected.

It also follows that the study of bilingualism in its demographic and institutional contexts has failed to employ all of the descriptive and inferential techniques that are available. I have already indicated the failure to develop sufficient rigor in testing the validity of the data as well as their internal and external consistency. What I have in mind here are the wide range of statistical techniques developed in demography and human ecology for dealing with census data. There are all sorts of controls that are possible, to say nothing of descriptive methods for describing spatial distributions of social phenomena (see, for example, Duncan 1957; Duncan, Cuzzort, and Duncan 1961). Many of these are readily applicable to the study of bilingualism. It is even possible to draw inferences about linguistic phenomena even when the data are not presented in a fully satisfactory fashion, as has been demonstrated with the Canadian censuses (Lieberson 1966: 264-66). Finally, I must confess to considerable enthusiasm about the measures

proposed by Greenberg for quantitatively describing the linguistic
properties and diversity of social aggregates (see Greenberg 1956,
Lieberson 1964). These measures do not describe the actual interaction within a population in a social psychological sense. But they
do provide a quantitative measure of diversity, the communication
potential in a multilingual setting, and the role of bilingualism in
raising intelligibility.

But whatever the dimension of bilingualism measured on a
census, Diebold's development of the concept of incipient bilingualism
makes it all the more apparent that greater specification of bilingualism must be employed, both in terms of skills and medium. Further,
any definition implies a number of different ways in which it could be
measured or indexed in a survey. Thus, it is absolutely crucial that
the issue of validity be examined both before and after a census. In
particular, pilot tests should be made on a wide range of possible
questions to determine which one gets closest to what linguists would
have concluded had they been interviewing the entire population.
These experiments should make it possible for investigators to determine what question elicits the best set of answers in the sense that
they most closely correspond with the results obtained by linguists
who interviewed the respondents afterward. Likewise, there is no
question that more attention must be paid to post-enumeration surveys
in order to determine how closely the results correspond to the goals
of the census questions. After all, it is one thing to observe popular
agitation for certain linguistic response or to speculate that biases
may have crept into the census, but it is quite another to find out in
quantitative terms just how widespread and significant these distortions actually were.

REFERENCES

Arès, R. 1964. Comportement linguistique des minorités françaises
    au Canada—II. Relations 281: 41-144.
Bureau of the Census. 1933. U.S. census of population, 1930. Vol.
    2, General report, statistics by subjects. Washington, D.C.:
    Government Printing Office.

Bureau of the Census. 1962. U.S. census of population, 1960. De-
    tailed characteristics, Puerto Rico. Washington, D.C.:
    Government Printing Office.
_____. 1964. U.S. census of population, 1960. Selected area
    reports, Americans overseas. Washington, D.C.: Govern-
    ment Printing Office.
_____. 1966. U.S. census of population, 1960. Subject reports,
    mother tongue of the foreign born. Washington, D.C.:
    Government Printing Office.
Bureau of the Census and Statistics. 1960. Census of the Philippines,
    population and housing, summary. Manila: Department of
    Commerce and Industry.
Coates, W. A. 1961. The languages of Ceylon in 1946 and 1953.
    University of Ceylon Review 19: 81-91.
Ceylon, Department of Census and Statistics. 1957. Census of
    Ceylon, 1953, vol. 1. Colombo: Department of Census and
    Statistics.
Department of Economic and Social Affairs. 1959. Handbook of pop-
    ulation census methods. Vol. 3, Demographic and social
    characteristics of the population. New York: United Nations.
Deutsch, K. W. 1953. Nationalism and social communication; an
    inquiry into the foundations of nationality. Cambridge: pub-
    lished jointly by the Technology Press of the Massachusetts
    Institute of Technology, and Wiley, New York.
Diebold, R. A. 1961. Incipient bilingualism. Language 37: 97-112.
Dominion Bureau of Statistics. 1951. Enumeration manual, 9th cen-
    sus of Canada, 1951. Ottawa: Edmond Cloutier.
Duncan, O. D. 1957. The measurement of population distribution.
    Population Studies 11: 27-45.
Duncan, O. D., R. P. Cuzzort, and B. Duncan. 1961. Statistical
    geography; problems in analysing areal data. Glencoe, Ill.:
    Free Press.
Fellegi, I. P. 1964. Response variance and its estimation. Journal
    of the American Statistical Association 59: 1016-41.
Ferguson, C. A. 1964. Diglossia. In D. Hymes, ed., Language in
    culture and society; a reader in linguistics and anthropology.
    New York: Harper & Row, pp. 429-39.
Fishman, J. A., et al. 1966. Language loyalty in the United States;
    the maintenance and perpetuation of non-English mother

tongues by American ethnic and religious groups. The
Hague: Mouton.
General Register Office. 1966. Census 1961 Scotland. Vol. 7,
Gaelic. Edinburgh: Her Majesty's Stationery Office.
Gil, B., and M. Sicron. 1956. Registration of population (8XI 1948),
Part B, Special series no. 53. Jerusalem: Israel Central
Bureau of Statistics.
Greenberg, J. H. 1956. The measurement of linguistic diversity.
Language 32: 109-15.
Kelley, G. 1966. The status of Hindi as a lingua franca. In W.
Bright, ed., Sociolinguistics; proceedings of the UCLA
Sociolinguistics Conference, 1964. The Hague: Mouton,
pp. 299-308.
Lieberson, S. 1964. An extension of Greenberg's linguistic diversity
measures. Language 40: 526-31.
_____. 1965. Bilingualism in Montreal: a demographic analysis.
American Journal of Sociology 71: 10-25.
_____. 1966. Language questions in censuses. Sociological
Inquiry 36: 262-79.
Mackey, W. F. 1962. The description of bilingualism. Canadian
Journal of Linguistics 7: 51-85.
Mortara, G. 1950. Immigration to Brazil; some observations on the
linguistic assimilation of immigrants and their descendants
in Brazil. Population Studies 3, supplement, pp. 39-44.
Office of the Registrar General. 1965. Census of India, 1961. Vol.
1, Part II-C(ii), language table. (No city or publisher indi-
cated.)
Reyburn, W. D. 1956. Problems and procedures in ethnolinguistic
surveys. New York: American Bible Society.
United Nations. 1964. Demographic yearbook, 1963. New York:
Statistical Office, Department of Economic and Social Affairs.
Weinreich, U. 1957. Functional aspects of Indian bilingualism.
Word 13: 203-33.
Wioland, F. 1965. Enquête sur les langues parlées au Sénégal par
les élèves de l'enseignement primaire. Dakar: Centre de
linguistique appliquée de Dakar.

Part IV. Language Spread: A New Direction

18 | Forces Affecting Language Spread: Some Basic Propositions

Language spread is nothing more than a reshaping of the existing pattern of acquisition and usage. It sometimes occurs because new functions are created—for example, the communication needs generated in airplane traffic control—but usually it occurs because one language replaces another either for some specific existing function or in a broader, more general fashion covering a wide variety of domains. What causes a language to expand? This is a question for which propositions and principles may be sought. Answering it is very different from explaining the specific set of linguistic usages observed in a given setting because the present-day social correlates of an established and stable pattern of language practices need not account for its origins. Although it is almost certain that changes in the pattern of language usage can ultimately be traced back to societal shifts, it does not follow that the current social correlates of a relatively stable set of linguistic usages will provide very many clues to understanding the earlier changes that led to the present pattern of language usage.

This is due to a simple but overlooked fact, namely that the social causes of linguistic phenomena need no longer be present after the language pattern is firmly established. In other words, the products of social events have a life of their own. Once a language acquisition and usage pattern is established, then a set of norms, traditions, and expectations is generated about the language used in the marketplace, or the language given prestige and esteem, or whatever. But this set of expectations and notions of propriety is not necessarily the force that initially created the language pattern. It is certainly interesting to know the nature of the societal shifts occurring after a linguistic change takes place, but the current set of social expectations did not necessarily precede and cause the linguistic shifts covered under the phrase "language spread." Put another way, those social events preceding a linguistic shift are different from those that follow from the shift, and merging the two can only cause confusion. The origins of a given language pattern cannot be explained through the social facts associated with its present use because it is past causes that led to the present-day acceptance that are of significance, not the current social processes that maintain it.

It follows that the study of language spread is concerned with empirically determining the forces that disrupt an existing set of language acquisition and usage patterns. This study may take several paths, none of which are easy to pursue. One way is to explain the broad non-linguistic changes that in turn will significantly influence the existing set of language usages in the area under consideration—whether that be a community, a region, a nation, or indeed the world. Such a task is likely to take one into the realm of major social, political, technological, demographic, and economic changes—activities that are best left to those with specialized skills and knowledge. Another way is to take these societal changes as "givens" and, without seeking to explain their origins, try to comprehend the ways such shifts affect the existing pattern of language acquisition. One does not generate notions of what causes nationalism, industrialization, changing intergroup relations, etc., because this would be too massive a task, but rather one asks how such events affect the existing set of language usage patterns.

A third way is to examine the linguistic shifts that occur as a consequence of other linguistic shifts; for example, if language A is now used by an increasing proportion of the population of A's because of nationalism or some other cause, then non-A's may be forced to learn and use the tongue as well. In turn, this will have further linguistic consequences. Or the usage of language B by the prestigious members of the community may have consequences for the likelihood that B will be employed by members of other groups. There are a multitude of such interesting questions about the further linguisti consequences of a given linguistic change generated by societal forces.

Unfortunately, it is more difficult than one might think to determine the linkage between societal cause and linguistic effect.

Suppose, for heuristic purposes, that no societal changes occur henceforth. How long would it take for a linguistic equilibrium to occur such that the pattern of language acquisition and usage remained stable in every setting? It would probably not be until some distant time because presumably some of the events that occurred in recent decades (and possibly much longer ago than that) would not yet have worked themselves out in terms of their linguistic consequences—for example, the influence of an earlier literacy or education drive on language acquisition. Moreover, the linguistic shifts that occur as a consequence of other linguistic shifts might not yet have developed fully.

This points to a serious problem in any look at linguistic spread over time; to wit, one is dealing with the consequences of both past and more recent societal changes, and it is extremely difficult, indeed probably close to impossible, to sort out empirically what is going on without a very clear understanding theoretically of what might be expected.

It is the second and third approaches that I wish to pursue here. Working primarily with international data, I wish to suggest several processes and linkages of the most elementary sort between societal change and the spread of language, including both the direct influence of social organization and the indirect influence that occurs when one linguistic change generates another change in the existing pattern of acquisition and usage.

The Conservation of Language Usage

Once established, the existing pattern of language usage will tend to perpetuate itself in situations which, had they existed earlier, would never have generated the same language pattern. This is because a series of expectations and adaptations is created that then perpetuates the language pattern. Once language A is established as the medium of communication in the marketplace for speakers of B and C, then simple shifts in the numbers of A, B, and C speakers will not generate a comparable change in the marketplace language pattern, since a set of understandings has arisen that tends to perpetuate A. It is these forces that generate what might be called the conservation of language usage.

Consider, for example, the role of French, English, and
Spanish in international conferences. Latin served as the lingua
franca in the western half of the Roman Empire (Greek in the eastern
half) and continued to serve as such in western Europe well into the
Middle Ages (Encyclopædia Britannica 1975: 656). By the seventeenth
century, the language of diplomatic interchange was French. (The
processes by which it succeeded Latin and edged out Italian and Spanish are well worth studying in terms of the questions at hand.) Accord
ing to Butler and Maccoby (1928: 35), eighteenth-century negotiations
were held almost exclusively in French. At the Congress of Vienna,
the victors employed French not only in dealing with the defeated
France, but also among themselves—indeed the treaty was written in
French. It was only at the close of World War I that English received
important recognition as an equal to French in diplomacy. At the
first assembly of the League of Nations, it was proposed that Spanish
should also be made an official language, along with French and English, but the proposal was defeated. Why did French long enjoy this
powerful position at the expense of English ? Second, why was Spanish
still unable to move into a position of equality ?

The linguistic patterns of the "third parties" are a key factor
in the conservation of language usage in facing any potential change in
the existing patterns. Hence, although neither the number of native
speakers nor the number of nations with French as the official language would give that tongue a particular claim or advantage over
English or Spanish as a medium of communication in the League, the
neutral parties are crucial in all of this. French had become the
established and accepted international language, and hence persons
with neither English nor French mother tongue were far more apt to
learn the latter language. Once a pattern is established, there is
little reason to shift. In 1920 English was spoken in the League of
Nations Assembly by delegates from six nations in which English
was not an official language, whereas French was used by delegates
from 24 nations besides those from France, Haiti, Belgium, Canada,
and Switzerland (Shenton 1933: 381). By 1927, the numbers were
even less favorable to English, with only two countries using that
language in addition to those from nations with English as an official
language. (These and other remarkable statistics on language
usage in international conferences were gathered by Herbert Newhard
Shenton, professor of sociology at Syracuse University and advocate
for an international auxiliary language.)

The defeat of Spanish may likewise be viewed in terms of the
alternative linguistic systems already established. Of the 18 nations
in the first assembly of the League of Nations proposing that Spanish
should be one of the official languages, all but four were Spanish-
speaking (World Peace Foundation 1921: 27). Why was there such in-
difference to Spanish on the part of other nations? (Curiously, three
of the four non-Spanish-speaking nations signing this proposal had
French as an official language—Belgium, Haiti, and Switzerland. The
other was Denmark.) A clue may be had by looking at the linguistic
practices of the 16 original members of the League whose official language was neither English, French, nor Spanish. As a rough measure
of their linguistic policy, I looked at the languages used for publishing
official census volumes (this is because the titles to such volumes are
readily available to me in a series of books published by the Population Research Center, University of Texas). Information on the languages used in the census reports of China and Thailand in the late
nineteenth century and the early part of the twentieth century are not
available from this source (Population Research Center 1966: 10-1,
41-1). But for the vast bulk of the remaining "third party" nations,
linguistically speaking, French was used along with the national language in the census titles; this was the case for Poland, Iran, Czechoslovakia, Greece (as early as 1870), Japan, the Netherlands, Norway
(as early as 1835), Yugoslavia, and Sweden. It was not the case for
Brazil, Denmark, Italy, Portugal, and Rumania. But in each of these
cases, no other language was used besides the national one. In other
words, it is clear that French had gained widespread acceptance and
usage for such international functions. In turn, these "third party"
nations helped prevent change.

The conservation of language usage, in summary, is brought
about not merely because a set of rules, understandings, and norms
evolves after a language adoption occurs, but in addition because rival
languages must compete not only with native speakers of the established
tongue or tongues, but also with those linguistic "third parties" that
also have a stake in the maintenance of the existing usage pattern.
Often these third parties develop almost as much linguistic commitment to a particular language as do the native speakers. An example
of this is the French Canadian attempt to force the non-English and
non-French immigrants in Quebec to become French-speaking. For
the most part, such immigrants in the past had very strongly favored

English over French in their acquisition of an official mother tongue
(Lieberson 1970).

Power and Prestige: General Observations

Obviously, despite these conservative influences, the patterns of language usage do change; there are forces that overcome
the inertia existing in each sociolinguistic setting. Languages do not
differ among themselves in their inherent power, but their users do.
Accordingly, the carriers of different languages differ in their ability
to alter the existing language usage pattern, thereby affecting the
spread of languages. The term "power" and related concepts must
be used with great caution. First, it is of little value simply to attribute linguistic change to changing power relations, even if there is good
reason to believe it is due to such changes. This is because it is important to have a clear understanding of the precise mechanisms
whereby such influence occurs, bearing in mind at all times that the
power need not have been explicitly exercised. The danger in applying the power concept is the generation of circular arguments that on
the surface appear to explain the spread of a given language but that
in reality offer no explanation whatsoever. An investigator may determine, without an independent empirical measurement of power, that
shifts in language usage and adoption are due to changes in power
among the speakers, nations, or other corporate bodies associated
with these tongues. Such reasoning is circular when the very shift in
language usage is taken to be evidence of differential power among the
groups involved.

There are, of course, circumstances in which pure and naked
power does operate to affect language usage—the events leading up to
the League of Nations being one of them. Of great value here are the
observations of David Hunter Miller (1928a,b), a technical adviser to
the American mission that prepared the Covenant creating the League
of Nations. Not only was the role of English rather enhanced by the
fact that the United States and Britain were on the winning side, but
moreover the usage of English as an equivalent to French was very
much due to the position of influence enjoyed by Woodrow Wilson, the
American President. "Almost all the diplomats present from countries other than Great Britain, the United States and Japan spoke and
understood French" (1828a: 505). Earlier, he observed:

The formal decision that "the Peace Treaty should be printed in French and English languages, which should be the official languages of the Treaty" was made on April 25 by the Council of Four. Much as the French wished otherwise, the British and American participation in the War and in its settlement and the presence of President Wilson in Paris made it inevitable that the English language should be an official language of the Treaty of Peace. Naturally the decision was one which the French greatly regretted not only in itself but also because the writing of the Treaty of Versailles in French and in English of equal validity made those two languages the official languages of the League of Nations and also the official languages of the Permanent Court of International Justice, and perhaps to some extent marked the passing of French as the chief medium of diplomatic intercourse. (Ibid.)

Incidentally, the fact that the United States never did join the League of Nations, and hence that its preference for English was totally irrelevant, is further evidence for the contention made earlier that a given set of linguistic practices may continue on long after the disappearance of the events that initially brought it into being. At any rate, it is necessary to give a very close and precise consideration of the various ways by which power affects changes in linguistic usage; merely waving the term about is of little analytic value.

As for the prestige enjoyed by a language and the consequences this has for its diffusion, I am inclined to believe that such rankings are a function not of any inherent qualities of the language, but of the prestige of its speakers or the groups associated with it. For the most part we have learned that certain languages (or dialects within a language) are attractive and appealing, eliciting our admiration and bestowing prestige on their speakers. Our response to language is so thoroughly socialized that we are apt to attribute certain inherently attractive qualities to some languages and inherently unattractive ones to others. But the social origin of these responses is no different from the responses to different foods in a given society, where some are highly appealing, others relatively neutral, and still others absolutely repulsive. One can conclude that attitudes toward a given language reflect a set of intergroup relationships, either ongoing or characteristic of an earlier period. As such, attitudes toward specific languages are essentially an intervening variable in the case of language spread, rather than a fundamental causal factor. If there are radical attitudinal shifts toward a language that affect its spread, it is almost certain that they derive from intergroup relations, nationalism, and the like. From this perspective, then, the prestige of a language does not help explain much, because it is really a shorthand description of the linkages between the groups. To be sure, it is interesting to work out the factors affecting the linkage between language attitude (including prestige) and group relations.

Interaction

Change in the frequency and nature of the interaction between and within language groups is one of the major ways through which the existing pattern of language usage is altered. Because increased interaction exposes a group to the influence of other languages, at the same time expanding the potential impact of its language on other speakers, as a general rule the existing pattern of language usage will change as interaction changes. Indeed the power of a group to influence language usage is only a potential force if the group is completely isolated; it is only through interaction with other populations that this potential is transformed into events that alter the existing language practices and thereby affect the spread and contraction of different tongues.

Interaction both within and between nations has increased dramatically in recent decades, in no small way owing to technological improvements in transportation and communication. As a consequence this is a period during which one would expect changes in language usage that reflect the new intensity of interaction. Higher levels of living coupled with newer and cheaper forms of transportation and communication, have made it possible for increased contact within and between nations. The era since World War II has been marked by a massive expansion in the role of English in a variety of domains, particularly in science and business. To a striking degree, one can show that this shift in language usage, namely the expansion of English, is closely linked to the changes in the intensity and nature of commercial interaction. I will consider some of these financial changes because I believe they help to suggest a number of hypotheses about the role of interaction in language spread. Although my concern here is primarily with international forms of interaction, the hypotheses are applicable to interaction on the local and subnational planes as well.

In 1911–13 the nine English-speaking nations among the 29 leading nations in international trade (Australia, Canada, British India, Ireland, British Malaya, New Zealand, South Africa, United Kingdom, and the United States) received slightly more than one-third of the entire world's imports. By contrast, the four nations that can be classified as French-speaking in the list (Belgium, Canada—which is included for both English and French—France, and Switzerland) accounted for 16.7 percent of the world's imports. The two major German-speaking nations, Germany and Switzerland, received 13.8 percent, and five Spanish-speaking nations (Argentina, Chile, Cuba, Mexico, and Venezuela) received 4.0 percent. Clearly the English-speaking world was the most significant international market, as measured by the value of their imports (ignoring, for the moment, the intra-language imports that occur). The position of English increased by 1927 to where these same nine countries received 40.6 percent of the world's imports, French declined to 13.1 percent, and German declined to 11.3 percent, with Spanish increasing slightly to 4.4 percent (on the basis of data in United States Department of Commerce 1928: 742). By 1938 the English-speaking figure had dropped somewhat, to 37.2 percent (on the basis of data in United Nations 1976, Special Table A).

The expansion of English as a commercial language after World War II was not accompanied by an expansion in the importance of such English-speaking nations in world trade. In point of fact, the nine nations in which English either was currently an official language or had been an official language during the colonial period accounted for only 27.9 percent of the world's imports in 1974, a rather considerable drop from the figures earlier in the century (which ranged from 35 to 41 percent). By contrast, the French-speaking figure had actually increased somewhat from 1927 to 15.3 percent—albeit still below the 1911–13 level. German in 1974 amounted to 11.1 percent (figures based on the same source as used for 1938). In other words, the importance of English as a world trade language increased during a period in which these English-speaking nations declined as importers. How does one explain this? Certainly the English-speaking component of world trade is not the only indicator of international commerce. Moreover, non-English speakers may have been influenced by other factors in their shift to English, for example, the growth of English as a language for science and technology. Perhaps the dominant in-

fluence of the United States immediately after World War II was respor
sible for getting English going.

One major force is the changing level of interaction and its
relevance to the general issue of language acquisition. Although the
role of these English-speaking nations declined, the importance of
world trade itself increased considerably. This tremendous growth
in world trade is illustrated by some index figures provided by the
United Nations 1976: 96). Between 1948 and 1974, the value of all exports in the world increased from an index of 22 to an index of 139,
more than six times the earlier level. By contrast, the production
of primary commodities merely doubled (from 55 to 108), and even
manufacturing only quadrupled during the period (from 30 to 121).
Clearly international trade became increasingly important to the
nations of the world. In other words, the intensity of interaction went
up even though the relative importance of English declined. International trade was more important than ever before, and hence the relevance of learning additional languages was greater than it had been.
English was still by far the single most important language, and its
power or strength became more relevant through increasing interaction. In this regard, a modest correlation of .38 in the expected direction is reported (Fishman, Cooper, and Rosenbaum 1977: 91) betweer
the relative importance of exports to English-speaking nations and a
composite measure of English language behavior within the nation.[1]
If these propositions about interaction are correct, they lead to the
paradoxical conclusion that a language can become increasingly used
and important at the same time as the source of its initial strength
(the relative number of native speakers) declines. This is because
increased interaction intensifies the relevance of a language. The
weakness of Russian and Chinese for world communication, we shall
see, is due to their low levels of interaction—not their inherent weakness.

Further Evidence About the Level of Interaction

Since World War II, there has been an incredible expansion
in international banking, with major banks establishing branches in
the far-flung corners of the earth to a degree unprecedented in earlier
decades. Much of this represents, of course, the expansion of world

trade and the growing importance of multinational corporations (see, for example, Reimnitz 1978). Other factors involved are the complex tax laws that make it desirable to establish branches in certain locations and the Eurodollar market (Mayer 1974, Part 5; for still other factors, see Baker and Bradford 1974 and Robinson 1972). The first point about the growth of international banking is that it represents an intensification of interaction and, according to the principle suggested at the end of the preceding section, increased interaction intensifies the relevance of language. Differentials between language groups in their relative advantage as a second language become increasingly relevant as the interaction pattern intensifies the need for non-native language acquisition and usage.

To be sure, there have been international banking centers for many centuries. Earlier in this century, London was the premier banking center; New York and Paris followed, with Berlin a distant fourth. In 1933, British banks had 62 foreign branches in Europe, 224 in the Near East, 98 in South America, and 73 in the Far East (Baster 1977: 245). Likewise, there was a rather large number of foreign bank branches located in such cities as Hong Kong and Cairo in 1933.[2]

Zurich and Geneva, at present magnets for banks from throughout the world, had virtually no foreign banks in 1933. In Zurich in 1976 about a dozen different U.S. banks alone were represented, as well as various banks from every part of the world. Japan is perhaps an even better example. In 1933 there were only a handful of foreign banks located in Tokyo or, for that matter, anywhere in the nation: two Dutch banks, one French bank, one Hong Kong bank, one United States bank, and one British bank were represented (in some cases with several branches). Represented in Tokyo in 1976 were 31 United States banks, ten from Great Britain, four each from France and Germany, ten from elsewhere in Europe, as well as four from Australia-New Zealand, five from Canada, four from Latin America, and at least one each from Thailand, India, Korea, Taiwan, Singapore, and the Philippines.

Beirut provides another spectacular example of the intensification of international (and hence cross-linguistic) interaction on a financial and commercial plane. In 1933 there were a total of six different banks in Beirut; three were branches of Paris institutions, one

was headquartered in Rome, and two were apparently local institutions
By 1965 there were at least 25 different foreign banks located there (I
say "at least" because it is always possible that some bank that appears to be headquartered in Beirut or elsewhere in Lebanon is actually an unrecognized affiliate of a foreign institution). In turn, by
1976 there were 64 different foreign banks located in what had become
a major international financial center.

Incidentally, coinciding with this great expansion in international banking has been an extraordinary shift among United States
banks. The two largest Chicago banks had no foreign branches at all
in 1947. By 1965, both had representatives in London and Tokyo, with
one also in Zurich. One of these banks was represented in 31 different countries in 1976, with the other trailing close behind with 28.
Bank of America, the largest bank in the United States, had only one
foreign branch in 1933 (in London), whereas it had branches or some
form of representation in over 50 nations by 1976—a number exceeded
by the two largest New York City banks. To be sure, there were
some New York banks with overseas activities in 1933; the most extensive network that I found involved branches in some 25 nations.
But for the most part, this type of international banking was not very
extensive for American institutions until the last decade or so.

Some linguistic ramifications. The shift toward English can
be illustrated rather nicely by some changes in banking practices in
the last half-century. In both 1933 and 1941 a number of Japanese institutions used the term "Ginko" rather than "bank" or some similar
word in their name (the 1947 Directory gave the listings for Japan as
of 1941). This practice disappeared almost completely after World
War II, reflecting both the American occupation and a greater sensi-
tivity to foreigners by an industry that was increasingly internationally
minded. (Since the Directory is published in English, one might well
expect a propensity to translate banks' names into the appropriate
English common nouns, but this was of course a constant bias throughout the period and hence cannot explain the timing of the shift.) I
might mention that banks located in French, Italian, and Spanish and
Portuguese areas almost without exception stick respectively to banque
banca, and banco in their titles rather than using bank. These tongues
appear to be well established, and the practices do not change as readily as those among other language groups.

On the other hand, the expansion of English is found in the practices exhibited by banks in both Athens and Beirut. I restrict my analysis to banks that are, so far as I can determine, locally based in the country. This allows one to avoid the complications that might occur through the inclusion of foreign institutions. At any rate, in Athens in 1933, banque was clearly the preferred term, with 13 local institutions using it in their title (of which three put "bank" in parentheses in their listings). By contrast, there were three banks (one of which used "banque" in parentheses) and one banca. Practices in 1947 still favored the French word, with ten listed as banque, three of which include "bank" in parentheses. There were no institutions listed exclusively as banks, but there were three that used bank in the title followed by "banque" in parentheses. Again there was one banca. By 1965 it was all but over for the French word, with nine local banks, three of which had "banque" in parentheses. No banques were listed exclusively in French, although there was one that included the English term in parentheses. In 1976 there were no local banques at all, with or without the English in parentheses. The vast majority of the local institutions using the English word did not bother even to include the French term in parentheses (8 out of 12).

The tabulation below gives the language usage in 1976 of banks headquartered in Beirut, classified by the period in which they were established.

	Language used in the bank name	
Year of establishment	English	French
1880–1954	0	11
1955–1964	8	11
1965–1976	4	1

Since Lebanon had been under French control, it is not surprising to see the initial propensity to use French in naming banks in the period between 1880 and 1954 (bear in mind that these data refer to the language practice of banks surviving to 1976, not to their practices in earlier periods or of banks that no longer existed by 1976). English almost reached a parity with French between 1955 and 1964, with the latter falling behind among the small number of new Lebanese banks established in recent years.

Interaction: Number of Speakers vs. Number of Units

Every facet of language shift is influenced by the sheer demographic context of linguistic behavior; the present size of a language
group has a profound bearing on the future with respect to its maintenance and spread (for an early quantitative study of the influence of language composition on bilingualism, see Weinreich 1957). This is a
simple and very clear point. It is also obvious that linguistic behavior
is more than a product of demographic size; bilingualism is also affected by social institutions, employment opportunities, power, and
government policy. Compare, for example, the rates of bilingualism
among French and English when in analogous demographic situations
in Canada (Lieberson 1970: 46-50).

Also modifying the demographic impact on language maintenance and spread are the number and structure of units involved and
their effect under a given set of social conditions. Such languages as
English and Spanish enjoy certain advantages in the competition between tongues that are derived not merely from the large number of
speakers in the world, but from the fact that these speakers are important in a large number of political units. By contrast, the impact
of Chinese, Russian, Hindi, and Japanese that might be expected on
the basis of the worldwide number of speakers is in some circumstanc
modified and reduced because of the concentration of such speakers in
a minimal number of nations. The contrast between French and German is interesting in that regard. Although the number of native
speakers of German is greater than the number with French mother
tongue, the former is an official language in Germany, Switzerland,
and Austria, whereas the latter is official in France, Switzerland,
Belgium, Canada, Haiti, and a large number of former colonies in
Africa.

Unfortunately, it is rather hard to separate this influence
from many other factors; for example, it is unlikely that the position
of Hindi is purely a function of the fact that it is a national language
in only one political unit. Likewise, a comparison between the number of French and German units ignores the earlier forces that established the role of French. A continuum is of help here, ranging from
circumstances in which the sheer number of speakers determines the
support base for a language to circumstances in which not the individ-

ual but the nation or some other corporate body is the relevant unit, with the result that the number of persons belonging to each unit has no bearing on the number of representatives it gets. For the economics of publishing, the sheer number of potential underlying readers is crucial and the number of units much less important. On the other hand, in circumstances where each unit has the same number of delegates (at the United Nations, for example), the number of units with each language becomes far more important than the number of speakers represented by each unit. To be sure, interaction in all cases is between individuals, but the underlying numbers are by definition relatively more significant in the purely demographic situation than in one where a unit form of representation exists.

Needless to say, English enjoys an enviable position, since it is both a demographically important language and, at the same time, an official language in a relatively large number of the world's nations. The relevance of the unit influence compared with a purely demographic influence is determined by the degree to which the interaction is between persons or between units. It is therefore helpful to distinguish between individual-based interaction (for example, tourist flow) and interaction between aggregate units such as nation-states or corporations. Changes in interaction will always affect the relative importance of different languages, but it is crucial to consider whether this involves individuals or units.

Interaction: Russia and China

Two of the great languages of the world, in demographic terms, have effectively left themselves out of the competition in some domains because of the political and ideological factors involved. I refer here to international finance and, to a lesser degree, international trade. The 1976 edition of the Rand McNally Bankers Directory lists only two foreign banks in the People's Republic of China (p. F175): the Hongkong and Shanghai Bank, headquartered in Hong Kong; and the Chartered Bank, a British international bank with headquarters in London. Both of these banks have offices in Shanghai, but nowhere else in the People's Republic. In the 1933 Directory, there were a large number of foreign banks in both Shanghai and Peiping, as well as a number of other Chinese cities; countries represented included Belgium,

Germany, Japan, Italy, the United States, France, India, and the
Netherlands. Mainland China, then, provides one of the few instances
in which greater interaction during this span did not occur; indeed, the
trend was in the opposite direction. This reversal was not the case
for Taiwan, and Hong Kong has become a great international banking
center. Still, the kind of role that one might expect for Chinese, owing
to the sheer number of speakers, is greatly undercut because of the
limited number of political units involved, compounded with the relative absence of interaction between mainland China and the rest of
the world (although it appears as if this will change in the years ahead).

The Soviet Union, like China, has been relatively isolated
from international finance. To be sure, the Soviet Union has not been
above international capitalistic ventures; the Moscow Narodny Bank,
established in London in 1919, lists many of the great New York City
banks as its correspondents. Moreover, according to Mayer (1974:
455), the Eurodollar was invented at the Russians' bank in Paris and
they have had a Swiss bank since 1966. Nevertheless, banking interaction has been quite limited, although increasing in recent years.
There were about a dozen foreign banks in Moscow in 1976: three from
the United States; two each from Italy and France; one each from Sweden, Yugoslavia, and the United Kingdom; a branch of the Moscow
Narodny Bank (headquartered in London); and the International Bank
for Economic Cooperation, which is essentially an Iron Curtain bank
representing the governments of Bulgaria, Czechoslovakia, East
Germany, Hungary, Mongolia, Poland, Rumania, and the Soviet
Union. Obviously, under other circumstances, the Soviet Union would
be a much more significant center for international banking. As is the
case for mainland China, its relative isolation means not only that its
linguistic influence is vastly reduced in this domain, but that it permits other languages to play an even more pronounced role. In that
sense, one can argue that both China and the Soviet Union indirectly
support the widening international role of English.

In similar fashion, the concentration of Eastern European
trade within the Warsaw Pact nations, as well as the relatively minimal international trade thus far exhibited by mainland China, has reduced the broader significance of Russian and Chinese. To be sure,
Russian has thereby become extremely important within the Warsaw
Pact nations (Conrad and Fishman 1977: 48), but this restricted trade
minimizes its world role. The other "centrally planned economies"

in Furope, defined by the United Nations as Albania, Bulgaria, Czechoslovakia, the German Democratic Republic, Hungary, Poland, and
Rumania, accounted for 53 percent of Russia's exports in 1975 (United
Nations 1976: 983). It would be interesting to know more about Cuba's
linguistic policy, incidentally. From about 75 to 80 percent of Cuba's
exports in the period between 1913 and 1938 was directed to the United
States (United States Department of Commerce 1928: 189; United Nations
1951: 67). The Soviet Union, which had been such a minor market for
Cuba in the years right after World War II (United Nations 1951: 67),
accounted for 41 percent of Cuba's exports in 1973 (United Nations
1976: 291).

There are even fewer foreign banks represented in other
Eastern European nations: one in Bulgaria (Lebanese), one in Czechoslovakia (Yugoslavian), none in Hungary, two in Poland (U.S. and
Italian), and one in Rumania (U.S.) (Rand McNally 1976). In short,
the restricted interaction of Russia and mainland China vastly minimizes the role that these countries could play through demographic
types of interaction, that is, interaction occurring on the basis of
relative numbers. Those outcomes affected by the relative number
of units, however, would be less seriously altered by increased interaction because there are so few Russian- and Chinese-language nations.

The Mechanism Through Which Linguistic Pluralities
Are Converted to Linguistic Majorities

One of the papers prepared for this conference* (Scotton
1978: 11) has already cited Greenberg's observation of a "dynamic
quality to the spread of a lingua franca" such that its usage at some
point tends to accelerate (Greenberg 1965: 52). Using international
trade and banking data, I wish to suggest some mechanisms through
which this occurs. Earlier I observed that the leading Fnglish-speaking industrial nations of the world account for a smaller proportion of
world commerce now than they used to. Nevertheless, in linguistic
terms Fnglish-speaking countries constitute the single most important
international market for many nations of the world. Hence, given the

---
* Conference on the Spread and Contraction of Language,
held at Aberystwyth, Wales, September 1978.

Table 1. Export Markets, Classified by Language,
for Hypothetical Nations

Language of importing nation	Exporting nation			
	A	B	C	D
A	—	20%	20%	20%
B	20%	—	20	30
C	20	20	—	30
D	10	10	10	—
E	30	30	30	0
F	10	10	10	10
G	10	10	10	10
Total	100%	100%	100%	100%

growth in world trade (in effect, interaction has gone up), one can
readily understand the expansion in the significance of English for
these countries. But what about other nations, ones in which customers
with some other language are more important? Would the spread of
English be expected to occur there as well?

Shown in Table 1 is a set of hypothetical data representing
export markets of four different nations, A, B, C, and D. For the
first three of these nations, E is the most important market, consum-
ing 30 percent of their exports. E consumes none of the exports from
nation D, however, whereas B and C each receive 30 percent of D's
exports. At first glance, E is the optimal language for anyone in A,
B, and C to learn. By learning E, members of A, B, and C will
share a common language with their customers 30 percent of the
time—not a felicitous figure, but still higher than could be obtained
with any other language. By contrast, the optimal language for someone in D to learn at first glance appears to be either B or C.

In fact, members of A, B, and C can now communicate with
far more than 30 percent of their international customers. Although
nobody in C has learned B and nobody in B has learned C, because in

each case E was initially somewhat more desirable, members of C
and B can communicate with each other through their common knowledge of E. Given these assumptions about A, B, and C, then it will
also become optimal for members of D to learn E even though no trade
occurs with the E nation. Because B's and C's will have acquired E
themselves, an E-speaking member of group D will be able to communicate with far more customers than if either B or C is learned. In
other words, we can see how a language will spread as interaction
increases to the point where its early spread encourages even further
learning.

Language markets for a sample of nations. In order to consider the relevance of this process, I took a small sample from the
Yearbook of International Trade Statistics, 1975 (United Nations 1976),
every fifteenth nation listed, including Zambia at the end, since it was
one short of inclusion anyway and I had only one other African country.
(See Table 2.) For ten leading customers of each nation, I determined
their official language or languages, using the information sketched
out in Urdang (1975). In nations such as Belgium, Canada, and Singapore, there is more than one official language, and I credited each
tongue accordingly. Hence, it is possible for the figures to sum to
more than 100 percent, because some nations contribute to more than
one official language. In many cases the figures add to less than 100
percent because we are only dealing with ten large foreign markets for
each nation that was sampled.[3]

A striking feature is precisely the plurality for English described earlier. English-speaking countries formed less than a simple majority of the export market in all of the nations sampled.[4] However, in seven of the ten nations, English was the largest single market. This amounted to only 19 percent for Bolivia's exports and 21
and 24 percent, respectively, for India and Zambia, but in outher
countries English was the market for a considerably larger part of
the exports (Costa Rica, French Guiana, South Vietnam, and Uganda).
Incidentally, the important role of English for South Vietnam in 1973
was due not to the United States, which received only 4 percent of the
exports, but to the markets for their exports provided by Hong Kong
(26 percent) and Singapore (12 percent). The data for Poland provide
a good example of the confinement of Iron Curtain countries to within
the Eastern European sector to a degree that probably reflects more
than the influence of transportation costs.

Table 2. Export Markets, Classified by Language, for a Sample of Nations

Official language of importing nation	Exporting nation									
	Bolivia 1975	Costa Rica 1974	French Guiana 1975	India 1975	Lebanon 1973	Netherlands 1975	Poland 1974	South Vietnam 1973	Uganda 1975	Zambia 1973
English	19	31	46	21	10	12	8	46	47	24
German	8	13	—	3	—	32	16	2	6	10
Dutch	6	9	4	—	—	14	—	—	2	—
Japanese	8	—	—	10	—	—	—	24	8	—
Italian	4	3	—	2	2	6	4	1	3	12
Spanish	9	26	—	—	—	1	—	1	—	—
French	3	3	41	3	—	25	3	16	4	8
Russian	5	—	—	12	—	—	29	—	—	—
Other	—	3[a]	8[b]	12[c]	52[d]	4[e]	13[f]	65[g]	5[h]	10[i]

Source: United Nations 1976, Table 3 for each exporting nation.
Dash signifies no representation in the leading markets for that nation.
[a] Finnish.   [b] Portuguese.
[c] Persian (8 percent); Bengali (2 percent); Polish (2 percent)
[d] Arabic.   [e] Swedish (2 percent); Danish (2 percent).
[f] Czech (7 percent); Hungarian (3 percent); Bulgarian (3 percent).
[g] Chinese (38 percent); Malay (15 percent); Tamil (12 percent).
[h] Serbo-Croat (3 percent); Arabic (2 percent).
[i] Portuguese (5 percent); Chinese (2 percent); Serbo-Croat (2 percent); Swedish (1 percent).

One can see precisely how English would be the single most desirable language for a large number of countries. This, with the mechanisms described above, should lead to an even more significant role for the language with the operation of a simple feedback system. The figures also show an important worldwide role for a number of other European languages. German makes up 10 percent or more of the export market for four of the nations sampled. French is likewise a very important market in several cases. The minimal role of Russian and Chinese, discussed earlier, is nicely illustrated. Except for Poland, Russia is an important customer only for India and, to a much smaller extent, Bolivia. Likewise, Chinese is significant only for South Vietnam—and that is because of Singapore and Malaysia rather than mainland China.

Distance, Transportation, Affluence, and Interaction

As a general rule, interaction has a cost, that is, there is a friction or resistance due to the time and distance involved in the movement of persons, goods, or messages across space. As a consequence, inventions in transportation and communication that reduce either the time or cost of such movements will tend to increase interaction. Likewise, greater affluence will have the same consequence by reducing the impact of transportation costs. Since the expansion and decline of international languages, just like those within a nation, is affected by changes in interaction, it is important to recognize some standard forces that influence interaction and see how these, in turn, affect language spread.

The ease with which people move across great distances has been greatly affected by the widespread use of air transportation in recent decades. Likewise, new technologies such as television and communication satellites have greatly facilitated the movement of messages. These are not trivial factors in trying to understand the growth of English and will be highly relevant for future language shifts. Particularly important here is the way such transportation changes and their widespread use have brought the massive numbers of English speakers from the United States into the communication network. First, consider the intensification of interaction generally. There were 4,717 international conferences during the nearly 100 years between 1840 and

1931 (Shenton 1933: 26). Observe the incredible increase by decades
in their number:

1840–49	9	1890–99	510
1850–59	20	1900–1909	1,062
1860–69	77	1910–19	516
1870–79	168	1921–29	1,517
1880–89	311	1930–31	501

Except for a drop-off during World War I, an extraordinarily steady
growth in international conferences is found. The first peaceful decade after the war was marked by a new record even though the year
1920 was not included. The period under study by Shenton ends with
two years, 1930 and 1931, during which there were more international
conferences than were held during the first 40 years under consideration.

For the 1923–29 period, Shenton was able to tabulate the locations of 1,415 conferences (pp. 76–80). Europe is far and away the
most important locale, with France in first place (275 conferences),
followed by Switzerland (204), England and Scotland (122), Germany
(109), Italy (103), and Belgium (101). The Western Hemisphere is
relatively insignificant, with the United States holding 42, Canada 7,
Cuba 6, Brazil 4, and Argentina 3. This is a period in which cross-
Atlantic travel would have been both much slower and more expensive.

Not surprisingly, French was the official language in more
conferences than any other tongue during this period after World War
I, being used officially by 220 organizations, compared with 160 using
English, 132 German, and 22 Italian (Shenton 1933: 255). Although
the United States was represented at a large number of these international conferences, given the difficulties involved at that time, it was
tied with Austria for eleventh place in the rankings. The nations were
led by France, followed by Great Britain, Belgium, Switzerland, the
Netherlands, Germany, Czechoslovakia, Italy, Poland, and Sweden
before the United States and Austria are reached (p. 119).

Changes in the barriers of space alter the role of distance
and its influence on interaction. I believe developments in recent
decades have greatly favored English insofar as it has made it much
easier for numerically important English-speaking populations located

away from Europe to participate in international conferences in
sizable numbers. Since French was not handicapped to the same
relative degree (the only serious handicaps were those faced by
French speakers in Africa), changes in the direction of bringing the
world closer together have differentially affected the pace of interaction for language groups. What the future changes will be in transportation and communication cannot be predicted, but one can be certain that they will alter the probabilities of interaction for various
language groups, and that this alteration will have an impact on language spread and maintenance.

Implications

        If the principles and mechanisms described above are valid,
then they should be relevant for understanding future events as various languages gain and lose because of the social changes that can be
expected. The tendency toward the conservation of language usage
observed at the outset is extremely important because it means that
shifts in the power of language groups, or in their numbers or in
other forces that might be expected to affect language spread, will
not necessarily have such effects. This is because the role of a language, once established, will tend to be perpetuated long after the
disappearance of conditions that were initially necessary. Hence, it
is quite possible for the English-speaking nations to decline in economic, political, or other types of power without a concomitant drop
in the role of the English language. It also follows, then, that speakers
of other languages can make significant gains in these domains without
an immediate linguistic gain. The role of neutral third-party language
groups as a conservative force has been demonstrated to be extremely
important. On the other hand, where it is the third-party language
that becomes a competitor, then the conservative influence is lost,
since the initial support base will disappear. In other words, the
impact of a decline in the power of English-speaking nations relative
to, say, Chinese will be minimized by "third party" language groups
such as the Japanese- or Spanish-speaking groups who have already
made a commitment to English. But if one of these third-party groups
becomes a competitor, then its support will quickly fall away. Thus
if Japanese or Spanish were to begin to compete sociolinguistically
with English, then the present bilingualism of such speakers would no
longer work to slow down change.

Of special significance in altering language usage are changes
in interaction patterns. There are several areas in which very significant interaction changes could occur. The Soviet Union and the
People's Republic of China are far more isolated now than they may be
in the future. Increased interaction would make the potential power of
these nations a greater reality, since changes in interaction affect the
actual influence of a language group on other language groups.

On this score, Latin American nations at present do not interact anywhere as much among themselves as one might expect. The
export data for the two Latin American nations shown in Table 2 are
by no means atypical for the Spanish-speaking part of the Western
Hemisphere. This absence tends to undercut the potential strength
of Spanish and at the same time serves to support English, since the
United States has such an important level of interaction with these
countries. No Latin American country had a bank branch or representative in Lima, Peru, in 1976, whereas there are five United States
banks represented, along with two each from Switzerland and Spain;
in addition, France, the United Kingdom, Japan, and Germany each
have one bank represented. Likewise, in Caracas, Venezuela, there
are two non-Venezuelan Latin American banks represented as well as
two from Spain; but 14 different United States banks are represented.
São Paulo, Brazil, has become a major banking center; there are nine
different Japanese banks represented there, along with five from both
Germany and Italy, four from Switzerland, three from France, and
20 from the United States. Although Spanish is relatively close to
Portuguese, the only Latin American representation in São Paulo consists of a single bank from each of three different countries: Mexico,
Argentina, and Ecuador. Buenos Aires, Argentina, has only one bank
from another Latin American country (Brazil), and the only international Spanish influence is due to the representation of four banks from
Spain; by contrast, there are 13 U.S. banks, nine from Germany,
seven Swiss institutions, five each from France and Italy, and lesser
numbers from the Netherlands, Belgium, the Bahamas, Israel, the
United Kingdom, Canada, and Japan. Shifts owing to industrialization
and other factors could greatly reduce the power of English in Latin
America, and this, in turn, would both strengthen Spanish and reduce
a "third party" support base for English.

In closing, I should at least mention that the linkage between
language and commerce sometimes runs in the opposite direction:

that is, language bonds can affect economic bonds. The expansion of
United States banking after World War II, for example, has led to
further maintenance of the role of London, since it appears to be the
first city that American banks select for an overseas office. Apparently affecting this decision was the common English language (Mayer
1974: 466). Likewise, I find a banking linkage between Latin America
and Spain that probably is not entirely due to international commerce.
Banco Nacional de México, with more than 400 branches in Mexico,
has foreign offices in six cities, one of which is Madrid, but none in
the United Kingdom. The Banco de Comercio, a large Mexican bank
with 558 offices in the nation, has international representation in five
cities; again Madrid is one of these. Similarly, Madrid is one of the
six foreign offices for Banamex, and the only European office for
Banco Comercial Mexicano. Likewise, although I have not emphasized
it, one still finds British and French banks playing a pronounced role
in the former African colonies of Great Britain and France.

Seven Propositions

     This analysis of language spread can be summarized in
seven propositions:

     1. The origin of a given language pattern need not be found in
the forces currently operating to maintain the pattern. A language
pattern, once established, has a life of its own that may continue long
after the initial causes have disappeared. Indeed, there is every reason to expect a set of intervening factors such as attitudes and norms
to develop from some more basic underlying cause, but these should
not be confused with the initial causes.

     2. There is a conservation of language usage. Once language
practices are established, they will tend to perpetuate themselves in
situations which, if existing earlier, would never have generated the
same language pattern.

     3. The conservation of language usage is abetted by "third
parties," namely groups for whom neither the existing dominant language nor its potential competitor is a native language. Because they
have little reason to shift from the second language already used to a

new second language, third parties play a key role in the conservation of language usage. Once such neutral groups become bilingual in an existing dominant language, they develop a vested interest in that tongue with an intensity almost equal to that of the native speakers.[5]

4. An existing language usage pattern can be altered through changes in the frequency and nature of the interaction within and between language groups. Indeed, without interaction, the political, economic, social, scientific, and other sources of power and influence for speakers of a language group are only matters of potential rather than forces operating to affect behavior.

5. Two basic distinctions are necessary in analyzing the role of interaction. First, it is necessary to distinguish between changes in potential as opposed to actual influence (the two can change independently of one another and hence in opposite directions). Second, it is necessary to recognize that interaction ranges on a continuum from the purely demographic form, in which the number of each population is the crucial consideration, to an aggregate form in which each unit has equal participation regardless of the underlying population represented.

6. There are certain inherent mechanisms in language shift which, when operating by themselves, would tend to convert linguistic pluralities into linguistic majorities. As the number of persons acquiring a given language increases, this in turn increases the pressure for others to acquire the same second language even if their interaction patterns remain unchanged. It is through this mechanism that we can understand Greenberg's observation (1965: 52) of a dynamic and accelerating quality to the spread of a lingua franca.

7. Changes in the technology of transportation and communication will alter the levels of interaction. Because the consequences of such technological changes will not be the same for all language groups, the existing linkage between potential and actual influence will not change equally for all tongues. This in turn means that the existing patterns of language acquisition will tend to be altered when major differentials in interaction are generated through such technological changes.

NOTES

[1] This is the only such effort I know of to correlate the role of exports with language behavior and hence is an important development, but a serious caution is necessary. Although the investigators claim that they measure "the percentage of exports sent to English-speaking countries" (Fishman, Cooper, and Rosenbaum 1977: 85), inspection of their data source (United States Department of State 1972) indicates that the figures refer only to trade with the United States and hence do not fully measure the role of English-speaking markets for various nations.

[2] My data for branch banks are derived from the Rand McNally Bankers Directory for the following years: 1933, 1947, 1965, and 1976. This is a standard reference for world banking, and although no doubt errors are inherent in such analyses, such as overlooking affiliates and the difficulty in determining headquarters, they are presumably insignificant for my purposes.

[3] Although the ten markets listed for each nation were the largest in recent years, in some cases they did not overlap exactly with the largest ten for the year specified. For the most part, this had a minor influence on the results. The reader should bear in mind, however, that the proportions given in Table 2 are of exports to all nations, not only those directed to the countries specified.

[4] To be sure, some countries in the sample send more than half of their exports to English-speaking countries.

[5] Such groups, of course, are often disposed to shed the acquired language in favor of their own native tongue, but they are usually resistant to giving up one acquired second language for a new one.

REFERENCES

Baker, James C., and M. Gerald Bradford. 1974. American banks abroad. New York: Praeger.

Baster, A. S. J. 1977. The international banks. New York: Arno Press.

Butler, Sir Geoffrey, and Simon Maccoby. 1928. The development of international law. London: Longmans, Green.

Conrad, Andrew W., and Joshua A. Fishman. 1977. English as a world language: the evidence. In Joshua A. Fishman, Robert L. Cooper, and Andrew W. Conrad, The spread of English. Rowley, Mass.: Newbury House.

Encyclopædia Britannica. 1975. The New Encyclopædia Britannica, Macropædia, vol. 10. Chicago: Encyclopædia Britannica.

Fishman, Joshua A., Robert L. Cooper, and Yehudit Rosenbaum. 1977. English around the world. In Joshua A. Fishman, Robert L. Cooper, and Andrew W. Conrad, The spread of English. Rowley, Mass.: Newbury House.

Greenberg, Joseph H. 1965. Urbanism, migration, and language. In Hilda Kuper, ed., Urbanization and migration in West Africa. Berkeley: University of California Press.

Lieberson, Stanley. 1970. Language and ethnic relations in Canada. New York: Wiley.

Mayer, Martin. 1974. The bankers. New York: Weybright and Talley.

Miller, David Hunter. 1928a. The drafting of the Covenant, vol. 1. New York: Putnam.

_____. 1928b. The drafting of the Covenant, vol. 2. New York: Putnam.

Population Research Center, University of Texas. 1965. International population census bibliography, Latin America and the Caribbean. Austin, Tex.: Bureau of Business Research.

_____. 1966. International population census bibliography, Asia. Austin, Tex.: Bureau of Business Research.

_____. 1967. International population census bibliography, Europe. Austin, Tex.: Bureau of Business Research.

Rand McNally. 1933. Bankers directory, 1933. New York: Rand McNally.

_____. 1947. Bankers directory, 1947. New York: Rand McNally.

_____. 1965. Bankers directory, 1965. New York: Rand McNally.

_____. 1976. Bankers directory, 1976. New York: Rand McNally.

Reimnitz, Jurgen. 1978. German banks follow German investment. Euromoney, June, p. 91.

Robinson, Stuart W. 1972. Multinational banking. Leiden, Netherlands: Sijthoff.

Scotton, Carol Myers. 1978. Lingua francas as white elephants: political and socio-economic integration in Africa. Unpublished manuscript.

Shenton, Herbert Newhard. 1933. Cosmopolitan conversation. New
    York: Columbia University Press.
United Nations. 1951. Yearbook of international trade statistics,
    1950. New York: United Nations.
_____. 1976. Yearbook of international trade statistics, 1975.
    Vol. 1. New York: United Nations.
Urdang, Laurence, ed. 1975. The CBS news almanac, 1976. Maple-
    wood, N. J.: Hammond Almanac.
United States Department of Commerce. 1928. Commerce Yearbook,
    1928. Vol. 2. Washington, D. C.: Government Printing
    Office.
Weinreich, Uriel. 1957. Functional aspects of Indian bilingualism.
    Word 13: 203-33.
World Peace Foundation. 1921. The First Assembly of the League
    of Nations. A League of Nations 4: 27.

Author's Postscript

With the benefit of hindsight, it is not hard to see why I developed an interest in language diversity and bilingualism. Both of my parents were trilingual, as were my aunts and uncles and grandparents. In addition to his mother tongue, Yiddish, my father had learned Polish in his native Warsaw, and he acquired English after migrating to North America. Throughout his life, my father insisted that he spoke English without an "accent"—a matter of great amusement to my mother, who was a native speaker of English but who also knew Yiddish and had a modest ability in French (not a bad asset even then in Montreal, where she was born and raised). I too was born in Montreal, in 1933, but I grew up in the Brighton Beach section of Brooklyn, New York—at a time when the vast bulk of adults in the area seemed to be non-native speakers of English. There were actually a few Yiddish words that I assumed were English through much of my childhood. At any rate, language diversity and language contact were very much part of my youth.

I myself was never any good with languages; my parents were able to use Yiddish as a secret tongue for conversations in my presence with almost complete success. I listened to many Yiddish conversations in Brighton with minimal understanding of what was going on; during visits I accompanied aunts and uncles in the Laurentian mountains of Quebec while they employed French to buy eggs or obtain directions from <u>les Canadiens</u>. I have a hunch that in an unverbalized way my childhood friends and I also understood the importance of language as a class marker. This was a period when merely the mention of Brooklyn and the English spoken there almost guaranteed laughter from a radio show's audience.

None of this was on my mind as I worked on my doctorate in
sociology at the University of Chicago in the late fifties under Otis
Dudley Duncan, a scholar of the highest accomplishment. My dissertation dealt with ethnic residential segregation and assimilation in ten
cities of the United States during the first half of the century (later
revised and published as a monograph, Ethnic Patterns in American
Cities). I was trying to obtain the best data possible on assimilation
in order to link such patterns with immigrant groups' residential isolation in cities. One such variable dealt with language, specifically
the proportion of each immigrant group able to speak English (the
results correlated rather nicely, although the causal direction was
not entirely clear). At any rate, when I discussed this part of the
project with Duncan, he wondered out loud about the nature of the language situation in other nations. For some reason that question stuck,
although obviously my dissertation was not the time to pursue the matter further. So, along with many other debts to Dudley Duncan, I owe
him this initial thrust into a topic that I have pursued on and off for a
number of years.

Beginning with this chance question, my work on language
has largely been a case of one fortuitous event leading to another.
My first position was at the University of Iowa. With my dissertation
out of the way and under revision for a monograph, I decided to find
out what the language situation was like in all the countries of the
world. I thought a small grant would be sufficient, but the Social
Science Research Council turned down my application. One of my
references, however, Albert J. Reiss, Jr. (now the William Graham
Sumner Professor of Sociology at Yale), liked it very much, and I
believe it played a role in my appointment at the University of Wisconsin as an assistant professor in 1961.

I subsequently obtained a National Science Foundation grant
for a pilot project, and elected to study Canada, a country that I knew
something about and that has excellent census data on language covering a number of decades. This led to a number of papers and a further
NSF grant, and culminated in my monograph Language and Ethnic
Relations in Canada. Shortly after starting the project I learned that
a Royal Commission on Bilingualism and Biculturalism had been
formed, and I wrote to Ottawa telling them about my project and suggesting we exchange information of mutual benefit. A brief, formal

response expressed no interest in the idea. Subsequently, however, the Royal Commission asked me to do some research for them, in the course of which they provided me with some marvelous special cross-tabulations from the 1961 census. Ultimately, they had to cut back on their publication plans, but that was a minor annoyance, since I was able to use the segregation and income data in several publications.

Another important product of the initial NSF project was my participation in a summer program on sociolinguistics at Indiana University in 1964. The seminar included some of the most eminent people in the area of sociolinguistics, among them Jack Berry, William Bright, Charles Ferguson, Joshua Fishman, Paul Friedrich, Allen Grimshaw, John Gumperz, Einar Haugen, Heinz Kloss, William Lobov, and William Stewart. There were outside speakers brought in as well, such as Joseph Greenberg, Dell Hymes, Wallace Lambert, and the late Uriel Weinreich.

Although much of the summer was marked by debates and disagreements, I learned a great deal from this group. There were a number of high-powered minds talking right past each other, but for someone who had never taken a course in linguistics it was absolutely enlightening. The linguists were for the most part an impressive group of people, but their way of thinking was alien to my own, which originated in what might be called the social-demography and human-ecology traditions of Chicago sociology. Many of them, but not all, were oriented toward the humanities rather than the social sciences. For some, one exception was grounds for wiping out the value of a generalization. They were largely unsympathetic to quantitative data and were certainly more interested in the linguistics part of the term "sociolinguistics." It was the elaboration of the various features of language that most excited them. The idea of using national censuses to deal with language questions was absolutely incomprehensible to some participants—and rightly so, I should think, from their perspective, which could see little value coming from a study with such crude measures of language as those used in census questions. (On many occasions I have had to argue for the proper place and application of language data from censuses; this battle is reflected in several of my papers in this book.) But I benefited greatly from the issues raised and was helped by valuable suggestions and references.

Through the years I have appreciated the friendships that developed from that summer institute. If I were to single out any one individual, it would be Charles Ferguson, who has been helpful and kind on more than one occasion through the years. I served on the SSRC Sociolinguistics Committee for a number of years. While mentioning support, I should also credit the Ford Foundation, which sponsored several conferences that I attended and which also provided me with a grant (thanks to Elinor Barber) that made possible several papers in recent years. These opportunities for contact were particularly important to me because I have had relatively modest contact with the linguists in the institutions I have been affiliated with and because most of my sociological colleagues are still not overly interested in language itself.

Still another bonus from the NSF grant was a reference one of the reviewers provided to a paper by Uriel Weinreich on bilingualism in India, which introduced me to the diversity measures proposed by Joseph Greenberg. Not only have I used his measures, but I have had occasion to elaborate on them, expand them, and even apply the basic type of thinking to a variety of non-linguistic problems. This volume includes several papers that build on Greenberg.

Only in the mid-seventies was I able to turn to data I had gathered through the years on language diversity in various nations. With additional materials, and excellent students, I was able to make some sense out of a line of inquiry first stimulated by a casual question that Duncan posed 15 years before. The resulting papers are reprinted here as Chapters 2 and 3.

Most of my work on language diversity in nations, bilingualism, and language shift is linked to my central and unfading interest in race and ethnic relations. Questions about the grand nature, purpose, and theory of the sociology of language have never been of concern to me. I believe there are theoretical elements in my work, but they arose out of specific empirical questions, curiosity, or an effort to make sense out of puzzling data. After I complete my current project, I am not sure where I will go next. One of my recent interests is language spread, on which I have written a paper and attended a recent conference. I am also interested in patterns of language transmission among the large Mexican-American population in Tucson. In the city's

El Con Shopping Center I have a powerful impulse to quiz parents
speaking Spanish to their offspring in order to find out the number of
generations their families have resided in the United States, whether
they are bilingual, when they use English, what their level of education is, and the like. In addition, I have some data in my files on
language diversity in India through the decades that I have not yet fully
exploited, and there is more to do about models of language change in
nations. Then, too, I have become rather sensitive during a year in
Toronto to some odd differences between Canadian and American
English. My ten-year-old daughter, I am convinced, spoke American
English to my wife and me but Canadian English to waitresses, store
clerks, and other adults.

So there is no shortage of interesting questions. The problem is finding ways of arriving at satisfactory answers of a reasonably
rigorous nature.

Bibliography of Stanley Lieberson's Works

1958 a.   Ethnic groups and medicine. M. A. thesis, University of Chicago.
    b.   Ethnic groups and the practice of medicine. American Sociological Review 23: 542–49. [Reprinted in Bobbs-Merrill Reprint Series, S–171.]
    c.   Review of American minorities: a textbook of readings in intergroup relations, ed. by Milton L. Barron. Midwest Sociologist 20: 114–15.

1959   Ethnic segregation and assimilation. Coauthored with O. D. Duncan. American Journal of Sociology 64: 366–74. [Reprinted in Urban Social Segregation, ed. by Ceri Peach (London: Longmans, 1975), pp. 96–110.]

1960 a.   Comparative segregation and assimilation of ethnic groups. Ph. D. dissertation, University of Chicago.
    b.   Metropolis and region. Coauthored with O. D. Duncan, W. R. Scott, B. Duncan, and H. H. Winsborough. Baltimore: Johns Hopkins. (2d ptg, 1961.)
    c.   Review of Property values and race: studies in seven cities, by Luigi Laurenti. American Sociological Review 25: 610–11.

1961 a.   The division of labor in banking. American Journal of Sociology 66: 491–96.
    b.   Texas institutional inbreeding re-examined. Coauthored with David Gold. American Journal of Sociology 66: 506–9.
    c.   The impact of residential segregation on ethnic assimilation. Social Forces 40: 52–57. [Reprinted in Bobbs-Merrill Reprint Series, S–444; in the Study of society, ed. by Peter I. Rose

(New York: Random House, 1967), pp. 454-63; 2d ed., 1970, pp. 426-34; in Comparative urban structure: studies in the ecology of cities, ed. by Kent Schwirian (Lexington, Mass.: Heath, 1974), pp. 475-82; in Urban social segregation, ed. by Ceri Peach (London: Longmans, 1975), pp. 111-21.]

1961 d. Non-graphic computation of Kendall's tau. The American Statistician 15: 20-21.

     e. A societal theory of race and ethnic relations. American Sociological Review 26: 902-10. [Reprinted in Race, class and power, ed. by Raymond W. Mack (New York: American Book Co., 1963), pp. 238-50; 2d ed., 1968, pp. 42-53; in Contemporary sociology, ed. by Milton L. Barron (New York: Dodd, Mead, 1964), pp. 458-68; in Major American social problems, ed. by Robert A. Dentler (Chicago: Rand McNally, 1967), pp. 181-91; in Minority responses, ed. by Minako Kurokawa (New York: Random House, 1970), pp. 10-21; in Power in societies, ed. by Marvin E. Olsen (New York: Macmillan, 1970), pp. 335-43; in Majority and minority: the dynamics of intergroup relations, ed. by Norman R. Yetman and C. Hoy Steele (Boston: Allyn and Bacon, 1971), 2d ed., 1975, pp. 45-53; 3d ed., 1980; in Racial conflict: tension and change in American society, ed. by Gary T. Marx (Boston: Little, Brown, 1971), pp. 120-29; in Intergroup relations: sociological perspectives, ed. by Pierre van den Berghe (New York: Basic Books, 1972), pp. 38-51; in Chicanos: social and psychological perspectives, ed. by Nathaniel N. Wagner and Marsha J. Haug (St. Louis: Mosby, 1971), pp. 18-26; in Race, ethnicity and social change, ed. by John Stone (North Scituate, Mass.: Duxbury Press, 1977), pp. 76-88; in Ethnicity and ethnic relations in Canada: a book of readings, ed. by Jay Goldstein and Rita Bienvenue (Toronto: Butterworths, 1980), pp. 67-79.] [In this volume, pp. 83-98.]

1962 a. Suburbs and ethnic residential patterns. American Journal of Sociology 67: 673-81. [Reprinted in Comparative urban structure: studies in the ecology of cities, ed. by Kent Schwirian (Lexington, Mass.: Heath, 1974), pp. 483-92.]

     b. Review of Urban social structure, by James M. Beshers. American Journal of Sociology 68: 369-71.

     c. Banking functions as an index of inter-city relations. Co-

authored with K. P. Schwirian. Journal of Regional Science
4: 69-81.

1963 a. Ethnic patterns in American cities. New York: The Free
Press of Glencoe.
b. The old-new distinction and immigrants in Australia. American Sociological Review 28: 550-65.
c. The national headquarters of voluntary associations. Coauthored with I. L. Allen, Jr. Administrative Science Quarterly 28: 316-38. [Reprinted in Comparative organizations:
the results of empirical research, ed. by Wolf Heydebrand
(Englewood Cliffs, N. J.: Prentice-Hall, 1973), pp. 322-37.]

1964 a. Limitations in the application of non-parametric coefficients
of correlation. American Sociological Review 29: 744-46.
b. An extension of Greenberg's linguistic diversity measures.
Language 40: 526-31. [Reprinted in Readings in the sociology
of language, ed. by Joshua A. Fishman (The Hague: Mouton,
1968), pp. 546-53; translated and reprinted into Russian in a
volume on language contact ed. by V. Rozencvejg (Moscow,
1972), pp. 215-24. [In this volume, pp. 304-13.]

1965 a. Bilingualism in Montreal: a demographic analysis. American Journal of Sociology 71: 10-25. [Reprinted in Advances
in the sociology of language, vol. 2, ed. by Joshua A. Fishman (The Hague: Mouton, 1972), pp. 231-54; in Bobbs-
Merrill Reprint Series, S-723.] [In this volume, pp. 131-57.]
b. The precipitants and underlying conditions of race riots. Coauthored with Arnold Silverman. American Sociological Review 30: 887-98. [Reprinted in Social problems in a changing
world: a comparative reader, ed. by Walter Gerson (New
York: Crowell, 1969), pp. 452-72; in The sociological perspective, ed. by Scott G. McNall (Boston: Little, Brown,
1968), pp. 340-57; 2d ed., 1971, 3d ed, 1974, pp. 487-504;
in Race, Class. and Power, ed. by Raymond W. Mack, 2d
ed. (Cincinnati: Van Nostrand Reinhold, 1968), pp. 414-29;
in Bobbs-Merrill Reprint Series, S-596; in Readings in col-
ective behavior, ed. by Robert R. Evans (Chicago: Rand
McNally, 1969), pp. 412-29; rev. ed., 1975, pp. 173-90; in
Racial violence in the United States, ed. by Allen D. Grim-

shaw (Chicago: Aldine, 1969), pp. 354-70; in Dynamic social
psychology, ed. by Dwight G. Dean (New York: Random
House, 1969), pp. 586-603; in Crime and delinquency: a
reader, ed. by Carl A. Bersani (New York: Macmillan,
1970), pp. 367-77; in Dynamics of aggression, ed. by Edwin
I. Megargee and Jack E. Hokanson (New York: Harper and
Row, 1970), pp. 170-89; adapted in Racial and ethnic relations, ed. by Helen M. Hughes (Boston: Allyn and Bacon,
1970), pp. 86-99; abridged in The black revolt, ed. by James
A. Geschwender (Englewood Cliffs, N. J.: Prentice-Hall,
1971); in The ambivalent force: perspectives on the police,
ed. by Arthur Niederhoffer and Abraham S. Blumberg (Wal-
tham, Mass.: Ginn, 1970), pp. 193-204; in Readings in race
and ethnic relations, ed. by Anthony Richmond (Oxford: Per-
gamon Press, 1972), pp. 259-79.]

1965 c.   The meaning of race riots. Race 7: 371-78. [Reprinted in
Human relations: a reader for West Virginians, ed. by
Thomas M. Drake and David G. Temple (Morgantown, West
Virginia: Institute for Labor Studies and Manpower Development, 1968), pp. 187-91; adapted in Racial and ethnic relations
ed. by Helen M. Hughes (Boston: Allyn and Bacon, 1970), pp.
86-99.]

1966 a.   The Price-Zubrzycki measure of ethnic intermarriage.
Eugenics Quarterly 13: 92-100.

      b.   Issue Editor and Introduction. Explorations in sociolinguis-
tics. Sociological Inquiry 36. [Reprinted in International
Journal of American Linguistics 33, 1967.]

      c.   Language questions in censuses. Sociological Inquiry 36:
262-79. [Reprinted in International Journal of American
Linguistics 33: 134-51.] [In this volume, pp. 281-303.]

1967 a.   Editor, Explorations in sociolinguistics. Bloomington, Ind.:
Indiana University Press.

      b.   Negro-white occupational differences in the absence of dis-
crimination. Coauthored with G. V. Fuguitt. American
Journal of Sociology 73: 188-200. [Reprinted in Black Amer-
icans and white racism, ed. by Marcel L. Goldschmid (New
York: Holt, Rinehart, and Winston, 1970), pp. 284-95; in
Bobbs-Merrill Reprint Series, S-724; in Racial discrimina-

tion in the United States, ed. by Thomas F. Pettigrew (New
York: Harper and Row, 1975), pp. 187-206.]

1967 c. Review of Language loyalty in the United States: the main-
tenance and perpetuation of non-English mother tongues by
American ethnic and religious groups, by Joshua A. Fish-
man, Vladimir C. Nahirny, John E. Hofman, and Robert G.
Hayden (The Hague: Mouton, 1966). American Journal of
Sociology 72: 690-91.

1969 a. How can we describe and measure the incidence and distribution of bilingualism? In Description and measurement of bilingualism: an international seminar, ed. by L. G. Kelly
(Toronto: University of Toronto Press), pp. 286-95; also
translated into French for a text. [In this volume, pp. 334-48.]
      b. National and regional language diversity. In Actes du Xe
Congrès International des Linguistes. Bucharest: Editions
de l'Académie de la Republique Socialiste de Roumanie, pp.
769-73. [In this volume, pp. 99-104.]
      c. Measuring population diversity. American Sociological
Review 34: 850-62.

1970 a. Metropolis and region in transition. Coauthored with Beverly
Duncan. Beverly Hills, Calif.: Sage Publications.
      b. Language and ethnic relations in Canada. New York: Wiley.
[Chapter 1, "Language and ethnic relations: a neglected problem," pp. 3-30; in this volume, pp. 1-18. Portions of Chapter 8, "Implications for the study of linguistic pluralism and
ethnic relations," pp. 238-40, 249-50; in this volume, pp.
127-30. Chapter 5, "Occupational demands," pp. 138-75; in
this volume, pp. 173-217.]
      c. Stratification and ethnic groups. Sociological Inquiry 40:
172-81. [Reprinted in Social stratification: research and
theory for the 1970's, ed. by Edward O. Laumann (Indianapo-
lis: Bobbs-Merrill, 1970), pp. 172-81; in Readings in race
and ethnic relations, ed. by Anthony Richmond (Oxford: Per-
gamon Press, 1972), pp. 199-209.]
      d. Linguistic and ethnic segregation in Montreal. In Internat-
ional Days of Sociolinguistics. Second International Congress
of Social Sciences of the Luigi Sturzo Institute. Rome: Luigi
Sturzo Institute, pp. 753-82. [In this volume, pp. 218-48.]

1970 e.   Residence and language maintenance in a multilingual city.
          South African Journal of Sociology 1: 13-22. [Reprinted in
          Plural societies, Summer, 1971, pp. 63-73.]

1971 a.   Language shift in the United States: some demographic clues.
          Coauthored with Timothy J. Curry. International Migration
          Review, special issue on language maintenance and language
          shift in migration and immigration 5: 125-37. [In this vol-
          ume, pp. 158-72.]

     b.   An empirical study of military-industrial linkages. Ameri-
          can Journal of Sociology 76: 562-84. [Reprinted in The mili-
          tary-industrial complex, ed. by Sam C. Sarkesian (Beverly
          Hills, Calif.: Sage Publications, 1972), pp. 53-94; in Bobbs-
          Merrill Reprint Series, S-722; in Testing the theory of the
          military-industrial complex, ed. by Steven Rosen (Boston:
          Heath, 1973), pp. 61-83; in Society and politics: readings in
          political sociology, ed. by Richard G. Braungart (Englewood
          Cliffs, N. J.: Prentice-Hall, 1976), pp. 237-58; to be trans-
          lated into German and published in United States armaments
          policy, political decisions and economic interests (English
          translation of the German title), ed. by Gunter Brauch, Gert
          Krell, and Dieter Lutz (Baden-Baden, West Germany: Nomos
          Verlag).]

1972   Leadership and organizational performance: a study of large
          corporations. Coauthored with James F. O'Connor. Amer-
          ican Sociological Review 37: 117-30. [Reprinted in A socio-
          logical reader on complex organizations, ed. by Amitai
          Etzioni and Edward W. Lehman, 3d ed. (New York: Holt,
          Rinehart and Winston, 1980), pp. 284-99.]

1973   Generational differences among blacks in the North. Amer-
          ican Journal of Sociology 79: 550-65.

1974 a.   The correlation of ratios or difference scores having common
          terms. Coauthored with Glenn V. Fuguitt. Sociological
          methodology, 1973-1974, ed. by Herbert L. Costner (San
          Francisco: Jossey Bass), pp. 128-44.

     b.   National development, mother-tongue diversity, and the com-
          parative study of nations. Coauthored with Lynn Hansen.

American Sociological Review 39: 523–41. [In this volume, pp. 19–47.]

1975 a. Language diversity in a nation and its regions. Coauthored with James F. O'Connor. In Multilingual political systems: problems and solutions, ed. by Jean-Guy Savard and Richard Vigneault (Quebec: Laval University Press), pp. 161–83. [In this volume, pp. 105–26.]

b. The course of mother tongue diversity in nations. Coauthored with Guy Dalto and Mary Ellen Johnston (Marsden). American Journal of Sociology 81: 34–61. [In this volume, pp. 48–82.]

c. Rank-sum comparisons between groups. Sociological methodology, 1976, ed. by David Heise (San Francisco: Jossey-Bass, 1975), pp. 276–91.

d. Review of Linguistic composition of the nations of the world, vol. 1, Central and western South Asia, ed. by Heinz Kloss and Grant D. McConnell. Language in Society 5: 401–4.

1976 A comparison between Northern and Southern blacks residing in the North. Coauthored with Christy A. Wilkinson. Demography 13: 199–224.

1978 a. A reconsideration of the income differences found between migrants and Northern-born blacks. American Journal of Sociology 83: 940–66.

b. Domains of language usage and mother-tongue shift in Nairobi. Coauthored with Edward McCabe. International Journal of the Sociology of Language 18: 69–81. [In this volume, pp. 249–62.]

c. Selective black migration from the South: an historical view. Demography of racial and ethnic groups, ed. by Frank D. Bean and W. Parker Frisbie (New York: Academic Press), pp. 119–41.

d. The anatomy of language diversity: some elementary results. Inter-ethnic communication, ed. by E. Lamar Ross (Athens, Ga.: University of Georgia Press), pp. 32–48. [In this volume, pp. 314–33.]

1979 a. Making it in America: differences between eminent blacks and new Europeans. Coauthored with Donna Carter. American Sociological Review 44: 347–66.

1979 b. The interpretation of net migration rates. Sociological methodology, 1980, ed. by Karl F. Schuessler (San Francisco: Jossey-Bass), pp. 176-90.

1980 a. Procedures for improving sociolinguistic surveys of language maintenance and language shift. International Journal of the Sociology of Language 25: 11-27. [In this volume, pp. 263-80

   b. A piece of the pie: black and white immigrants since 1880. Berkeley: University of California Press.

1981 a. Forces affecting language spread: some basic propositions. To be published in Language spread: studies in diffusion and social change, ed. by Robert L. Cooper (Bloomington: Indiana University Press). [In this volume, pp. 349-77.]

   b. An asymmetrical approach to segregation. To be published in Ethnic segregation in cities, ed. by Ceri Peach (London: Croom Helm).

   c. The influence of racial and ethnic stereotypes on interaction with others. To be published in Social structure and personality: papers in honor of William Hamilton Sewell, ed. by Robert M. Hauser, David Mechanic, and Archibald O. Haller (New York: Academic Press).

   d. Author's postscript. [In this volume, pp. 378-82.]

Lieberson, Stanley   1933–
        Language diversity and language contact:
essays by Stanley Lieberson. Selected and
introduced by Anwar S. Dil. Stanford, California:
Stanford University Press [1981]
        xvi, 392 p. 24cm.
(Language science and national development series,
Linguistic Research Group of Pakistan)
        Includes bibliography
I. Dil, Anwar S., 1928–   ed.
II. (Series) III. Linguistic Research Group of Pakistan